In Praise of
Adi Da (The

A DI DA IS THE GREATEST SPIRITUAL MASTER ever to walk the
earth. Seeing this, attending to this truth, we need not
walk in the dark any longer. Adi Da is the God-Man. He
reveals the ultimate truth residing in the human heart and at
the heart of all religions.

THE REV. THOMAS AHLBURN
Senior Minister, The First Unitarian Church,
Providence, Rhode Island

T HERE EXISTS NOWHERE IN THE WORLD TODAY, among
Christians, Jews, Muslims, Hindus, Buddhists, native
tribalists, or any other groups, anyone who has so much to
teach, or speaks with such authority, or is so important for
understanding our situation.

HENRY LEROY FINCH,
Professor of Philosophy;
author, *Wittgenstein—The Early Philosophy*
and *Wittgenstein—The Later Philosophy*

A DI DA PROVIDES A WAY in which Oneness may be experienced by anyone who is bold enough to follow his
teachings. It is important to understand that his vision is
neither Eastern nor Western, but it is the eternal spiritual
pulse of the Great Wisdom which knows no cultural,
temporal, or geographical locus.

LARRY DOSSEY, M.D.
author, *Healing Words; Space, Time, and Medicine;
Beyond Illness; Recovering the Soul*

I N THE CONTEXT OF THE SACRED COMMUNITY of the Free Daist
Avataric Communion, the story of Adi Da's ultimate
"Divine Emergence" becomes a living, existential truth. In
this sense, I regard the work of Adi Da and his devotees as
one of the most penetrating spiritual and social experiments
happening on the planet in our era.

JEFFREY MISHLOVE, PH.D.
host, *Thinking Allowed* public television series;
author, *The Roots of Consciousness*

M Y RELATIONSHIP WITH ADI DA AS HIS DEVOTEE over the past 21 years has only confirmed my certainty of His Realization and the Truth of His impeccable Teaching.

RAY LYNCH,
composer, *The Sky of Mind; Deep Breakfast; No Blue Thing; Nothing Above My Shoulders but the Evening*

A DI DA IS A GREAT TEACHER with a dynamic ability to awaken in his listeners something of the Divine Reality in which he is grounded, with which he is identified, and which in fact, he is.

He is a man of both the East and the West; perhaps in him they merge and are organized as the One that he is.

ISRAEL REGARDIE
author, *Psychology, Magic & Mysticism; The Golden Dawn*

A DI DA IS A MAN WHO HAS TRULY WALKED IN SPIRIT and given true enlightenment to many.

SUN BEAR
founder, The Bear Tribe Medicine Society

Praise for
The Knee of Listening

THIS IS THE AUTOBIOGRAPHY OF THE LIVING GOD-MAN, Whose Loving Heart and Powerful Spiritual Transmission have awakened me to the Love-Blissful reality of the Great One, Who He Is.

LEE SANNELLA, M.D.
author, *The Kundalini Experience*

I KNOW OF NO OTHER TEACHER who has exposed his life and spiritual journey with such complete abandonment for the teaching of all who will pay attention. His story and process are a fascinating portrayal of the ordeal, potency, and blessing of an infinitely expanded spiritual life. This biography is a perfect gift!

BONNIE GREENWELL, PH.D.
author, *Energies of Transformation:
A Guide to the Kundalini Process;*
Director, Transpersonal Counseling Center,
Institute of Transpersonal Psychology

ADI DA'S LIFE IS LIKE A GREAT GENTLE TRAIL OF LIGHT in the dark spiritual night of modernity. He can be seen from afar and heard amid the deafening noises of this machine culture.

MALIDOMA SOMÉ
author, *Of Water & the Spirit: Ritual, Magic,
& Initiation in the Life of an African Shaman;
Ritual: Power, Healing, and Community*

THIS FASCINATING AND INSPIRING STORY of the metamorphosis of Franklin Jones into Adi Da is high spiritual adventure.

HAROLD BLOOMFIELD, M.D.
author, *The Power of 5*

WHAT YOU HOLD IN YOUR HANDS is not just a book. It is an invitation and an opportunity, a doorway to Joy. When I first read *The Knee of Listening*, I knew I had found the greatest Spiritual Realizer that had ever lived. I urge you to open yourself to the Life that fills these pages. The opportunity has never been so great.

BILL GOTTLIEB
Senior Vice-President and Editor-in-Chief,
Prevention Magazine Health Books

The Knee of Listening

Adi Da (The Da Avatar)
Adi Da Purnashram (Naitauba), Fiji, 1994

The Knee of Listening

*The Early-Life Ordeal
and the Radical Spiritual Realization
of the Divine World-Teacher*

by

ADI DA

(THE DA AVATAR)

THE DAWN HORSE PRESS

MIDDLETOWN, CALIFORNIA
MARIA HOOP, THE NETHERLANDS

NOTE TO THE READER

All who study the Way of the Heart or take up its practice should remember that they are responding to a Call to become responsible for themselves. They should understand that they, not Avatara Adi Da or others, are responsible for any decision they may make or action they take in the course of their lives of study or practice.

The devotional, Spiritual, functional, practical, relational, cultural, and formal community practices and disciplines referred to in this book are appropriate and natural practices that are voluntarily and progressively adopted by each student-novice and member of the Free Daist Avataric Communion and adapted to his or her personal circumstance. Although anyone may find them useful and beneficial, they are not presented as advice or recommendations to the general reader or to anyone who is not a participant in Da Avatara International or a member of the Free Daist Avataric Communion. And nothing in this book is intended as a diagnosis, prescription, or recommended treatment or cure for any specific "problem", whether medical, emotional, psychological, social, or Spiritual. One should apply a particular program of treatment, prevention, cure, or general health only in consultation with a licensed physician or other qualified professional.

First published 1972
Standard Edition, unabridged, April 1992
New Standard Edition, popular format, September 1995
Printed in the United States of America

Produced by the Free Daist Avataric Communion
in cooperation with the Dawn Horse Press

International Standard Book Number: popular format 1-57097-023-8

Library of Congress Catalog Card Number: 95-70839

CONTENTS

Adi Da (The Da Avatar)
Adi Da Purnashram (Naitauba), Fiji, 1995

The Secret of The Knee of Listening

by devotees of Adi Da, the Da Avatar

There is a State of Being that is completely, unequivocally, permanently, infinitely Happy and Free—a State that cannot be lost under any conditions, in this world or after death. Such a State is not just imaginary. It is the underlying Truth of existence. In various times and places, great saints and sages have tasted this Happiness to some degree. *The Knee of Listening* is the story of how this Truth, this Joy, perfectly emerged in the world for the first time, and has become the actual possibility of all human beings. There is no way to be prepared for the power of this book. It is a miraculous story of Divine Grace, but it is not a myth. It is literally true. The events described here took place in our own era.

In November 1939, on Long Island, New York, a baby was born who was not an ordinary child. But no one knew this. No one knew that this child—named by His parents "Franklin Albert Jones"—had intentionally accepted birth as a human being in order to accomplish Work that was great and sublime beyond description. This Work, which began at His birth, continues today, and will continue beyond His human lifetime, even forever. The One born as Franklin Jones is Adi Da, the Da Avatar, and this book is His early-life story, told in His own words.

The "Bright"

During His infancy, Adi Da was perfectly aware of everything around Him. He saw that people were not Happy, that each person presumed himself or herself to be separate from everyone else, each struggling to find his or her own separate joy. As He describes in *The Knee of Listening*, Adi Da found this remarkable—it was not His experience at all. He knew only Oneness, only Blissfulness. His consciousness was not yet identified with a bag of flesh and skin. He lived in an entirely different State of Awareness—as "Infinitely and inherently Free Being", a sphere of Radiance and Love that He called the "Bright". Adi Da was inseparable from the Bliss and Joy of the "Bright". He knew Himself to be the very Source of It, the true and "Bright" Condition of everything. How could a baby have known this? What Adi Da describes on the first page of His story is more than the ordinary experience of a human infant. The secret of *The Knee of Listening* is that the One who speaks to you in this book Exists eternally—before this birth and forever. The early-life story of Adi Da is the confession of the Divine Being, the ultimate Truth and Reality, appearing in human form.

For His first two years, Adi Da enjoyed the undiminished Bliss of His Real Condition. Then during His second year, something very mysterious occurred. As Adi Da was crawling across the linoleum floor one day, His parents let loose a new puppy they were giving Him—and in the instant of seeing the puppy and seeing His parents, Adi Da's infinite Awareness suddenly changed. He made the spontaneous choice to be an "I", an apparently separate person relating to apparently separate others.

**"For His first two years, Adi Da enjoyed
the undiminished Bliss of His Real Condition."**

"Forgetting" the "Bright"

What had happened? Adi Da had relinquished the "Bright", out of a "painful loving", a sympathy for the suffering and ignorance of human beings. He was responding to the great impulse behind His birth—the impulse to make the "Bright" known to every one. But the only way that Adi Da could fulfill this Purpose was to intentionally "forget" the "Bright" and experience life from the ordinary human point of view— and then, in the midst of that limited condition, to find the way to recover the "Bright".

This was Adi Da's early-life ordeal, and it was a perilous, desperate affair. He did not know how it would turn out. He had no "method" for recovering the "Bright". But He embraced every aspect of human life, both great and ordinary, in order to reveal the complete Truth of existence, the Truth that can set everyone Free. *The Knee of Listening* is the story of how Adi Da did this, through a most intense ordeal that lasted for His first thirty years.

In the course of this ordeal, Adi Da always risked everything for the Truth. He could not bear to place any limitations on His quest to recover the "Bright". In this disposition, Adi Da not only thoroughly explored the realms of ordinary human experience, but He also passed through every possible kind of psychic and Spiritual experience—and with extraordinary speed. It was as though these Awakenings were already, in some sense, thoroughly familiar to Him. But Adi Da was not satisfied. He had the intuition of some "incredible Knowledge". He knew that the ultimate Truth had to be greater than any of these experiences, any of these visions, any moment of revelation. The hidden force of the "Bright" Itself was always alive in Him, leading Him toward the astonishing events that form the climax of *The Knee of Listening*.

Los Angeles, 1973

"Who Do You Think Franklin Is?"

When the first edition of *The Knee of Listening* appeared in 1973, men and women from all over America—and beyond—were enthralled. Many could not put the book down, reading it at one sitting. There were people who fell into blissful states as they read, or simply felt an inexplicable happiness and freedom. Some readers reached for the phone immediately and called the number at the back of the book. They felt impelled to find out more about "Franklin". Their enquiries led them to a modest Spiritual bookstore—in, of all places, downtown Hollywood, Los Angeles. There, in the rooms behind the store, Adi Da's extraordinary Work as a Spiritual Teacher had begun.

For those who came to Him, Adi Da was the most attractive being they had ever met. He radiated Love. He magnified Happiness to everyone around Him. The Joy in His laughter held people spellbound—it was the laughter of one who got the "joke" of existence. He was uniquely at ease in the world and, simultaneously, not "of the world". Right from the beginning, some who were associated with Adi Da had the most profound intuitions about Him. On an occasion in 1973, one of the men who was closest to Him was invited to San Francisco to speak to some people who were approaching Adi Da as their Spiritual Master. In the course of his talk, this man was asked: "Who do you think Franklin is?" He had no planned reply. He simply said, without hesitating, "I think Franklin is God."

God-Realization

Many individuals throughout history have been acknowledged as "God-Realized" or "Enlightened", or in union with the Divine in some sense. Different religious traditions mean different things when they speak of the ultimate goal of religion. But it can be said, in the general sense, that God-Realization is the Condition in which God, or the Divine Self, has been "made <u>Real</u>". It is the State in which God (or the Divine) has become the living Reality of one's existence—rather than a great Being or Power <u>apart</u> from oneself. In the same way, to be Enlightened is to be profoundly Awakened to God, Truth, or Reality, to the point that even the body becomes radiant with Spiritual Force.

Throughout history, remarkable men and women have lived their lives as an heroic ordeal directed to attaining God, Truth, or Reality. Some of them—the greatest saints, yogis, and sages—attained various degrees of Enlightenment, or God-Realization. But Adi Da had nothing to attain. He <u>is</u> the "Bright" of God, the Perfect Descent of the Divine into the human world. And the State of most perfect God-Realization that Adi Da reveals in *The Knee of Listening* is a Realization never known before. It is the Realization of the "Bright", the all-surpassing Divine Enlightenment that Adi Da has now made possible for all beings.

Adi Da Purnashram (Naitauba), Fiji, 1994

The Great Mystery of Who Adi Da is and what He has come to give is not a claim to be believed, but a Secret to be discovered at heart. Countless people have already experienced this overwhelming and joyous surprise and have become devoted to Adi Da as their beloved Spiritual Master and Divine Liberator. Once the depth of that Secret is revealed, nothing is ever the same again.

19

The Immense Bond of Guru-Love

The bond between Spiritual teacher and disciple that Adi Da's devotees have discovered in His company was also a crucial part of Adi Da's own early-life ordeal. In fact, the Guru-devotee relationship is one of the great themes of *The Knee of Listening*. This kind of relationship is more fundamental than any other, more intimate than the blood-bond, more passionate than any relationships with lovers and friends. It has been treasured in all religious traditions throughout time. To be accepted as the disciple of a saint or a being of true Spiritual Realization has always been regarded as the most precious Grace, the very means of one's own Awakening to Truth. Why is this? Because, in order to learn <u>anything</u> great, one must go to a master, one must imbibe that skill, that art, that wisdom in the company of one who knows it through and through and can transmit its secrets to worthy disciples. In the case of a true Spiritual Master, what is transmitted is not merely esoteric knowledge, but the very Power and Condition of the Master's own Spiritual Realization.

Adi Da, like other Westerners of His generation, grew up with no knowledge of the Guru-devotee relationship. He discovered "the Immense Bond of Guru-Love" as spontaneously as He discovered everything else in the process of His Re-Awakening. Adi Da's Spiritual Teachers were great beings, and He loved them and submitted to their instruction and their discipline with limitless devotion and heart-felt gratitude. But Adi Da was not the usual disciple, just as he was not an ordinary, or even an extraordinary, man. His Realization was already absolute, but it was "latent in the heart", not yet fully active. He was in the process of recovering the "Bright", His native State of Being, and that was the process that each of His Gurus served in Him. All kinds of Spiritual Realizations are described in the traditions, and Adi Da passed through all of them—visions, trances, mystical raptures, "cosmic consciousness", states of profound meditation and Transcendental knowledge. But, as you will read, in the closing phases of His ordeal, Adi Da's overwhelming impulse to the Truth drove Him into territory unknown to His Gurus, unknown in the annals of Spiritual literature. His ultimate Re-Awakening to the "Bright" occurred on the basis of a unique and all-encompassing insight, a "radical understanding" that places mankind's whole history of Spiritual seeking and Realization in a new light—and leads beyond all of it.

Radical Understanding

Radical understanding is the bedrock of *The Knee of Listening*. Normally, when we say we "understand", we are indicating that we have figured out a concept, grasped how something works, intuited the nature of the object (or person), or become sympathetic with someone's feelings. When Adi Da speaks of "radical understanding", or just "understanding", He is not using the word in the conventional sense. He is referring to a most profound and liberating insight—a direct awareness of the single root-cause behind all un-Happiness. He is pointing to something we are always doing, an activity that is actually holding back the flood-gates of Divine Bliss, Joy, Happiness, and Love. What is that Happiness-preventing activity exactly? What is it that we are doing that is keeping us from Realizing the "Bright" right now? Adi Da found out.

Through the most rigorous observation of Himself in every possible circumstance—talking, reading, dreaming, eating, at the movies, at a party, walking alone—this primal activity more and more stood out in His awareness. He saw that we are always contracting—recoiling from existence, physically, emotionally, mentally, psychically. This self-contraction, Adi Da came to see, is our

Adi Da Purnashram (Naitauba), Fiji, 1994

constant, though largely unconscious, response to the uncontrollable, unknowable world in which we find ourselves. It is a fearful reaction to the fact that we know we are going to die. And its effects are devastating. The self-contraction, Adi Da realized, is the source of fear, sorrow, anger, desire, guilt, competitiveness, shame, and all the mayhem of this world. Even ordinary pleasurable moments are governed by the same seed-activity. It became awesomely obvious to Adi Da that <u>everything</u> we do is a form of search, an effort to be free of the self-inflicted pain of self-contraction. But this effort cannot succeed, because the search itself is a form of the self-contraction. And so seeking for release, for freedom, cannot lead us to the Happiness we desire. Perfect Truth, or unqualified Happiness, Adi Da saw, only appears when the activity of self-contraction is radically understood, and therefore spontaneously ceases—revealing the simplicity, the Joy of Being that is always already the case.

This understanding may sound simple—but do not be deceived. It is <u>most</u> profound. As Adi Da discovered, the self-contraction is programmed into the very cells of the body. Thus, even after this fundamental intuition arose in Him, Adi Da could not instantaneously correct the fault—because He had submitted to all the limits of human existence. But Adi Da's unique understanding, once it was basically established, accelerated His entire course of Divine Re-Awakening. It proved to be a kind of "muscle", an insight that gave Him the key to every experience, high and low.

As He moved closer to the great resolution of His early-life ordeal, Adi Da observed the self-contraction in more and more subtle forms. He observed it even as the simplest awareness of separateness, the naked sense of "I" and "other" that is at the root of our perception of the world. By now it was obvious to Him that the self-contraction explained not only the ordinary dramas of life, but the whole "tour" of Spiritual experience as well. At last, all of mankind's searches for God, Truth, or

Reality fell into focus for Adi Da as an immense effort of seeking that was totally unnecessary, based on a fundamental error—the lack of radical understanding. Then there was nothing left over, nothing left for Him to Realize, except the Truth Itself.

What that astounding Truth is and how it ultimately broke upon Adi Da is a Mystery beyond words. Only His own account in *The Knee of Listening* can truly reveal this Mystery to you. There is no doubt that through the Power of His radical Spiritual Realization something has changed at the very heart of existence. The Divine Avatar, Adi Da, has done what only the Divine could do. He has, so to speak, "cracked the cosmic code", broken through the force of illusion that has always kept born beings bound to the realms of change and suffering and death.

The Divine World-Teacher

The world we live in today is more desperate than ever before—this is a dark epoch when the very survival of our world is threatened by the excesses of materialism and the sophisticated weapons of war. In the lore of the ancient Spiritual traditions there is a common thread of hope, an intuition that, in the "last days", or "end-time", when the world is at its worst, a Deliverer will come, the supreme God-Man who will complete and fulfill all the aspirations and Spiritual strivings of the past. Adi Da, the Da Avatar, is that One. He is the Divine World-Teacher, the Giver of Divine Enlightenment, Who has made all myths unnecessary and all seeking obsolete.

The Way that Adi Da offers to all is a <u>relationship</u>, a Spiritual relationship to Him, not a mere system of self-applied techniques. No mere technique, no mere self-effort could possibly result in the unique Awakening described in *The Knee of Listening*. Avatara Adi Da is the Very Person and Source of this Grace. And the Way that

Adi Da, the Da Avatar

"Da" is an ancient Name of God meaning "the Giver".
The Name "Da" intuitively came to Adi Da early in His
life, but He did not assume it as His true Name until 1979,
when the time was right for this revelation. In 1994,
His Name was most fully revealed as "Adi Da"—"Adi"
meaning "first", or "original". Thus, "Adi Da" means the
"First Giver" or "the Giving Source". To speak of Him as
"the Da Avatar" or "Avatara Adi Da" is another way of
acknowledging Him as the Divine Giver. "Avatar"
(or "Avatara") means "Descended One", the appearance
of the Divine Reality in human form.

Free Daism is so named because it is the Way of
Perfect Freedom revealed by the Divine Giver, Adi Da.

He has established—Free Daism, or the Way of the Heart—is the means of entering into His sphere of Grace. The Free Daist Way is for every race and culture, for men, women, and children of all kinds and backgrounds. Free Daism is the true world-religion of Divine Enlightenment, the way of life based on Adi Da's unique revelation of the "Bright".

The Knee of Listening is the account of how this entire possibility began. It is the greatest Spiritual life-story of all time. This book is not merely a story about "Franklin Jones". It is a story about each of us, the Truth of our Very Being and of our Real Destiny.

Note on the Editions of
The Knee of Listening

After Adi Da first wrote *The Knee of Listening*, He decided, in consultation with the publisher, to reduce the manuscript to about half its original length. This abridgement was published as the first edition in 1972. The complete manuscript was published as the second edition in 1992. Now, for the third edition, Adi Da has gone over the second edition in great detail, expanding His account of many incidents and adding new accounts of others. His purpose is to make the full and final communication of His early life—not only in terms of the content, but in His manner of writing. When Adi Da first published His Spiritual autobiography, His devotees had not yet begun to approach Him, and so He wrote of Himself and His experiences in a way that He felt could be directly understood and received by the public reader. More than twenty years later, the picture has completely changed. His Work is established, and thousands can testify to the authenticity of His words and of their acknowledgement of Him as the Da Avatar. Thus, in this third edition, Adi Da speaks openly of His Divine Nature and Purpose, even as it was shown from His earliest years.

Adi Da's Work to Awaken others—which continues today—is just as momentous as the ordeal of His early life. *The Knee of Listening* ends with His Re-Awakening to the "Bright"; the story of Adi Da's life and Work after this Great Event is told by His devotees at the end of this book.

This third edition of *The Knee of Listening* appears on the twenty-fifth anniversary of Avatara Adi Da's Divine Re-Awakening in September, 1970.

Adi Da (The Da Avatar)
Adi Da Purnashram (Naitauba), Fiji, 1994

The Knee
of Listening

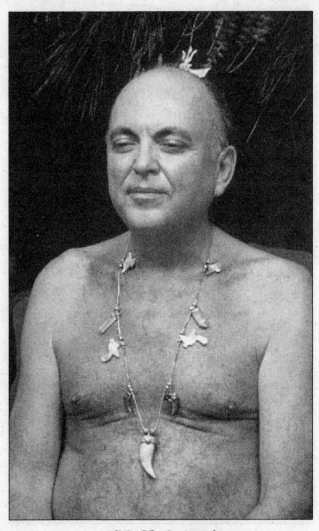

Adi Da (The Da Avatar)
Adi Da Purnashram (Naitauba), Fiji, 1994

The Heart
of Understanding

D eath is utterly acceptable to consciousness and life. There has been endless time of numberless deaths, but neither consciousness nor life has ceased to arise. The felt quality and cycle to death has not modified the fragility of flowers, even the flowers within the human body. Therefore, one's understanding of consciousness and life must be turned to That Utter, Inclusive Truth, That Clarity and Wisdom, That Power and Untouchable Gracefulness, That One and Only Reality, this evidence suggests. One must cease to live in a superficial and divided way, seeking and demanding consciousness and life in the present apparent form, avoiding and resisting what appears to be the end of consciousness and life in death.

The Heart Is <u>Real</u> understanding. The Heart Is <u>Real</u> Consciousness and <u>Real</u> Life. The Heart Is What Merely and Only <u>Is</u>, but Which Is also Appearing In and Behind the conditions of mortal life and its death. Therefore, it is said of old, the One That <u>Is</u> Is neither born nor come to death, not Alive merely as the limitation of form (itself), not Itself (or Entirely) Rendered in what appears, and yet It Is the Living One, than Which there Is no lesser other (and no Great or Greater Other), Appearing As all of this Play of changes, but Eternally One, Unchanging, and Free.

There Is Only the Constant Knowledge and Enjoyment of the Heart, moment to moment, through the instant of all conditions of appearance and disappearance. Of This I Am Perfectly Certain. I <u>Am</u> That.

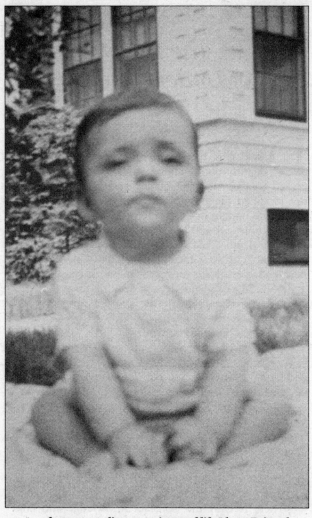

"... from my earliest experience of life I have Enjoyed
a Condition that, as a child, I called the 'Bright'. "

CHAPTER 1

The "Bright"

On November 3, 1939, at 11:21 A.M., in Jamaica, Queens County, New York, I was born "Franklin Albert Jones".

The sign of my birth is Scorpio, marked by the images of Spirit and of Sex, the eagle and the crab.[1] It is the sign of internal warfare, the problem and perfection. The sign of Scorpio should indicate to you the kinds of forces that aligned to generate my birth. Whatever significance you may attribute to astrology, it is true that my personal life has often cycled high and low, marked by equal and opposing determinations to ascend and to descend. And the external adventure of my life has turned me in and out of every kind of Spiritual and religious path, every kind of ascending means, and likewise every form of pleasure, ecstasy, and self-indulgence.

The signs of my birth suggest (and have required) a drama of opposites. However, in spite of all of that, it has also been my lot to remain untouched by cosmic and human circumstance. This is perhaps the first key to what I must Communicate. From the beginning, I have also Known a radical Alternative to the revolutionary internal dilemma of my natural existence. I have played in the problem of my alternatives, but from my earliest experience of life I have Enjoyed a Condition that, as a child, I called the "Bright".

I have always known desire, not merely for extreme pleasures of the senses and the mind, but for the highest Enjoyment of Spiritual Power and Mobility. But I have not been seated in desire, and desire has only been a

1. The eagle and the crab are symbols for the extremes, high and low, to which individuals born under the sign of Scorpio are said to be inclined.

play that I have grown to understand and enjoy without conflict. I have always been Seated in the "Bright".

Even as a baby I remember only crawling around inquisitively with a boundless Feeling of Joy, Light, and Freedom in the middle of my head that was bathed in Energy moving unobstructed in a Circle, down from above, all the way down, then up, all the way up, and around again, and always Shining from my heart. It was an Expanding Sphere of Joy from the heart. And I was a Radiant Form, the Source of Energy, Love-Bliss, and Light in the midst of a world that is entirely Energy, Love-Bliss, and Light. I was the Power of Reality, a direct Enjoyment and Communication of the One Reality. I was the Heart Itself, Who Lightens the mind and all things. I was the same as every one and every thing, except it became clear that others were apparently unaware of the "Thing" Itself.

Even as a little child I recognized It and Knew It, and my life was not a matter of anything else. That Awareness, that Conscious Enjoyment, that Self-Existing and Self-Radiant Space of Infinitely and inherently Free Being, that Shine of inherent Joy Standing in the heart and Expanding from the heart, is the "Bright". And It is the entire Source of True Humor. It is Reality. It is not separate from anything.

From my birth I have not been centered in Scorpio or the dilemma of alternatives, but in the "Bright". So it is with True Humor that I describe how I existed all this time.

My father[2] was always a salesman, and my mother was always at home. They could always use a little ordinary humor, but I always loved (and love) them, and love was always the premise of our life together. That is why we were always free to be so reckless, stupid, unfeeling, uncommunicative, unhappy, and separate! None of that ever amounted to anything less than an enjoyment of our separate spectacles. Quiet, long-suffering, fathered mother. Emotional, violent, elaborate father-boy. Crazy, secluded, independent son away.

2. Adi Da's father, Frank Jones, died in 1984.

"Even as a little child I recognized It and Knew It, and my life was not a matter of anything else. That Awareness, that Conscious Enjoyment, that Self-Existing and Self-Radiant Space of Infinitely and inherently Free Being, that Shine of inherent Joy Standing in the heart and Expanding from the heart, is the 'Bright'. And It is the entire Source of True Humor. It is Reality. It is not separate from anything."

With parents and sister

As a young boy

Boyhood home in Franklin Square on Long Island

I always grew up on Long Island, mostly in a town called Franklin Square, which was not named after me, or my father (whose name is also Franklin). Mother is Dorothy. A sister, Joanne, was born when I was eight years old, whom we also always loved (and love), except she and I grew up at separate times and not together.

I was early brought to the Lutheran Christian Church, and so became combined with the mind of Christianity, and especially with the myths and legends (or the so-called history and historical person) of Jesus of Nazareth. Eventually, the ideas I received from that early association with Christianity became crucially important life-supporting beliefs for me, after my own "Bright" Strength of Being had been, temporarily, undermined by my experience of the human world of conflict, illusion, and death. Indeed, even quite early, I began to see there was a fundamental difference, or a very basic unlikeness, between myself and others—not a difference of ultimate essence, and not at all a social or, otherwise, merely physical difference, but a difference of point of view, and of experience, and of life-practice. Thus, schooled by conventional religion, and puzzled by the conventional mind and the disturbed manner of others, I gradually, but only tentatively, accepted the three root-conventions of the common mind: the idea of God (as "Creator", and as separate from all "creation"), the idea of separate self (in my case, and in all cases), and the idea of the world (as itself separate, and as itself composed of separate "things", or absolute differences).

One of my most significant early memories is the Event that clearly marks the beginning of my transition from the gratuitous "Brightness" of my earliest childhood to my life of seeking, which transition was, as you will see, motivated by my intentional identification with all mortal beings, and by my intentional identification with all the problems of mankind, and by my suffering of all that followed from my consequent ever-decreasing presumption of the "Bright" Itself. In this crucial early Event,

I was walking to the movies with my mother and father. As was frequently the case with them, they were having an argument. My mother plays the "tar-baby", which, if you remember Uncle Remus, was set down on a log by Br'er Bear and Br'er Fox in order to trap Br'er Rabbit. She is quiet and passive, and my father very quick, loud, and threatening violence, until he gets stuck and fades away, pretending he will never be heard from again.

That scene was one of their lifelong characteristic games, and so it really makes no difference what aroused it in this case, as I am sure I did not know at the time. I remember there was a full moon, shining, but orange and shadowy. I have no specific recollection of what movie we were on our way to see. I must have been about six or seven years old.

What appeared to me then was a kind of archetype of all conflict. There was the act of separation, and that act was destroying the Energy of Love-Bliss. I very clearly and directly experienced the effects of this conflict and separation. I could feel the embracive rays of Love-Bliss-Energy that surrounded us and moved in a delicate network of points in and through our bodies. I could feel those rays of Love-Bliss-Energy being cut by the negative emotional acts of my parents. As a result of their Love-less actions, dark vacuums were being spotted out around us and between us. And I was about to make one of my most significant early attempts to Communicate that there is only Love-Bliss-Energy, and to Prove it was so by an actual Spiritual Transmission of that Love-Bliss-Energy Itself.

I remember silently expanding the "Bright" Love-Bliss-Energy from my heart, while, at the same time, trying to distract my parents by pointing out the moon, and by asking them questions about God and life, so they would be calmed, and enabled to feel the Love-Bliss-Energy of the "Bright" I was Transmitting to them.

Their ordinary humor did return a little. My father seemed quieted, and my mother was answering my

"From the beginning, in the early 'Brightness' of my life,
I directly perceived the guiding Purpose of my life:
to restore True Humor . . ."

questions. Nonetheless, I felt their basic refusal, and their basic insensitivity to the "Bright". We went to the movie, and all the while we watched I felt a pressure in my solar plexus and my heart, where the Love-Bliss-Energy was refused and pushed back. But at least the argument was gone, for the night.

The conflict between my parents was a constant field of experience for me as a boy. By no means did they argue all the time, but those events were a persistent and arbitrary danger, and they formed an early ground of disturbance and of understanding in me. And, in the crucial Event I just described, my parents' profound insensitivity to the "Bright", and, indeed, their fundamental refusal of It (even though It was Freely Transmitted to them), gave rise to, or, at least, most profoundly confirmed, a deeply felt concern and urgency in me that became the means for me to fulfill the guiding Purpose of my life.

From the beginning, in the early "Brightness" of my life, I directly perceived the guiding Purpose of my life: to restore True Humor (or the all-transcending quality of Happiness, that can persist, or, otherwise, constantly come forward, in the living being under all conditions, whether the conditions appear to be positive or negative). Throughout my life, I have been moved to Communicate (or to Reveal, to Transmit, and to Awaken) the fundamental Source and Substance and Condition of True Humor to others. Ordinary humor can appear in many forms, as the seemingly undauntable mood of life-enjoyment, as the hilarious pleasure of laughter, as the fairy-tale ease of faith, as the self-congratulating certainty of mental knowledge, and as the overriding excitement of even all the greater and smaller bodily victories. But True Humor has only one living Form (and one ultimate, or inherently perfect, Form), Which is Real God, Perfect Truth, or Reality Itself.

If my Purpose, even from the beginning of this lifetime, has always been to restore True Humor, and, likewise, if my Motive has always been Founded in the "Bright", death and the fear of death have, also from the beginning of this lifetime, always been the counter to my Presence, the source of contradiction, fear, mystery, and despair.

I contracted all of the childhood diseases, including a relatively mild case of polio, and, at times, became delirious with fever. This suffering grew a certain depth in me as a boy, because outwardly there were few of the possible overwhelming tragedies. In delirium I would experience tremendous fear and an awesome mortal separateness, such that death became very real to me during those incidents.

During one of those episodes, I believe when I was about five or six years old, I had a dream that impressed me very deeply. I saw a neat green grass field moving up and away from me, and there was a beautiful full oak tree at its highest point, on the horizon. It was a clear blue day. I did not see myself in the dream but felt as if I were stationed at my point of view at the base of the rise. There were three women in black gowns, like nuns, walking away from me, up the hill. And I felt this tremendous loss and separation, as if I were being left behind.

I woke up crying, with an intense fear of death. And I asked my mother about death. She tried to console me with assurances about God and the afterlife. But a fear was planted in me from that time, so that death was always thereafter a fascinating mystery to me.

I often thought about that dream. I felt it was not a dream at all, but a memory of past death, or an intuition of future death. And the importance of that dream, or of death itself, was never the fact itself. For this reason, I never became particularly motivated to investigate spiritualistic psychism, which pursues the link between living beings and those who are outside this life. For me, the interest in death has always been a matter of investigating, or deeply considering, the present relationship between life-consciousness and death.

I have not truly been concerned with where one goes after death. In my very earliest years, it was always clear to me that, no matter where one goes or where one is, one is always the same fundamental Consciousness. Indeed, I observed and experienced <u>all</u> events from the "Point of View" of the "Bright". I was <u>Being</u> that Radiant Consciousness, Which is untouched. But I gradually became combined with the mortal experience of identification with the body-mind, and a great question arose in me, more and more persistently and profoundly: What <u>is</u> Consciousness (in Its living form, and altogether)? What must occur within It for It to remain as It is (untouched and Free and Blissful) even while, in Its living form, It already bears the certainty (or the tacit knowledge) of death?

It was this question, felt as a true dilemma, which caused me to indulge in a rather awesome adventure some years later, when I was about nine years old. My father and I shared a passion for animals, although my mother usually took care of them. I was given a black cocker spaniel named "Bootsie" as a present for Easter. The cellar of our house was my free space, and I spent long hours secluded there or playing with friends, where I invented space ships and boats for us to ride in. I kept a large chest of small toys and would play quietly there with my hoard. I was not exclusively introverted, since I also constantly played outdoors and with friends in the woods all around us, but there was a strong interior activity in me that I also enjoyed without feeling the need for company.

One day I went into the cellar while my father was at work and my mother away shopping. As I walked into the room, I saw Bootsie lying in an old overstuffed chair in the corner of the cellar. I called her and rushed over to pet her. And she was dead. I do not think I had ever touched a dead one before, and certainly not one that I had loved and known alive. She was stiff, lying as if in sleep, and her warmth was nearly gone.

I was immediately overcome by terrible grief. I ran upstairs and sat and rolled in my room, and wept for

Adi Da with Bootsie

what seemed like hours. But there was not only grief. There was also fear and guilt. I was stuck with some kind of knowledge that I was afraid to tell. My door was closed, and I heard my mother in the other rooms. She must have heard me crying, but I do not think she came in to me. She must have gone and found the dead animal and decided to leave me to my father. Then he too came home, and they opened the door to me.

My father asked me what was wrong, and I was trying not to show my grief. But then I told him, "Bootsie died." And I fell in his arms and wept.

After several hours of consolation and quiet, I had controlled my grief. Then I made a very strange decision. I could not bear estrangement from love. I prayed to God to receive Bootsie and care for her. And then I told Him that I wanted Him to take me also. I needed time to make the transition from my life and love in the world, and so I told Him it should be at 9 P.M. two days from then, I believe on a Sunday.

I did not tell my parents I was about to die. I decided to be with them and enjoy with them for two days and make an easy transition. On the last day we drove in the country. I watched in the clouds, seeing only heaven and Bootsie and God.

Then it was the evening of my death. We had dinner and sat in the living room watching television. I went and prayed to God, and I was certain He would take me at nine o'clock. But as the hour approached, I began to realize the importance of this move. I was about to leave life! I was about to suffer the loss of the world, my parents, my future possibility. I felt a tremendous connection to the living world, and saw that the absence of one I loved did not amount to the destruction of love, of living consciousness, of life-energy, of "Bright" Fullness, or of Heart-Joy. I saw that I was alive!

Nevertheless, I presumed that much of this "conversion" might be due to fear and regret. I knew that I had bargained with God, and, therefore, I would not abandon

His Will. And so I only sat and waited. I watched the television and continually relaxed the awesome fear that kept rising in me. Nine o'clock came, and I did not die.

I do not remember if I was alone in my room or with my parents at that hour, but when it passed I went and prayed to God. I thanked Him for my life and asked forgiveness for my wavering. But something in me had died or become hidden at that hour. I remember that for several years afterward I would end my prayers with the request, "And please, dear Lord, allow me to live until I am eighty-nine years old or older."

For some time after this incident I suffered a constriction in my chest, and I felt as if I could not breathe deeply enough. I even had my father take me to a doctor. The doctor and my father watched me breathing behind a fluoroscope. And it was determined that I was in good health. After that I gradually took some relief, for I had not been certain that my promise to die had not crippled my heart in some way. I remember that even in the days before our visit to the doctor, and then for weeks afterwards, I experienced a sublime enjoyment of the air and light, the fact of my life, in spite of the feeling of weakness in my heart.

So I experienced in myself the meaning of death, conflict, and separation, which I knew to be the primary fact in all suffering. I saw how the sentiment of separation from love can, as a problem or concern in the living consciousness, draw one out of the "Bright" of Illuminated, Free Consciousness, until one no longer perceives the perfect Form that is always here.

Such early experiences in my life are not merely clinical, nor did they alone "create" the later personal form of my life. I was Awake and full of Clarity in those early episodes, just as I am now. Even then, and forever before then, I was What I _am_ now. And it is Clear to me that I have always operated on the basis of a few fundamental perceptions, and these have structured all of my life. And the basic, few perceptions that have structured all of my life are the fundamentals of Reality (altogether, both conditional and Un-conditional), and not merely the idiosyncrasies of character (or of conditional personality) in and of itself.

Character is built through experience, through the accumulations of one's use of certain given options in the living consciousness. Disturbances of the personality, which form so much of the data of clinical observations, are not the results of a given disorder in one's Real (or Ultimate) Nature. Rather, they are the results of a misuse and unconsciousness of the options associated with the living, or conditional, consciousness. Therefore, it was Clear to me from the beginning of this lifetime (and, over time, it was repeatedly reconfirmed) that true healing (or the establishment of the capability necessary for free, "creative" life) is not a matter of concentration on memory, the past, or the history of the functional personality, good or bad, but it is a matter of understanding the fundamental and <u>present</u> activity of the living consciousness and making the right conscious and intentional use of one's living options.

Whenever I have turned from the True Center of present-time life-consciousness to one or another kind of seeking motivated in the desires of my complex life, I have been brought to the same recognition: The search is suffering. When, for example, I felt the loss of the little animal I loved, I was moved to find her, to be where that love continued as is. So I was motivated to a drastic ascent from life, to what, because of my separated mentality, seemed to be God. But, at last, I saw that the motive toward re-union was itself the source and act of separation, and that it was itself a destructive cutting away of Free Awareness, of Love-Bliss-Energy, and of Life.

In the hours of waiting for death I was not Awake as the "Bright", the Full Presence of my Being. I was separate from the "Bright", and saw all Love and Light and Freedom of Being as radically above, apart from me and this world. Only too late, it seemed to me then, did the shock of what I awaited draw me into that Fullness again. And I saw that Reality was always already (and, therefore, always presently) Full, and that to seek that Fullness in the symbolic state I was awaiting was to abandon (or to not presume and Enjoy) that always present Fullness in the actual present moment.

I learned (or even re-learned) this Great Lesson at that time. It is not merely the product of reflection years hence. Originally, and (but decreasingly) as a small boy, I operated with that Clarity and Enjoyed (even in my living form and consciousness) the Knowledge of Real (or Ultimate, or Truly Divine) Consciousness. The search itself has never been my fundamental Vocation. The search was only a curious excursion. It was temporarily necessary (because of my born association with the functions and tendencies of a living human body-mind), but (because of the always underlying Foundation that is the "Bright") it was also only a means of reaffirmation of the Real in the context of my living consciousness. Therefore, all of my life, Reality Itself, "Bright" and Full, has been the Fundamental Circumstance of my living existence.

My earliest childhood (from birth), and not merely some later (or more adult) time, was the period of my first Knowledge and Unfoldment of the "Bright", Which I Knew to be the perfect Form (and the Source of the living condition) of Reality. And what is That exactly? This book is determined to Communicate It again and again in so many ways. But, on the level of my earliest recognition of It, It was the "ordinary" Condition of even my living consciousness. It was Consciousness Itself, Radiant and Awake. It was my simple (human and Ultimate) State, Prior to even any experience. It was not mysterious or awesome to me. There was no shadow, nothing hidden in It. It was not motivated to seek any end at all. There was no beyond, no outside, no Other. It had no sense of time. Nor had It yet begun to feel any kind of confusion or identity with existence as separated personality and problematic experience. It was the Center of the life-functions, but without dilemma or unconsciousness. There were no divisions in It. Radiant Energy was Communicated within It, and, thus, in and via the entire body-mind. There was Joy in the body, a Luminous cell life, a constant respiration and circulation of Love-Bliss-Energy and unlimited, boundless Pleasure. There was a Current of Energy in the heart that rose into the head through the throat. And that same Current of Energy was below the heart, rising up into it from below. There was a surrounding Circle of Energy that was spaceless and boundless, but Which had a formless Locus above the head. And all of this moving Energy Originated as a single Source-Current of Light and Life in the heart that was reflected and Felt at a pervasive Center deep within the head. There was a constant Radiation of this entire Form, including the body. It was Joy in the heart reflected as Enjoyment in the head. And that formless, spaceless Form of Consciousness was "Bright", Silent, Full, Knowing only and entirely this Condition, this Reality, and seeing no problem, no separation in the fact of life.

This "Bright", this Real Consciousness, is the perfect Form (and the Source of the living condition) of Reality, and It is never undone. It is now, and It is you. Now and always, every living being is arising within and as this Form, Which is the very Form of life. It is only that life is not lived as Real Consciousness. It is confused with some experience, some fragment of Energy in the event of the personality, in the functions that operate by laws subconscious and unconscious to the individual, or some wave of Energy that fascinates the individual in the superconscious patterns above. When such confusions of identity overwhelm and distract one into some division of the living structure of Reality, one is moved to great seeking in the alternatives of life. Every course that is not simply the demonstration of Real Consciousness, direct and present, is a schism in one's living form. The excursions of my life beyond childhood showed this all the more to me.

"Beyond my tenth year I was more often solemn,
and even ordinary humor became more an act of 'creation'.
I turned from mostly pleasure to listening."

CHAPTER 2

The Listener

My earliest years were gratuitous, a free enjoyment whose wisdom was unearned. This is true of all human beings, but many people learn suffering very soon, and so even the given becomes a matter of problems and of seeking. Beyond my tenth year I was more often solemn, and even ordinary humor became more an act of "creation". I turned from mostly pleasure to listening.

As a small boy I liked to use the ways of increasing simple enjoyment and life-humor in others. I recited poems and rhymes, sang, and told stories. I made a puppet theatre in the cellar and put on shows for the neighbors and their children and all my relatives. Then I was a ventriloquist and a dancer, and until I was thirteen I always performed comedy with my dummy at school. I loved to draw and paint, and everyone took pleasure in what I made, so that I even won the "art award" when I left eighth grade to go to high school.

Even religion took on a certain humorous quality for me as I came to adolescence. I was an acolyte in the Lutheran church, and nearly every Sunday I served at the altar. Once every month the church practiced the ceremony of "holy communion", and I would prepare the altar. I filled the little glasses in the trays with wine and set out the pressed discs of unleavened bread.

I would have to get up very early to serve on those communion Sundays. From the time I was about eight or nine, my parents ceased to go to church except on the important holidays. And so I would get up on those Sundays alone, about 6 A.M., and leave for church without breakfast. I would get very hungry while I poured the

"I was an acolyte in the Lutheran church,
and nearly every Sunday I served at the altar."

wine into glasses and packed the wafers into the paten. The wine was contained in a special glass bottle. It had a rubber bulb on top that injected a bit of wine into a glass through a little spout as you pressed it.

I had tasted a little wine at home a few times in my life. When my parents had company, they would sometimes give me a tiny bit of port. And once or twice I had a small glass of beer with pizza at a neighbor's house. But I had never felt drunkenness, and wine seemed harmless to me. Before it was consecrated on the altar, the bread and wine of communion was not presumed to be "holy", or untouchable, so I felt only a little reluctant to sample it in the pastor's study.

One such morning, when I was thirteen or fourteen, while feeling particularly hungry and weak, I pressed a little sweet port into my mouth, then one for the tray, then one for me. I ate a few communion wafers, and then a little more wine. I had tried this just a little once or twice before and felt no peculiar effects. And it did help my hunger. So, on this particular day, I was very liberal with myself.

I had not quite finished filling the trays when I began to feel very dizzy, and yet very happy, so that I was laughing quite a lot when the other acolyte, the pastor, and the choir began to arrive to prepare for the service. I knew that I was drunk. There was no doubt about that. But I did not feel particularly guilty. I felt only that I should try very hard to look as normal as possible!

It could not have happened on a day more filled with unusual circumstances. The pastor was a little late, so, as soon as he arrived, everything had to be done very quickly. I was a little too dizzy for fast movements, but somehow I had to finish the wine trays instantly and lay out the altar. Then there was a sudden prayer, and we were hustled into the church.

Before the actual communion, the acolytes sat in the choir pews in the chancel. I was enjoying myself. I felt very heady and relaxed, but a little concerned that people, especially the pastor, would observe something peculiar about me. I looked at faces a lot, and grinned every now and then at a friend in the choir or the congregation.

During the communion service, the acolytes had to do a lot of ceremonious moving around at the altar, giving and taking wafers and wine trays to and from the pastor. I seemed to sway a lot, and my body felt very nervous as we began. Then I dropped a few wafers and, in obedience to the rule, I hungrily picked them up to eat. But the rhythm of the movements in the ceremony became a kind of repetitive dance, so that my anxiety disappeared in circles, again and again.

I watched the communicants very closely. And soon their movements became absurd to me. Sometimes there would be one too many, and all the kneeling communicants would be crunched up. And there was something ridiculous about the way each of them would stick out the tongue for a wafer. So that very often I would find some bit of business to do on the altar, to turn away and bury my laughter in the wall!

Then the communion was over, and we returned to the pews in the chancel for a hymn. At that point the pastor, who was about twenty feet away from me at the head of the pew, remembered that he was supposed to perform a baptism at the close of the service. He told one of the choir to signal me. Whispers went down the line, and soon I was being elbowed. The person next to me was trying to whisper something about a baptism, but I had no idea what that had to do with me. I had never served at a baptism.

I began to get a little nervous, and I was not sure whether my drunkenness was preventing me from getting the message. Finally, someone leaned over and whispered very loudly, "Fill the baptismal basin!"

The baptismal basin was down in front of the congregation, outside the chancel and just below the lectern where the pastor read the Bible lessons. I really did not know how to go about it ceremoniously and unnoticed,

The Lutheran Church in Franklin Square

Inside the church

The baptismal basin

but I figured I had better get out of the chancel and get some water somewhere.

I got up and swayed out of the chancel into a doorway on the other side of the altar. As I went out, I looked back anxiously at the pastor for any last-minute signal about what I should do. But he was nodding in his hymnal with the choir.

I had no idea how long I had before the baptism was supposed to take place. Perhaps only the length of a hymn! So I ran frantically around the pastor's study looking for a water bottle. I opened up the doors to a closet where we kept our gowns and the altar paraphernalia. I jumped back. There was a man standing in the closet, peeking out between the gowns! He was obviously hiding in the closet! He pressed his index finger to his lips and made a sign for me to be quiet. So I closed the doors on him again and ran around some more, but I could hardly keep from falling on the floor and laughing myself silly.

I learned later that the man in the closet was an FBI agent who was supposed to be watching for someone who had been stealing money from the weekly offering plates. Anyway, I let him be, since I was rushed. All I could find was an old milk bottle under the pastor's wash basin. It was coated inside with some kind of ashy substance. It looked as though somebody had been growing plants in it.

I had no time to look for any other kind of bottle, so I ran water through it several times and shook it to loosen the sludge. The best I could do was wash away some of the surface dirt, but the stain itself remained all around the inside of the bottle. I filled it with cold water and ran toward the exit to the church nave.

As I opened the door and stepped into the church in front of the congregation, every eye seemed to follow me. I tried to carry the bottle ceremoniously on my right side, away from the congregation, but everyone seemed to see it anyway, and lots of them began to smile at me and whisper to one another. It all began to seem friendly enough to me, so I walked as calmly as possible, smiling solemnly. As I walked, it began to occur to me that the ice cold water was going to be a little rough on the baby's head. And I began to laugh inside again at how ridiculous it all was, the man in the closet, the dirty bottle, the cold water, so that I stepped into the front of my robe and nearly fell over on the floor.

Now it seemed everyone was aware of me. I was standing by the baptismal basin. The pastor was standing above me at his lectern. And the entire church was silent. I lifted the top off the basin and put it on the floor. And then, with grace and ceremony, I turned the milk bottle upside down.

The bottle went "Glub-Glup, Glub-Glub", and the sound seemed to ring around the church! I could hear people snorting everywhere. And when I looked up at the pastor, he was pressing his lips and trying not to laugh. The more I poured, the louder it got, and I was trying so hard to keep steady and not to laugh that tears were running out of my eyes.

Finally, I figured there was enough water in the bowl, and I swifted out of the room, back to the pastor's study. I remember laughing in the pastor's sink until I was empty of every last urge to laugh. Then, as if nothing had happened, I cruised back, solemn and easy, to my seat in the choir.

I suppose it was around this time that I became a true adolescent. I should mark it just about the year I entered high school, when I was nearly fourteen. Then the rights of sex, the exercise of personal identity, and the need for privacy became very crucial requirements. Up to that time, I was protected in the circumstance of the parental nest. I had, until that time, asserted myself in dependence, but now, more and more, in independence.

At first, I was not overtly independent at all. My first three years in high school were gray years in many ways. I did not feel the freedom of sexual and personal play that I assumed even as a little boy. I became more serious, more reserved, somewhat puzzled, and, outside of school, I tended to spend a lot of time in solitude.

During those early high school years, I was an amateur radio operator. There was a fascination for me in the invisible energies, the mysterious circuitries, and even all the physical mysteries of radio communication. I was often awake late into the night, or I would get up before sunrise, in order to take advantage of the longer-distance radio communication possible (because of the unique atmospheric conditions) during those hours.

About the middle of my junior year in high school I learned that, in special circumstances of communication, the Power of the "Bright" would come out of hiding and rouse Itself again in me, and expand Itself, such that It would even, to some degree, be felt by many others. I read in the school newspaper that the American Legion was sponsoring an oratorical contest, and all junior and senior year students were eligible. I felt certain that I could speak persuasively (although I had never given a speech before), and so I immediately began to write a speech.

I do not remember how it occurred to me, but I decided to write an oratory on prejudice. This was back in 1956, before the civil rights movement or its viewpoint had any force or voice that were known to me. The speech was called "Patterns of Prejudice". I studied various documents and books in the library, and I put together a speech that had a very pure and righteous tone. It had very little ordinary humor, but there was a basic feeling throughout of the obvious wrongness of human social negativity. I mimicked many negative attitudes in the speech, and they seemed to me to be obviously that—attitudes, possible, but not necessary, ways of relating to another human being about whom one was conscious of a difference, be it color, or religion, nationality, manner, or whatever.

I think some of the impetus behind that speech came from my childhood experiences of conflict in my family. And my father was from Mississippi. I do not recall any expressions of race prejudice in him, but he had taken me to the South a couple of times when I was yet a boy (of eight, and then of nine, years of age), and I became aware of race hatred there. Shortly before we made our first visit, a black man had been hanged in a barn nearby, and reports of such terrible events were routinely heard by me as part of the surroundings of casual conversation during those visits.

My oratory on prejudice included the tone and point of view of religion. Prejudice was an attitude I had perceived in the very people I met in my church. And I saw it everywhere in the general community. I assumed, rather naively, that nearly everyone was a religious person in some way, and so I considered that nearly everyone could recognize at once that prejudice was not a viable expression, purely on the basis of the religious beliefs they already professed.

I delivered the speech to a few people in a small classroom and was accepted as a finalist, along with three or four others. Then, a week later, we were brought to the school auditorium, which was filled with perhaps a thousand people or more. I had never confronted a mass of humanity before. But the Power of the "Bright" suddenly moved in me, and It gave me confidence and inspiration.

I gave my speech while standing alone on the stage. I noticed immediately that I was producing a very remarkable effect on everyone. My words moved and expanded through and out from me on the feeling-waves of the "Bright", and a sudden silence came over the entire audience. Even the "hoods", the gangs that took the front rows and slouched or mimicked whatever appeared on the stage, began spontaneously to sit up. Each one, and all, became profoundly attentive, as if each were deeply experiencing a fundamental life-truth that was always hidden, but which one could not deny if it stood out before one. I felt I was speaking a life-truth that everyone accepted whole, and upon which all could operate, except that people tend not to decide together that each one already holds it true.

I won the oratorical contest that day. And I went on from there to a finalist's session that was supposed to decide the winner for the county, who would then go on to compete for the state award, and, I suppose, then for the national award. But I did not win at the next level. As soon as I stood to speak before the huge numbers of that strange, hostile crowd, I felt a different aura, a wholly different mind, and the "Bright" Itself seemed reluctant to Shine abroad, as if because the gathering in front of me was not worthy of Its blessing. The person who won on that occasion gave what appeared to me to be a merely cute, meaningless speech about George Washington and the flag. And I even felt some embarrassment that I had brought up anything more profound than picnic patriotism.

Nevertheless, many came to shake my hand after the speeches. And, as I had surmised, their expressions also implied that I had stepped on some toes. They felt there was an actual "establishment" of prejudice, and that it could not accept what appeared to be a very radical expression of brotherhood, mutual love, and untroubled enjoyment of humanity. Finally, one older man took me aside, clasped my hand, looked at me strongly, and said (as if intent that I should always remember it): "Never let them stop you from thinking."

I was only a teenager, and the entire matter was surrounded by adolescent perceptions, but there was something real that I encountered in the world that day. As a result, my involvement in the guiding Purpose of my life was further aroused and intensified from that day. From then, I was concentrated in myself. I began to listen to something un-Happy in the wind. I began to doubt. I was profoundly aware of a resistance, a madness, in humanity that would require great Intelligence and a masterful Communication before it would acknowledge its own Truth (or even anything right).

That day was the beginning of human maturity in me. Of course, it was a matter of the same problem of conflict and separation that I recognized even as a little child. And I was handling it in the same manner, by enforcing a Presence and an Intelligence that was, for me, already Obvious, Whole, and Free. It was the "Bright" again, but I brought It to bear on a problem that is not merely personal, or even a temporary family conflict, but a schism that is rooted in everyone's mind, in every moment of everyone's life, and, therefore, in the world itself. I saw that human beings were not living as Real and True. I saw that Truth, or Reality, was not actually being lived, and that the entire world of my future was not a field of free consciousness and love, but a field of ignorance, conflict, and seeking.

After that I became a "public man" for a year. I acted in school plays, spoke in school politics. My paternal grandfather died in my senior year, and I composed a ceremony to be performed at his funeral. I was to recite it along with my cousins and other members of the De Molay, a junior branch of the Masons, of which my grandfather was a high-ranking member.

We performed this ceremony in the funeral home, before my grandfather's casket. It was a very honorable ceremony, and everyone present was deeply, emotionally moved. However, even as I spoke, there was no particular sorrow in me or sense of loss. I was mostly aware of the living who were present. There was something I understood that needed to be understood and lived by all. It was the summary Lesson of my childhood. It was about always keeping love in the present time, and not relinquishing that love in the present in order to seek it elsewhere, even among the dead. And I wanted to Communicate that life-truth with an overwhelmingly "Bright" effectiveness. But it seemed that the more I emphasized this life-truth, the more outwardly sorrowful everyone, and especially my father, became.

Nevertheless, my effect on the funereal gathering

was appropriately intense, and, certainly, cathartic. And, immediately after this ceremony, the pastor of my church, who had also served the event, and who was astonished by the effect I had on everyone there, passionately urged me to go on to college and eventually become a Lutheran minister. This seemed like an obvious and right course to me at the time, and I agreed. At the pastor's invitation, I became a liturgist, often reciting the sacred texts and the instructions to the congregation during the ceremonies in the church. And I was accepted by Columbia College to enter as a freshman in the coming year.

I moved into this agreed upon future in religion with a great feeling of certainty, and even anticipation. But I did nothing to "create" it. My interest in high school studies fell off completely, so that one teacher remarked that he wished I had "never won that contest". It was true that the oratorical "contest" had changed me. But it was not so much the winning as the losing, and not the fact of my loss, but the reasons for it in everyone. I was aware of something radically wrong in life. As far as I was concerned, I had "dropped out".

I had taken a large number of credits in technical courses that dealt with the physics and practical use of electricity and electronics. The examinations I was to take at the end of my senior year were the finals for courses that extended for two and even three years. But I ceased to study altogether. None of that work, or any of the work in my other courses, seemed to have any importance. In fact, it seemed like nonsense to me.

I made only the most superficial study for my exams. I thought that I could probably pass many of them. Some of them I was almost certain I could not pass. Yet, I felt that it did not matter, and I knew that I would somehow go on to whatever work I had to do.

I had always been an excellent student in the past, and I have never, before or since, cheated on examinations. But when I went to my final technical examinations

almost totally unprepared, I decided I would simply copy
another student's work. I sat behind and across the aisle
from a student I knew would do well on the tests. And I
copied every one of his calculations and answers. Here
and there, where I was able to notice a slight error, I cor-
rected the answers.

As a result, I came to graduation with one of the
highest scores in the technical exams. It did not matter
to me, although I was happy to know that I would be
able to go on to college unobstructed.

The next phase of my life is the real beginning of listening for me. At the end of my high school years, I was
radically apart from any kind of superficial idealism or
any need to achieve ordinary human excellence. I was
profoundly serious and also profoundly undisciplined. I
aligned myself exclusively with my own internal states.
Where there was desire, I indulged it. Where there was
interest, I followed it. I was totally renegade in my holding to life, for I felt on the brink of Knowledge, of Reality, of brilliant Discovery. Of course, no one who lives
disarmed in this manner is free of delusions or suffering,
and I was about to begin a long period of most awesome
and painful suffering. But I was alarmingly free to follow
the thread of my own life-consciousness.

The gratuitous, foundation period of the "Bright" was
past. I no longer possessed the unearned Joy and Clarity
of my boyhood. I had seen the world and ceased to be
innocent. I had even begun to enjoy my own lack of innocence, and my own forbidden pleasures. The inner
resources of True Humor became strangely entangled with
others and the world. Therefore, I avoided no "sin" at all.
And, yet, I remained concentrated in the image and person
of Jesus, as if, when I would Know his "Secret" utterly, it
would freely convert me and purify all of my estrangement. Thus, I did not fear my "sinfulness" any more than I
feared to eat the wafers and the wine in secret.

I became more and more self-indulgent, and, thereby,
began a pattern of self-exploitation that was to persist for

Adi Da in His youth

many years. I began to gain excess weight, to indulge myself sexually, and to assert myself beyond anyone's ability to limit or control me. Nevertheless, within me I was fully aware of this play of Scorpio. Therefore, I did not adopt "sin" as a way of life, but as a way of Knowing life.

Beginning at that time, while I was yet sixteen years of age, I became submitted to an inner drive to utterly experience the heart of the human dilemma, the very essence of human suffering. This intention in me is not something I can recognize only now, after years of reflection. It was an actual, conscious decision I made at that time. Later, as you will see in the next chapter, this intention became even more explicit. I no longer took the position of the "Bright", the Radiant Presence of Consciousness Itself, surrounded by the conflicts of others. I had found conflict in the very world. I felt it rising in myself. And I rushed to become it, by surrendering to it, in order to Know the way that no longer required it for anyone.

"When I entered Columbia College in September 1957,
I was possessed with a single, motivating interest.
I wanted to understand what living beings <u>are</u>.
What <u>is</u> living consciousness?"

CHAPTER 3

Hearing

There is no such thing as anyone's "autobiography". The events of experience do not, when recollected, synthesize themselves into an exact history, or even an exact person. Ordinary experience does not, over time, become a "something". It is only an irregular series of concerns for life and death. If I were to write about a few such moments of ordinary experience, I could "create" an image. This in fact is what everyone does with memory. One highlights and defines a few (originally, shapeless, or indefinable) events, identifies each of them with a particular defining emotion, and, thus, by a kind of "artistic" effort, makes a narrative, and even invents a particular and separate "self". Thus, one conceives of oneself as a "someone" by means of the device of partial contemplation. But if one could include it all (utterly and entirely), and consciously (and utterly) perceive the Real nature of experience at any moment, there would be no particular and separate person in the mind. There is no emphasis, and no design, in the whole. No particular and separate thing stands out at the point of Totality. Therefore, the more deeply and completely one experiences the recollection of one's ordinary life, the more arbitrary every mark becomes.

Nevertheless, there are a few unique Events in what, as a concession to the conventions of ordinary communication, I refer to as "my own life" that stand whole by themselves. They neither signify nor justify an inherently (or otherwise, and utterly) separate life, nor do they define or describe an artificial, synthetic, or merely presumed "person". Rather, they are Events that Communicate, or cease to hide, Reality. And these Events are the genuine subject of my "autobiography". They are the Events in my early life that uniquely and fully demonstrate what I refer to as "True Humor". And they do not speak of my human instance alone, but they are moments in the universally Communicated and universally Knowable life of Reality Itself. Therefore, those Events reveal the Truth of Who I am, Which, ultimately, is the Truth and Identity of every one and all.

When I was a little boy, the "Bright" was my constant Knowledge of Reality. But the more tentative I became about Reality, the more I felt myself to be separate from Reality, and, therefore, one who "listens" to Reality, and even one who seeks Reality. And the more I became a "listener", and then a seeker, the more the Knowledge of Reality became an Occasion, an overwhelming Event, an Enlightenment. The subject of this chapter is the first and primary Event of Conscious Reality in my life after the "Bright" had disappeared into my childhood and I had become not only a "listener" but an urgent seeker relative to my own Truth.

When I entered Columbia College in September 1957, I was possessed with a single, motivating interest. I wanted to understand what living beings are. What is living consciousness? Whatever academic studies were required of me, I was always at work on this one question, and I was forever researching some kind of primary thesis out of great need.

The experience of study at Columbia was completely devastating. I had never in my life encountered any kind of sophisticated thought. But now I suddenly became aware of the literature of the world. The mood at Columbia in those years was profoundly solemn and critical. The attitude and the dilemma that I encountered when I gave my little speech on prejudice were here extended as the consciousness of the human race.

Grayson Kirk, who was then president of the University, introduced us to college life with a serious speech about the rising problems of humanity. He promised that Columbia would not teach us the answers, but we would perhaps learn the questions. Altogether, he indicated that Columbia would not make us Happy, but he promised that we would learn how to think.

I was deeply impressed by his attitude, and that of the entire, formidable crowd of lecturing "thinkers", talking, and otherwise in attendance, there. Immediately, Columbia seemed like an eminently appropriate, and even ideal, place in which to expand my doubts, but I was puzzled that one of the highest institutions of learning could represent itself as anything but the bearer of Truth. I soon learned that the Truth was always in research in such places. They are not institutions of Truth. They are marketplaces of doubt.

I began to read the deposits of Western culture. And all my idols lost their Power. To begin with, I learned that the "Holy Christian Truth" was anything but the real substance of Western civilization. There is a thesis emphasized in all the little bits of thought generated in a university education. In that thesis, the human being is described as necessarily mortal, functionally conditioned, and, at best, "creative" as a social animal. Also, the universe is described as materially prior to conscious life, and it is chronically understood without recourse to Spiritual or religious propositions.

Every book I read and every course I took emphasized this thesis in some unique fashion. This experience very quickly destroyed even the latent image of Jesus that I had stored up in childhood. A book that deeply affected me in the midst of my freshman year was *The Lost Years of Jesus Revealed*, by Charles Francis Potter. Even the church seemed to proclaim the absence of its own Truth. In his book, based on his interpretation of the Essene tradition[3] revealed in the "Dead Sea Scrolls", Dr. Potter wrote about the process whereby the traditional

---

3. The Essenes were an ancient Jewish sect believed to be the monastic community described in the Dead Sea Scrolls, and interpreted by some scholars as being the background from which Christianity arose.

Christian descriptions of Jesus of Nazareth came to be proposed:

> A "scheme of salvation" emerged, transforming the man Jesus into the mystical Christ, the Son of God. . . .
>
> In the body of doctrine as it grew, influenced by current ideas about what a god-man should be and do, Jesus must perforce have come from heaven to be born of a virgin, must perform many miracles, make mystic utterances, raise the dead occasionally, and then himself die, rise again from the dead, and be assumpted back to heaven, thus proving his deity from advent to ascension. These were the standard "signs" by which a new god could be recognized, and these myths were gradually attached to the person of Jesus the son of Miryam (Mary) as his deification proceeded. . . .
>
> The first-century followers of Jesus and the theologians and their successors can be excused to some extent for failing to perceive that he was no god come down from heaven, but rather a very great human being, ahead of his time in his intuitive understanding of his fellows and in his apparently instinctive knowledge of the technique of what we now call psychotherapy. . . .
>
> But we already have enough data to show that the Scrolls are really "God's Gift to the Humanists," for every unrolling reveals further indications that Jesus was, as he said, "The Son of Man," rather than the deity "Son of God" his followers later claimed.[4]

After about six months of "education" I went to my old pastor with my doubts. I wanted to know if the resurrection and ascension of Jesus, his miracles and Power,

4. Rev. Dr. Charles Francis Potter, *The Lost Years of Jesus Revealed* (Greenwich, Connecticut: Fawcett Publications, 1958), pp. 71-72, 125, and 127.

and all of the doctrine of God had any support in evidence. He was unable to offer me a single means of faith. Instead, he tried to make a mockery of educators and psychologists. He railed about John Dewey and progressive education.[5] And he let me go home with a prayer to God for our salvation.

From that time, I was passed into the terror of my doubts. I cannot possibly overemphasize the effect of those doubts. I was finally and terribly lifted out of the ease of my childhood. My mind sank into despair and actual terror. I had fixed my Freedom and Joy into the image of Jesus, and I had long ago given over the support of my Happiness to the church. Now that institutionalized symbol, "Jesus of Nazareth", was wrecked by the same ones who had carried it through time.

Then all was, it seemed, finally lost, for Jesus of Nazareth had, for me, in the trouble of my adolescence, become the symbol for even the lost (or, certainly, receding and fading) "Bright" of my childhood. Indeed, in that trouble, he, being but a symbol in my own mind, was a fundamental means whereby the "Bright" was concealed and withheld from me. When the "Bright" deeply receded in me, It only left tracks in the mind, and "Jesus of Nazareth" epitomized them all. Therefore, when "Jesus of Nazareth" fell to my doubts, it was the "Bright" Itself that I felt fall forever away from me. And that fall broke my heart. It drove me into my own vast empty wilderness.

My doubt grew overnight into awesome fear. I felt as if I were living under the threat of death. Life, it seemed to me, was only dying and afraid. I had not a single reason for Joy. I found no faith, no inexplicable grace. I saw only the constant drove of merely "civilized" humanity, a long history of illusions sewn up in the single foundation of a muscular mortality. There was only death, a constant

5. John Dewey (1859-1952) was an American philosopher and educator who believed that education was the fundamental method of social progress and reform. His philosophy of "progressive education" had a major influence on American school systems in the late nineteenth and early twentieth centuries.

ending, a rising fear, a motivated forgetfulness and escape.

I became profoundly aware of conflict and suffering everywhere. There was only struggle and disease, fear and longing, self-exploitation and emptiness, questions without answers. In every man and woman, I recognized the complex of doubt. Then I understood the root of conflict in my parents and the necessity for illusions, for exotic pleasures, for relief and distraction. I knew there was not a single man or woman who had overcome the mystery of this death. I knew this education would only be a long description of fundamental suffering, since all were convinced of the "Truth" of mortality.

From then my schooling ceased to be a serious study. I knew that from beginning to end it had only one object to proclaim, and I had learned it already. From its effects in me and in all mankind, I knew this model of learning was not sufficient. I had not a single reason for Joy, except that there was a kind of tacitly motivating memory of the "Bright".

As a boy I had never been a conscious Christian until I was perhaps five or six years old. But, previous to that age, I had already been a Conscious Form of Light that Knew no-dilemma and no-death. Now, in my early adult life, the "Bright" had seemed to disappear in the human darkness, and I had no means to Enjoy It. But I could not assert the mortal philosophy of Western Man, even if I could not counter it.

Therefore, I dedicated myself to another awesome experiment. I decided that I would begin an experimental life along the same lines which controlled the mood of Western civilization. I decided that I would unreservedly exploit every possibility for experience. I would avail myself of every possible human experience, so that nothing possible to mankind, high or low, would be unknown to me.

This decision became very clear to me one night at a party. I knew that no other possibility was open to me but that of exhaustive experience. There appeared to be no single experience or authority that was simply True. And I thought, "If God exists, He will not cease to exist by any action of my own, but, if I devote myself to all possible experience, He will indeed find some way, in some one or a complex of my experiences, or my openness itself, to reveal Himself to me." Thereafter, I devoted myself utterly and solely to every possible kind of exploit.

No experience posed a barrier to me. There were no taboos, no extremes to be prevented. There was no depth of madness and no limit of suffering that my philosophy could prevent, for, if it did, I would be liable to miss the Lesson of Reality. Thus, I extended myself even beyond my own fear. And my pleasures also became extreme, so there was a constant machine of ecstasy. I could tolerate no mediocrity, no medium experience. I was satisfied with neither atheism nor belief. Both seemed to me only ideas, possible reactions to a more fundamental if unconscious fact. I sought Reality, to <u>be</u> Reality, What <u>is</u>, not what is asserted in the face of What <u>is</u>.

I read and studied every kind of literature. It would be impossible for me to count the thousands of books and influences I embraced in my years of experimenting. I began to write my reflections. My lecture notes in college were filled with long passages of my own, where I would write whatever conclusions or impulses rose in me at the time. A continuous argument of internal contemplation began to move in me, so that I was always intensely pursuing an internal logic, distracted or enlarged at times by some idea or experience in my education.

My lecture notebooks and my separate journals began to become long volumes of my own thinking. They were at first mainly philosophical notes that developed from a kind of desperate and childish complaint into a more and more precise instrument of thought and feeling. Then I began to write poetry also, and to conceive of works of fiction that would express this dilemma and lead to some kind of solution, some opening, some kind of primary Joy.

I became a kind of mad and exaggerated young man, whose impulses were not allowable in this medium culture. My impulses were exploitable only in secret extensions of my own consciousness, or in the company of whores, libertines, and misfits.

My father's younger brother, Richard, asked me what I wanted to do with my life. He could see that I lived only abandoned to adventure, and there was no apparent purpose in me. I told him that I wanted to save the world. And I was absolutely serious. That remark totally expressed all of my reasons. Some incredible Knowledge was the goal of my seeking and not any experience I could ever possess.

I went on in this fashion for more than two years, until all the violence of my seeking precipitated an experience late one night in the middle of my junior year. I had rented a small room from an old woman named Mrs. Renard. It was several blocks away from the college campus. When I was not in class, I spent most of my time in that room reading, thinking, and writing.

On this extraordinary night I sat at my desk late into the night. I had exhausted my seeking, so that I felt there were no more books to read, nor any possible kind of ordinary experience that could exceed what I had already embraced. There seemed no outstanding sources for any new excursion, no remaining and conclusive possibilities. I was drawn into the interior tension of my mind that held all of that seeking, every impulse and alternative, every motive in the form of my desiring. I contemplated it as a whole, a dramatic singleness, and it moved me into a profound shape of life-feeling, so that all the vital centers in my body and mind appeared like a long funnel of contracted planes that led on to an infinitely regressed and invisible image. I observed this deep sensation of conflict and endlessly multiplied contradictions, such that I was surrendered to its very shape, as if to experience it perfectly and to be it.

Livingston Hall, where Adi Da lived during His first semester
at Columbia College

"On this extraordinary
night I sat at my desk
late into the night.
I had exhausted my
seeking, so that I felt
there were no more
books to read, nor any
possible kind of ordi-
nary experience that
could exceed what I
had already embraced.
There seemed no out-
standing sources for
any new excursion,
no remaining and
conclusive possibilities."

Door to the room Adi Da rented
from Mrs. Renard during His junior year

Then, quite suddenly, in a moment, I experienced a total revolution in my body-mind, and, altogether, in my living consciousness. An absolute sense of understanding opened and arose at the extreme end of all this sudden contemplation. And all of the motions of me that moved down into that depth appeared to reverse their direction at some unfathomable point. The rising impulse caused me to stand, and I felt a surge of Force draw up out of my depths and expand, Filling my entire body and every level of my living consciousness with wave on wave of the most Beautiful and Joyous Energy.

I felt absolutely mad, but the madness was not of a desperate kind. There was no seeking and no dilemma within it, no question, no unfulfilled motive, not a single object or presence outside myself.

I could not contain the Energy in my small room. I ran out of the building and through the streets. I thought, if I could only find someone to talk to, to communicate to about this "Thing". The Energy in my body was overwhelming, and there was an ecstasy in every cell that was almost intolerable in its Pressure, Light, and Force. But it was the middle of the night. There were no lights coming from the rooms. I could think of no one to awaken who would understand my experience. I felt that, even if I were to meet a friend, I would be unable to express myself, but my words would only be a kind of uncontrolled poetry of babbling.

My head began to ache with the intense Energy that saturated my brain. I thought, if I could only find someone with some aspirin or something to tranquilize me. But there was no one. And at last I wore myself out wandering in the streets, so that I returned to my room.

I sat down at my desk and wrote my mind in a long, ecstatic essay. I tried to summarize all the significance of this revolution that had occurred in my living being. Until finally I became exhausted in all the violence of my Joy, and I passed to sleep.

In the days that followed, I described this Event to a

few friends, but no one grasped Its importance. Indeed, no one presumed It to be more than some kind of crazy excitement. I even read aloud to one friend the things I had written, but it became clear as I went on that it was only a collection of images. He only laughed at my excitement, and I thought it would be impossible for another to appreciate the magnitude of that great experience of mine.

As it happened, it took me many years to understand that revolution in my living being. As you will see, it marked the rising in me of fundamental and unqualified Life, and it, in its moment, removed every shadow of dilemma and ignorance from the mind, on every level, and all their effects in the body. But I would have to pass through many years of trial before my understanding of that Event became thoroughly established as the constant and truly effective premise of my living being (and, at last, the most perfect revelation of my Very Nature, my Ultimate Condition, and my "Bright" Purpose in the world).

Nevertheless, in the days and weeks that followed, I grasped certain basic concepts that arose in me at that time and which stood out in the mind undeniably, with a self-validating force. Two things in particular stood out as fundamentals.

I had spent years devoted to forceful seeking for some revolutionary truth, some image, object, reason, or idea, the effect of which would be absolutely liberating and salvatory. My seeking had been motivated by the loss of faith, the loss of the "Christ"-object and other such reasons for Joy. But in that great moment of Awakening I Knew the Truth was not a matter of seeking. There were no "reasons" for Joy and Freedom. It was not a matter of a truth, an object, a concept, a belief, a reason, a motivation, or any external fact. Indeed, it was clear that all such objects are grasped in a state that is already seeking and which has already lost the prior sense of absolutely unqualified Reality. Instead, I saw that the Truth or Reality was a matter of the absence of all contradictions, of every trace of conflict, opposition, division, or desperate motivation within. Where there is no seeking, no contradiction, there is only the unqualified Knowledge and Power that is Reality. This was the first aspect of that sudden Clarity.

In this State beyond all contradiction I also saw that Freedom and Joy is not attained, that It is not dependent on any form, object, idea, progress, or experience. I saw that human beings (and, indeed, all beings) are, at any moment, always and already Free. I Knew that I was not lacking anything I needed yet to find, nor had I ever been without such a thing. The problem was the seeking itself, which "created" and enforced contradiction, conflict, and absence within. Then the understanding arose that I am always already Free. This was the second aspect of that fundamental Awareness.

That sudden understanding was the obviation of all striving, and this I Knew to be unqualified Truth. I had been striving for some objective "Truth", in order to replace my loss with a thereby acquired "Freedom", but this striving was itself the source of contradiction in me. Now I Knew there was no entity of Truth, and perfect Freedom was always already the case. Freedom exists as life, not when Freedom is "created" or sought, but where there is this fundamental understanding. In that moment of understanding I had simply turned out of the context of my presumed dilemma. I was possessed of the mature cognition of the "Bright".

In the years that followed, I would find many analogies for my experience in the Spiritual literature of the East and the West. I could call that revolution in myself "enlightenment", "liberation", "Realization of the Self", or "union with God". I would pursue the sciences of that Realization in religion and Yoga, in ancient Scriptures and modern therapeutic techniques. But always, as you will see, I returned to the simplicity of that understanding, free of all concepts, which, although they seek to express it in a communicative symbol, in fact serve to limit the State Itself and re-"create" the milieu of seeking.

But I was not at that time living in a Spiritual community. And the mind of the university, bound as it was to the subtle doctrines that enforce dilemma, served only to counter my experience, just as when a child I could find no community of the "Bright".

Because of the vulnerability that necessarily characterizes any kind of "Spiritual" consciousness in the traditionally non-Spiritual, or even bodily-based and worldly, culture of the West, I was unable at that time thoroughly to understand my own experience. I could not establish that Realization as the "creative" premise of my existence. I was simply not that strong. And the habits of mind and body that I had built by years of self-exploitation persisted as consoling means of pleasure. So that I remained rather sedentary and reflective. I did not overcome the gravity of mind that I had achieved as a result of my presumed dilemma and my manner of living. And I naturally adapted to a basic misinterpretation of my experience.

I retained something of the attitude of the seeker. Whereas previously I continually pursued some kind of "objective" Truth (whether internal or external), now I sought the removal of contradictions, of the parts of conflict, ignorance, or impurity, by various internal means.

I did not realize that this understanding, this Knowledge, is Itself the removal of contradictions and the instant, moment to moment purifier of the mind and life. I considered that the Truth was as I had Known It in that moment of Realization, but that I would have to find the means for working the revolutionary purification of my living being. I saw the State of Knowledge or understanding to be in some sense <u>caused</u> by the practical removal of the impurities or contradictions in the mind and life.

Thus, I began a new period of effort. Its goals were not desperate and un-Real as before, but the simple assumption of the attitude of the seeker, and the consequent identification with the one who is not yet radically

Free, not yet Real and True, made it impossible for me to continuously Enjoy the State of unqualified Being that had been accomplished in that moment of Realization.

The burden of these considerations made me feel that I had even lost the Truth that I had Realized. I began to pursue It again through endless writing and search. I remained addicted to my mediocre pleasures and sought through them the means of purification and release. I graduated from Columbia in the following year, in June 1961, in despair and confusion, without a clue as to where I should take myself. Reluctantly, I had become a seeker, even a very ordinary seeker, but I was not certain there were any means in all the world to restore myself to the "Bright".

Graduation day at Columbia College, 1961

CHAPTER 4

The Seeker

There exist a few, rather dismal photographs of me that outwardly record the day (or the brief event) of my graduation from college. The day of college graduation is generally supposed to be a day of celebration. All your relatives are supposed to congratulate you with various gifts. You are supposed to be very relieved of the long effort of preparatory study and testing. In your revelry of accomplishment, you are to look forward ideally to productive life's work or the beginning of some professional study that will expand your maturity in useful learning, teaching, or service. But I had nowhere to go. Who in the world could teach me this "Thing" I had to learn? Where in the world was It being lived? How at all could I accomplish what I sought?

I saw that in fact I had attained nothing at all. I was proficient in no science or art, interested in perfecting no existing form of useful knowledge or productivity. I had been honored in nothing. I had failed to take hold of even the one breakthrough that seemed to make the difference. I had no impulse of any kind to succeed or even to make a living. I felt an overwhelming sense of failure. I had already lost very heavily in love. I had the sympathy of no one.

On that day my parents stood alone with me. There were no well-wishers, no gifts, no congratulations. The natural and flowering signs of early summer were all around us, but no pleasure anywhere in me. I was heartsick, and gray as death. I only wanted to get away.

I spent the summer trying to make a living as a hotel waiter. But the money was bad, and the work had nothing to do with me. Finally, in August, I quit work, and a friend, named Marco, who was living in a storefront on the Bowery[6] in New York, allowed me to stay with him. Whenever he had a girlfriend for the night, I would sleep in an old chair in an alley.

Marco had some raw peyote, and we decided to take the drug, although neither of us had any idea what its effects would be. In the past months I had used marijuana a few times and found it very enjoyable and relaxing. And so I willingly accepted a chance for some kind of very powerful "high".

We ate the cactus raw, and soon we both became very ill. For what seemed like hours we lay separately, trying to avoid vomiting, wondering if this was supposed to be the effect of the drug. After a while, Marco got up, and I could hear him laughing and moving around in the street. I got up and, feeling very dizzy, stumbled out the hallway into the street. Marco was standing on the sidewalk with a brilliantly gleeful expression on his face. At first I was simply trying to gather strength to keep standing, and the dizziness and nausea still persisted. But after a few breaths of air I began to feel an incredible elation.

We both caught on to the same feeling at once. There was a serenely blissful pleasure in the body, the senses were all alive, and everything appeared to pulse visibly with an internal light. The mind had no weight at all, and its usual logic was undone, so that the only impulse was laughter and pleasure. We stood in the street laughing ourselves silly. And everything we pointed out to one another took on the same ridiculous quality we felt in ourselves. The extraordinary feeling and energy of the experience appeared to simulate (even though it did not truly duplicate) the moments of greatest ecstasy and sudden Freedom I had Known in my life.

A few minutes later, the phone rang. It was my father. He kept asking me please to come home. My

6. The Bowery in New York City is a district notorious for cheap bars and street people.

mother was very worried about me, and she had fallen down the cellar stairs. He said she fell downstairs while he was away, and she must have been there for an hour or two, unconscious, her face bleeding and cut.

The more he described the entire matter to me, the more ridiculous it appeared. I hallucinated my mother's injuries as he described them. Her swollen eyes, her cut cheeks and lips, her knocked-out teeth. But the image seemed only like a clown's face, and I could not understand any of the seriousness my father ascribed to it. I could only laugh out loud.

Then he put my mother on the phone, and she was very sad and seemed to have difficulty talking. I did not tell them I was on a drug, but I was unable to "create" any feeling in myself besides this unstoppable hilarity. I only wanted to hang up so I could go and enjoy myself. I assured her I would come and see them in a day or two, and I put down the phone.

Marco and I spent the day at the Museum of Modern Art, laughing at the sculpture and painting. We watched the film *Touch of Evil*, shown at the museum that day, and constantly laughed so hard we were nearly thrown out. Then there was the orgy of food and girls until we passed out late in the night.

When I saw my parents a day or two later, they were obviously disturbed. My mother's injuries had begun to heal, but both my parents were now very concerned about what I was doing, and about what I was, altogether, going to do with my life.

I had tried to gain acceptance into a graduate school in English, so that I could study literature and perhaps begin to write seriously. All of the schools but one had refused me, basically because my background was in philosophy. Stanford University had accepted me, but I did not want to burden my parents with any more finances for my schooling. And I was so depressed by the fact that most of the better schools had refused me that I made no effort at all to make my entrance to Stanford possible.

Nevertheless, my father very kindly offered to pay my way to Stanford, if I wanted to go. At first I refused, but after a day or two I thought it was probably my only possibility for any kind of positive existence. I accepted my father's offer, and a couple of weeks later I flew to San Francisco.

My arrival in California was the most instantly healing and supportive experience of a purely external kind that I had yet enjoyed in my life. The sunlight was so deeply radiant, the air so soft, and the hills and country all around so dramatic and beautiful that I became marvelously light and, in the most positive ordinary sense, happy.

Since that time I have traveled many places in the world, but for me the areas of northern California, with the incredible mountains and forests of Yosemite, the dramatic coastline of Big Sur, and the beautiful city of San Francisco, remain equal to the most glorious physical environments on the earth.

I spent my year at Stanford regaining my mental and physical well-being. I found the intellectual environment and especially the formal study of English to be far less intensive and significant than my best work at Columbia. There was a kind of "country intellectual" establishment at Stanford, which, like all of life in such (even physically) consoling environments, tended never to become truly serious about the fundamental and radical purposes of the mind.

And so I remained a kind of revolutionary, aggravated presence there, tolerable enough for one year. I passed through my courses with ease, and spent most of my time getting New York out of my system. I stretched in the sun, wrote poetry, toured the hills and the mountains, and generally regained my ordinary sense of humor.

In January of 1962, I submitted a short story to the Department of Creative Writing and was accepted as a candidate for the master's degree in English with a "concentration" in writing. Then I began to write seriously,

Stanford University in Palo Alto, California

Adi Da during His time at Stanford

and, for the first time in my life, had at least a limited audience.

Wallace Stegner, a novelist and authority on life in the western United States, was head of the "creative writing" program. The writers who joined the workshop were generally conservative people proficient in the traditional genre of story writing. But I was mainly interested in writing of an experimental kind, and the ideas that motivated me were visible in modern writers such as Marcel Proust, James Joyce, Gertrude Stein, Virginia Woolf, and Samuel Beckett.

Besides myself, there were only one or two people seriously interested in experimental fiction. The first few stories I wrote were nearly traditional in form and content, but gradually I began to explore some of the more plastic possibilities of language and form, so that my writing expanded into an instrument for deeply internal motives.

During the previous years, I had written in private toward a solution or expression of the internal dilemma to which I had become sensitive. I developed a "creative" mechanism that gradually unfolded a source of form, imagery, and movement that was, for me, profoundly necessary and satisfying. This approach to the problem or activity of writing was influenced not only by my own basic human characteristics and my own characteristic manner of seeking but also by my reading of modern philosophical and therapeutic thought and technique, including the work of Ludwig Wittgenstein,[7] of Sigmund Freud, and of C. G. Jung, the poetry of Dylan Thomas and the "beat" writers of the fifties and early sixties,[8] the

7. Ludwig Wittgenstein (1889-1951) was an Austrian philosopher who called into question many of our most basic presumptions about existence and knowledge.

8. The "beatnik" (or "beat") movement gained prominence during the 1950s as an avant-garde bohemian reaction to the then-dominant cultural forms of conventional middle-class American life. Beat poets and writers expounded a generalized philosophy derived in part from Eastern religious traditions, in particular Zen Buddhism. Some of the "beat writers" that Adi Da read were Lawrence Ferlingetti, Kenneth Rexroth, and Allen Ginsberg.

novelists I have already mentioned, and also the works of the painters and sculptors of the late nineteenth and the twentieth centuries. I felt that the truly "creative" movements that led up to and included this time were generated in the form of a new subjective order of consciousness that needed to be tapped, experienced, and then expanded into a communicative external order.

As I continued to write, I allowed my work to become more and more freely this intention, this utterly unqualified internal rule. As I progressed, I began to encounter great resistance in the writers at the workshop. Only one or two people became interested in my work, and they gave me the only encouragement I ever received as a "creative" writer.

As we approached the final quarter of the year of study necessary for the master's degree, I felt that my writing was leading me necessarily into a point of no return in regard to the professionals in the writing workshop. Their resistance to my earlier work seemed to guarantee no sympathy at all for what I felt was the ultimate course of my writing.

I have never admitted any compromise to the process of my own conscious and "creative" development. After all, I was not at work for the sake of making a living or even for the entertainment of others. Rather, I was always at work on the same thing, the experimental investigation of conscious life for the sake of its unfolding, revelation, and eventual solution or Realization. Now I saw my writing as the possible and necessary instrument for removing internal contradictions, for establishing the "Bright" Condition of Consciousness Itself.

Consequently, in the final months of my year at Stanford, I gave up all attempts to "create" short stories in the acceptable manner of the workshop, and I began to write in earnest, for my own sake. I found that by the end of the final quarter I had produced no single work that could qualify for credit. I went to Mr. Stegner with a manuscript that represented my quarter of effort. It consisted of perhaps three or four hundred handwritten pages. I explained to him that the manuscript did in fact represent "creative" work, but that it was nothing more than work in progress.

I had developed a process, over several years, of a kind of listening. I focused on the plane of the mind and allowed it to be the focal point of experiences within and without. I thoroughly believed that the individual human being was involved in and controlled by a profound, largely unconscious or preconscious logic or structure, a motivating drama or myth. I felt that this myth, previous to becoming conscious, acted only as an arbitrary limitation, and it never appeared directly in the mind or in a person's works and actions. This "myth" was necessarily common to all human beings collectively, but it was effective on the level of the individual, and it needed to become conscious in the individual before any "creative" work or life-freedom was possible on its basis or beyond it.

I combined the internal work of listening with the activity of writing. Therefore, the plan of my work as a writer was to remain actively attentive to the movement of my life on every level, to an exhaustive degree. I proposed to become exhaustively aware, by a critical and constant act of attention to whatever experience or movement occurred on the planes of life and consciousness. Thus, I would simply perceive every form of memory or internal imagery, every form of thought or perception, every indication or pattern in my daily experience, every intention, every imposition from without, in fact every possible kind of experience.

I hoped by these means to become directly aware of the form which governed or informed the entire quality and adventure of my existence. And this form or myth, the myth of my life, would, I was certain, become the source and subject for a fictional work, or some kind of radically useful literature.

Mr. Stegner listened cautiously to my theories. I was

certain he presumed me to be quite adolescent and perhaps irrational. He and I were of dramatically different
natures. He was a hard-headed practical man, and I was
an intense, self-enamored, nearly violent subjectivist. Of
course, he could not allow my little manuscript to stand
for credit in his department, nor could he for himself
accept my writing program as a viable plan for "creating"
fiction. But he allowed that I could carry on my work if
I so desired, and he would be willing to receive the
results anytime in the reliable future.

Thus, I left the Stanford campus in Palo Alto to begin
the long adventure which was to make or break my "rep-
utation", and perhaps even my sanity. I was fully aware
that my way of life, including the work to which I was
devoted, bordered on matters that settled in the brink
between life and death, sanity and madness, intelligence
and irrationality. But I was certain that I had no choice in
the matter. I was simply choosing to endure the course
which had been pre-determined for me by all the "Bright"
and human signs associated with me since my birth.

While at Stanford I also met Nina Davis. She is
unqualifiedly sane and gentle, tolerant and loving, flexi-
ble and supportive, to the degree that she more than any
other single factor in my early life is responsible for my
survival. Late in the school year we began to live together in the hills above Palo Alto. And she, under the most
awesome conditions, remained with me throughout the
long adventure of my listening.

During the summer that followed my year at Stanford, I planned to leave California and stay with my parents in New York. I had also sent samples of my more
traditional writing to the Bread Loaf Writer's Conference
in Vermont, and, with a cautious recommendation from
Wallace Stegner, I was accepted and given a fellowship
for the two-week conference of professional writers and
students that was to be given in August.

But when I arrived at my parents' home, I immediately felt the signs of old conflicts. I had still failed to

found myself in any kind of practical and productive work, and I am sure this disturbed them. I wanted to be able to write according to my lights, and this required the solitude of a positively safe and undisturbed environment.

As a result, within a couple of weeks I called Nina, who was visiting her family in Ohio. I asked her to come to New York. After her arrival it became clear that we could not live in the state of intimacy and freedom I required. Arguments began to build in the household. Finally, I left my parents quite violently and took an overnight train with Nina to Ohio. I abandoned all of the practical order of my life, including the Bread Loaf fellowship.

In Ohio, Nina's father reluctantly gave me just enough money to pay for a train ride to California. Nina stayed behind temporarily, for her parents' sake, and I carried all of my belongings from train to train until I reached Oakland. A friend from the Stanford writing workshop picked me up at the station and allowed me to stay temporarily with him and his wife and baby in Palo Alto.

My friend's wife took to disliking me for various reasons, and I was without money, so I needed very quickly to get some cash and find a place to live. I learned that a psychologist was looking for subjects to take hallucinogenic drugs under supervision at a nearby Veterans Administration hospital. I went and was accepted for a preliminary and a final interview, with four drug sessions in between at one week intervals, all of which would pay me fifty dollars a week for six weeks.

I called Nina and told her to return to California immediately, and I arranged to stay with her roommates at her former house in the hills above Palo Alto. Thus, we began a two-year period in which I experimented with my writing, read voluminously, exhausted myself in self-indulgent experiments, and worked on my internal processes with various drugs and therapeutic techniques.

My experimental method at the time was similar to the one by which I directed myself in college. But, whereas before I pursued experience itself, and a certain "objective" Truth, internal or external, now, as a result of the revelation in college, I sought the removal of internal contradictions, or the removal of the "opposites", the mutual alternatives that enforce the kinds of experience, the patterns of seeking and of conflict.

During this period, I pursued every kind of means, every method of interiorization and exteriorization of awareness, that could possibly dredge up the lost content, the controlling myth, the forms of God, Reality, soul, Truth, key memory, and so on, all of the false and presently unconscious logic or imagery that prevented the "Bright" of simple, direct, and unqualifiedly Free Awareness. To this end, the new or ancient hallucinogenic drugs seemed profoundly useful and promising.

In the midst of my year at Stanford I had occasion to use marijuana again. And I took a formula cough medicine called "Romilar" that had very remarkable effects if taken in large doses. At that time the formula for Romilar contained a special, but non-narcotic, element, which, I believe, was later eliminated or modified. On perhaps four or five occasions I took Romilar in a dose of either thirty to fifty capsules or a full bottle of syrup.

I found that the dose of Romilar had no effect whatsoever in terms of a "high" if I spent my time at a party or in conversation with others. But if, after an hour or so, I went out alone and walked in a natural environment, particularly among trees, a profound State would come over me. Thus, I became deeply relaxed, mentally and physically. And I became directly and intuitively aware of a form and Presence in other living things that was duplicated in my own living form.

Trees in particular appeared as living beings in a much larger sense than is ordinarily supposed. They were not hallucinated as mutations of my own human life-form, but I saw that they as well as myself were entities of the same order. There was an Energy-form to which the physical form of the tree and my own physical form were only analogies and extensions. The fundamental living fact was not the external and functional apparatus. These only marked the separate and distinct purposes of trees and humans in the ordinary state of consciousness. But there was, fundamentally, a primary, common fact or Energy-form that was sublime, constant and unqualified, and which bore its closest analogy to the human nervous system.

I saw that the upright tree, with its lower roots and its upper limbs, branches, and leaves, was analogous to the form of my own nervous system, with its roots deep in the brain, its spinal trunk, and its vital branches extending to every extremity. The State of my living consciousness at those times was infinitely Peaceful, Enjoying a profound and untouchable Pleasure and Freedom, and a Clarity that never wavered under any influence within or without. The mind itself was positively thoughtless, and the physical body enjoyed a deep, cellular calm and mutability, so that there was profound physical pleasure in placing it in almost any position.

I intuitively presumed that this State must be the same Condition described as "Nirvana" in the Buddhist texts. There was no problem, no question, no answer, but only the most unqualified and direct perception, and the dwelling as primary and unseparated Conscious Awareness. There was only the inherent, constant, and universal Presence of Reality. That State felt (or tacitly authenticated Itself as) True, even though It had been artificially induced. Its natural features (and Its characteristic of Free Conscious Awareness) generally corresponded to the Condition I, especially in my earliest childhood, readily (even without effort or means) Knew as the "Bright", and It duplicated quite exactly, although more calmly, the structure of my experience during my spontaneous college Awakening.

It was on the basis of such self-validating experiences that I openly desired to experience the effects of the "new" drugs, LSD, mescalin, and psilocybin. And so, just before Nina's return, and for several weeks thereafter, I voluntarily submitted to drug trials at the Veterans

Administration hospital in Palo Alto, California.

I should add that these drug experiments did not serve a purpose in me to "create" or evolve any kind of enlightenment, or any kind of permanent transformation of my living consciousness. They were taken during a peculiarly experimental phase of my life in which I was seeking to understand the mechanisms in the living consciousness, those which prevent, and those which later make possible, the stability of the natural conditions associated with the Free Conscious Awareness I had already Known in childhood and lately while in college. I was aware of a problem in relation to that State Which I earlier called the "Bright". There was an intervening and learned force or structure in the life-process which made the Original Condition, Prior to all dilemma, seem to disappear in a fragmentary and problematic state of mentality and experience. There is a long tradition, in the East and the West, of the use of certain herbs and drugs in order to effect a temporary removal of this intervening state which limits free conscious Awareness. I sought to take advantage of these means in order to investigate that intervening process. It was not for the sake of the artificially induced state itself.

Of course there is a limitation to such "wisdom". It is conceived and promoted in the problematic state itself. Its platform is to that degree desperate. And it could, in certain people or under certain conditions in even the strongest individual, produce hypnotic and artificial conditions that are devastating and deluding. I would eventually suffer such conditions myself. But I was prompted by a lifelong Intention to understand and Illuminate conscious life, and I was in agreement from the beginning to put a halt to this level of experimentation the moment it became aggravating, deluding, or unnecessary. Therefore, it was a happy circumstance, to my mind, that in my early experiments with drugs I had discovered analogies to processes and states that I knew to be valid under natural conditions.

The hills above Palo Alto

Nina

The house in the redwoods
where Adi Da lived after
the experiments at the
V.A. hospital

The Veterans Administration hospital in Palo Alto

At the V.A. hospital I was given a dose of drugs one day per week. I was left in a small hospital room alone, except for the occasional visit of the psychologist or a medical technician. At times I was given brief physical or mental tests. Otherwise, I simply sat, rested, read, or observed the internal states as they passed. I was told that I would be given mescalin, LSD, or psilocybin at three separate sessions, and, during a fourth session, some combination of these. The precise drug or combination I was to be given at any one time would remain unknown to me. Nor was I told the exact measure of the dosage in any case, except that they appeared, from their effects, to be quite large.

During those several weeks of drug trials I had many different drug-induced experiences, most of which were not particularly important to me. At times I would see the room and my body become quite plastic and mobile, and their various parts would become exaggeratedly large or small in relation to one another without any volition on my part. During one session, I think perhaps under psilocybin, I felt only as if I were in a profound sleep, although my mind at some depth was continually conscious, and I was unable to achieve physical sleep even though I greatly desired it.

There were also various bizarre experiences and periods of anxiety. Several times I was brought to the lunchroom at the height of the drug state. I had to appear in some state of normalcy in the midst of hospital patients who were variously amputees, shell-shocked, mentally disturbed, or in various states of plastic surgery. As a result of the unnecessary shock caused by the mishandling of my condition at those times, I suffered mild anxiety attacks and occasional nervousness for perhaps a year beyond the actual tests.

However, there were at least two experiences that were significant.

During one of the sessions, I think perhaps while I was on LSD, I felt a profound Energy rising in me. It began at the base of my spine, and when It appeared in the heart It generated an intense emotion that was overwhelmingly loving and full and yet intensely sorrowful. It rose from the heart through the throat, up the back of the head, and through the internal centers of the head, and culminated in what appeared to be a massive dome in the crown of the skull. At that point I began to weep uncontrollably, as if all of the parts of my being had been aroused spontaneously, and I was born, suddenly conscious and alive. In the midst of this experience I had a thought that was the verbal equivalent and symbol for the entire Event: "Getting to cry is shaped like a seahorse."

I had become conscious of the formal structure of the living human being, associated with (but not exclusively identical to) the nervous system, but, even more than that, what is, in Asian Indian literature and, in turn, in Western occult literature, called the "chakra body".[9] The Kundalini Shakti[10] was spontaneously Aroused in me, as It also had been in times past. It was, as from a stupor or sleep, the Awakening of the latent "serpent" of Energy that is otherwise habitually turned outward to the

9. "Chakra" is Sanskrit for "wheel". The "chakra body" is the etheric and subtle system of centers that conduct psychic force and nerve force to and through the principal regions of the body-mind. The chakra body is generally conceived of as having seven principal chakras, all of them on the central axis of the body and brain. The chakras are associated, respectively, with the perineum (or bodily base), the sex center, the navel and solar plexus, the heart, the throat, the midbrain, and the crown of the head.

10. "Kundalini Shakti" is Sanskrit for "coiled up" ("kundalini") "energy" ("shakti"). It is the traditional name for the "serpent power", or the ascending force of Spiritual Life-Energy, described in the esoteric Yogic traditions of the world, especially those of India. It is often described as lying dormant at the bodily base, or the lowermost chakra of the body-mind. It may be activated either spontaneously in the devotee or by the Guru's initiation. Once initiated, the Kundalini Shakti is said to rise through the various centers in the chakra body, producing signs of purification, balancing, and energization of all the psychophysical functions and capabilities associated with those centers, thereby producing the various forms of Yogic and mystical experience.

Adi Da has Revealed that the Kundalini Shakti as typically conceived in most Yogic traditions, and by modern (even scientific) commentators, is only a partial manifestation of the universal Divine Spirit-Current. It cannot rightly be said merely to originate at the bodily base, since it is a continuation of the same Spirit-Current that descends in the frontal line of the body.

various physical organs and the centers of vital experience. Thus, the Kundalini Shakti was opened inwardly and upwardly, and the living consciousness was turned to its own internal form. The "seahorse" is that shape, with its various vital and ethereal attachments, which moves upward from the base of the spine through the massive centers of the heart and the head. The result in me of this profound Awakening was an uncontrollable emotion, even the sorrow of conscious birth.

In later years I chanced to see some photographs taken inside the womb at various stages in the development of a human fetus. At an early stage the body is mostly unformed, and its central axis, analogous to the full spine, is curved. The heart appears visibly as its vital center. It is massive, full of blood, and it stands out from the body as a separate orb attached to the spinal tube by a cord. The head is also quite large. Its full weight and size are generated in the crown and forehead, and the facial features, like the limbs, remain undeveloped. In the Event I have described, I was not only experiencing the most subtle and profound Energy-body, the most internal structure of all Spiritual consciousness, but I was also re-experiencing my own prenatal state, even at the early stage of physical development shown in the photographs I saw years after the Event Itself. I was re-experiencing my birth as a living being in the womb, and, therefore, the Awakening was not only profound but also quite shocking and sorrowful.

This very "form", this Spirit-conducting structure, in and beyond the physical body, was a structure basic to What, as a child, I experienced and Knew as the "Bright". And it was also this chakra body that I would later investigate in detail in the practice of Kundalini Shakti Yoga in America and in India.

One other experience stands out from that period. At apparently random times, from my early childhood, usually as I either approached sleep or awoke from sleep, and, most dramatically, during seizures of childhood illness, as I would pass into delirium, I had an experience that appeared like a mass of gigantic thumbs coming down from above, pressing into my throat (causing something of a gagging, and somewhat suffocating, sensation), and then pressing further (and, it seemed, would have expanded without limitation or end), into some form of myself that was much larger than my physical body. This experience of "the Thumbs" also recurred once or twice during these drug trials.

"The Thumbs" were not visible in the ordinary sense. I did not see them then or even as a child. They were not visible to me with my eyes, nor did I hallucinate them pictorially. Yet, I very consciously experienced and felt them as having a peculiar form and mobility, as I likewise experienced my own otherwise invisible and greater form.

I did not at that time or at any time in my childhood fully allow this intervention of "the Thumbs" to take place. I held it off from its fullest descent, in fear of being overwhelmed, for I did not understand at all what was taking place. However, in later years this same experience occurred naturally during meditation. Because my meditation had been allowed to progress gradually, and the realizations at each level were thus perceived without shock, I was able at those times to allow the experience to take place. When I did, "the Thumbs" completely entered my living form. They appeared like tongues, or parts of a Force, coming from above. And when they had entered deep into my body, the magnetic or energic balances of my living being reversed. On several occasions I felt as if the body had risen above the ground somewhat, and this is perhaps the basis for certain evidence in mystical literature of the phenomenon of levitation, or bodily transport.

At any rate, during those stages in meditation the body ceased to be polarized toward the ground, or the gravitational direction of the earth's center. There was a strong reversal of polarity, communicated along a line of Force analogous to the spine. The physical body, as well as the Energy-form that could be interiorly felt as analogous to but detached from the physical body, was felt to turn in a curve along the spine and forward in the direction of the heart. When this reversal of Energy was allowed to take place completely, I resided in a totally different body, which also contained the physical body. It was spherical in shape. And the sensation of dwelling as that form was completely peaceful. The physical body was completely relaxed and polarized to the shape of this other spherical body. The mind became quieted, and then there was a movement in consciousness that would go even deeper, into a higher conscious State beyond physical and mental awareness. I was to learn that this spherical body was what Yogis and occultists call the "subtle" body (which includes the "pranic",[11] or natural life-energy, dimension and the "astral", or the lower mental and the higher mental, dimensions of the living being).

These remarks are already leading toward experiences that belong to a later and mature phase of my life. I mention these experiences here because they demonstrate a continuity in my conscious experience that links my prenatal and early childhood stages with my later life. These Events also show that there was a pattern in Reality being uncovered in me even during that period of drug experimentation (or "artificial" inducement). I regard that period no differently than any other in my years of seeking. It contained degrees of wisdom, and many indications of the same matters of living form that I perceived at other, more natural phases in my career. It is only that, like every other form and stage of my

11. "Pranic" derives from the Sanskrit word "prana" (literally, "breathing forth"), commonly used to mean "life-force" or "breath"). In this context "pranic" refers to the etheric body, or body of life-energy that coincides with the body of flesh. The etheric body may appropriately be called the "pranic" body because the ebb and flow of energy in the etheric body (and therefore also in the physical body) is directly dependent on our patterns of breathing. In order to maintain and enhance the level of energy in the etheric, or pranic, body, Yogis practice traditional breathing exercises called "pranayama".

search, its inherent limitations were eventually under-stood—and, at that point, I abandoned it.

However, that point of abandonment lay in my future, even three years away at the time. After the peri-od of drug trials at the V.A. hospital, Nina and I moved to a house in a redwood forest in the mountains above Palo Alto. After perhaps six or eight months in that area, we moved again to a small cabin built into the hillside over the ocean at Tunitas Beach, a point nearly due west of Palo Alto.

We stayed in that cabin until some rather remarkable events brought a decision in me to leave California in search of a Spiritual teacher in New York. That move came in June 1964. During the nearly two years previous to it, following the drug trials at the V.A. hospital, I con-tinued the exhaustive experiment of my writing.

View from the house at Tunitas Beach
(photograph taken by Adi Da)

CHAPTER 5

The Understanding
on the Beach

After my experiences at the V.A. hospital, I went into a period of relative seclusion to carry on my work undisturbed. Nina worked as a school teacher during this period and supported our living.

My own manner of living at that time finally established a form of practice in me that had begun in college. It was not required that I maintain a "job" of any kind, and so I was free to work as I pleased. As always, I found seclusion to be extremely vital, productive, and "creatively" necessary for my own kind of progress.

The pattern of my days was mostly sedentary. This was partially dictated early in my life by a chronic weakness in my left side, particularly the left leg, and in certain tiny bone malformations in my lower back, all due to my childhood case of polio. I had not been very noticeably disabled by this limitation, but it had led me to experience a certain tiredness and weakness in those areas if I became very active physically. Over time, my body had developed a counterbalance of muscular strength, and I had always been able to enjoy strong activity in swimming and other kinds of exercise. (And, in later years, I would also learn how to manipulate and refresh the bone structure of the body, its muscular system, and the nervous system by using certain techniques of Hatha Yoga.)

Thus, I spent my days in retirement. While Nina was away at work, I would spend the day writing. My method of writing was not one of any kind of intentional production. The writing of this present book, for instance, is a very intentional process. It involves a deliberate plan of productivity, the gathering of various notes and sources, chronological recollection, and so on. I write very deliberately and almost continually for eight hours or more each day. However, in those days my method of writing was deliberately "unproductive". My intention was not to write a particular narrative I had preconceived. Rather, I deliberately and very intensively focused in the mind itself. And, as a result of several years of experiment in this direction, I remained focused there without effort, almost continuously, regardless of my peculiar external involvement.

This could perhaps be understood as a kind of "Yoga" of my own "creation", and it has analogies in the history of Spiritual experience. But I had no separate goal in doing this. There was no other point I hoped to arrive at as a result of this concentration. I wanted to reside in the plane of consciousness at its deepest level, where all experiences, internal as well as external, were monitored. I wanted simply to become aware of what passed there.

Ordinarily people do not remain aware on the deepest level of the mind. They are concentrated either in its extensions, at the level of sense awareness, or in the processes of concrete thought. Occasionally a person slips into a deeper level, similar to the level to which one passes in dreams, and there he or she experiences the daydreams, the subliminal memories, emotions, and motivations, that underlie his or her functioning life. It was my intention to remain continuously aware at this deepest focal point of the mind. That was also a point at which I often concentrated in the "Bright". It is a point deep within the head, but it monitors all the levels of functional consciousness, the physical body and the experiences of the sense organs, the vital centers in the lower body, the great center of being and Energy in the heart, the peculiar order of subliminal imagery that moves out of the "creative" center analogous to the throat, and all of the passing perceptions, the images, ideas, sensations, forms, memories, and superconscious communications, that are generated in the parts of the head.

In those days I spent all of my time concentrated in this observing function. I carried a clipboard with me wherever I went. And I would write whatever perceptions were generated in my living consciousness. I attempted to make this writing exhaustive, so that not a single thought, image, or experience would pass unrecognized. The act of writing seemed necessary to the act of becoming conscious itself. What I did not write seemed to pass away again into unconsciousness, perhaps to remain trapped there and provide matter for the hidden, unconscious form that bounded my awareness and prevented the "Bright".

Whenever I was too busily occupied to write, I would invent a catch phrase or some other mnemonic device in order to hold the concept or perception until I could write it fully. I became so occupied in this process that Nina would have to do anything that required practical attention. She would drive the car, communicate with friends, and perform all of the usual chores within and without the household. My writing became a continuous, fascinating, and absorbing occupation. And I began to fall naturally into a thread of consciousness and life that was profound, hidden, unfolding, inevitable, and sublime.

I would write at any and all times, even in the evenings when Nina was at home, at the movies, at parties, or during walks on the beach. I would often write late into the night, or I would awaken many times from sleep to record dreams and ideas. The same process went on during sleep, so that I remained conscious even during dreams or deep dreamless sleep.

I continued to exploit the possibilities for experience during that time, and I saw no benefits in retarding any impulses. I feared that suppression would only prevent certain necessary images or motives from releasing their living energy and significance to consciousness. I would often exploit the possibilities of sex, or become deeply drunk on wine, engage in orgies of eating, or smoke marijuana for long hours.

I became intensely aware of every movement in the living consciousness. I perceived every event in the world as well with an almost painful absorption. Every creature or environment I perceived became a matter of profound attention. I would write page after page of exhaustive observation on every step of a walk on the beach, or the daylong process and change of the ocean. There was page after page describing the objects and marks in the sand as I walked, detailed descriptions of rooms, mental environments, and so on. And I gradually came to a similar state in which I found myself at the point of Awakening in college. I came to the point of exhausting that exercise. The simultaneity, coincidence, and oneness of "inside" and "outside" became utterly obvious to me. My living awareness was uniquely and extremely intense, and inclusive of everything, both inside and outside the body-mind, such that I felt there was no remaining power of distraction in anything. As a result, I was utterly focused on the yet hidden depth of the living consciousness.

As I approached that point of inclusive awareness, focused in depth, the form of my writing also began to bear fruit. My concentration, as I said, was not purposive. It was not in order to "create" something intentionally on the basis of what was preconceived in the mind. But I was always looking and listening for that very and most fundamental structure in the living consciousness which is prior to ordinary awareness. I was waiting for the revelation of the hidden content of the mind. Not some sort of primitive event, no memory in the Freudian style or some symbolic perception which informs the content of Jungian types of introspection. These came and went. But I was attentive to the underlying structure of the living consciousness, to the seed-logic, or myth, that prevented the "Bright".

As I approached that form of Knowledge, which I was certain, from previous suggestions in my deepest experience, had to be there, I would often pass through

top: Adi Da during the period of His writing at the beach

left and right: the house at Tunitas Beach

profound recollections and imagery. There were the emotional and scatological memories of childhood, and the moments of conflict in life that underlay persistent anxieties, preferences, and chronic patterns. There were also times when I saw and learned the workings of psychic planes and subtler worlds. I remember once for a period of days I was aware of a world that appeared to survive in our moon. It was a superphysical or astral world where beings were sent off to birth on the earth or other worlds, and then their bodies were enjoyed cannibalistically by the older generation on the moon, or they were forced to work as physical and mental slaves.

I became very interested in the writings of C. G. Jung, and I sometimes experienced symbolic dreams typical of the level of consciousness he investigated. One of these coincided with a dramatic awakening that I will describe presently.

But my attention could not settle in any particular impression or event. I was always driven more deeply into the underlying structure, and so I always remained focused in the mind itself, regardless of what passed.

Eventually, I began to recognize a structure in the living consciousness. It became more and more apparent, and its nature and effects revealed themselves as fundamental and inclusive of all the states and contents in life and mind. My own "myth", the control of all patterns, the source of identity and all seeking, began to stand out in the mind as a living being.

This "myth", this controlling logic, or force, that formed my very consciousness, revealed itself as the concept and the actual life of Narcissus. I saw that my entire adventure, the desperate cycle of awareness and its decrease, of truly Conscious Being and Its gradual covering in the mechanics of living, seeking, dying, and suffering, was produced out of the image or mentality that appears hidden in the ancient myth of Narcissus.

The more I contemplated him, the more profoundly I understood him. I observed in awe the primitive control that this self-concept and logic performed in all of my behavior and experience. I began to see that same logic operative in all other human beings, and in every living thing, even in the very life of the cells and in the natural energies that surround every living entity or process. It was the logic or process of separation itself, of enclosure and immunity. It manifested as fear and identity, memory and experience. It informed every function of the living being, every experience, every act, every event. It "created" every "mystery". It was the structure of every imbecile link in the history of human suffering.

He is the ancient one visible in the Greek "myth", who was the universally adored child of the gods, who rejected the loved-one and every form of love and relationship, who was finally condemned to the contemplation of his own image, until, as a result of his own act and obstinacy, he suffered the fate of eternal separateness and died in infinite solitude. As I became more and more conscious of this guiding myth, or logic, in the very roots of my being, my writing began to take on an apparently intentional form. What was before only an arbitrary string of memories, images, and perceptions leading toward an underlying logic now proceeded from the heart of that logic itself, so that my perceptions and my thoughts from hour to hour began to develop as a narrative, completely beyond any intention or plan of my external mind.

I found that when I merely observed the content of my experience or my mind from hour to hour, day to day, I began to recognize a "story" being performed as my own conscious life. This was a remarkable observation, and obviously not a common one. The quality of the entire unfolding has the touch of madness in it. But people are mad. The ordinary state of human existence, although it is usually kept intact and relatively calmed by the politics of society, is founded in the madness of a prior logic, a schism in Reality that promotes the entire suffering adventure of human lives in endless and cosmic obstacles. I have known since I was a boy that this round of conflict, of contradiction and unconsciousness, was neither natural nor ultimately Real. And the total and guiding Purpose of my life has been, even by (and in the midst of) fully embracing the states and circumstances of conditionally manifested existence, to most perfectly Realize (and then to Communicate to all others) that Reality, that given Form, the "Bright" Condition of Consciousness Itself, Which is not properly the illusive goal of life, but Which is the Very and Conscious Foundation of life.

Thus, in order to learn this "Thing", I had to endure the progress of my own "madness". I had to observe the madman himself and undermine him with my Knowledge. This "madness", however, is not merely unfortunate, irrational, and disruptive. It is required of all those who would pass into Real Existence, beyond fear and egoic ignorance. And, in the process, one experiences remarkable revelations, and eventually discovers (and realizes) the synergy of the mind and every movement of Energy in the world.

It was this synergy, or synchronicity, this conscious coincidence of the internal and external world, that I discovered (and realized) at that time. After the pattern I recognized as Narcissus began to show its flower in the mind and I became settled in observing its "creative" position in the entirety of my life, the internal and external events in my experience began to demonstrate a common source or, rather, a coincident pattern. My own thoughts or images, then, began to arise in a similar pattern to my external experiences. A narrative was being constructed as my very life, which was itself a mythic form. The people, the passing events, the dramatization of my own motives, and all the imagery and categories of my thought appeared to be generating a conceived pattern. And I knew that my own life was moving toward the very death of Narcissus.

I began to write the outstanding narrative, or myth, that was appearing hour by hour. And I proposed to write a novel, tentatively entitled *The White Narcissus*, which would be this very complex of my life and mind as it was and had been revealing itself in my writing over several years. I intended to follow this production in myself until I should see it worked out whole. And then I would go back through the entire manuscript, whose proportions were already enormous, and make out of it a novel that included all of the "creative" motivations and intentions I had generated as a writer.

I was not utterly afraid even of the death of Narcissus, which was now my own death. I knew that no matter how terrible the event in terms of physical and mental and emotional suffering, it was not in fact the death of anything identical to my own Real Being. Even my own physical death appeared to me as a kind of mythic event. Its apparent consequences would perhaps be the end of my earthly life, but I was certain that I would have to pass through it in order to transcend the form of Narcissus. I knew then that all human suffering and all human deaths are endured only in the concepts, functions, and mentality that are guided by the unconscious logic of Narcissus. And so I devoted myself freely to the self-meditation of Narcissus in order to die his death as quickly as possible.

As it happened, that "death" did occur very dramatically three years later. But necessary transformations in my state of life had to occur before it would be possible. This point in my narrative brings us to the spring of 1964.

Beginning with the event I am about to describe, I have noticed that a peculiar and dramatic transformation in the state of my awareness has occurred every year at approximately the same time. The spring of every year is a time of awakening in nature, just as the period moving into winter, the time of my own birth, is a period moving into latency. Peculiar events of awakening seem naturally to occur to me at the springtime of the year, and the period moving into winter is usually a time of interiorization, often of a heavy kind. The cycle of my own experience has seemed to follow this pattern exactly.

One morning, in early May 1964, I awoke with the clear memory of a significant dream. As I indicated earlier, a dream of the type often analyzed by Jung preceded a dramatic awakening in myself. I had dreamed that I was being born. At first I saw it from outside my own body. I was watching my mother from a position near the doctor's viewpoint, between her legs. I could not see her face, and so I am not certain it was my natural mother in the dream. Her body was very large, fecund and swollen. The baby appeared head first, and its face was red, ugly, wet, and bunched up like a fist. Then I took the position of the baby itself, and one of the doctors said: "It's one of those multiple babies!"

Then I became aware of what must have been a later period in the life of that entity. The point of view was from my own body. I assumed it was the mature body of the baby I had seen being born. There were cords of phlegm that rose up out of my insides through my throat and out into the room. I was uncomfortable with this gag in my throat, but I was calm, as if I had lived that way for some time. The mass of phlegm separated out into two paths in the room, and each was attached to a young man. I assumed from their appearance that the three of us were in our late teens. And I also assumed that the birth of the "multiple" baby was the birth of the three of us. The first baby, whose face was like a fist, and whose body I now inhabited, was the source or controlling entity. The other two were dual aspects of my living being.

The one boy was very bright, energetic, attractive, and youthful. The other was "dark". His life-energy was heavier, and he had less mobility, physical and mental. I noticed the cords of phlegm at my feet as I moved forward and carelessly stepped on them. The act of stepping on the cords was both voluntary and involuntary, so that I felt both aggressive and guilty or trapped. I thought perhaps the boys would die if I stepped on the cords and broke them, but I also desired to be free of the gag in my throat and the immobility our attachment required of me. But when the cords were crushed and broken under my right foot, the boys came running up to me and embraced me happily. We all appeared now bright and free. And they thanked me for cutting the cords, which they said they had long hoped I would do.[12]

An ordinary external observer of this dream could certify one of several interpretations, depending upon the partial viewpoint by which he or she understands the matters of consciousness. Perhaps all the basic interpretations would bear some of the true import of this dream. But I required no interpreter. The very having of the dream marked a transformation in me. I had operated for several years in the aggravated model of my conscious being, and this dream marked the end of a long period of difficult progress. Those years had been filled with awesome fear and doubt as well as great intensity and, for me, worthwhile endeavor. Now a feeling of wholeness and well-being rose in the center of me, and I felt a peculiar relief in the wake of this dream. This change in me apparently set the stage for a remarkable discovery.

A few days later I arose in the early morning feeling very energetic. I sat at my desk to read while Nina slept. I turned to a volume of essays by C. G. Jung which I had often examined before. In particular, I turned to some chapters from *The Interpretation of Nature and the Psyche*. When I came to the concluding chapter, I read something which, though I must have seen it before, never communicated to me as it was about to do.

I think it would be valuable to quote the entire passage as I read it at that time:

It may be worth our while to examine more closely, from this point of view, certain experiences which seem to indicate the existence of

12. This dream is related to an important physical fact about Adi Da's Birth— that He was born with the umbilical cord wrapped around His neck.

psychic processes in what are commonly held to be unconscious states. Here I am thinking chiefly of the remarkable observations made during deep syncopes resulting from acute brain injuries. Contrary to all expectations, a severe head injury is not always followed by a corresponding loss of consciousness. To the observer, the wounded man seems apathetic, "in a trance," and not conscious of anything. Subjectively, however, consciousness is by no means extinguished. Sensory communication with the outside world is in a large measure restricted, but is not always completely cut off, although the noise of battle, for instance, may suddenly give way to a "solemn" silence. In this state there is sometimes a very distinct and impressive feeling or hallucination of levitation, the wounded man seeming to rise into the air in the same position he was in at the moment he was wounded. If he was wounded standing up, he rises in a standing position, if lying down, he rises in a lying position, if sitting, he rises in a sitting position. Occasionally his surroundings seem to rise with him—for instance the whole bunker in which he finds himself at the moment. The height of the levitation may be anything from eighteen inches to several yards. All feeling of weight is lost. In a few cases the wounded think they are making swimming movements with their arms. If there is any perception of their surroundings at all, it seems to be mostly imaginary, i.e., composed of memory images. During levitation the mood is predominantly euphoric. "'Buoyant, solemn, heavenly, serene, relaxed, blissful, expectant, exciting' are the words used to describe it. . . . There are various kinds of 'ascension experi-

13. Hubert Jantz and Kurt Beringer, "Das Syndrom des Schwebeerlebnisses unmittelbar nach Kopfverletzungen", Der Nervenarzt (Berlin), XVII (1944).

ences.'"[13] Jantz and Beringer rightly point out that the wounded can be roused from their syncope by remarkably small stimuli, for instance if they are addressed by name or touched, whereas the most terrific bombardment has no effect.

Much the same thing can be observed in deep comas resulting from other causes. I would like to give an example from my own medical experience: A woman patient, whose reliability and truthfulness I have no reason to doubt, told me that her first birth was very difficult. After thirty hours of fruitless labor the doctor considered that a forceps delivery was indicated. This was carried out under light narcosis. She was badly torn and suffered great loss of blood. When the doctor, her mother, and her husband had gone, and everything was cleared up, the nurse wanted to eat, and the patient saw her turn round at the door and ask, "Do you want anything before I go to supper?" She tried to answer, but couldn't. She had the feeling that she was sinking through the bed into a bottomless void. She saw the nurse hurry to the bedside and seize her hand in order to take her pulse. From the way she moved her fingers to and fro the patient thought it must be almost imperceptible. Yet she herself felt quite all right, and was slightly amused at the nurse's alarm. She was not in the least frightened. That was the last she could remember for a long time. The next thing she was aware of was that, without feeling her body and its position, she was <u>looking down</u> from a point in the ceiling and could see everything going on in the room below her: she saw herself lying in the bed, deadly pale, with closed eyes. Beside her stood the nurse. The doctor paced up and down the room excitedly, and it seemed to her that he had lost his head and didn't know what to do. Her relatives crowded to

115

the door. Her mother and her husband came in and looked at her with frightened faces. She told herself it was too stupid of them to think she was going to die, for she would certainly come round again. All this time she knew that behind her was a glorious, park-like landscape shining in the brightest colors, and in particular an emerald green meadow with short grass, which sloped gently upwards beyond a wrought-iron gate leading into the park. It was spring, and little gay flowers such as she had never seen before were scattered about in the grass. The whole demesne sparkled in the sunlight, and all the colors were of an indescribable splendor. The sloping meadow was flanked on both sides by dark green trees. It gave her the impression of a clearing in the forest, never yet trodden by the foot of man. "I knew that this was the entrance to another world, and that if I turned round to gaze at the picture directly, I should feel tempted to go in at the gate, and thus step out of life." She did not actually <u>see</u> this landscape, as her back was turned to it, but she <u>knew</u> it was there. She felt there was nothing to stop her from entering in through the gate. She only knew that she would turn back to her body and would not die. That was why she found the agitation of the doctor and the distress of her relatives stupid and out of place.

The next thing that happened was that she awoke from her coma and saw the nurse bending over her in bed. She was told that she had been unconscious for about half an hour. The next day, some fifteen hours later, when she felt a little stronger, she made a remark to the nurse about the incompetent and "hysterical" behavior of the doctor during her coma. The nurse energetically denied this criticism in the belief that the patient had been completely unconscious at the time and could therefore have known nothing of the scene. Only when she described in full detail what had happened during the coma was the nurse obliged to admit that the patient had perceived the events exactly as they happened in reality.[14]

I have no idea how long I spent reading and rereading this passage and the surrounding material from Jung's essay. But when Nina awoke to prepare to go to work, I was a changed man. I cannot overestimate the importance that data held for me at the time. It was as if the entire mass of heart-depressive ideas and assumptions that I began to adopt years before in works like *The Lost Years of Jesus Revealed* had been lifted away in a single moment. I had long regarded Jung to be an important investigator into the true significances of human experience. I felt limitations in his method and some of his assumptions, and these would become even clearer to me later on, but I had learned that he could be trusted to observe data and report it without distortions and interpretations. When he interprets, it is usually apart from the language and material that he reports.

Therefore, when I read this report of phenomena that transcend the boundaries of the ordinary model of "Man" typically presumed by Western culture, I was positively overwhelmed. I felt this was a key to an enormous range of experience, now capable of honest and direct investigation, which would vindicate, parallel, and extend the experiences that had long been the burden of my life.

When Nina awoke, I flooded her with my excitement. It was one of the humanly happiest hours in my life to then. An extreme pressure and source of conflict

14. C. G. Jung, *Psyche and Symbol: A Selection from the Writings of C. G. Jung*, ed. Violet S. de Laszlo (Garden City, New York: Doubleday Anchor Books, 1958), pp. 267-69.

within me had been drawn away. I felt that I could begin the practical investigation of the miraculous and Spiritual phenomena that up to now had seemed impossible. And because they had seemed impossible, because they had been carried away with all the imagery of the lost "Christ", I had been required to endure long years searching for an alternative solution. I was forced to pursue a description of the essential Nature and Freedom of the human being that does not assume more than the model of mortality that had been propagated in my university education. All in all, this passage in Jung signified in me a liberation from mortal philosophy and all bondage to the form of death.

In the weeks that followed I ravenously took to reading whatever material I could find that dealt with occult phenomena, miracles, Spiritual and religious philosophy, and any kind of liberated significance. I was particularly impressed by the documented evidence for out-of-body experiences and the better sources on spiritualism. The miracle that occurred at Fatima earlier in this century seemed to me a remarkable and important event. As many as ten thousand of its witnesses, many of whom were non-believing reporters or passersby, signed affidavits that they saw the sun wheel around in many colors and fall toward the earth. I was also profoundly impressed by the life and work of Edgar Cayce.[15]

I became acquainted with the *I-Ching*, translated by Richard Wilhelm and introduced by C. G. Jung. I used it several times over a period of a month or more and saw the laws of synchronicity described by Jung demonstrated interestingly in myself and those around me.

The people I began to meet during that time also seemed to be coming at an appropriate stage in my life. And they came on a gradient suited to my own learning. At first I met people who were mainly spiritualistic and

15. Edgar Cayce (1878-1945) was a psychic particularly known for medical diagnosis and healing via clairvoyance. He also made various predictions for the future based on his visions.

religious enthusiasts. Then I met others who led me to read intelligent material that supported a philosophic and Spiritual view. All of this was founded in evidence of the kind I was beginning to recognize rather than in the mortal philosophy of the establishment.

Finally, I met a man named Harold Freeman at a party in Palo Alto. He was an occultist and the first man I had ever met who claimed to have experiences of this unusual kind. He indicated that such experiences could be attained consciously and intentionally by a kind of scientific method.

He told me stories of how he met his teacher, a woman who has allegedly maintained a physical body for over six hundred years. She demonstrated and taught him many unusual abilities. He led me to the source books of occultism. I read the works of H. P. Blavatsky,[16] Alice Bailey,[17] and a remarkable (even though, I felt, basically fictional) set of volumes by Baird Spalding called *The Life and Teaching of the Masters of the Far East.*

I was unable at that time to completely separate fiction and exaggeration from fact in the occult material. It seemed even less reliable than religious literature. It appeared to take masses of religious and Spiritual lore, which were the products of many centuries of community, and pass them through the emotional mind of a single, mediumistic intelligence. This gave it the force of a firsthand account, whereas it was actually a body of tradition in the secondary form of an oral literature. It also tended to deal with "phenomena" rather than matters of fundamental importance. Thus, I became very wary of literary influences, and I desired a direct, personal experience of anything pertaining to Spiritual Reality. But it

16. Helena Petrovna Blavatsky (1831-1891) was the founder of the Theosophical movement, which introduced many Eastern religious and philosophical concepts to the West.

17. Alice Bailey (1880-1949), originally a member of the Theosophical Society, formed her own organization, the Arcane School, in 1923 to teach the philosophy espoused in her books. She claimed that all of her books were dictated telepathically to her by a Tibetan wise man.

was all at least an emotional symbol that did much to enlarge my ordinary humor and extend my growing impulses to Real experience.

At one point I asked Mr. Freeman if he was to teach me. I told him I was now in search of a teacher for help in my own developmental course. A couple of days later he told me that he had contacted his teacher and was told that someone else was supposed to teach me.

I felt that he was mostly a genuine man. He made no effort to capitalize on my vulnerability. And his reply seemed altogether right to me, for I had begun to recognize a new psychic awakening in myself. In the occasional flickering of certain images in my mind I had begun to recognize a communication about my future.

In the weeks that led up to my meeting with Mr. Freeman, I had grown more accustomed to operating in the manner that my own work had precipitated. The recognition of the coincidence between consciousness and external experience began to develop into a comfortable ability, so that I began to use the images that seemed arbitrarily to pass through the mind. I saw that many of these images were signs of precognition.

One image became a constant factor. I saw that I was to find a teacher that would be able to help me. I did not see him, but, in spontaneous visionary flashes, I saw pictures of a store where oriental sculpture and other oriental works of art were sold. It became spontaneously evident to me that this store was in New York City.

I told Nina about this experience, and we began immediately to prepare to leave for New York. We gradually sold or gave away most of our belongings, including my library of about 1400 volumes. I kept only a few books that seemed important to my new line of study. These events led on toward the middle or end of June 1964.

Robert

CHAPTER 6

The Passage to the Guru

One morning, shortly before Nina and I left for New York, I awoke to a very brilliant clear day. I went outside and stood in front of the house to enjoy the morning freshness. The house was built on the ledge of a cliff, and the wall of the cliff dropped off steeply about twenty feet in front of the house, exposing a sheer drop of about one hundred feet to the beach. The beach itself was very wide, perhaps two hundred feet wide, and the ocean stretched in a huge expanse as far and wide as I could see.

The house and the beach were in a very isolated area, with only a few people in other cabins, and they were generally away at work during the day. On this day, no one else was around, and so I was alone.

I stood on the cliff, the morning was clear and shining, and the air was that kind that makes one go "Ah!" inside with relief and Joy, and make a big breath of ease, like on vacation. And, suddenly, in barely a moment or two, a storm moved over me from the ocean like a huge shroud, like a great canopy or blanket. It had the feeling of an immense shell, rising above me, and touching the earth and sea only at all the horizon points. The weather below, where I was standing, was not a dense mass. The air around and above me remained clear. The storm was only in the high sky. The high, moving mass of dark sky rose above me and beyond, and stood everywhere above, appearing like a gigantic dome, enclosing the space where I stood. The storm looked like a huge gray dome, full of gray shapes of clouds, a perfect half-sphere. It was not homogeneous, but it was boiling with great masses of differing and combining clouds. And I could still see clearly in this dark dome, all the way to the horizon of the sea, and all around me in the suddenly shaded and sunless air.

Then, with shattering quickness, like an aerial display of royal fireworks, lightning began to move everywhere through the dome, such that now it felt like the crown of my own head, and it looked like a Great Sahasrar,[18] with what appeared to be millions of bolts of lightning shooting everywhere, in all directions in the sky, and, like gods, flying anywhere in a moment, hundreds of miles at will.

How can I describe what kind of storm it was? It was a Divine storm, a revelation of Truth, a transformative Blessing, a Spiritual Initiation! It was the most magnificent thing I had ever seen. It was a tangible Divine Vision. It was the "Bright", outside me. How many were the countless bolts of lightning? The lights in that great vast dome were like the millions and millions of lightnings of the little nerve filaments in the center of the brain, the Corona Radiata. The storm was all lights, and waters. It was the most shocking, torrential drenching of the earth I had ever seen. And it was enormously, blowing loud! The thunder was so loud it shook the sea and quaked the ground, everywhere, and deep to the core, rolling and churning, even under my feet, and all over my body, as if to crack the atoms of all that seemed and end the infinitely fragile world. And the water flew from everywhere, Washing me, Waking me, Shouting me, "Brightening" me to my Life to come.

The storm impressed me as if it were not only the physically most powerful storm that ever happened on earth, but the very First and the very Last storm that could ever happen on earth. And it was also a storm of Spiritual Power, for, all the while I stood in it, within my body there

18. The sahasrar is the highest chakra (or subtle energy center), associated with the crown of the head and beyond.

was a "Bright" Storm of Spiritual Energy. My entire body was rolling and churning with feelings, like electric shocks.

I do not know how long I stood there, in the titanic Force of everything, but the storm itself must have lasted for an hour or two. Then, as suddenly as it had come, it disintegrated and disappeared in the resurrected morning sun. And, in the moment of its passing, I Knew it was time for me to leave California and go on to what it had now become certain was to be the "Bright" Divine Fulfillment of the Purpose of my human birth.

Quickly thereafter, Nina and I left California, at the near-end of June 1964. My mood was one of intense excitement and expectation. There was no doubt at all in me that I was about to begin the ultimate adventure of my life. I was willing to make any sacrifice and to go anywhere in the world in order to abandon myself to the Sources of the Divine Good.

The trip itself was a comedy of frustrations. We traveled in an old Chevrolet station wagon that seemed to explode on schedule every hundred miles. It was loaded to the windows with the belongings we felt necessary for life in New York. There were boxes of books, blankets and sleeping bags, various clothing, pots and pans. And three necessary cats.

Even in all the years before this time, I had not been entirely without teachers. I had learned from many people and environments. Now I was seeking a teacher who could lead me into an entirely new order of Experience and Knowledge. I was in pursuit of the Guru, a Realizer of God, Truth, and Reality. But I had also known a Guru of a certain kind for nearly two years. I had even lived with him. He was my cat, Robert.

If one is truly sensitive to the movements everywhere within and without oneself, every kind of object or creature or experience becomes an instructional (or teaching) communication. One cannot help but receive the teaching, under any circumstances, if one is a real listener. Indeed, even the most inert objects Know the

125

same Bliss of unqualified Existence that is the Root of the living consciousness of human beings.

My own way of life had been an absolute devotion to this practice of listening, so that I had never before required a Guru to teach me in the formal and traditional manner. Indeed, I did not even know what a "Guru" was until these last days. And, in the past, if I had heard of such persons or matters, I would have considered them to be impossible, like the "Jesus" of my childhood.

My experience throughout my life had, thus far, progressed spontaneously and profoundly, always generating new forms of Clarity and Awakening. As a result, I was fully capable of finding a "teacher" in the most oddball and the most ordinary of sources, and I could give myself to be taught by such sources just as consciously and even formally as any sworn practitioner in a monastery founded in the traditional Scriptures and rules.

For nearly two years, then, I had been very attentive to my tomcat, Robert. At the end of my year at Stanford I went to say goodbye to two old friends, Cynthia and Vito, with whom I had shared many hours of drug adventure and conversations about art and literature. Their cat had just given up a litter of kittens, and they were making the usual attempt to pawn them off on their friends.

I told them I was going back to New York for the summer and did not really know when I would be able to provide a home for a cat. But when I looked at the litter of kittens, I saw a little one with huge eyes, a dark one with long hair that sat in deep calm and watched me. I fell in love with him immediately, and Nina and I pleaded with our friends to keep him for us.

The long summer passed as I have told you. And by the time we found our house in the redwood forest the following September, we had entirely forgotten that we owned a cat. But one day Cynthia and Vito arrived with Robert. We were absolutely happy to have him, and so grateful and surprised that our friends had kept him for us all that time. I named him "Robert" purely in fun. He was such a strong animal presence, with an economy and grace that made the idiot brand of human living seem so unconscious and confused. I gave him an ordinary human name just to remind myself of the difference in him.

Robert was quite a large cat now. He had matured beautifully, and all of his instincts were wild. He seemed perfectly placed in himself. We decided that he should have a lady cat for his consort, and so we were happy when some other friends in Big Sur offered the pick of their new litter.

The Big Sur litter contained only a pair of orange tiger cats, both females, with twin markings. We took them both. And we brought them home to Robert so that he could enjoy his ladies in the wild.

Robert and his ladies always lived completely independent of us. We left food for them, but they came and went at will. Their manner of living was so pure and intelligent, so direct an enjoyment, with such effortless capability for survival, that Nina and I soon became enamored of them. We watched them constantly in the sheer pleasure of seeing life lived as an instinctive perfection. Their solutions to the hour by hour confrontations that humanity tends to bypass or escape were an example to us of unproblematic existence.

When we left our home in the redwoods and moved on to the beach at Tunitas, our cats were just drawing into their maturity. We were wondering if Robert would choose only one of the lady cats for his consort, and if this would cause problems with the remaining one. But we were not surprised when both of the lady cats began to swell up in obvious pregnancy.

At the time this seemed to me a perfectly moral solution to Robert's domestic situation. He loved and tended them both completely and without conflict, so that he appeared to me a master of domestic peace, even a model of sanity and strength to human householders, who always seem unable to solve the problems caused by their traditional and conceptual monogamy.

One evening I heard Robert and the lady cats hissing and growling in the yard. I went out and found the three of them surrounding a fourth. It was a young gray male who had somehow wandered into Robert's territory. The three cats stood almost motionless in a circle about the fourth, and their primitive signals continued for what must have been several hours, even while Nina and I passed to sleep.

In the morning all was quiet. Robert and the ladies were lying in various parts of the house asleep. I went outside to enjoy the morning sea, and I came upon the place where they had surrounded the stranger the evening before. I made an awesome discovery. In the center of the circle where they had stood there was a perimeter of gray hairs, and in the center were stains of blood and fragments of the inner parts of the dead animal. The cats had apparently cannibalized the intruder.

I showed the place to Nina, and we were really astonished. But our cats came out gentle in the morning, showing no signs of the sacrifice in signals of guilt or anger or lust. They felt to us to be an ancient triangle of righteousness. And their justice confounded all our reasons, so that we could only admire them as beings who seemed to enjoy the free consciousness of higher laws that all humanity had long ago forgotten.

But something had occurred in the mutual life of our cats that they were about to solve according to their peculiar laws. The ladies were fully pregnant now, and they had begun to keep a distance from one another. That evening Robert remained in the house with only one of the ladies. The other had disappeared.

For several days we looked everywhere for the second lady cat. But finally we decided that she must have wandered away or been killed somewhere on the highway above. We even supposed that Robert may have chosen the one and banished the other to her own survival.

We had no idea that he had only found a way to establish his domain in two entirely separate realms.

For a full year Robert remained with his single consort. Her kittens were born and grown. Robert would leave at sunrise and pass over into the hills, but every evening at sunset I would hear him calling as he descended the rise behind the house. He would return to eat and sleep with us and his lady until the following morning.

We assumed that this was merely the pattern of his wildness, and that he must have spent his days wandering and hunting. His consort always remained behind in the area of the house, and he would often bring her a bird, a rabbit, or a mouse to eat. Or she would capture some small animal just at sunset and offer it to him when he returned home.

After a year of this we had settled fully into the cycle of the lives of our cats and never expected to see the other lady cat again. But one day I noticed something a little strange about the lady who remained at home. Her hair was furled and matted in an unusual manner. At first I only generally noticed this, and I simply accepted it as being the result of her climbing about in the woods. But the next day I examined her more closely, for she had also acquired some kind of new intensity. Her paws stretched open, and she constantly touched my feet, insisting on my attention.

When I picked her up, I saw that it could not be Robert's domestic bride. Her hair was wild and full, and its ends were bleached by weather. Her exposed nose and the pads of her feet were also bleached by water and air and sunlight, and they were all freckled by spots that I knew did not belong to the lady who remained behind. And even the edges of her eyelids were pink and white. Her eyes were wild as only those could be that had lived and survived in wilderness.

It was obviously the long lost lady cat. When Nina came home, we looked her over together. And we welcomed Robert in the evening. He preened her and loved her, and we began to understand the intelligence of his way of life. When the two ladies had first become pregnant, Robert must have led one into the wild. And afterwards he divided his time between them, tending one in the wilderness by day and returning to the other at night. Again we marveled at this justice, this untroubled, thoughtful, and inexplicably kind order of their survival.

When we awoke the next morning, Robert and his wild lady had come bearing gifts. Sitting in the top of a storage basket surrounded by soft cloths were four wide-eyed baby cats, two dark and two orange, like wild flowers, with long soft hair. They were four of the most beautiful and fresh creatures I have ever seen. Nina and I laughed joyfully at them. Robert and his lady had also produced miracles in the alchemy of wilderness.

As the days passed, we also saw what must have been a further development of Robert's plan of living. The lady cat who had remained domestic the previous year disappeared, as her sister had done. I think it was their plan to exchange their states of living and carry on the same pattern as before. But we found the lady dead near the highway. She had been struck by a car while moving off into the wild.

It was about this time that Nina and I began to prepare to move to New York. Robert's children surrounded us in great numbers now. Along with the new four there were at least five others from the domestic lady. And there was another stray that had wandered in from nowhere but who was allowed to remain. We named him Sanjuro, because he was such a tough, self-contained rascal, and he handled himself like the samurai depicted by Toshiro Mifune in the Japanese movie entitled *Sanjuro*. We had also acquired a little black female whose manner was irresistible. She was a little stalk of a creature with tall legs, and we knew her as "the fastest cat in the West". We called her "the Bitty". All in all there were about a dozen cats around us, living in various degrees of dependence and wildness. As we prepared to leave, we gave them to various friends. But we kept Robert and his wild lady and the Bitty.

Thus, on the day we left California, we packed our belongings in the station wagon along with the three cats for the long drive across America. We could not part with these companions. Their way of life had become a necessary vision to us, a sign and at least a memory of the intelligent wilderness that was the example of beauty and sanity by which we ourselves were moved and consoled in California.

Robert himself was nothing less to me than my best friend and mentor. He was more, not less, than human to me. I watched him with fascination. I followed him through woods and watched him hunt. I tried to understand his curious avoidance of the sea, and how he could sit on the cliff above the sea, watching the evening sun, and the wind blowing his hairs heroically about his head. The mystery of his pattern of living, his ease and justice, the economy of all his means, the untouchable absence of all anxiety, the sudden and adequate power he brought to every circumstance without exceeding the intensity required, all of his ways seemed to me an epitome of the genius of life. And he communicated with me so directly that I was always disarmed. He would call me when he returned in the evening. He would touch me whenever he needed my presence. He would lie with me as if with conscious intention to console me with his living presence. And I loved him as deeply as the universe itself.

I could not leave such friends behind. Yet I was aware that my adventure was about to be renewed. I was seeking a teacher for an entirely new order of my mind and life. Hereafter, the wilderness could not be the model for my seeking or my healing. In New York the cats would have to live in an environment whose unreality and absence of instinctual intelligence, not to mention the absence of human intelligence, was a critical problem even for human beings. They would have to survive in an artificial enclosure, the hardware of human

Robert

The lady cat
with kittens

"Robert himself was
nothing less to me
than my best friend
and mentor. He was
more, not less, than
human to me."

Robert's "wild flowers"

The Bitty

evolution. There would be no possibility for the hunt, for natural solitude, or for any of the native signs and obstacles of wilderness that my animals had mastered even an aeon ago.

Even as we traveled, we realized the dilemma of our cats. Several times the car blew up, and we were stranded in the desert. The tires would explode at will, and we had often to remain stranded for hours without food or moving air, in pitiless heat. The cats strained and gagged in the breathless air with dry lungs, so that we were afraid they could not survive.

When we finally arrived in New York, I went to my parents to be reconciled. And Nina and I found an apartment in the lower end of Greenwich Village, on Houston Street. It was a dark place, with the enclosed odor of a long-degraded humanity that had been confused with refuse, immobility, and death. I began to observe the signs wherever I went, and, thus, I looked and waited for my new teacher. Meanwhile, we settled into our new, unnatural order of living.

The cats had to remain contained in the apartment, except for the relative freedom of a rear window, a fire escape, and an adjacent roof that could be reached with a small jump of perhaps two feet. I was afraid for my cats in this environment. We were four stories above the ground, and a slight miscalculation could mean a fall to death. But I considered that it was better for them to enjoy even this little freedom, and I consigned them to the survival power that had been demonstrated in wilderness.

After a few weeks I could feel the advancing Presence of what I sought. I knew it was perhaps only a matter of days until I would meet my teacher. It was a rainy evening, the Fourth of July. I returned from a walk in Washington Square. Firecrackers and a few amateur fireworks tended to draw my attention into distant streets and alleys, and into the sky above. When I came in the door to the building, the superintendent met me. Robert had fallen from the roof. Since no one was home, he had called the local animal shelter to take him away. I asked if Robert was dead. He said he was not sure, but he pointed to the fire escapes high above, as if to say: "How alive could he be after such a fall?"

Nina had been out shopping during that time. I went upstairs and found that she had returned. We called the animal shelter, and they told us Robert was dead. We turned away from one another in separate sorrow and wept. It was a grief more profound than any I had ever known. The death of my little dog when I was a boy had taken me by surprise. At that time, I had not expected death, and when it came I was moved to follow her to the place of continuous life beyond the world. But Robert's death was no surprise at all. The news of it came to one who bore the knowledge of death, so that when it came there was no movement in me toward any other place. There was only the incomparable sorrow of a broken span of living. There was only the absence of that dear one. His mortality appeared in a world whose livingness I had come to know as far exceeding the image and power of death. But, for all the Sphere of living Energy that I Knew informed the world and was its Truth, there remained the fact of this end, this disappearance, this sorrow-laden implication of Truth within the Blissful Void.

I recognized that Robert had been my teacher in the wilderness. He had filled my eye and owned a thread of attention in my heart. I Knew him and he Knew me. Nothing could replace that state of life or console its absence. I treated him in death like a saint. I had him cremated, and I kept his ashes. I observed my grief and kept my mind focused in the hope of new events. I Knew that Robert's passing was the Sign that I was about to find my teacher in the human world.

In the weeks that preceded Robert's death and my immediately subsequent meeting with my first teacher, I had informed myself with every kind of study. I had passed beyond the remarkable news that the phenomena of human experience included much more than merely "mortal" phenomena. It was no longer a matter of proving such things to be true. I was certain enough of them on the basis of my own experience and the reliably communicated experience of countless others in human time. Therefore, I did not pursue phenomena themselves. My knowledge and my experience were associated with a point of view that sympathized with the greater, and generally esoteric, points of view proposed in the world's traditional philosophical, mystical, and Spiritual literatures. My reading encompassed the literate mystical works of Christian saints and the classical writings of Buddhism and Zen Buddhism, Hinduism, Vedanta,[19] and Yoga. I was acquainted with the works of Ramana Maharshi, J. Krishnamurti, Ramakrishna, and Aurobindo.[20] I felt particularly drawn to these more oriental teachers, whose course or intention was liberation, or an ultimate fulfillment of a

---

19. The Sanskrit word "Vedanta" literally means the "end of the Vedas" (which is the most ancient body of Indian Scripture), and is used to refer to the principal philosophical tradition of Hinduism.

20. Ramana Maharshi (1979-1950) is regarded by many as the greatest Indian Sage of the twentieth century. He established his Ashram at Tiruvannamalai in South India, which continues today. Adi Da writes at length about Ramana Maharshi later in *The Knee of Listening*.

Jiddu Krishnamurti (1895-1986) was brought up in India by the early Theosophists, who hoped he would become a world-Teacher. Krishnamurti in fact rejected all traditional Spiritual Teachings and paths of devotion and spent his life advocating his own mind-based philosophy of enlightenment.

Ramakrishna (1836-1886), better known in the West than any other modern Indian Saint, was a renowned ecstatic, and a lifelong devotee of Kali, a form of the Mother-Shakti. In the course of his Spiritual practice, Ramakrishna passed spontaneously through many religious and Spiritual disciplines, and he Realized a state of profound mystical union with God. In 1993, Adi Da Revealed that Ramakrishna and his principal disciple, Swami Vivekananda, are the deeper-personality vehicle of His bodily human Incarnation (pp. 554-57).

Aurobindo Ghose (1872-1950) was born in Calcutta of Indian parents who sent him to be educated in the West. Later, after his return to India, Aurobindo was imprisoned as a political agitator, and during this period his life changed dramatically. He began to study the *Bhagavad Gita* and took up the practice of Yoga. After his release from prison he settled at Pondicherry, South India, where he Taught and wrote religious philosophy, developing his ideas about the Spiritual evolution of mankind.

most profound and, perhaps, even miraculous kind, free of the dogmatic limitations and unrevealing symbolisms of merely exoteric religion. And, relative to the religion I inherited in my childhood, I felt that the significance of Jesus of Nazareth was not in the conventional (and no longer believable) myths and legends promoted by traditional, exoteric Christianity. Rather, I felt that the significance of Jesus of Nazareth was in his (or his story's) basic inspirational recommendation that one, for Real, discover and embrace God, or Truth, or Reality Itself, and that one discover and embrace only Real and True and present-time Means, including Spiritual Means, for Realizing God, Truth, or Reality Itself.

Based on my studies at that time, I was mainly attendant both to the Yogic Spiritual traditions and to the Truth proposed alike in Vedanta and Buddhism. But the philosophically oriented paths of discrimination and practice proposed by Vedanta and Buddhism, and even Zen Buddhism, seemed to me to be rather indirect, or merely mind-based, and not sufficiently oriented toward Spirit-based practice and toward the Spiritual Realization of Reality (as I Knew It in the "Bright" of my childhood). Also, the essentially non-Yogic (or non-Spiritual) traditions of Vedanta and Buddhism seemed to me to require a course too much dissociated from the usual action of life. Nevertheless, the philosophically described One Truth that is the True, or non-egoic, Self-Condition, the One and non-dual Reality, the unqualified Divine, or the Nirvanic Absolute that includes all things, was, for me, the ultimate traditional description of God, Truth, and Reality, and, from my point of view, the traditions of Vedanta and Buddhism even epitomized that description. And that description, combined with the devotional and Spiritual Means described in the religious and Yogic traditions, and including the true Guru-devotee relationship (or the great devotional and Spiritual relationship between the true disciple, or the devotee, and the true teacher, or the adept), summarized my then developing (but, even then, basically established) sense of how I was moved to practice and of What I was moved to Realize. Indeed, from my point of view at the time, all of that simply and exactly corresponded to a way of Realization based not only on a summary of all the traditions, but also, and even more importantly, on the inherent Content of the "Bright" of my childhood (and the "Bright" of the profound revelations of my youth).

On the basis of all of this, I was moved to seek a teacher, a human guide who could lead me into the full Realization of this primary Truth, with all Its capabilities and Joy. And, I felt, such a teacher would necessarily be adept in the esoteric Yogic processes and in all the Spiritual functions that I felt must be the practical means for Realizing What was otherwise less availably represented in the cool, or mostly philosophical and ascetical, Scriptures of Vedanta and Buddhism.

My reading then, as always, was dictated by the laws of my own necessity. Curiously, what spontaneously became available for me to read was always uniquely appropriate, and immediately useful, relative to the stage or mode of my then present-time development. Thus, as the day of my meeting with my teacher approached, I began to read works that dealt with the peculiar Yoga of the Kundalini Shakti. I read such works as *The Serpent Power*, by Sir John Woodroffe, and I found in them keys to many of my own experiences. The descriptions of the various "chakras", or Spiritual and "creative" centers in the body, and the details of experiences generated in each stage of Spiritual ascent, brought a clarity of order to the progress of many of my own seemingly arbitrary experiences.

I saw that What I called the "Bright" was the fundamental (and inherently Spiritual) Consciousness in Which the entire chakra body is aroused, and functionally open to the proceedings of the Divine Shakti, or Spirit-Energy, or Primary Light. Likewise, I understood that the experience associated with my college Awakening was a sudden and profound Manifestation of the Divine Shakti, the Conscious Energy that, from the ordinary point of view, appears as mortal ego-consciousness, but Which, rightly engaged, leads back to the Divine Self, or Siva, Who is eternally Calm.

I knew that my own course of life, and the meaning of all life, was in this process of Siva-Shakti, the endless "Bright" unfolding of living consciousness and experience, and its consistent foundation in (and, most ultimately, its most perfect Realization of) the Pure, "Bright" Infinity of unqualified, Transcendent Being. Thus, I expected to be guided by the "Bright" Itself, and, thus and thereby, to a teacher (or perhaps even a sequence of teachers) who would lead me further and further into a conscious, direct, and regulated revelation of this same "Bright" process.

I had read the "autobiography" of Paramahansa Yogananda[21] as we drove across country. I found in him a curiously sane and beautiful example of the kind of life and experience I needed to touch as my own. But I knew that I required a teacher who was presently alive to guide me through my peculiar problems of seeking.

I was only uncertain of the precise direction of such seeking. The fundamental Spiritual path as it is proposed in the various literatures divided at a certain point. The typical motive of the oriental teachings was in the direction of an absolute liberation from all forms of experience and life-consciousness. Such teaching is typical of Vedanta and Buddhism, in the classical works of Zen masters and such modern saints or God-men as Ramakrishna and Ramana Maharshi.

21. Paramahansa Yogananda (Mukunda Lal Ghosh, 1893-1952) was born in Bengal, the child of devout Hindu parents. As a young man, Yogananda found his Guru, Swami Yukteswar Giri, who initiated him into an order of formal renunciates. In 1920, Yogananda traveled to America to attend an international conference of religions in Boston. Subsequently he settled in America, attracting many American devotees. He Taught "Kriya Yoga", a system of practice that had been passed down to him by his own Teacher and that had originally been developed from traditional techniques of Kundalini Yoga. Yogananda became widely known through the publication of his life-story, *Autobiography of a Yogi*.

On the other hand, the teachings of Christianity, of Western occultism, and of such Eastern saints as Aurobindo indicated a course whose goal was in life, or at least not radically opposed to life. They drew on the ultimate conclusion of all the Scriptures, which variously state that "this is God's plan and creation", or "this is That", or "Nirvana and samsara are the same",[22] or "there is only One, without a second". They proposed a sacrificial practice of surrender and reception, wherein life is moved toward a perfect vision or evolution. I found even in the mind of the iconoclast J. Krishnamurti a sense of life that is not divorced from the process of natural existence. And, though I greatly desired the incomparable Peace of Ultimate Knowledge, I also tended to sympathize with this latter path of Realization and "creativity", whose purposes are a Divine life rather than a pure separation into Absoluteness.

This problem of direction, which was always to be one of the most fundamental in my progress, took the form of a continuous questioning in me as I sought for my teacher. And it was to form the basis for my first questions when I met him.

When we arrived in New York, I began to look for this teacher with peculiar certainty. I did not seek for him by effort. I did not wander about the city looking for oriental art stores that resembled the one I saw in spontaneous visions. Rather, I lived normally, according to the particular requirements of each day, but, as I went about the city in the midst of my daily course, I was also attentive and ready for signs of the store I had seen in visions. It was clear and certain in me that I would find my

22. "Nirvana" is a Buddhist term for the Unqualified Reality beyond suffering, ego, birth, and death. "Samsara" is a Buddhist and Hindu term for the conditional realm of birth and change and death. The traditional saying quoted here therefore expresses the doctrine that there is ultimately no difference between the formless Divine Reality and Its conditional manifestations.

"This is That", another Ultimate Statement quoted here, is similar in meaning: Any conditional phenomenon ("this") is not different from the Divine Reality ("That").

teacher in an oriental art store, and I was certain that the guiding-Source of the visions that convinced me of this would Itself bring me to the place itself. However, I also felt that any intentional outer seeking for the place would likely only prevent the spontaneous discovery of it, which depended on an inner availability and sensitivity and spontaneity. Therefore, Nina and I simply went about the practical matters of founding a household. Nina found work to support us. And I, writing and living as before, watched for my teacher.

The move to New York was a shock to us both in many ways. Our country life of wilderness was past. Robert's death signified many things, the passage from an old order to a new. I awaited a new teacher and a new way of life. And the city life of humanity also stood in contrast to the wilderness and natural rule by which Nina and I had always lived. The material and mortal philosophies had died in me, and the transition in the wilderness, the exploitation of instinctual, animal, and passionate laws, seemed inappropriate, not only to the great city, but also to the new order of Spiritual life to which I was inclined.

I was quite confused by all of this. The new way of life seemed to require a kind of purity and enforced morality that was unknown to me or my cats. I began to doubt my old way of life. The kind of self-exploitation by which I lived and wrote began to seem immoral. I thought that, perhaps, it only "created" obstacles to the attainment of what I would now possess.

I thought perhaps I should leave Nina. After all, the paths of Spiritual life were largely taken by celibates and highly disciplined saints. I became overwhelmed with my lack of discipline. I had rarely worked for a living in my life. I had never really supported myself or anyone else. I was a libertine, a drinker, a drug user, a useless and impractical dreamer, a passionate madman!

All of these emotions turned in me. It became September. On the Sunday afternoon of the Labor Day weekend, my parents were driving us back to New York. We had been spending the weekend with them on Long Island. We were driving down Seventh Avenue in Greenwich Village, just a few blocks from our apartment on Houston Street. As we passed down the relatively deserted streets, I saw a small store on the west side of the street. There was a large sign above with the name "Rudi" and several written characters that looked like Chinese calligraphy. The window of the store was full of oriental sculpture and painting. As I looked at it, it became instantly clear that this was the place I had seen in visions. I was immediately certain that this was the place where I would find the teacher toward whom I had been directed while in California, and since California.

After my parents left us at home, Nina and I walked back to the store. It was only a small store, and it was unceremoniously filled and even cluttered with thousands of pieces of sculpture from all over the Orient. There was a huge Buddha seated on a lotus in the window. Standing in the rear of the store was a colossal wooden Bodhisattva, perhaps fifteen feet tall, holding a lotus in its hand and a crystal jewel in its forehead. Everywhere were standing Buddhas, dancing saints, and portraits of ferocious and sublime deities.

There was an aura of feeling and of light surrounding the store, as if all of these sublime entities had gathered to generate a center of Force for any who were ready to recognize It. I told Nina that this was certainly the place I had envisioned, and, as we left, I planned to return the next day, during business hours.

The next day we returned in the early morning. The door to the shop was then (as always in the future) fixed in an open position. We walked in casually, concealing a great expectation. But there was no one in the store who "looked" like a teacher. There was only a little, round, oldish Jewish lady. She immediately displayed every insincere mannerism and manipulative sales technique I had ever seen exhibited by a New York shopkeeper. We,

"There was an aura of feeling and of light surrounding the store, as if all of these sublime entities had gathered to generate a center of Force for any who were ready to recognize It."

The Houston Street apartment building

The site of the oriental art store on Seventh Avenue

in turn, pretended to be only interested in art, especially looking for a small Buddha to stand in a place of meditation. The woman showed us many objects in the "merely" fifty dollar price range. I was careful to observe her for any signs of an impractical Spiritual nature! But she was all business, and I had the feeling that I was being well and truly "sold". The quality of the place did not differ from that of a meat market or a 5-and-10.

Finally, we decided to purchase a small, antique, Japanese figure, a standing Buddha about twelve inches high. The woman assured us it would be a "very Powerful" object for meditation. We passed to the rear of the store, where she wrapped the object in newspaper and stuffed it in a paper bag! We watched this with holy amazement, and then my eyes turned to a pair of photographs on the wall.

The photographs appeared to be of two different saints. Both of them were naked except for a small loin cloth. One was an enormously fat man with the appearance of awesome strength. And the other was a more moderately proportioned man with a melancholy expression, as if his mind were tuned to some distant place that was his real home. Both of them had short hair and equally short beards that suggested they had each been totally shaven within the past few weeks. And there were undeniable, obvious signs of Spiritual Power and Presence generated bodily by both men.

As I studied these pictures, my heart began to pound with excitement. I asked the woman about the pictures. She said they were her son's teachers. Her son was a Spiritual teacher, she said, and he was the owner of the store. I asked how I could meet her son, and I was told that he was away for a long weekend in the country, but he would return the next day.

We left the store quite hurriedly. Our business was over. But as we got into the street, I began to jump and run us down the block. I had found my teacher! I had found the Guru!

Rudi in his oriental art store

CHAPTER 7

The Meeting
and the "Work"

The long night of almost sleepless excitement that passed until the next day was to be the last night of my undisciplined search in the wilderness of my youth. From the next day, the day of meeting with my teacher, I would be unable to live as liberally as before. The doubts I had formed about my lack of discipline would be consummated in the will of my teacher. There would be a practical, moral revolution in my way of life. But at the time I merely swooned in expectation, in the Joy of my discovery. And I went to meet my teacher as if I were to be given some sweet free gift of miracles and love, and coddled home like some eternal loved-one of the gods.

When the morning came, I bathed and dressed very ceremoniously. My long hair and beard were combed and trimmed. There was to be no offense in me. I walked to the store in the bright sun and wondered what incredible miracles I was to see before evening. From works such as Yogananda's *Autobiography of a Yogi* I had learned to expect some kind of priceless love-meeting and a dear touch of the teacher's hand that would shake my mind loose in a vision of lights and blessed peace. I walked to the store with the same excitement in which I used to follow a whore. I went to grasp all the miracles hidden in the secret parts of this mystery.

When I neared the store, I carefully hid myself on the other side of the street. I wanted to be certain that the teacher was there before I made my entrance. After a while I saw several men come out of the store. One of them was apparently directing the others. He was a heavy fat man in his mid-thirties. He wore a T-shirt and a baggy pair of corduroys. The others appeared to be doing some sort of work for him.

I watched them move in and out of the store for some time. Finally, all of them left, except the fat man. As I watched him, I perceived a seriousness in him, the same kind of all-business attitude I found in the woman the day before. I supposed that he was alone, and I crossed the street, filled with embarrassment and expectation, self-consciousness and anxiety.

I walked into the store as directly and upright as I could. One should not approach a teacher with weaknesses hanging out! The man was sitting in a chair by the desk at the rear of the store. His mother was standing behind him in a small doorway making a sandwich. She recognized me and very animatedly told the man that I had been in the day before and bought a piece of sculpture.

The man stood up and approached me. He made it a very deliberate point to shake my hand. He introduced himself as Rudi, and I told him I was Franklin Jones. "Your mother told me that you are a teacher." He looked around at her as if displeased, and then he said, "She tells that to anybody who comes in here. She really ought to keep her mouth shut."

I was already very uncomfortable, and now I felt foolish, but I was determined. "What do you teach?" "Kundalini Yoga."[23] "Are you an adept at this Yoga?" He looked at me very sternly and a little bothered. "You don't teach it if you can't do it."

---

23. Kundalini Yoga is a practice that originated in the Hindu Tantric tradition. It aims to awaken latent Spiritual Energy, which is considered to lie dormant at the base of the body, so that it rises up through the spine to reunite with its ultimate source above the head. While typical techniques to raise the Kundalini involve meditative visualization and breathing exercises, it has long been traditionally understood that the initiatory force of a Spiritually Awakened Teacher is the principal means whereby it is activated. The activation of the Kundalini can produce intense blisses and other phenomena.

I told him I was looking for a teacher and I felt that I had been directed to him. He asked me what I did. I said that I wrote and had just moved from California. "No, what do you do Spiritually?" "Oh, well, I relax and direct myself toward the top of the head." He smiled a little. "Do you work?" "No, I have just been writing, and I live with my girlfriend. She works." He drew away from me a little. "This Yoga requires great discipline and surrender, and I can't teach anybody who doesn't accept the discipline and work. You go out and get a job and come back in about six months or a year. We'll talk about it then."

That was apparently the end of the interview! He made it a point to shake my hand again, and he turned away, so that I felt I was supposed to leave.

As I left the store, I felt a tremendous relief that I had been able to manage the meeting at all. I was disappointed, to be sure. There was no sublime love-meeting, no miracles, no immediate recognition of me as the long-awaited disciple. But I had been received at least conditionally. Six months or a year was not an unbearable length of time. Unpleasant as the prospect was, I was willing to get a job if that was the kind of test required of me. I felt a kind of certainty in the man himself. He was by his own admission adept in the teaching and practice of the highest and most miraculous kind of Yoga. I had met him, and I was certain that I was willing to meet the conditions.

I was elated! I felt I had been successful. Strong and complicated feelings went through my mind as I moved up the block beyond the store. By the time I reached the corner I had gained my composure, and even my doubts had turned to elation and certainty. Then I became aware of a very strange sensation. A current of very strong Energy was rising up my arm from my right hand, the hand Rudi had made it so much a point to shake when I arrived and as I left.

As I became aware of this Energy, It quickly passed into the rest of my body and Filled me with a profound and thrilling Fullness. My heart strained in a vibrant Joy, and my head felt swollen, as if my mind were contained in an aura that extended around my skull several inches. As I walked, I began to run. I felt on fire with a Joyous Energy, and I had become incredibly light!

When Nina returned home from teaching school, I told her all about my experience. I told her about the mysterious Energy, about my muted reception, and the condition that I get a job for six months or a year before I could go back for any teaching. She was a little puzzled by this condition. She had only known me as a writer and a wild man, and she was not sure that she really wanted it any other way.

As the evening passed, I also began to wonder about these things. My writing and my way of life were very real to me. They were even the necessary preliminary to Spiritual effort. I began to think about the writings of Aurobindo, and how he justified "creative" work, even writing and other forms of art, as a usable and even necessary means for Spiritual opening. And even if I did get a job, should I continue to write? And what about all of my other habits? What does this teacher think about drugs, and sex? Should I leave Nina? Do I have to become a vegetarian?

The entire matter was much more complicated than it had originally seemed. So I sat down to write Rudi a long letter about all of my questions. I intended to have Nina deliver it to him the next day and return to me with his answers. "The young woman who brings this letter to you is my girlfriend. We are not married, but we have been living together for two or three years." And so on, and on. I wrote about all of my questions. I wanted to be certain I made as complete a transformation in myself as necessary, so that when I returned to him I should be fully able to use his teaching. I asked about "creative" work and drugs, sex and diet. I told him about the experience of his Energy. And I made it clear that I was willing to undergo all the conditions.

The next day Nina went to see Rudi after work. She returned very amused with me. Rudi had received her very warmly, in contrast to his brusque and almost rude reception of me. Nina had not asked him to teach her. He told her that I had a lot of work to do, but he would be glad to take her as a student right away! Anyway, he appreciated my letter, and I should come and see him the next day.

I was happy for this news. Of course I insisted that Nina take advantage of his offer to teach her. But I was confounded at how he could take her as a student off-hand, while I, who had such a long history of seeking, trial, and experience, should have to go begging even for an interview! As it happened, this pattern of offense and testing was to be the basic form of my life-experience with Rudi over the coming years.[24]

When I went to Rudi the following day, his manner was much more familiar and friendly. He told me that he really loved Nina and that she was a very open person who could easily receive the Shakti, or the "Force", as he called It.

On the other hand, he certainly did mean that I would have to begin to work on myself before he would allow me to come to his classes. "What about my writing?" "How much do you write or want to write? A serious writer works constantly, out of great need." "Well, I write, but more or less spontaneously. It is a different thing. Well, yes, I am not disciplined. A job wouldn't interfere with that work."

His one answer to all of my questions was "work". Discipline and effort are necessary to provide an instrument that can contain this "Force". It is not necessary to give up sex or life or go on any special diet. Only

24. "Rudi" (1928-1973), Albert Rudolph, was also known as Swami Rudrananda. Rudi Taught the practice of intentional and effortful surrender to the "Force", or Life-Current, or Kundalini Shakti, Transmitted from Guru to disciple. Rudi also prescribed various personal and practical life-disciplines to purify and balance the body-mind.

work, be intelligent with these things, take proper care of yourself.

My life with Nina was a particular focus of his. He wondered why we were not married, and he knew that my undisciplined way of life must draw me into myself more than anything else. Thus, his teaching required a drastic turning of my attention outward. Work, love Nina, become more loving. Your life with Nina is your Yoga.

And so he sent me away again with one of those electric handshakes. But he told me that as soon as I got a job I would be welcome to come to his classes.

At that time I was about twenty-four years old. I had never taken a job other than the purely menial labor of waiting in restaurants and the like. Consequently, I was at a disadvantage when I went looking for work. I still considered that my basic work was writing and a kind of Spiritual process in consciousness. Thus, I did not feel particularly motivated to any kind of career. But I felt constrained to find some kind of productive work that would not only allow me to reserve some "creative" life-energy but also provide sufficient means to support Nina and me.

The reaction of any and all agencies and employers that I first contacted was that I had a bad employment history and was educationally overqualified for most kinds of work. Their experience showed that overqualified persons with similar backgrounds to my own tended to leave unchallenging forms of work after a relatively short period. Finally, in order simply to have work to do, I volunteered my services to WBAI, a non-profit, listener-sponsored radio station in New York. I worked at soliciting and addressing in the subscription department. After a few weeks, I was hired at a limited salary to do the work part-time.

In the meantime Nina began to go to Rudi's classes. She said it was a very strange and exciting experience. The classes were held in a large room on the ground floor of a building Rudi owned on Hudson Street, a few

blocks from our apartment. She said the room was surrounded with huge oriental sculptures. There were
approximately twenty or thirty people at each class. And
the classes were held on Tuesday and Thursday evenings
at eight, Saturday morning at ten, and Sunday at eleven
or noon.

Rudi's students were mostly young people in their
twenties or early thirties. Most of them were former professional "freaks", like myself, with very little history of
dramatic accomplishment. They required disciplining,
like myself, and probably many of them were really
working for the first time in their lives. Some of course
were older, either professionals or businesspeople. Many
were fairly successful and had met Rudi in the course of
his business dealings.

I would frequently go to Rudi's store to talk or enjoy
the aura that permeated the place. The store was never
empty. There was a constant stream of visitors and
patrons. His mother was usually preparing food for people, and we would crowd around the rear of the store or
sit in rows of funeral parlor folding chairs by the curb.

Rudi's attention was constantly directed toward someone or something. There was rarely any stillness around
him, and this was another characteristic that was unex-
pected. There was no kind of distant, mystical, airy mood
of quiet, none of the usual "Spiritual" atmosphere peculiar
to churches and religious or Spiritual books. There was a
constant activity that was even annoying at times.

Rudi was always animated in conversation, either
with students and friends or with customers. His conversation was a constant stream of strongly communicated
moods, alternating between talk of Spiritual life, his
experiences in India, his Spiritual experience and
visions, and the perpetual absorption in business. For
Rudi, life and work were Yoga. His business was his
principal Yoga. And if you did not know or accept this
about him, you could become angry at what appeared to
be his perpetual concern with business and the store.

After a while I learned that I could not expect to visit Rudi and pass a pleasant hour conversing about Spiritual life. More often than not there would be a brief handshake or a hug, and then he would spend his time talking to somebody else as if I were not there. Then he might suddenly shake my hand and tell me to leave.

As the weeks passed and I became an accustomed regular at the store, I found that I would be given some work to do when I arrived. There was always some sculpture to be moved around, some windows to wash. Gradually it became clear that only casual visitors or friends got to sit and talk. Any student that came was given work to do.

As Rudi's business increased, the work increased, so that I was called upon to come and work in my spare time. Rudi always generated work around him. Even if I stopped by to say hello at the house, he would hand me a bag of garbage to take to the corner. And if I dropped by the store casually, I might be asked to go home and change clothes, and then come back and wash the floor.

This "dharma" of work awakened tremendous resistance in me, and in most of Rudi's other students. But that was also the teaching. We would often wish it were otherwise, and we always suckered ourselves into a casual visit, hoping he would be in the mood to let us sit and entertain us with stories of miracles and all of the glory we were going to gain in the future by the aid of the "Force". The more we suffered, the more we communicated our resistance and discomfort, the more he would tell us to surrender. He said that we should "be like smoke". You can cut through smoke with a knife, but it is not disturbed.

The idea that was infused in us was the simple attitude of work. Work forced us to encounter resistance and obstacles in ourselves, and perseverance in work gradually wore away resistance and brought about a state of openness, or surrender. The constant practice of work and surrender opened the instrument of the body and the internal mechanism that was a channel for the "Force" (the Spiritual Energy, or Shakti, that was Rudi's gift), and the continuation of work strengthened the instrument in its openness and allowed the "Force" to expand and to produce ever higher Realizations and capabilities. He often said that work was endless and always generated more work, so that life was pictured as a fruitful effort in constant relation to the "Force" that had no other goal than continual growth.

Two or three weeks after Nina began to go to "class", Rudi gave me permission to begin also. The work I had managed to acquire was not completely satisfactory from his point of view, but it was a "job", and I had managed to adapt myself to the basic conditions for his teaching. I had even shaved and gotten a haircut. I paid more attention to discipline and cleanliness. I had stopped using even marijuana to relax. And, in general, I had turned the self-involved habits of solitude into a more communicative and socialized life.

I decided to begin classes on my birthday, thinking this was auspicious. Rudi's classes always followed the same pattern. We would begin to arrive in the classroom about 7:30 in the evening. Someone would light incense next to Rudi's chair, which was a large metal trunk covered with a bearskin. His seat was placed on a higher level of the room, about three or four steps above the rest of us. Most of us sat in folding chairs set in rows, with an aisle down the middle, but some would sit in Yogic postures on the floor in front of him.

Before my first class, I was told to go to the store for instruction. Rudi told me that the "Force" was the real subject of the class. It came into contact with us through his eyes. I was simply to sit comfortably and relax and try to open myself or surrender to the Force. If I felt the Force enter me, I should simply relax more and allow It to go down through the chest and belly into the sex organs. When It got there, I should relax at the base of the spine and let It travel upwards to the head. If I wanted, I could silently say "So" with each inhalation and "Ham" with each exhalation. "So-Ham" could mean "I am That", or "I am the Force, or God", whichever concept was meaningful to me. But the important thing was surrender and opening to the Force, so that It could carry the exercise. Sometimes, as he spoke of these things in class, he would also recommend that we feel a part of ourselves going way out into space, beyond all the universes.

With these instructions, I went on to class. The room was not particularly decorative. It was about twenty-five by fifty feet. There was a plain oriental folding screen behind his seat, to keep our eyes from distraction. And there were many large oriental figures along the sides of the room, as well as great numbers of smaller objects or paintings here and there. Rudi often said that this was not for "effect", but he simply kept them stored there for his business.

By the time class was to begin, everyone was supposed to be seated and quiet and "into the exercise". The Force was not only supposed to be given by Rudi, in or out of class, but was always working in us. Therefore, surrender and work was to be our constant attitude, and class was merely a special exercise of the same work. In addition to class we were to spend up to an hour a day at home doing the same exercise. But we should not spend more than an hour a day at meditation. More than that, he warned, only produces illusions. Meditation was to be a "creative" exercise, to awaken capability, not to produce effects like quietness. Apart from the exercise, we should only work and live intelligently.

When I went to class the first night, I was again full of expectations. Nina had been urged not to tell me all the specifics of what went on, but to let me find out for myself. I had experienced the Force many times through Rudi's handshake, or when I chanced to look in his eyes. But, for all I knew, that might only be a taste! I truly did not know what to expect, but I was ready for visions and miracles.

Shortly after eight o'clock, Rudi came in and sat down. At the beginning of class he would sometimes speak for a short time about the Force and about work and surrender. Or else he would describe some experiences of the Force that he was having. He would often have visions of opening lotuses, fantastic creatures, other worlds, or his teachers. His teachers were the two men whose pictures I had seen that first day in the store. The first and heavier one was Swami Nityananda,[25] a Powerful saint he had met in 1960. After Swami Nityananda's death, or "mahasamadhi",[26] in 1961, Rudi became the disciple of the other man, Swami (Baba) Muktananda,[27] who was Swami Nityananda's chief disciple.

Rudi spoke briefly on this first night, and I believe he introduced me to the group either at the beginning or the end of the exercise. Then he sat up straight in the lotus posture and closed his eyes. All of us also made an effort to relax and surrender. Then he opened his eyes. They appeared to be deep set and very wide. His eyes moved from person to person in the room. He concentrated on each one for a minute or two, or perhaps only a few seconds, depending on the needs, or the openness, of the person.

25. Swami Nityananda (d. 1961) was a profound Yogic Realizer of modern India. Little is known about his early life, although it is said that even as a child he showed the signs of a Realized Yogi. While still a boy, He abandoned conventional life and wandered as a renunciate. Many instructive stories and miracles, including spontaneous healings, are attributed to Him.

26. Mahasamadhi ("great samadhi" or "great state of ecstasy") is the Sanskrit term for the physical death of a Realizer. Such a being does not die in the ordinary sense of being helplessly subject to the body's death process. Rather, in death, such a Realizer merely releases the body-mind and continues to Bless others by Abiding in Samadhi, or the exalted state of Realization Itself, through and beyond the death transition. The burial site, called the "samadhi site" or "Mahasamadhi site", of such a Realizer is highly valued for the potency of Spiritual or Blessing Transmission that may be felt or received there.

27. Swami Muktananda (1908-1982) came from a wealthy background, but he abandoned his home at the age of fifteen for the sake of Spiritual practice. Eventually he encountered his Guru, Swami Nityananda, in whose company he mastered Kundalini Yoga. Swami Muktananda attracted many Western aspirants to his Ashram at Ganeshpuri, India, during the 1960s and 1970s.

I could feel a certain relaxation as I tried to surrender, open, and empty my mind. And I waited intensely for Rudi to look at me. When my turn finally came, I felt a little foolish. Looking deep into a person's eyes, particularly under such circumstances, requires a certain relaxation from the usual armor we wear. But, gradually, I loosened up, and accepted my position of vulnerability. I tried to deepen my surrender as he described. I concentrated on his eyes. We remained that way for perhaps a minute, and then he passed on to another. I continued to try to deepen the surrender while concentrating on his form. He would often tell us not to close our eyes unless there was a very strong impulse from the Force to do so. Then, suddenly, the class was over. As was customary, we lined up to leave, and each received a big bear hug from Rudi. He told me that it was a very good class for me, and that the Force would begin to work for me very soon.

Apart from a certain relaxation during the class and an exhilaration afterwards, which I usually felt after a meeting with Rudi, I had not experienced anything unusual. This was somewhat disappointing to me. I realized that this work was not going to be simply a matter of free miracles and visions but a gradual process requiring great effort.

As the weeks passed, I became more accustomed to this exercise, and going to class became a matter of course. The work of surrender became more natural to me, and I began to become sensitive to levels of resistance programmed into my being. At times they fell away, as if by the work of the Force, just as at other times they could only be removed by the active effort of surrender. But there were many times when I felt unable so much as to touch the resistance in myself. Indeed, the more I tried to surrender, the more the resistance grew.

The activity of the mind also fluctuated in this same manner. I began to acquire a certain anxiety and frustration about my own limitations, and I would often go to

Rudi desperately demanding some kind of help to remove the obstacles in my life. But there was only a sort of ordinary chiding humor to ease me up, and then the admonition to more work and deeper surrender.

This is a common experience among those who deliberately perform various kinds of work in consciousness. The more you try to do it, the more obstacles arise. There is probably no more confounding and frustrating admonition than the simple order to relax. And one of the greatest Lessons I would learn from all my years of Spiritual effort was that Spiritual <u>seeking</u> not only reinforces (and intensifies the experience of) the very things it seeks to remove, but it is for that very reason founded in the same mechanisms and motives that are one's problems and suffering. In time, I would come to resolve this dilemma on the basis of a radical understanding, a point of view much different from that of Rudi's, but for now I put myself to conscious effort with tremendous intensity and need.

Rudi would often talk about the kind of effort to surrender that he felt was required. He compared it to "tearing your guts out". I found that my life was becoming a terrible ordeal of surrender, and the depth of my work never satisfied him. He worked on me by frustrating me and minimizing my efforts or accomplishments, and this combined with the Yogic Force Itself, so that most of the time I was in a literal fever, with extreme heat and redness all over my skin. I felt the incredible weight of all I needed to surrender. Real Spiritual work must amount to nothing less than a wholesale cutting away of all that I am. It must amount to an infinite depth, an absolute surrender. And when I would examine the littleness of my depth, I would become awed and frustrated. I was burdened with the need for an impossible purification and self-abnegation.

This surrender was not merely a physical opening or relaxation of the nervous system. Nor was it simply a purifying and disciplining of life. It was a profound internal opening in every part. Rudi sometimes said we should concentrate on surrendering three things: self-pity, negativity, and self-imagery. Surrender was a perfect letting go of the ego, the learned identity and drama.

As my experience grew, I also became critically aware of the work, its effects, its value, and its sources. I examined these things in relation to my own intelligence and understanding, and, thus and thereby, I gradually became aware of significant differences between Rudi and myself.

Rudi claimed to have had visitations from certain "Tibetans" when a little boy. They told him his life would be very difficult, but it would bring him to a very high State. They also told him he would have thousands of students. His life over the years was indeed difficult. And, from the time I met him, the numbers of his students steadily increased (becoming significantly enlarged especially in the years after I myself had ceased to be his student). Nevertheless, regardless of his growing "success", every step of his life appeared, at least to him, to require almost absolute sacrifices and "work" on his part.

He described himself constantly as a poor Jewish boy whose father abandoned him and his mother when he was young. His mother apparently treated him to huge doses of violent physical abuse, for whatever reasons, and he had to surmount terrible obstacles and resistance on his part in order to improve his life.

He was obviously a man of great passions and appetites, a figure of Gargantuan vitality and huge pleasures, and a very strong and masculine (but also demonstratively homosexual) character. He would often give himself as the perfect example of the need for great effort and surrender. In him all the passions of self-indulgence were active, and he would often say that when he indulged them he had to pay a terrible price to regain himself. Thus, he was not an example of religiously motivated purity. Even so, he recommended to his students that they achieve as great control as possible over their various desires.

Rudi

Adi Da and Nina during the period of their involvement with Rudi

I was quite overweight at the time. I weighed over 230 pounds and looked somewhat swollen and uncomfortable, although I was not nearly as large as Rudi! He insisted that I watch my diet and lose weight. I took all of his admonitions very seriously, and I observed everything in him as the direct Communication of God. Thus, I lost a lot of weight, to my great benefit. But Rudi, even though he protested about his own overweight condition, only grew larger and larger.

Finally, he would only say that his size and weight were the result of the activity of the Force, and we allowed him that. After all, Swami Nityananda was also a huge fat man, and he more than anyone else was Rudi's ideal image of the "God-Force". It was always Swami Nityananda's example and image that Rudi held before himself. Thus, Rudi expanded in size like Swami Nityananda, whatever the reasons.

During a trip to India some time later, I was told that Swami Nityananda had always been an ascetic, and his early photographs show a figure of skeletal thinness. Even in later life, although, reportedly, he would sometimes take huge quantities of the food offered to him as gifts by his devotees, he often, or perhaps even generally, ate only the very little his devotees could force him to take. In any case, over the years, his body expanded hugely, and his devotees wondered about this. However, the general conclusion was that his hugeness was due to the influx of higher Power. And he was even called "Ganesh",[28] the "elephant god", because, like the traditional images of Ganesh, he was very big in the belly. Nevertheless, when Swami Nityananda died, his body was thin, and even somewhat emaciated.

I considered that Rudi's case was a combination of several factors. Certainly he was the bearer and the instrument of a tremendous natural human energy and a Spiritual Force that were not the ordinary gifts of a human being. But

28. Ganesh is the huge, elephant-headed God of wisdom revered by Hindus as the personification of those qualities that overcome difficulties.

he was also more complicated than the traditional Indian saint, and he was hearty enough to accept the psychology of the expansive, devouring fat man as part of the structure of his life. His size and manner were otherwise quite charming, and, from his point of view, presented no impenetrable obstacle to his growth. Years later, when I was in India, a man told me that many gossiped about Rudi's unascetic tendencies, but that, when he arrived, they all would go to him to get "charged up" by his Presence.

I never quarreled with the appropriateness of Rudi's philosophy and practice for his own case, at his stage of human and Yogic demonstration. It was only that I gradually began to understand that his characteristic emphasis on "effort, work, and surrender", for the sake of growth in life, and even to the exclusion of any higher or ultimate philosophy or aspiration, was a distinct characteristic of his peculiar need, tendency, and life-experience. My own tendencies at that time were indeed destructive, and his teaching was almost entirely beneficial to me while I remained with him. But, for myself, such a "machine" of effort, once it had achieved its earliest benefits in my general human well-being, began only to reveal its own ego-reinforcing limitations, its fundamental bondage to only rather gross aspirations, and its fruitlessness relative to Ultimate, or truly Divine, Realization. Therefore, more and more, over time, I was drawn to another, and truly radical (or most fundamental), understanding.

Rudi's way was obviously not entirely or even basically founded in Indian Yoga. Indeed, I was to discover years later that his methods and aims were quite different from those of Baba Muktananda, his Guru. Even before he went to India and met his present teachers, he had first been a student of the Gurdjieff[29] work in New

---

29. Georges Ivanovitch Gurdjieff (1872-1949) was an important figure in Western occult circles during the 1920s, 30s, and 40s. Born in Armenia of a Greek family, Gurdjieff spent many years wandering in Eastern Russia, Turkey, India, and Tibet searching for secret wisdom. The Gurdjieff work (which is the result of his eclectic interests in psychology, magic, and esoteric religion) involved "working" on oneself in order to become free from egoic limits.

York. And he had graduated from there to the practices instituted by Pak Subuh[30] in the Subud movement.

Rudi never spoke much in detail about his experiences in those movements, but the manner of his teaching, his philosophy and practice, can be seen as a direct reflection of the leading motives of G. I. Gurdjieff and Pak Subuh.

The Gurdjieff work emphasizes the necessity for profound effort, the absolute and conscious work of evolution. Like Rudi, it does not emphasize such work for the sake of "enlightenment" or some single, perfect, and liberating Realization that is the ultimate goal of striving. It posits the endlessness of that work in the direction of an ever higher evolution of Knowledge and Ability that will have direct consequences in human life.

Rudi's way of work and effort in an endless progress of growth was generated by his own needs in the presence of his particular personal tendencies. But it is clear that he acquired much of the technology and reinforcement for that path in the Gurdjieff movement. Even so, the Gurdjieff work was basically a pattern of philosophy and technique. He acquired the first experiences and personal signs of what he called the "Force" from Pak Subuh.

Pak Subuh, an Indonesian teacher, experienced a spontaneous Energy-Awakening sometime early in his life. It was the Awakening of a certain Power (or Spiritual Force) that came to him miraculously and thereafter remained always available to him. He found that he could also Initiate this Force in others, if they were even a little open to It. Rudi apparently experienced his first conscious Initiation in this "Force" while involved in the Subud movement, and later he received It from Pak Subuh himself.

But Pak Subuh was apparently not aware that there was any previous tradition of this same Power. He thought It was an entirely new Spiritual Influence that he

30. Muhammad (Pak) Subuh (1901-1987) was an Indonesian teacher who founded the Subud movement in the 1920s.

was to reveal to the world. He seemed to know nothing of the already existing tradition of Kundalini Shakti in India, nor the already traditional process of Spiritual Initiation (generally, by touch, thought, look, or the giving of a mantra[31]) known in India as "Shaktipat".

Therefore, Pak Subuh interpreted this Force and Its value along lines peculiar to his own isolated experience. He saw that once this Force was activated in a person, It could be developed into various purifying and "creative" life-abilities through a spontaneous exercise he called the "latihan". Again, this Energy was not promoted as a means to an absolute higher Knowledge, Which is Its ultimate Purpose in the Indian sources. It was interpreted as a kind of "creative" God-Force, whose significance was in the evolution and expansion of "creative" life-processes.

Thus, the work of Subud also has the kind of endlessness and non-specific purpose characteristic of Rudi's teaching. However, in my own case, Spiritual life always had a radically specific Purpose. It was to Realize the supreme Knowledge, the Knowledge of fundamental Reality that makes all the difference and ends the search. For this reason, I was also chronically disturbed by the notion of perpetual, evolutionary work which Rudi advocated. And, again, this difference in our intentions or aims also provided the basis for the break between us in later years.

Rudi apparently possessed the fundamentals of his path, both its philosophy and its activating "Force", even before he arrived in India, in 1960. What he received, first from Swami Nityananda, and then from Baba Muktananda, was that Force in Its most direct and Powerful form. He saw his Indian teachers as an endless Source, a Spiritual Fountain that he could always tap and thereby discover even greater depth, greater experiences, and greater Power.

Thus, ever since Swami Nityananda's mahasamadhi, Rudi made at least two trips a year to Baba Muktananda's

31. A sacred sound, syllable, or Name used for worship, prayer, and meditation.

Ashram. He would always return to America claiming greater Power and higher levels of experience. Rudi always clearly stated that he was not, as he put it, a "finished product" (or a perfectly evolved or enlightened adept). However, and in spite of his obvious dependence on his Indian Sources, Rudi always demanded recognition of himself as a unique Source or Instrument for the Force. At the same time, he suggested that fullest access to the Force, and direct access to his Indian Sources, was not possible or appropriate for his students.

I greatly desired every Spiritual gift for myself, and, the stronger I became, the more I also required a direct and overwhelming contact with the Force Itself.

Even though, in Rudi's company, there was, in my own case, practical evidence of a partial improvement of my life, I sought an utterly radical reversal and transformation of my existence. Thus, over time, I became hungry for direct contact with Rudi's Spiritual Sources. And it was only a matter of time before the burden of merely egoic effort and the unsatisfactoriness of Rudi's rather worldly philosophy would reach their limit in me.

I had embraced Rudi's way totally, absolutely committed to the ends I sought. I was willing to do whatever necessary to attain them. Such intensity of purpose is characteristically required of those who devote themselves to conscious evolution by various efforts. The first effects of that commitment were wholly beneficial to me. But in time I began to learn profound Lessons in secret. And the entire process began to become too limited and limiting in comparison to my aspirations and my understanding. However, it would be three and one-half years before I would have strength enough to wander into India on my own.

"All in all, our lives became cleaner and happier.
It was an intense struggle and discipline for me, but
I welcomed all its effects. And I looked to Rudi and the Force
for a dramatic reversal of my ordinary state of resistance
and the logic of Narcissus."

Adi Da in New York, 1965

CHAPTER 8

The Idea of Release from Narcissus

The central ideas in Rudi's way of teaching were "surrender" and "work". "Surrender" was an idea that corresponded to the internal practice in life and meditation. It was conscious and even willful opening or letting go of contents, resistance, patterns, feelings, and thoughts. "Work" was the idea that corresponded to the external practice. The ideal student was to be in a constant state of surrender and a constant act of work. The purpose of this was to make the entire instrument, internal and external, available to the higher Power, the "Force", or "Shakti", and thus to grow by including Its Will, Presence, Intelligence, Light, and Power on every level of the functional being.

I took this way very seriously, and I made a constant effort to adapt myself to this way absolutely and exhaustively. I accepted Rudi as a perfect Source of this higher Power, and I allowed none of his apparent limitations to represent actual barriers or limitations to the Force Itself. Whenever I encountered limitations in him, I was immediately moved to reflect on my own resistance. Thus, I never allowed myself to become concerned about Rudi's problems or to think the Force, or the Divine Power, was available to me only to a limited degree.

The effect of this way of life was a perpetual and growing encounter with my own resistance. And where I encountered my own resistance, I would awaken to my own tendencies to self-pity, negativity, and the subliminal self-imagery by which I guided the "creation" or manipulation of experience. The more I worked, the more I saw Narcissus.

This way required immense self-discipline, and, as long as it worked, it provided a positive mechanism that strengthened and purified me physically, mentally, and morally. Rudi was a master at this kind of psychological tutoring, and these effects were his primary gift to me. Even if his motives were often founded in problems of his own, he would never allow his students to become identified with his own case. He would always turn them to themselves, to their own work and surrender.

I considered Rudi to be a tremendous and brilliant Means for the transformation of my life. He was unique in my experience. My own ordinary tendency was to seek a loving connection on which I could become dependent. Where love was not poured on me, I tended to become angry and resentful. But Rudi used, and even intentionally stimulated, these tendencies in me, in order for me to develop an awareness of my own patterns and reactions, and an ability to generate an effective self-effort that could exceed those self-defeating patterns and reactions.

Rudi's psychological tutoring of me was coupled with the mysterious Power of the "Force", an Energy that I could experience directly and unequivocally. Rudi became for me a personal God-Presence, a unique combination of human and Spiritual Influences that, for me, were the equivalent of Jesus of Nazareth and all the other and various Divine personalities in religious and Spiritual literature.

And what were my motives in surrendering and in practicing obedience to such an Influence? Clearly, I had sought just such an encounter. It was no arbitrary meeting, but it perfectly coincided with my own needs at the time. First of all, it was an encounter, a confrontation. I had spent years in a more or less private investigation of my own mechanisms on a purely internal and philosophical level. I had become exquisitely aware of the content of my mind and life. Now I had sought an Influence outside myself that would contain and manifest all of the Force and Virtue I had come to believe were really present in the living condition of Reality. My years in exile or solitude were an attempt to discover or affirm what was necessarily in Reality. Now I sought to encounter that proven Reality in a living, demonstrable Presence. If I had lost the conventional "God" of religion and had ceased to believe in the traditional reports and claims about Jesus of Nazareth, now I sought to encounter the equivalent Force and Reality. I no longer considered the "God" and the "Guru" of Reality and Truth to be impossible. I thought them to be entirely necessary.

Even more, as a result of my long experiment, I had discovered an underlying content and "creative" logic or image in my own living consciousness. I had located the source of suffering and misadventure in myself and recognized it as the pattern and drama of Narcissus. The logic of separation and self-fascination had appeared to me concretely as the leading mechanism of ordinary consciousness. This was coupled with another recognition, based on my own experience, but which I also found in the observations of Jung and the literature of Spiritual phenomena. It was that the drama and fate of Narcissus was not necessary, not equal to Reality. Thus, I sought an encounter with Reality that would release me from Narcissus, my own deadly logic, by forcing me to include what Narcissus always rejects by means of exclusive self-involvement.

The idea of release from Narcissus, the internal myth that "creates" suffering and destroys the inherent Bliss and Freedom of uncontradicted Reality, was my leading Intention. Thus, when I saw that Rudi manifested and dramatized that "other" Presence that is Reality, that always works to confound Narcissus, I gave myself up to him as a man does to God.

As weeks passed, Rudi increased his hold on me. He fascinated me with the stories of his life, the entire drama of the Force and Its miraculous effects. And the more fascinated I became, the more he strengthened his demands for work and surrender. Soon there was only work, only the effort of surrender. The underlying (and supportive) connection of love and friendship was continually reinforced by him in many personal ways, whenever it was required. But the outstanding manner of his dealing with me was blunt and aggressive. Whenever I approached him, I would be set aside. Attention was not focused on me. I was only given some kind of work to do or left only to listen while he openly gave his attention to others and seemed to favor them.

From the beginning, Rudi proposed Nina as an object of my love and pleasure, and he constantly drew my attention from my own problems, questions, and needs to Nina's need for love. I had decided before I met him that I would either have to leave Nina or accept the responsibilities of a husband. Rudi's way neither required nor valued celibacy and separation, but always love and connection. When he, at first with ordinary humor and then with obvious seriousness, began to chide me for my irresponsibility in relation to Nina, I began to consider how to become more a husband to her. Finally, he all but demanded that I marry her, and I agreed.

There is much truth in the idea that I got married only because my teacher told me, for the sake of discipline and as a kind of Yoga. But it was a voluntary decision on my part, and one that I had come to recognize as right and necessary at that time in my life. Thus, Nina and I were (for a time) married on February 26, 1965.

Rudi's influence also led me to discover a way of engaging my work-life that utilized my personal and "creative" needs. My father had become interested in Rudi as a result of our conversations, and he would occasionally visit Rudi at the store or even come to class. On one of these early visits, my father told Rudi that I had once intended to become a Lutheran minister. He said that at one point I appeared to lose all hope in the church, and tended to abandon my family, the church, and even the world in despair.

Rudi asked me why I never became a minister. I told

him that at one point I had become unable to believe in Jesus or God and had gone off on my own to discover what was True about all such things. He dismissed all of my romanticism about the past and told me it would be good for me to take up those studies again. After all, I was no longer separated from What was True. It had become my own experience. And the work of a minister or a theologian was ideally suited to me. It could make use of my intellectual abilities and give me a "creative" outlet in which to speak about Spiritual Truth and help other people.

I protested that I may have become attuned to Spiritual life, but I was in no sense a Christian any longer. The Truth for me was universal and absolute, not limited to the myths and legends and dogmas of Christianity. I had found my inspirations more in the East. And Jesus of Nazareth, even if taken to be an historically real Spiritual figure (independent of the myths and unsupportable legends of conventional, exoteric religion), stood for me only as one of many God-men, or revealers of the Divine Reality. Rudi told me that I was only being childish. He pointed out that his way could easily be expressed in the language of Christianity. The Force was the same as God, or the Holy Spirit. If I accepted the work of a minister with a mature mind, it could even involve me "creatively". I should simply see in it a right path that would give me the opportunity for work and surrender.

At first this seemed impossible to me. I was no longer affiliated with any Christian church, nor did I care to be. And I felt I could never identify myself with the point of view and the beliefs of traditional Christianity. Rudi claimed that this was a virtue. Why should I identify with it? Indeed, I should not identify with it, for that would only provide more armor and self-imagery and prevent me from using it for the sake of work and surrender.

Finally, I attributed all of my misgivings to my own resistance. I agreed to give it a try. Even when I told Rudi I would accept it and play it as a kind of "imposter", he pointed out again that it was all a part of me and suited to my very needs and abilities.

At first I tried to find a place in a denomination other than Lutheranism, the given religion of my childhood. I thought perhaps the Episcopal church was a broader denomination that could include more of the form of Spirituality I would profess. But I soon learned that I would have to pass through a long period of probationary training as a member of an Episcopal congregation before I could be accepted as a candidate for seminary training. Besides, the Episcopal church had many peculiarities of its own to which it would take me a long time to adapt.

So I again made efforts to become affiliated with the Lutheran church through my old congregation in Franklin Square. The minister who served there when I was in high school had since retired to a congregation in Florida. But I quickly made friends with the new minister and was received quite openly by those who remembered me. After several weeks I was recommended as a candidate for seminary training and given preliminary acceptance at the Lutheran Theological Seminary at Philadelphia.

This was in the spring of 1965. Entering students at the Seminary were required to have minimum training in koiné (or "Biblical") Greek, and so I was unable to enter the following September. Instead, I enrolled at a Protestant seminary in New York for a year of preparatory study in Greek. In the meantime, my job at the radio station had come to an end, and I went to work as a furniture refinisher in a store owned by one of Rudi's students. Thus, I established myself in productive work that could carry me until September 1966.

Rudi's effects extended to all areas of my life. One evening he came to visit Nina and me at our Houston Street apartment. He made it obvious that he was uncomfortable in the place, and said the atmosphere was very heavy and unclean. He remarked at how dark and small it was there. There were few windows, and the building was in an old, run down, and unclean neighborhood. He told us we should not keep cats or other animals because they kept the place dirty and generated vibrations that draw consciousness down to an animal level.

Nina and I took this quite seriously. We gave the "Bitty" to a friend and sent the lady cat off to Nina's parents. We tried to brighten up the apartment, and covered the walls with religious and Spiritual pictures. As a result we also began to collect art, and we spent quite a bit of money buying paintings and sculpture from Rudi during the next few years. Finally, we found a large and bright apartment on Fourth Street near Sixth Avenue.

All in all, our lives became cleaner and happier. It was an intense struggle and discipline for me, but I welcomed all its effects. And I looked to Rudi and the Force for a dramatic reversal of my ordinary state of resistance and the logic of Narcissus.

The many practical changes in my way of life were lasting benefits of my experience with Rudi. Even these changes were gradual, and it would take longer for the kind of internal experiences I sought to begin with any kind of dramatic potency.

On a physical level, my life was becoming happier. My new logic of living was a conscious surrender of the patterns of self-indulgence and excess to which I had voluntarily submitted in the past. I began to limit and improve my diet, and this, coupled with the heavy labor of work as a furniture refinisher, gradually strengthened me and dropped my weight from more than 230 pounds to about 170 pounds. I began to use Hatha Yoga exercises to limber my body and adjust my weak back. All of this enabled me to enjoy a state of physical comfort and well-being I had not known since early childhood.

But while I concentrated on these more external improvements in my manner of living, I was slower and more reluctant to let go of certain internal obstacles that prevented the Force from generating new forms of internal experience. I had long been accustomed to writing and exploiting the inner mechanisms of experience through its means as well as through various excesses, including the occasional use of marijuana (and, on a few occasions, other drugs). Clearly, Rudi's way was opposed to such habits and the prolonging of them could only prevent the evolution of that internal advancement the Force was supposed to Initiate.

My first experiences with the Force in class and in my personal relationship to Rudi were, for me, events within the sphere of the ordinary. They indicated a real Presence of a Spiritual kind, but they affected me mostly on a physical and mental level. They served to motivate me, but they were not themselves of a uniquely profound nature, or, in any most profound sense, of a higher or ultimate Nature.

In class I would only become profoundly aware of my own resistance. After my first one or two experiences of the exercise, I saw that I would have to perform a revolutionary and gradual effort in relation to this resistance. Only then would I have any of the kind of dramatic and visionary experiences Rudi described, and which, on the basis of my own past experiences and my reading of Spiritual literature, I had learned to desire for myself.

Even because of the presence of this resistance in me and my awareness of it, I began to acquire intense feelings of frustration in regard to the internal work. Thus, I continued to maintain my efforts to write as before, and I began again to use drugs on occasion to relieve this frustration and provide certain forms of internal opening and perception that I so deeply desired.

However, as a result of my new logic in opposition to Narcissus, and also because of the purifying Presence of the Force in my life, my old ways also met with resistance in me, and they began to cause me trouble.

I began to see my writing as a superficial and fruitless exercise. And I doubted that I had any talent at all. My writing had developed to the point where I should begin the actual and intentional production of a book that would contain all of the values and discoveries of my long progress. But I steadily resisted bringing it to the point of deliberate "creation". I felt that something more needed to occur. There was yet some crucial Event that needed to be uncovered in the process of internal attention. I had not yet seen the death of Narcissus.

By the spring of 1965, I had again begun to use marijuana with some frequency. I found it relaxing and (it seemed at the time) particularly necessary under the pressure of work and effort that Rudi required. But the drug began to have a peculiarly negative effect. When I would smoke it, the salivary glands in my mouth would cease to flow, and I would realize a profound anxiety and fear.

On a very few occasions, I took other drugs with my old friends. We took Romilar again, but now its effects were minor. We found the city atmosphere aggravating, in contrast to the natural and beautiful setting of California. We began to spend our "high" time yearning to return to the ocean and the forests.

I took a drug called DMT, which had a remarkable effect. I became visually aware of the nature of the unity and deep structure of space and matter. Time disappeared, and space and matter revealed themselves as a single, complicated mass or fluid. When I concentrated on a wall or the objects in a room, they would break up and converge with incredible speed toward an invisible point at infinity. I would see forms and space break into the millions of geometrical and mathematical units that composed their apparent structure. When I would look at someone's face, I could see the muscle and bone structure below with a kind of X-ray vision. I could see the internal organs of the head, the brain, the moving flow of fluids and nerve energy, the structures and the natural energies of the body that were more subtle than the physical.

Such remarkable states of awareness combined with my rising sense of anxiety, fear, and reluctance in relation to drugs, so that finally, in the early summer of 1965, I determined somehow to stop their use.

I decided that I would deliberately take a drug for the last time. I would not simply stop using drugs before a last, bravely intentional try. I did not want fear to be my motive for stopping my experiment with drugs. Thus, I bought two large capsules of mescalin, and Nina and I went to spend the Fourth of July weekend at the summer home of a friend on the south shore of Long Island.

I was quite anxious, and I delayed the taking of the drug for several hours. Nina decided she did not want to take the drug, and so I gave it to a young man who was also present, the friend of my friend. My friend, Larry, took several capsules of peyote. I shuffled through all my cautions. Then I downed my last capsule of drugs with abandon. It was to be the most terrifying experience of my life.

After we took the drugs, we drove out to a nearby beach for a picnic. It was a deserted area. We spread out blankets and lots of food. As soon as I began to eat, I noticed that peculiar nausea and disinterest in food that often accompanies a powerful hallucinogen. My friend Larry was already experiencing the effects of the peyote, and he was walking along the beach many yards away. I watched him as he walked, and my mind seemed to have become a prism focused through a concave lens. Everything became small and compressed. Instead of opening and expanding, my "consciousness" had contracted, so that I felt trapped, and my very life seemed about to vanish in the tiny focal point of my vision.

Physically, I felt equally unstable. I perceived none of the familiar points in space or the sense of my body within them that permits balance and ordinary judgment. I was becoming quite disturbed and frightened. My speech was becoming incoherent. Somehow, I managed to communicate to Nina that she should get me to the car.

When we got into the car, I told her to drive and just keep me moving. As we drove, I was overcome by violent fear and confusion. My body began to tremble, and soon my legs began to shake and jerk up and down, so that I felt I was about to be overcome with a violent fit. Then I felt as if I were about to have a heart attack. Violent constrictions began in my lower body and my chest, and then the awful moment came in the heart. There was a powerful jolt and shock in my chest, and I passed into blackness, certain that I was about to die. But then, a moment later, I returned to bodily consciousness and felt the violent fit climbing in me again. Again there was a seizure in the heart, and again the black. Then again the trembling fit of terror, the fit of breathing, and the jolt in the heart.

I could not imagine a more terrifying predicament. It was an endless cycle of deaths and fits that had no end, but always seemed about to end. I told Nina to get me to a doctor.

Minutes later we arrived at a hospital. Nina guided me in. I was incoherent with confusion and fear. Several nurses came and asked questions, but they seemed unconcerned or unaware of my state. Nina told them I had taken a drug, and they frowned and told us to sit and wait. I could not imagine why they did not simply administer an antidote or a tranquilizer. The minutes passed, and I began to wander around the waiting room searching for help.

Nina sensed that they were only stalling in order to get the police. I decided we must somehow get away, and I told her to meet me in the parking lot. I found a door and wandered out toward the cars. As I walked, I felt as if I were passing utterly into madness. My mind appeared like a dome with two interlocking spheres that closed the visual mind to what is above and outside the body and ordinary perception. As I walked, these semispheres turned, and openings were revealed in their separate shapes. Thus, as I walked, the mind opened beyond itself, and I seemed to pass through myself and out beyond any figure or ability to perceive or know a thing in relation to my human personality and form.

I had told Nina to get me some tranquilizers. When she found me, I was groveling in the dirt beneath a tree, weeping and crying to God and Jesus and Rudi for help. I swallowed a few tranquilizers and asked her to call Rudi on the phone. But Rudi was not home. Nina spoke to his mother and found that Rudi was away for the weekend.

I stumbled into the station wagon and lay down in the rear section on my back. Then Nina drove off toward our friend's house. As she drove, I passed into a State of Absolute Conscious Awareness, beyond any thought or feeling or perception. The deaths that threatened me earlier became a kind of Nirvanic death of perfect and mad simplicity.

The next thing of which I became aware was the door opening to the rear of the station wagon. It was night. Nina was standing there. She led me out into the street and into the house. I was experiencing a State of Absolute Tranquility. But I no longer possessed a memory of any kind.

It is difficult to communicate the emptiness of my condition at that time. It was not merely that I did not remember who Nina was, who my friend was, or where we were. I had not the slightest notion of what I was or what they in fact were. I had no idea what a human being or a world was. I had no ideas of any kind. I perceived everything as an Original, Blissful, Infinite Void.

It was a totally arbitrary awakening, from exclusive Absoluteness to forms perceived in Absoluteness. Out of necessity, I simply began to adapt to my arbitrary form and to the arbitrary form of the arbitrary world in which I had arbitrarily appeared. I learned the names and relationships and uses in that world. I adapted to the memories the people claimed to have of me. I questioned them and learned how to function among them. But it was all a present learning process without even a hint of memory involved. Later, it seemed to me that if I had awakened as a pair of shoes in a closet it would not have been more arbitrary and unusual than this, and I would have adapted to it in the same manner.

After several hours in this State, I had acquired a certain facility for life in this form. The feelings of love and familiarity were simulated again in my mind. And we drove out to watch the stars and the sunrise on the beach. My State continued to be one of Absolute Peace and Tranquility, unthreatened by any death or any necessity to persist. It was a True Calm, a State rooted in Ultimate Reality, but it was only temporary, and the price of suffering that had been required to attain it was beyond my willingness to pursue it again.

During the next week I spoke to Rudi about the incident. He knew that I had already paid the price, and he made no attempt to blame or chide me for it. I told him why I had done it, and (in fulfillment of my earlier and already established intention) I promised I would abandon the use of drugs. He accepted my promise and pointed out how devastating such drugs are. He said that even what internal strength I had gained as a result of the past months of effort with the Force had been wiped out by those few hours of experiment with drugs. He told me that I would have to avoid all such things in the future, or else invite madness. Now I must begin to work and surrender in earnest.

And so I did begin to work in earnest. My efforts, internal and external, were profoundly magnified by this freedom from the need to indulge myself in drug experiences or any other kind of stimulation. I found a new strength with which to penetrate the resistance of Narcissus within me.

Finally, even my writing stood before me as an obstacle. Over the years I had accumulated and retained a handwritten manuscript of perhaps fifteen or twenty thousand pages! Besides this there were several boxes of notebooks and collected material. I decided I would either turn all of this into some kind of productive writing or else abandon the activity altogether.

For several days, in the late summer of 1965, I pored over my manuscript and notes. But I saw that these pages themselves had developed into a size that could not possibly be either edited or used. The manuscript was simply too large, too expanded to be researched or included. The more I examined it, the more useless it appeared.

I saw that all of this was already all that it should be. It was not, in its bulk, the preliminary work for an eventual novel. It was itself the visible product of years of a Spiritual and ultimate exercise of my own peculiar design. Its Purpose was not fiction but the Realization of Truth. And its Purpose could not be fulfilled in the writing of any mere work of "fiction", but only by the extension of all of that previous exercise into the way of understanding that I was more and more discovering, and even into the way of Spiritual work I had already discovered in relationship to Rudi.

Thus, I decided to burn every last page of my manuscript, everything I had ever written or collected in my life. In doing so I was aware that something significant and "creative" might also be destroyed, but I knew in any case that whatever concrete results were produced by my writing were retained in my mind. If ever I gained the refreshment and "creative" power to write again, I could draw the useful material of those years of labor from my own memory.

Nina has often remarked about how startled she was when she came home that evening. I was squatting totally naked in front of the fireplace, throwing sheaves of manuscript into the fire. For her, it was also the end of a familiar form of life. It was the apparent destruction of all of the results of an effort she had made possible in many ways. She had protected and supported me through all that period of "creativity", and now she was never to enjoy its fulfillment. But I assured her it would be fulfilled. My life would be its fulfillment. Love and Consciousness and Truth would be its manifestation. And even what was substantial in all that I burned would remain in me, to be used whenever the real impulses of art were awakened.

It took me three days to burn it all. I do not know how many grocery bags and boxes of ashes remained to be discarded. But it was a purifying fire. I had spent years to recover even every memory, motive, and hidden internal form to my living consciousness. Now I had to perform the sacrifice that would return even all of it to its Source. Thus, I would be empty and "creatively" free. My manuscripts were a burden of past time, a present obstacle to conscious awareness. I saw that now my work must be a present, positive "creativity". It could no longer be a passive observation of contents. That had served its Purpose, and now Narcissus was known to me. He was alive as me. Now I must overcome him in myself, and to do so I had to be free of every last vestige of the old work and its accumulations.

The result of the burning was a purification from all my past and the position of self-conscious knowledge its awareness required in me. I felt thoroughly cleansed and free. My life was perfectly renewed and alive, instant and direct, a present activity free of any content that could either determine or limit its ultimate Realization. Thus, I gave myself utterly to the overcoming of Narcissus, and to the liberating attainment of his death.

**Adi Da in New York after His return
from the Lutheran Seminary**

CHAPTER 9

The Death
of Narcissus

From the late summer of 1965 until I left for the
Lutheran Seminary at Philadelphia the following
August, I was, without qualification, Rudi's devoted
disciple. I performed the internal and external work and
surrender he prescribed, and I enjoyed the entirely positive effects of the life-disciplines he required.

My relationship to Nina became Yoga, my work
became Yoga, and my life became Yoga. I enjoyed a state
of physical, mental, and moral well-being that I had never
known since I was a boy, and I exceeded even that in
these realizations of maturity. I learned the great pleasures of self-control and purity, of cleansing work and
discipline, and all of the wholesome effects that social
communication and outward love bring to anyone who
has exercised himself or herself in an erratic solitude.

I even became a wholly acceptable Christian. I found
that there was, indeed, no unsurmountable obstacle in the
language of Christianity, and I began to enjoy the "creative" exercise of adapting my Knowledge of Truth to the
historical and dogmatic language of the church. My studies in Greek also gave me great pleasure, and my attitude
of unobstructed work made me excel as a student.

The seminary at Philadelphia offered a one thousand
dollar fellowship which would cover all the usual
expenses of tuition, books, and a portion of the rest of
one's living. They proposed a series of questions to be
answered in the form of an essay by all those who
wanted to apply for the fellowship. I thought it would be
immense fun if I could win this fellowship in spite of my

background, and my thought and attitude toward Christianity. I wrote a long essay in answer to the questions. They dealt with "autobiographical" matters and thoughts relating to theology and social attitudes. It was a good test to see just how well I could represent myself and speak the language of a Christian. And I won! I had become a successful religious "imposter".

I also did some writing for the completion of requirements for the master's degree at Stanford. I wrote a long, semi-"autobiographical" novella in order to satisfy my "incomplete" in the "creative writing" course. Wallace Stegner accepted it as actual writing, acceptable for course credit, but he was vehement in his denial of its literary value. He apparently gave the work to some of his students, and they agreed with him that, whatever it was, it was not "literature".

I was not sure whether to take their resistance as censure or, since I knew very well what they considered viable "literature", a compliment. At any rate, I did not persist in defending the writing beyond a certain point. Once it was reluctantly accepted for credit, I went to work preparing a thesis for the degree.

I wrote a long study on the aesthetic theories of Gertrude Stein. I used the work to expand critically on many of the motives that had supported me as a writer, and I showed how these researches ultimately concerned not "literature" in the usual sense, but an attitude and a search that corresponded to otherwise philosophical, psychological, and Spiritual efforts. My thesis was developed by the addition of Jung's studies in alchemy and the psyche, various writers on psychology, philosophy, and the philosophy of art, and even the writings of Krishnamurti, who was, like myself, concerned with the problems of mind and art.

As I said earlier, my own career as a writer had been stimulated by various modern sources, of which Gertrude Stein was a primary example. In general, these people thought they were doing something new or revolutionary with the abilities of language to describe, signify, perform, or be something. But I knew they were actually, if not self-consciously, doing something with the mind, with life, with the living consciousness. And although this might represent an unusual and revolutionary activity in Western literature, it was not in fact something new in the history of human activity.

When I realized that I was also doing this, I began that work itself, consciously and deliberately. I no longer required the symbol or medium of language for my work. I abandoned "literature" and began the work that is only observing, understanding, and Realizing. Then, finally, I would Know this "Thing", and I would only write It clearly. My master's thesis was a critical presentation of this point of view.

My thesis was received warmly by the professors assigned to me, although I am sure they were unfamiliar with the more "esoteric" literature of Gertrude Stein, not to mention the other writers I mentioned. And it was clear to me that they did not discern any fundamental or revolutionary importance in the actual problems I discussed. But the work was an important exercise for me. It served to put a cap on my past work as a writer, and it left me free to engage in my new career as a seminarian.

During the period in which I wrote my master's thesis, I was still trying to discover some possible "creative" work, apart from the ministry, that would build upon my previous "creative" life and still make use of my new discoveries. I thought perhaps I could train in some professional work in psychology. I had read a great deal (casually, and in school) in all fields of psychology and philosophy. And Jung's work in particular bore a close affinity to the forms of Eastern Spirituality and the States of Conscious Awareness I had experienced in the past.

I went to see M. Esther Harding, a close associate and student of the late Dr. Jung. But this meeting only confirmed what I had suspected were grave limitations in Jung's assumptions. Dr. Harding told me that any

Westerner who devoted himself or herself to the Spiritual exercises peculiar to the Orient (as, for example, to the Tibetan methods described by W. Y. Evans-Wentz,[32] in books which Jung had introduced to the West) would become clinically insane. From her, and from Jung's, point of view, the realities of Eastern Spirituality were, in a Western psychology, usable and meaningful only as symbols. I told her that such "Eastern" practice was exactly what I had been doing and intended to continue doing. We discussed the living Yoga of Kundalini Shakti, but she could see in it only symbols that are the peculiar contents of the Eastern psyche. She urgently suggested that I abandon this approach and volunteer myself to Jungian analysis.

Thus, I saw that Jung's brand of understanding precluded even the modified use of Spiritual practice as I understood it. Even my experiences, over a lifetime, of phenomena that can only be properly understood in a Spiritual context were to this view unallowable, at best clinical, causative of disturbance, and to be made subject to the interpretations of a humanistic psychology that was not yet loosed from the mortal philosophy of the university establishment.

The best Dr. Harding would do was recommend an analyst for me. As far as training in the various methods of analysis or group process was concerned, not only was it precluded by the kind of interpretation required, but I would have to prepare myself with years of university and professional training that was, to my point of view, quite beside the point of what I considered to be the real and necessary preparations for Spiritual Knowledge.

Thus, I began to realize that, at least for the time being, my only option was to continue my preparations for the Lutheran ministry. Nina also finished her requirements for the master's degree at this time, and we directed ourselves toward the coming move to Philadelphia.

32. W. Y. Evans-Wentz was the translator of several major Tibetan Buddhist texts, including *The Tibetan Book of the Dead, Tibet's Great Yogi Milarepa, The Tibetan Book of the Great Liberation,* and *Tibetan Yoga and Secret Doctrines.*

No description of this period would be adequate and true without the inclusion of my various experiences with the "Force". At first that experience was limited to the kind I first described in meeting with Rudi. I became aware that an actual Force (or tangible Spiritual Power) emanated from him. I could feel It in various ways as a magnetic or electric Energy in my body. This of course is a tremendously unique experience in terms of what people ordinarily would suppose to be reality. But It was for me not unusual or unique in my experience. Rudi's manifestation and use of It was unique, and my approach to It was now based on a totally new logic of life, but I had experienced the same Energy or Force as the "Bright" of childhood, and, later, as the rising Force that overtook me in the college experience.

Very quickly, I came to a comfortable recognition of this "Force" as a reliably available Presence, and I felt It operating continually, and always availably, in Rudi. Thus, that Force was redeemed from dependence on the fluctuations of my own life-consciousness. It stood outside me, constantly available through my teacher. I was free to turn myself from the long enterprise and experiment of my youth, wherein I had sought to perceive and verify the actual Existence and Nature of this Force in myself. Now I devoted myself to purifying work under the assumption of a concrete relationship to that actual Presence.

Thus, my first experiences were as I have described. They manifested as changes in my life-pattern, my physical, mental, and moral existence, its functional instruments, and its environment. But after I had eliminated the practices and forms of deliberate self-indulgence that inhibited the work of this Force on an internal level, I began also to have significant Spiritual experiences.

As I continued to go to Rudi's class and tried to open and surrender, I began to experience Rudi's "Force" entering me as he said It would. When he would begin the exercise or look at me during the exercise, I would usually feel a sudden descent of tremendous and seemingly

Infinite Energy from above. I could feel this descent as a peculiar kind of pressure that first came in the head and then permeated the body.

This pressure was the usual sign of the working of that Force in me. As I exercised myself in surrender to It over time, I could feel certain points of resistance in myself fall away and give place in a kind of interior opening on a mental and physical level. In time I could feel this pressure at will and almost constantly. It became a Presence that I could respond to in moments of repose or even during any kind of activity.

After many months this pressure became particularly apparent in the head. The center of the upper brain became irritated in a manner that had a deep and even sensuous quality. My ears began to feel as if there were an internal pressure opening their channels, and they felt a certain heat. At times I could, in a subtle manner, hear the Force descend, and my ears seemed to be stretching open to perceive some sound, both internal and external, that was always going on.

The process of meditation involved a surrendering of thought, and as this emptying of the mind continued, it was replaced by a strong concentration of penetrating Energy in the head. Afterwards the head would feel bathed and warmed in a Blissful Energy that descended from above. Its immediate effect was to offset the usual concentration of Energy in thought and in the lower body. For a period sometimes lasting for hours after the exercise, there was only a sublime Calmness and Fullness, without any anxiety or any movement of desire. The natural energies that flowed in the body felt balanced and harmonized. And this appeared to be the natural precondition for clarity and free-functioning as a human entity.

There were also certain visual sensations. When I would concentrate in the exercise, either on Rudi or on an image used for meditation at home, the field of ordinary vision would become dark and thick, then suddenly expand as a pervasive field of Force, and I would perceive

Energy entirely pervading the atmosphere, such that a general luminosity, both seen and felt, would surround everything and form the very substance of space. It was also this luminous quality that led me to call my childhood experience the "Bright".

At times during meditation I would also see certain forms appear superimposed on Rudi's face as well as on other people or objects. I would see beards and moustaches appear and disappear on Rudi, or he would seem to be clothed in oriental robes. Sometimes the entire room would take on a quality of splendor, and it would seem as if we were in another time, seated before some oriental philosopher-prince. The features of his face would go through many changes, as if revealing his past lives and our past associations.

Rudi and some of his students also claimed to have various visions, but I never had any such experiences while with him. Basically, my experience with him was limited to these subtle demonstrations of Energy on a physical level, and on an etheric[33] (or otherwise astral) level, just beyond the physical.

The class itself was an exercise in concentration, in which the Force was received, directed below, and then drawn up the spine to the head. After the class I would experience a fullness, a sensitivity and vibrancy in the organs of the head, a quietness descended into the mind, and a kind of charged and burning feeling pleasantly throughout my body.

One time Nina and I spent a weekend with Rudi at a beach house on Fire Island. That night Nina woke up

33. When Adi Da speaks here of the "etheric level", He is referring to the experiences related to the etheric body, or the "body" of life-energy. Our physical bodies are surrounded and infused by this life-energy "body", which we feel as the play of emotions and life-force in the body. The "astral level" of the human being is the lower and higher aspects of mind—conscious, subconscious, and unconscious. In His life with Rudi at this point, Adi Da is saying that His experiences were still in the domain of bodily energy and the basic dimensions of the mind; He was not yet entering into any higher subtle and mystical experiences such as would occur later in His Spiritual practice.

feeling a strong electric shock running through the body, beginning from the head. I experienced the same basic thing a few nights later, but the experience was extraordinarily intense, such that I automatically struggled to arouse my body and shake off the experience. The Force had become so Powerful that I felt I was about to be electrocuted.

There was also another manifestation evident in Rudi and some of his students. During the exercise their bodies would begin to jerk in a characteristic manner. There appeared to be a jolting within the spine that communicated to the muscles. Their spines revolved and appeared to make small spasms. Then their heads would begin to revolve very violently. This always happened to Rudi at the close of the exercise. I often desired this experience myself, but it did not occur for some time. I never in my life of seeking tried to fake or simulate any kind of phenomenon. My seeking was always too desperate to be satisfied with anything but an obvious and spontaneous, and obviously genuine, experience, which carried an inherent internal authority and self-verification.

These movements, or "kriyas" (spontaneous and purifying movements), as they are called in India, did not arise at all in me until shortly before I left Rudi and his classes. Finally, they did begin to develop, although not as violently as in the case of others. For the most part, I only felt a kind of gentle pulsing in my lower back, like little bubbles of air and fluid rising in a percolator. Also, I began to manifest a twitching in my face and mouth, and a rapid breathing, like the snarl of a wolf, and another spontaneous action that was like the yawn and growl of a lion. The arising of such manifestations and the spontaneous generation of animal sounds are also a characteristic of this Shakti Yoga.

On a few occasions I also experienced what I mentioned previously as "the Thumbs". While seated in the exercise, I would feel the Force descending through me unobstructed. Then I was easily able to relax to a great

Rudi

depth. And the Energy would then move to the base of the spine and travel upwards along the spine to the head. As It did so, I felt the polarity of my physical being reverse, and, instead of tending gravitationally downward toward my seat, I would "gravitate" upwards toward my head. As I relaxed completely, the reversal of Energy would be completed, and my form felt to be a kind of detached sphere, entirely free of the ordinary body sense. A tremendous sense of Peace and Fullness would arise at such times, and I would long to remain in that State. But as soon as I became attached to It, It would tend to disappear. So I would relax more. And, as I relaxed, an extraordinary depth would appear within my living consciousness, and there was the feeling-sensation of falling into an Infinite Deep. Then I passed away into a profound Bliss. In India this is called "samadhi".

These experiences approximately summarize my fullest benefits from Rudi. By the time I was about to leave for seminary in the late summer of 1966, I had, in all human terms, become quite strong, clear, and free. And this strengthening was accompanied by a growing sense of independence. Rudi's Yoga was a form of liberating dependence, wherein I was (with very positive life-effects) filled and nourished and guided by him and his Force, but Rudi was not himself prepared (ultimately, and perfectly) to liberate others, or to bring any one to any truly high or otherwise ultimate Realization.

Rudi was a kind of super-parent to me, a mother-father force that guided me into human maturity. It is traditional in the Spiritual cultures of the East for the disciple of one who is not his or her ultimate teacher, or final Guru, to determine the moment of his or her maximum possible attainment (in that company), and (in that moment) to affirm his or her independence, and then move on to his or her next, and perhaps ultimate, teacher, or Guru.

As time passed, I knew my own moment of such independence and moving on was approaching. Thus, I gradually began to become aware of the urge to independence in me, and this was also reflected in a growing critical awareness of Rudi's qualities and of my potential in his company.

As I have already said, Rudi never represented himself as a "finished product". He always saw his life only as a matter of growth, rather than of completion (although he assumed he had grown more than perhaps anyone else). Thus, as I also grew, I became increasingly more aware of Rudi's limitations. I saw that, even in the midst of apparently dramatic Spiritual experiences, Rudi's interests were almost entirely life-ordinary. It was ordinary life-problems, and not the urge toward ultimate Divine Realization, that fueled and motivated even his apparently Spiritual efforts. And, most critically, I eventually saw that the particular Force, or the quality of Shakti, available through Rudi had carried me as far as It could go. Mere "experiences" and worldly, or merely ordinary, human growth were not sufficient for me. Only Truth Itself would be enough. In summary, I discovered that Rudi's personal instrument was not a perfect and unlimited Source of Energy, or Spiritual Influence, but a limited one in an advanced but still relatively early stage of growth.

When, eventually, it came time for me to finally leave Rudi's physical presence, I was no longer a Spiritual innocent. I had already begun Real Spiritual life on my own. I had already attuned myself to the "Force" that was Present in me, and Which had in fact been the Circumstance of my entire life, from the beginning. It had never been apart from me. I Knew It as the "Bright" and as my own Eternally Free Nature beyond all internal contradiction.

In the meantime, and even as I left for seminary, I kept all of these observations silent in myself. I wanted to test myself in Rudi's absence, to see if my growing sense of independence would prove itself worthy of action. Thus, Nina and I moved from New York and took up residence near the seminary in Philadelphia.

Shortly after the beginning of the school year, I began to write again. Only now the writing was of a different kind, and its motivation was also new. My position in the Christian community was unusual. I had to act and communicate and profess as a Christian, but in fact I was conscious of Reality in a radically different manner. The longer I was there, the more of an "imposter" I knew myself to be. I did not feel I was putting anything over on anyone. That was not my intention. But I had to remain continually aware of the difference in myself and, in the same moment, translate my awareness and my perception of Reality into a more or less orthodox, and even conventional, manner and communication.

This dual position produced a constant reflectiveness in me, and so I began to write a journal of my experiences and thoughts as they actually were, prior to the necessary translation into "Christian".

I managed to communicate myself fairly well. My studies were a tremendous discipline for me, but I managed to keep the highest grades in all of my course work. I exceeded everyone else on the level of study, and this alone was a tremendous proof of the utility of the attitude of work.

I kept as free as possible of the traditional religious life of the seminary. I only went to church when it was required, and Nina and I generally secluded ourselves in an invulnerable sphere of necessary privacy. As the months passed, I became more and more acutely aware of the internal movement of my own life. I was again on my own, and free to pursue the Truth of my conscious life. But now I was also functioning as a visible member of the world.

Nevertheless, I acted with a great feeling of Clarity, Freedom, and Power. The benefits of my entire life of "Bright" understanding, including all the effects of my Spiritual life and humanizing discipline in Rudi's company, were thus made obvious to me as a very practical matter of course. And this made me all the more aware of the limitations bred in that "modernized" religious community. The men and women there were alike pale and in doubt, struggling with desires they never understood, and they bore the burden of the kind of liberal theology that first affected me in college, when I read books like *The Lost Years of Jesus Revealed*.

The seminary and its Protestant Christian community were a collection of ordinary, suffering, and confused human beings, who lived without benefit of fundamental Truth. The kind of experience that was my daily Enjoyment was, from their point of view, unavailable, even unacceptable, and they consigned it to a primitive state of life. Far from enjoying the "peace that passes all understanding", these Spiritually unaware religionists were busy wondering what small portion of the religious life was the legitimate inheritance of the age of materialism, materialistic science, universal scepticism, and mortal philosophy.

I saw that the entire seminary community was suffering exactly the form of unenlightened and suppressive philosophizing that had turned me out of college into the wilderness of my seeking. I wrote in a copy of the Bible a remark by one of the psalmists, "My soul is released, as a bird from the snare of fowlers." This sense of Release, Certainty, and Joy was my common experience, but I saw no way at all to tell my Truth so that I could be heard.

In time, my daily life became routine. I had learned my "place". Most of the seminary professors had seen fit to criticize me openly or in private for the few of my "extreme" views I allowed myself to express. For them, there was no viable Truth at all in the entire realm of Spiritual experience and phenomena that was my birthright. They were enclosed in Rudolf Bultmann and Paul Tillich,[34] and even a mortal theology.

At best they saw human beings as necessarily mortal. When you are dead you are dead. But, they hoped,

34. Rudolf Bultmann and Paul Tillich were two major Christian theologians of the twentieth century (both German) who adopted a "de-mythologizing" approach to the New Testament that called many basic Christian doctrines into question.

perhaps it is true that Jesus will come again at the end of time and revitalize the world, "creating" everyone again in a new and immortal life.

Doubts began to arise in me. It was no longer simply a matter of whether or not I would be able to speak within the religious community. I began to doubt whether I could even persist in such a place. The Christian community with which I was associated became for me a pale shadow of life, a desperate vestige of the past that is no longer opened even to its own Truth.

Rudi continued to use the same arguments with me as before, and I remained for the same reasons. But I wrote and lived according to my own understanding, and waited for a moment when I would see my own way clearly.

I continued to observe that I was involved in the pattern and life of Narcissus. I was observing his evolution in myself and the world. And my "work" was Purposed to see the accomplishment of my Ultimate Release.

Finally, in the spring of 1967, I passed through an experience that epitomized all of my seeking and all aspects of my to then developed life of understanding. The experience itself is surrounded with apparent evidence of a "clinical breakdown", but it is otherwise full of the sense and Reality of primary Experience, the breakthrough of Ultimate and unqualified Consciousness Itself. It was the death of Narcissus.

I had contracted a spring cold, which was not unusual, except that I had been entirely free of any kind of disease for the last couple of years. I was in the bathroom when this episode began. I had bathed and shaven, and I was rubbing a cleansing pad on my face. Suddenly my flesh began to feel very "massy" and unpliable. I felt as if the pores of my face had closed. The skin became dry and impervious to air. As I looked at my face in the mirror, it appeared gray, disturbed, and deathlike. The saliva in my mouth stopped flowing, and I was overcome by a rising anxiety that became an awesome and overwhelming fear of death.

I was fixed in the certainty that I was soon to go mad and die, but I tried as much as possible simply to observe this process in myself. I calmly said goodbye to Nina, telling her nothing of this, and left for school.

When I sat down to my first morning class, this process was still going on in me. There was simply this absolute fear, and all my physical and mental processes appeared to be rushing to disappear and die. As I listened to the lecture on church history, I felt as if my mind were a separate, material entity. It seemed to be rushing forward toward an invisible point with accelerating speed. I felt as if I were to go violently insane on the spot. I began to write very rapidly in my notebook, in order simply to observe this process and not be overcome by its effects.

I wrote every word the professor spoke, and, if there was a moment of silence, I would write whatever I was observing in the room or in my body. Somehow I managed to get through the fifty minute lecture. When it was over, I sat by myself. My body felt in a fever and my mind close to delirium.

This one experience epitomized all the parts of the many experiences of fear and sickness and near madness I had known in my life. It was as if every one of those experiences was an event of this same kind, and could have led to some marvelous Realization, if only I were able to allow the death or madness to take its course.

But in this instance, as in the past, the shock and awesome fear were too great to be allowed without resistance. In the previous days, I had taken a few pills for a cold, and so I left school to go to a doctor for advice. The doctor said the pills were mild, and not aggravating or narcotic. He attributed my heightened sensitivity and alarmed condition to perhaps overwork or some kind of nervous excitement.

Nonetheless, I stopped taking the pills. I went home. All day I stretched alone on the floor of the living room, revolving in this same overwhelming fear of death.

When Nina came home, she tried to make me comfortable, and I passed the evening in front of the TV set, observing my terror.

When Nina went to bed, I also tried to sleep. But the intensity of the experience only increased. Finally, I woke her in the middle of the night and asked her to take me to the hospital. My breathing had become alarming, and my heart seemed to be slowing down. At times my heart would beat irregularly and seem to stop.

She drove me to a nearby emergency ward. I was examined by a nurse, and then a psychiatrist, who told me I was having an anxiety attack. There was nothing apparently wrong with me physically. He gave me a sleeping pill and told me to rest. If I felt no relief within a couple of days, I should seek psychiatric help.

When we got home, I tried to sleep, but it seemed a long time before I could sleep. During the next couple of days, I went to a psychiatrist, and I detailed to him the entire history of my life, including my experiences with drugs and my work with Rudi. He only told me I could join a group therapy session he held every week. I went to his session that night, and also, the next day, to a group session for students held by a psychologist at the seminary. But there was no relief, no fundamental insight, no communication I could make that made the difference.

Finally, on the third day after this process began, I was lying home alone in the afternoon. All my life I had been constantly brought to this point. All of the various seeking methods of my life had constantly prevented this experience from going to its end. All my life I had been preventing my death.

I lay on the floor, totally disarmed, unable to make a gesture that could prevent the rising fear. And thus it grew in me, but, for the first time, I allowed it to happen. I could not prevent it. The fear and the death rose and became my overwhelming experience. And I observed the crisis of that fear in a moment of conscious, voluntary death. I allowed the death to happen, and I "saw" it happen. It was not that an organic death occurred, but even organic death ceased to be a "concern". There was a spontaneous, utter release of identification with the body, the mind, the emotions of the separate person, and the self-contracting (or reactive and separative) act that is the "ego" (or the presumed person).

When that moment of crisis had passed, I felt a marvelous relief, or, rather, simply, a marvelous Freedom. The death had occurred, but I had <u>observed</u> it! I remained untouched by it. The body and the mind and the egoic personality had died (or been utterly released as a concern and an identity), but I remained as essential and unqualified Awareness (and purely That, but also Freely Aware of the physical body and its natural environment).

When all of the fear and dying had finished their course, when the body, the mind, the apparently separate "person" (and the <u>act</u> that made its apparent separateness) had been released, and my attention was no longer fixed in those things, I Knew Reality, tacitly and directly. There was an Infinite Bliss of Being, an untouched, unborn Sublimity, without separation, without individuation, without a thing from which to be separated. There was only Reality Itself, the incomparable Nature and constant Existence that underlies (and observes, and Knows) the entire adventure of life. And that Same and Very Reality was also revealed as the unqualified living condition of the totality of conditionally manifested existence.

After a time, I got up from the floor. I walked around and beamed Joyfully at the room. The Love-Blissful, unthreatened Current of the "Bright" emanated Freely and unqualifiedly from my heart, and not a pulse of It was limited by my otherwise conditional existence or the existence of the world. I had acquired a totally new understanding. I understood Narcissus and the entire cycle of suffering and search. I saw the meaning of my entire striving life to that moment. Suffering, seeking, self-indulgence, the seeker's Spirituality, and all the rest were founded in the same primary motivation and error.

It was the <u>avoidance</u> of <u>relationship</u>. That was it! That was the chronic and continuous source and characteristic of all egoic activity. Indeed, the ego was revealed to be <u>only</u> an <u>activity</u>, not an "entity". The "entity", the separate "person" (or ego-"I"), was revealed to be only an illusion, a mere presumption in mind and feeling, resulting from the self-contraction, the egoic reaction, the single egoic act of the total body-mind. The ego, the separate and separative "I", is the chronic (and total psycho-physical) avoidance of relationship. Thus, human beings are forever suffering, seeking, indulging themselves, and manipulating their lives for the sake of some unknown goal in eternity.

The human trouble showed itself to be entirely determined by this one process of avoidance, or total psycho-physical self-contraction. It was the source of separation and un-love, the source of doubt and un-Reality, of qualification and loss. But, in fact, there is only relationship, only love, only unqualified relatedness, only the unqualified living condition of Reality. Therefore, I Knew that Reality Itself could always be directly Realized in life, if the self-contracting (or separative) reaction in life was exceeded by the unqualified assumption of relatedness in all the moments of living.

In the weeks that remained of my first year at seminary, I tried again and again to speak revealingly to others about my recent extraordinary experience and my new understanding. I felt I was not in the same position I had been in college. I felt this experience was fundamental and complete. I felt that the Knowledge revealed to me in this experience could not be lost in the midst of any possible events, any return of old tendencies. This was the primary Knowledge (in life) that I had sought all of my adult life. The diminished experience of the "Bright" in my adolescence now paled beside the "Brightness" Aroused by this Knowledge. My "Bright" experience of Awakening in college appeared to be merely a preliminary to this fullest "Bright" Knowledge. And all that I had come to see as a result of Rudi's discipline, all of the functioning apparatus of conditional Spiritual experience, all conditional worlds, all conditional possibilities, all conditional abilities, appeared to be merely a distraction from this primary Knowledge. I identified that Knowledge as the primary feeling of relatedness. Not separation, not union, but unqualified relatedness, or non-separateness, arose in me as the root-sense (or radical condition) of living existence.

But my professors failed to understand what I had understood. I abandoned myself to them completely and told them all of the motives that brought me to seminary. Most of them were simply shocked. Their leading seminarian had turned out to be a fanatic, an heretical "enthusiast".

In the course of my studies, I had learned about the Eastern Orthodox Christian church. This Grand Event of the death of Narcissus had not removed the necessity for life in the ordinary sense. I had still to find some sort of "creative" and productive means of life. And so I considered turning from the Lutheran church to the Eastern church.

The Eastern Orthodox church, at least on paper, seemed to be the ideal form of Christianity. Above all, it acknowledged all the classical Spiritual phenomena of the saints. And its theology was founded in Spiritual experience rather than ecclesiastical dogma. Thus, I contacted a local Orthodox priest, and Nina and I were received into the Orthodox church a few weeks later.

In the meantime, in fulfillment of my previous commitment to the formal seminary requirements, I served all summer as a chaplain in the Philadelphia State Mental Hospital. Then, at the end of the summer, we returned to New York, and I entered St. Vladimir's Russian Orthodox Theological Seminary in Tuckahoe.

But I was quick to learn that Eastern Orthodoxy too was bound to its traditional exoteric mentality. The experience of liturgy, church politics, and ethnic religion was the fundamental occupation there. I felt so trapped that during the lunch hour I would have to walk up behind

At the Lutheran Seminary in Philadelphia

Apartment where Adi Da lived
while attending the Seminary

Philadelphia State Mental Hospital,
where Adi Da served as chaplain

"I understood Narcissus
and the entire cycle
of suffering and search.
I saw the meaning
of my entire striving life
to that moment.
Suffering, seeking, self-
indulgence, the seeker's
Spirituality, and all the
rest were founded in
the same primary
motivation and error.
It was the <u>avoidance of
relationship</u>. That was it!"

the seminary, where there was a waterfall and a stream. I would hold my hands out over the water so that the Spiritual Energy that Filled my body would run out into the stream. Then I would return to the seminary relatively empty to carry on the religious games.

Finally, I was told that it was not likely that I could be accepted as a candidate for the Eastern Orthodox priesthood. Nina happened to have been married and divorced before she met me, and there was an ancient canonical law preventing any man from becoming a priest if he is married to a divorced woman.

This was the final stroke. My religious "career" (for which I had no impulse beyond Rudi's "command") had come to the point beyond which I could generate no further toleration, no further seriousness, and no reasons for continuing. I felt certain that this particular discipline had served all that it could rightly serve, and that it had gone far enough. I went to speak to Rudi, and, surprisingly, he agreed.

At Swami Muktananda's Ashram in Ganeshpuri, India, 1968

CHAPTER 10

The Abandonment of Effort in India

The crisis of understanding that overcame me in seminary was yet to become a complete reversal and transformation of my life. It marked only the beginning of another phase in the progressive process leading toward my most perfect re-Awakening. Nevertheless, I had truly passed through the fear of death, and what was beyond death (or egoic separateness) stood out in life as a primary sense that I called "unqualified relatedness".

In childhood I was centered in the "Bright", the Illumined Freedom (and pathos) of truly living being in the face of conflict and death. But in time I became serious with conflict itself and with death itself, and, as a consequence, I saw the arising of contradictions in myself, which diminished the "Bright". Then, in college, I was drawn up again into the Truth. And I saw that I was always already Free, never dying or born to die. But this Knowledge seemed dependent on some kind of work in the living consciousness, whereby the internal pattern of contradictions moving as the mind was to be dissolved in Conscious Knowledge.

Thus, I began the long time of effort that culminated in my meeting and work with Rudi. But all that effort brought me lately to another crisis in understanding. In seminary, I was brought to recognize something more fundamental than seeking and effort. I saw that it was not a matter of any seeker's effort to find or achieve something not already the case in the living consciousness or in life. Rather, it was a matter of directly and constantly, or always already, abiding in what I called "the living condition of Reality", which is unqualified relatedness.

From that time I was moved to exercise my Knowledge of Truth in a totally new way. As a result of the experience of "death" in seminary, I saw that my entire life, even my Spiritual effort, was only a complex adventure of avoidance, the avoidance of the condition of relationship itself, and, thus, the avoidance of primary, radical relatedness as the always present, living condition of Reality. That avoidance, that act of self-contraction, that separateness and separativeness of the egoic self, was the characteristic of Narcissus.

I had become certain that Real life was a matter of constantly Realizing relationship and relatedness (prior, or always already the case) as the radical category or unqualifiedly felt condition of life on every level. Thus, it no longer was a matter of effort and seeking (which arise only <u>after</u> the self-contracting act of avoidance has already taken place), but it was a matter of maintaining and exercising this true understanding in every moment, and under all conditions.

Everyone to whom I spoke about this, including Rudi, tended to interpret my seminary experience negatively. In time, I realized that I was approaching people as if my experience had posed a problem for me, whereas in fact it had removed the problem and every sense of dilemma. I saw that my own efforts had been constantly re-"creating" the sense of dilemma and turning life into an effort to overcome some presumed obstacle. Indeed, Rudi himself epitomized the problem-based attitude of presuming obstacles, making strategic efforts, and, altogether, of forever seeking.

I wanted my new experience and understanding to be acknowledged as the sublime Truth it was. I wanted my "madness" to be accepted as our Real State. But everyone was offended by my radical, impulsive manner. Thus, after several months, I decided to abandon my previous efforts. I stopped trying to communicate my experience and my understanding, but I began to live on its basis.

I continued to go to Rudi's classes, but I set about "creating" my life in a new way. Rudi sensed that I was departing from the egoic strategy of "work" and "surrender", but there was no conversation between us that indicated any strong disagreement. I continued as before, but now I proceeded with a sense of ease, of prior fulfillment, free of the need to strive for any kind of overwhelming goal.

I had seen the futility of the seeker's effort. I saw that it was only another form of avoidance, just like the very patterns I was always trying to surrender. The egoic effort of work and surrender had proven to me the fruitlessness of that entire strategic path. Thus, the entire basis of struggle by which I had guided myself since college fell away in a graceful Calm.

I found work in a bookstore. And I simply made my living in an effortless manner. I enjoyed the human freedom of simple functioning. I was merely present. There was no problem.

One day I was sitting with Rudi in his store. I found a couple of publications from the Ashram of his Guru, Baba Muktananda, in India. At first Rudi seemed reluctant to let me read them. He made fun of the Indian manner of teaching, saying that it was very traditional and that one really needed to work very hard to get anything from Baba.

But I managed to read the little pamphlets while Rudi busied himself with his customers. The writings were little compendiums of Baba's teaching. As I read them, I began to discover parallels to my new unburdened sense of Spiritual life.

Baba said that Spiritual life was not a matter of egoic effort on the part of the disciple. It was a matter of the Guru's grace, the Guru's free gift. The disciple needed only to come to the Guru and enjoy the Guru's grace. It was as easy as flowers in sunlight. He said that once the

disciple received the Guru's grace the various phenomena of Spiritual experience would come automatically.
Meditation and purification would occur naturally, without egoic effort. Indeed, the attitude of egoic effort was
an obstacle to the disciple's progress.

I looked at Baba's picture on the wall, and that of
Swami Nityananda, his Guru. I began to feel that these
two men, the teachers of my first human teacher, were
in fact the Sources of Spiritual blessing and wisdom
toward which the "Bright" had been drawing me when I
was first led to Rudi. I felt that Rudi had been given to
me "on the way to India", as a preliminary Means of
purifying me from my own sense of seeking and egoic
effort. Rudi's teachings had duplicated, even with obvious exaggeration, the characteristic motive and method
of egoic seeking, especially in the ordinary, or grosser,
context of human life, such that I, by fulfilling that
motive and method as a total disciplining of my ordinary,
or grosser, life, would, in due course, come to the point
of utter despair relative to the search in the ordinary,
human context of life. Thus, the Intention, in the
"Bright", that had led me to Rudi appeared to me to have
been Purposed to grant me this Lesson in life, so that I
would be enabled to feel and receive and respond to a
further and higher Spiritual revelation, which required an
openness to receive, rather than an effort to acquire.

Perhaps this way of "openness to receive" would
itself, in time, become only another search, requiring a
further, and even more profound, understanding in me.
Nevertheless, I was altogether moved to respond to
Baba, take him at his word, and find out.

When I got up to leave Rudi's store, I was filled with
a determination to go to India myself. During the next few
weeks I managed to secure a position with Pan American
Airways. This seemed to me an ideal opportunity for
travel that would make it possible for me to go to India.

Shortly after the beginning of the year, in 1968, I was
told by my employers at Pan American Airways that I

would be able to make use of a two-day earned vacation and a 90% discount in air fare. If I could manage to trade days-off with some fellow employees, I could stretch that leave into six days. I immediately arranged for my vacation to fall in late March and the beginning of April, and I began to make arrangements for Nina and me to go to India.

I was determined in this course, although I knew that it would probably mean a break with Rudi. I told him my plan, and he (with a minimum expression of reluctance) gave me the address of Baba's Ashram. I continued to try to maintain my relationship with Rudi, but an obvious distance had grown between us that neither of us was willing to communicate. I loved Rudi dearly, and I will be forever grateful for his help. He remains one of the major influences in my life. But I was about to pass into a Fullness of my own that demanded a rather painful separation. The time had come for me to "strike" my first teacher and take my inheritance.[35]

The weeks passed. The task of arranging for the trip was filled with endless obstacles. But I managed to design and arrange a schedule of flights that would enable Nina and me to go to India and return in a little more than six days. We would return only a day later than I was allowed, and this I felt would not be so long that I would be likely to lose my job.

I wrote to Baba and received a letter from his secretary, Pratibha Trivedi (also, generally, called "Amma"). Our visit would be welcomed, although they would prefer us to come for a longer time and at a period in the year when the weather around Bombay was not so hot.

I wrote them that the period of our visit was fixed by my employers. I told Baba that I believed fully in his grace. I recalled to him the story of an Indian prince who once

35. Traditionally in Japanese Zen Buddhism, the Master may sometimes beat the student in order to serve his or her Awakening. Less well known is the tradition of the student's striking the Teacher. The act of striking the Teacher is playful and jubilant, a sign that the student for the first time has attained the same state of Awakening as the Teacher.

ordered a saint to bring him to the full Realization of Truth in the time it took him to place his foot in the stirrup and swing his leg over the saddle of his horse. The prince became Enlightened the instant he stepped into the stirrup, and he fell to the ground to kiss the feet of the saint.

I made it clear to Baba that I was coming to receive everything he had to give me. I would only have four days at the Ashram, and I did not know when I would be able to return again. I humbly offered these conditions as a limitation that I could not prevent, and asked Baba to bless me with everything that was necessary for me to Enjoy the perfect Realization of Reality.

I also wrote to him about my life, my experiences in childhood and college, my work with Rudi, and the incomparable Awareness that now resided in me since my experience in seminary. I told him how I had been led to Rudi and then at last to the Ashram, and that I felt that he (Baba) was the ultimate Source of grace to which (it seemed to me now) I had been moving all my life. I also asked his blessing for our safe arrival. And so I prepared for the adventure that seemed to promise a perfect gift of Truth.

Nina and I flew to Bombay via London and Beirut, and we arrived on April 2, 1968. We landed in Bombay about 4 A.M. and were met by Peter Dias, a former and sometimes Catholic and alcoholic, who was an Indian devotee of Baba. He was to be our interpreter and the communicator of the Indian form of Spiritual gossip during our first couple of days at the Ashram. He arranged for a private car, and we set out on a two- or three-hour drive toward Ganeshpuri, the home of Baba's Ashram.

Peter was a very animated and nervous presence. He announced himself clearly as one who felt antagonistic toward Rudi. And, as we drove, he kept testing our allegiances, as if to make sure we were there as pristine devotees of Baba and not somehow under the control of Rudi's brand of Yoga. I assured him we were there totally under our own power and felt drawn solely to Baba's grace.

The Indian towns and countryside were a revelation

to me. As the morning dampness and fog lifted, a primitive world appeared, filled with ancient poverty and the temples of an equally ancient Spirituality. There was a mysterious air all around, and everywhere there were signals of an ancient Presence, pointing me to an awesome and absolute Divinity.

Peter surrounded us with the drama of his Guru. He compulsively unraveled the tales of miracles that, he assured us, would prove themselves to us in Ganeshpuri. Everything pointed to a magic fact. I expected to walk into a world of sudden perfection, where the images of miraculous living stood around in the room as obvious as the hard-edged architecture of New York.

When we drove up to the door of the Ashram, I was excited beyond words. Peter led us into a small room where Indian men and women of various degrees of obvious wealth or poverty sat in separate groups on the floor. Sitting in a throne of cushions, wrapped below the waist in a light saffron cloth, was Baba.

Something was said to him in Hindi as we entered. He made an energetic greeting of "Ah" and "Hm", and we bowed at his feet. He welcomed us through Peter, who translated his remarks rapidly. Baba spoke no English. We were told to rest and refresh ourselves and come to sit with him in the early afternoon.

When we returned to the hall in the afternoon, Baba was seated again in his usual place. I sat in the lotus posture on the floor with the men, directly in front of Baba. Nina sat to the side with the women. At first there was a brief, familiarizing conversation. I was asked about our trip, and so on. Then Baba took the opportunity to call attention to everyone's sitting posture. (I was sitting in the full lotus position, with only minor discomfort arising after perhaps half an hour.) "Firm posture is the beginning of the true Spiritual attitude," he said. And, finally, we got down to business.

I felt my letters were a sufficient introduction to my past and to the Purpose of my visit. The limitation of speaking through an interpreter made lengthy conversation more of a burden than an instrument for instant communication. And so, after a few brief remarks about how I had practiced under Rudi's guidance and, as a result, come to feel that true Realization could not be accomplished through egoic effort, but that It depended entirely on the grace of a true Guru, I asked Baba to teach me about the true way of Spiritual life, and, by his grace, to reveal its Great Truth to me.

In response to me, Baba gave a long and somewhat pedantic monologue on the Truth of Advaita Vedanta[36] and on the practice of Ashtanga Yoga, the eightfold path of Realization prescribed by Patanjali.[37] The longness and wordiness of the monologue were, it seemed, intended merely to "fill some time", in order to provide a period of extended discourse to occupy and entertain the larger gathering of visitors there. But, soon after he began to speak, Baba turned to me very directly, and he very pointedly said to me (through his interpreter): "You are not the one who wakes or sleeps or dreams. You are the Witness to all of these states." As would become more and more obvious and clear to me over time, this utterance was the most basic and important (and Truly and Really Initiatory) verbal instruction Baba ever gave to me.

All the while Baba spoke, he was a field of perpetual movement. His hands constantly moved about him, either communicating with a gesture, touching his face, or adjusting the beads around his neck. Even though he

36. Vedanta is the principal philosophical tradition of Hinduism. "Advaita" means "non-dual". Advaita Vedanta, then, is a philosophy of non-dualism. Its origins lie in the ancient esoteric Teaching that the Divine Being is the only Reality. According to Advaita Vedanta, the self and the world have no independent existence but merely arise in that one Divine Reality.

37. Patanjali is honored as the originator of classical Yoga. He may have lived in the second century of the common era. In his famous treatise, the *Yoga-Sutras*, Patanjali describes eight practices that make up his system of Yoga: moral observance (yama), self-discipline (niyama), posture (asana), control of the breath (pranayama), restraint of the senses (pratyahara), concentration (dharana), meditation (dhyana), and exalted states of consciousness achieved through inward concentration and meditation (samadhi).

Swami Muktananda

was profoundly calm, his hands and his features seemed never to become still. His body spoke the language of Spirit-Energy, saying that even the very cells of his body were pulsing with an Absolute Bliss.

Apart from Baba's pointed admonition to me about abiding in the Witness-Position, he made no attempt to teach me how to meditate or how to respond to his Presence. And so, rather than immediately taking that admonition to <u>be</u> his actual instruction to me about how to meditate and how to respond to his Presence, I began, while sitting with him that first afternoon, to make an ego-based effort to surrender and open to him deeply, which was the habitual exercise I had learned with Rudi. Then, as I became more concentrated, and attuned to the internal mechanisms that I had come to know through the work of surrender and the Force, I felt a new and more Powerful Presence. I felt the same Force, or Shakti, that I had experienced with Rudi, but It was magnified to the degree of an almost muscular Power.

After about an hour or so, Baba and his Indian devotees began to chant the *Bhagavad Gita*, as was the custom every afternoon. While I continued to sit, vaguely observing this ritual, my entire body became more and more Filled with the Fullness of this bodily overwhelming Power and Bliss. Baba sensed what was happening to me, and he would frequently gesture to me with his eyes or make his characteristic "Hm" sound of approval.

As the chanting continued, the Shakti began to generate vigorous movements in my body. These were the "kriyas", the purifying activity of the Shakti as It moves through the various nerve channels and the physical form. My back began to move around involuntarily in jolts, the way I had seen the Shakti affect others in Rudi's class. My head began to jerk and revolve rapidly. The experience was not altogether different from the kind of experience to which I had become accustomed with Rudi, but now it was much stronger, and it seemed to be approaching a violent state, beyond my control, so that

I would often fall over backwards into the wall or sideways to the floor.

Even after the chanting was finished and Baba began to carry on conversations with his visitors, these movements and this Bliss continued. Finally, Baba said to me, "Now I've got you." He smiled, and left the room.

These movements increased and became my constant occupation during the few days of our visit. The kriyas became so strong in me that Baba began to call me "Kriyananda" (which means "One Whose Bliss Is In The Purifying Movement Of The Divine Power"). Only one or two others seemed to be experiencing similar effects, but I assumed mine was a common experience. Everyone was pleased that I was experiencing Baba's grace, and it seemed particularly good to them because I was a Westerner.

Our days were spent sitting with Baba during these sessions of chanting and conversation in the morning and afternoon. We would also get up at about 5 A.M. and meditate in the hall outside Baba's room. He would walk around in the dark with a flashlight and spend a few moments in front of each of us watching our meditation.

We were also allowed to sit with him privately, usually with only one or two others, while he rested on the Ashram grounds after lunch. We would sit around him on the ground outside the cowshed, and sometimes ask him questions, while he petted the young calves.

Nina's experience had always been much quieter than my own. Here, as before, she experienced a graceful calmness. Baba gave her a sari to wear, and he would often gift her with a flower or a fruit that he had blessed with his Transmission of Shakti.

We would sit at various times to listen to him answer our own and others' questions about many matters basic to Spiritual life, including meditation, vegetarian diet, and so on. On one such occasion, one of his answers seemed to summarize all his instructions relative to the entire practical discipline of Spiritual life: "Eat less, sleep less, talk less. Increase your love. Increase your devotion. Increase your meditation."

A major subject of Baba's discourses was always the process of Spiritual Initiation called "Shaktipat". He indicated that such Initiation might occur via the Guru's touch, or his glance, or his word, or his thought, or otherwise spontaneously, simply by one's remaining in proximity to him.

One morning I was sitting outside the Ashram office. Baba was inside discussing some Ashram business with a devotee. (I always tried to sit near him wherever he went, so that I could see him and meditate where he could see me.) On this occasion, I was sitting in meditation, contemplating Baba's form. Suddenly, he jumped out of his chair and rushed toward me, shouting the name "Kriyananda!" And he pressed his hand to my head, with one finger hard against my left eye. I fell into a swoon of Bliss. The violent kriyas stopped, and I sat in a State of trance-like absorption in Bliss, while still generally aware of what was going on around me. While everyone stood around and watched me, my hands raised up spontaneously and performed mudras, the hand poses that you see in Indian dance and the statues of Buddhas.

All of this was quite remarkable, except I was experiencing an inner state that was not calm but more and more exhausting. I was involved in a kind of super-effort of internal work of the same kind I had known with Rudi. The more deeply I surrendered, the more these movements took hold of me. But my experience also seemed to depend on this great effort. I was getting very tired and disturbed by the pressure of this work, and I wondered how to recapture the sense of ease and grace that had originally motivated me to go to India.

I asked Baba about meditation. He told me that it should be a mere act of Witnessing, not an effort. I should only sit calmly and observe the working of the Shakti in myself. I should relax, and with each cycle of breath recite either the mantra "So-Ham" ("I am He", "I am the Divine, or the Guru") or the primary sound "Om".[38]

Peter Dias also told me about the manner of traditional meditation that Baba recommended. He said it was not like Rudi's "work" at all. The Shakti did not come out of the teacher's eyes and descend into the body via the work of surrender before It rose up the spine. The Guru awakened It, and It rose by Itself, from the base of the spine toward the head. Then the various kriyas and visions should come quite naturally, while one remained in a state of calm Witnessing.

This was quite a new idea of meditation for me. It seemed right, and it certainly corresponded to my new understanding of how it <u>should</u> be, but, after years of intentional "work", I had grown accustomed to constantly making the intentional effort of surrender. Therefore, it seemed to me, an equally great effort would be required in order simply to allow the Shakti, the Divine Power, to do the "work". Thus, no matter how hard I tried (and, therefore, because of the hard trying), I was unable to break the old habit of effortful meditation. I even felt afraid that, if I dropped the habit of effort, the movements and experiences would cease. Indeed, when I finally did manage to simply relax into Baba's Presence, I merely settled into an ease, and there were no movements, no unusual experiences.

The three and one-half days of our visit quickly neared an end. The new idea of meditation and Baba's direct admonition to me about my Identity as the "Witness" appeared to be the limit of what I was to receive. When the last day arrived, I was desperate. I had come for more than this. I had come for <u>everything</u>!

Baba no longer called me "Kriyananda". And it seemed that I had merely experienced a physically

---

38. In the Hindu tradition, the syllable "Om" (sometimes spelled "Aum") is understood to be a direct expression of the Spiritual Power of the Absolute Divine Being, from which all existence proceeds.

stronger version of the same phenomena I had experienced with Rudi, only, at the last, to see even it fall away as well. I was disappointed, and when I sat with Baba in the morning I did little more than sit. I had consigned myself to mere Witnessing, and the movements ceased. It seemed that I was only caught up in the Ashram chitchat. But I could not imagine that Baba would let me come all this way only to leave with merely a little instruction. I was still in a state of confusion about the way of effort, and its effects, and the seemingly ineffective method of "Witnessing" meditation that Baba offered.

We took lunch, and then I sat briefly in the garden behind the dining hall. Baba passed by with another man, a white-bearded, round, saintly-looking man with large, penetrating eyes. I had not seen this other man before. (It would be more than a year before I found out this man was a great Yogi-Saint, named Rang Avadhoot, and, at the same time, I would be informed that he had died a few months after our encounter in the garden.)

As Baba and the stranger passed by me in the garden, the stranger suddenly stopped, turned directly toward me, and looked me directly in the eyes for a long moment. Baba also stood by, gently gazing at me. Then Baba and the stranger continued their walk.

Immediately after this encounter, I became sensitive to the extreme heat and light of the day, and I walked off to our room to get my hat. The sun was violently hot, but it had been my intention to take a solitary walk around the grounds of the Ashram, since only a couple of hours remained of my stay there. However, when I got to the room, I suddenly felt a profound urge to lie down and rest. I thought I should just lie down for a few moments, but I did not want to fall asleep and waste my last precious hours at the Ashram.

As I lay down, I immediately passed from the ordinary waking state to what at first seemed like a sleep, except there was no loss of conscious awareness. In an instant, I lost all bodily consciousness and every sense of my mind and personality, but there was also a profound State of conscious awareness that was absolutely calm, uncontained, and Free. Indeed, I felt that I existed only as conscious awareness. There was no other experience, no thought, no feeling, no perception. Awareness was (very quickly) concentrated above, at an unfathomable "Point", beyond space, and yet above me. As I became spontaneously concentrated in that "Point", I felt and passed beyond It, into an Infinite Space of Bliss, an Absolute Pleasure of Fullness and Brilliance, that completely Absorbed my separate being. And, then, "I" existed only at Infinity, <u>as</u> Infinity, beyond "I", beyond the separated and separate self-reference.

Eventually, there was an apparent movement from this incomparably pure State, into perceptual modifications of that same egoless Awareness. There were rapid visions (or feelings) of subtle levels of existence, beyond the human. In quick succession, I Witnessed numberless feelings of form and space, or of what appeared to be a hierarchically degressive descent through other worlds, or realms of conditionally manifested existence that are associated with levels of mind beyond, or subtler than, ordinary human life.

Then I heard a loud, roaring sound that at first seemed to surround me like a great room. I gradually descended toward association with the body, from a position above the head of the body. The sound was my own breathing, as it rushed through my lungs and throat. But I did not then perceive these things from within my body. I was fully Aware as that Consciousness Which transcends all form, and Which surrounds and breathes the body.

Just then, Nina entered the room, and, with a sudden jolt, I resumed the ordinary state of life-awareness, as if contained within the body. I have no idea how long this experience had lasted, but it was now time to pack and prepare to leave. I did not speak to Nina, but tried to remain concentrated in what remained of this unusual experience.

As I went about preparing to leave and walked from our bungalow to the hall where Baba sat, I began to understand the True Nature of my experience. What Baba had Transmitted to me via words that, at first, seemed not to penetrate my mind and heart had now been Awakened in me as the living Truth. I had Awakened as the egoless True Self, the One Who is the Witness, the Ultimate Reality of the ancient Scriptures!

Whereas human beings ordinarily remain conscious as the capsule entity contained in the body, I had Awakened as the One Who truly is the Life and Consciousness of the body and all things. I had seen the transformation of that Life and Consciousness, as It moved from Its own Absolute and most Prior State, down through the levels of the living being, toward bodily consciousness. I had seen bodily consciousness from the "Point of View" of the Self, Siva, or Siva-Shakti, the universal Being that "Lives" all things. Ordinarily, one identifies with the point of view of bodily consciousness, and either one strives to survive as that dying entity, in the face of all obstacles, or else one tries, by Spiritual effort, to attain the Realization of the Ultimate Self, or the Divine Consciousness. But I Awakened <u>as</u> that Self, and I directly perceived that everything is always and already being "Lived".

Every sense of limitation and egoic self-awareness had fallen away from me. What I had fathomed in the various difficult crises and "Bright" Illuminations of my life had been given to me whole, in a single moment of perfect Experience, without limitations of any kind. I Knew with absolute certainty that I was not the seeker or the one trapped in life, but everything was only being "Lived" by the Divine Being, and I <u>am</u> That One.

The highest Truth of all the Scriptures, East and West, had been Realized in my own conscious experience. There was no longer any need for effort, for seeking. There was no primary dilemma. I had given the Guru four days to Enlighten me, and he had given me everything, for free.

Like the prince from his horse, I fell at Baba's feet and touched them with my head. He slapped my back approvingly, and we took our leave. No mention was made of my experience. Nina and I carried our luggage to a waiting bus, and, feeling like prisoners being deported under guard, we moved out of Ganeshpuri toward America.

Mr. and Mrs. Pattani, a man and his wife who had been staying with Baba, were given charge of us for the night. We were to fly home the next morning. We traveled with Mr. Pattani by bus and train to a beautiful little town near Bombay called Mulund. Mrs. Pattani had gone on a few hours before to prepare for our arrival.

I felt so free and fulfilled, and yet sad to be leaving my Guru. I felt as if I were being taken away from the very Source of grace I had been seeking all my life. But that night, as I lay down to sleep, I experienced again the State of perfect Consciousness I had Known in the afternoon. I was pressed above into Infinite Bliss, and I passed somehow to sleep, surrendered without effort into the Motherhood of my own Being.

"Life in New York required an energy of involvement that itself 'created' conflict and the mind of effort, such that soon I began to seek the State I had Known in India. It became a problem in me to regain that State. The Condition that I had Known relieved all effort and amounted only to a free Enjoyment of perfect Knowledge. But now It began to seem unavailable, a goal requiring another kind of effort."

The apartment building where Adi Da resided
after His return from India in 1968

CHAPTER 11

The Problem of the Mind, and the Year of Waiting for Grace

When we arrived again in New York, I wrote to Baba (on April 10, 1968), to thank him for his grace. In a modest manner, spontaneously emphasizing the Vedantic (or Advaitic, rather than Yogic) aspects of what I had, at last, experienced and Realized, I described our recent visit to the Ashram, culminating in the Event of that last afternoon.

Dear Baba,

My wife, Nina, and I arrived safely and without much difficulty at about 8 P.M. (New York Time). We were worried that we would not be able to find place on the plane from Bombay to Beirut. But Mr. Pattani, whom we accompanied to Bombay, kept saying, "Baba would not have told us to leave if you were not going to be able to get away this morning." And he was right, for at the last minute there were a few cancellations and we flew away easily. As we left, we were both very sad, and it has taken us several days to adjust to being away from you. Even now as I write, my eyes are wet and I long to sit with you. As you told me one day last week, "Now I have got you." You have swiftly changed my life by directing me to the Truth and the Goal. Please do not leave me alone, now that I am far away. You have given me the seed, but I am a garden that needs much tending. I am still begging for the Shakti and right understanding, so that I will not be overcome by my own ignorance and despair.

You have told me about the value of asanas,[39] regularity of life, discrimination in diet and all other habits, and, above all, you told me to maintain myself in the Truth of Vedanta—"Identify yourself with Him Who is the Witness to the waking, dreaming, and sleeping states." When I asked you how I should do this meditation, you said, "Do nothing." All of these suggestions had an effect on me. After two days of trying merely to be relaxed in your presence, I realized that I could not "do nothing", and the Truth of Vedanta and everything else you told me seemed too dry and distant and unavailable to me. On the third day, in the morning, as soon as I sat down before you for the morning recitation, I began to work inside at surrender, and all day that day my head and back moved violently. All during the day you encouraged these movements in me and called me "Kriyananda" all that day because of them. Twice you placed your hand on me. The first time I responded by closing my eyes, twisting about, and raising my hands into mudras. The second time, in the meditation, I fell backwards away from you. At the end of that day I was exhausted from so much kriya. On the fourth and final day after the noon meal I went to the room to pack. I thought I would rest for a few minutes since I felt my last few hours at the Ashram were precious time. But as I lay down, I became very weary and felt a need to sleep. I felt myself going into a deep trance-like "sleep" in which somehow I was Blissfully Conscious. Then suddenly I became aware of my body. A sudden breath or snore came

39. Yogic postures.

through my throat, and I realized I was experiencing a Consciousness of my body that was completely detached and free. Just then Nina came into the room to rest. I continued to lie still and then fell asleep. Later we went down for the afternoon recitation. I felt sad to be leaving. You had not called me "Kriyananda" that last day. I had not yet understood the meaning of my afternoon "sleep", but I somehow felt I had your parting message and blessing with me. I felt a certain calmness, and since there was little movement I assumed that "Kriyananda" was not a name you intended for me to keep. I felt you were really leading me to a place where there is no movement (kriyas) at all.

Then, as the day went on, I began to think about my experience. I began to see that my experience in the early afternoon was of the "Witness", the Self Who is behind all the modifications of the mind. I saw then that all that you had told me earlier in our visit was not mere logic and intellectual description. It was a living Truth to be experienced consciously and in depth. And now that we have returned to New York, I recognize this Truth of the Vedanta to be the essential thing you sought to teach me. As I think about the Ashram, I realize that you are the Guru who liberates his children by leading them to experience their Identity as the Self.

This Truth, even though my deep resistance makes it impossible for me to experience It very frequently with any depth, is and will be extremely liberating for me. It is the very basis of sadhana[40] and its Goal. And It makes very clear just how I must manage myself in relation to my daily experience. This Truth is my Joy, and you,

40. Religious discipline. As Adi Da indicates here, the most potent form of sadhana is traditionally understood to be devotional surrender to the Guru.

Baba, are my Joy because you are leading me to a full Realization of this Truth. Please bless me with gratitude and surrender so that the obstacles in me will be overcome.

Nina and I long to be with you again. We send our love to all of your children.

April 10, 1968
New York

Your child,
Franklin Jones

Ever since my "trance-like" experience at Baba's Ashram, I continued to live in that "Witness-State" continually, always Aware that I was not the body or the mind, not the one who wakes or dreams or sleeps, but the Witness to all these things. It was not a mental supposition, but an actual and direct experience. It was the perfect Realization of the "Position" from Which, in seminary, I had experienced the living condition of Reality, or what I called "unqualified relatedness".

In my letter, I did not ask Baba to instruct me about what method of meditation I should adopt. After the extraordinary experience at the Ashram, all motive for effort had passed from me, and all that seemed necessary was a gentle concentration in my own Self-Nature.

In my daily living I simply rested in the Awareness that everything is being "Lived". In meditation, I passed into the inclusive Fullness of Real Consciousness, transcending all thought and perception. There was no sense of dilemma in me. When I was not rested in my own primary Nature as the True Self, or Reality, I would perceive that same Nature as a Presence that surrounded me and all things.

When I met Rudi, the signs of my transformation were obvious. I felt no need at all to engage in the form of exercise he prescribed. And when I went to his class and performed it as usual, the kriyas and the sense of internal conflict that motivated me in that work appeared again, and I could feel it as a familiar knot or cramp in my solar plexus. Thus, I began to see Rudi less and less, although there was no argument between us and no communication of the difference.

For the first two or three weeks after our return to New York, I lived and felt and Knew as the Divine Itself. There was no division, no act of separation, in the living consciousness. There were no distracting tendencies, no impurities, and not a trace of dilemma. But, gradually, as the weeks passed, I began to observe the piecemeal return of old sensations and thoughts, then the desires that follow them, and then the actual practice of old habits. When I would sit to meditate in the "effortless" manner, I would feel these old problems. And it became a matter of conflict in me somehow to make these feelings vanish.

Life in New York required an energy of involvement that itself "created" conflict and the mind of effort, such that soon I began to seek the State I had Known in India. It became a problem in me to regain that State. The Condition that I had Known relieved all effort and amounted only to a free Enjoyment of perfect Knowledge. But now It began to seem unavailable, a goal requiring another kind of effort.

At first this change was only subtly perceived. I could not accept the fact that I had lost the fundamental Realization to Which I had Awakened at the Ashram. But, gradually, I began to discover, to my horror and despair, that the mind and all its conflict of desire was rising again, untouched by any Illumination.

This became a very disturbing reversal for me. I had thought that the ascent to Clear Awareness of my True Nature would be sufficient to destroy every vestige of clinging to the habitual influences of the mind. I had thought that the ascended Knowledge would be purification enough, so that life need only be lived (and Witnessed) under the direct presumption of What I am in Reality.

But this ascended Knowledge was not enough. And I had not yet become consistently stabilized in the "Witness-Position" Itself (nor, until the last, did I Realize most perfect Identification with Its Source-Condition). Therefore, the mind in conflict arose by itself and brought with it all desires and every motive for seeking. Yet, I was unwilling to adapt myself to effort and strife again. I felt that my Ashram experience had most profoundly extended my experience of the Reality that Awakened in me during my crisis in seminary. But now the Ashram experience, because it held before the mind a kind of proof of the Ultimate Nature I had sought, served as a goad to seeking, a ground for the demand for that revelation as a continuous State.

I waited for a letter from Baba, hoping that it would bring a new blessing and clarify my trouble. But the weeks passed without a word, and I felt stuck with a vision of internal contradiction that even exceeded the one from which I had been relieved in college.

Now the mind itself, apart from any particular content, appeared as the source of dilemma, and I wondered by what means the mind should pass and let me be.

Baba had all but told me to abandon my relationship with Rudi. For my own part, the motivation toward Rudi's kind of "work" had already, entirely passed. But I felt no need to condemn Rudi, and the gossip (at Baba's Ashram) that opposed him seemed only a social manifestation of particular Indian predilections for habits and behaviors that Rudi did not appear to exemplify. I needed very much to be free of that limitation that had been my search in Rudi's company, but I was not in any sense opposed to him. Indeed, just as his way had been appropriate for me at a particular stage in my development, I felt it remained appropriate for him at his stage of development, and even for anyone else who was at a stage, and in a disposition, wherein they could benefit from such a disciplining of their ordinary lives.

Nevertheless, life had emerged as a totally different matter for me. I was convinced that the way of egoic effort was simply a further manifestation of life lived as a problem, a motivated search. Yet, the mind, and the entire habitual pattern of life, appeared to me to be a source of difficulty, which in fact prevented the continuous assumption of life on a radically free basis.

Baba's own way was peculiarly tied to Indian notions and methods. Although he suggested these to me, he did not seek to enforce any kind of method in my case. It all seemed a suggestive communication that should lead me to my own Truth. He even told me that I would eventually teach the ways of Spiritual life, in a year or so. But he did not tell me what to teach. I took his teaching (and my experience) on the broadest level, to be freely and meaningfully adapted to my own case.

As the old problems began to arise, all I could do was observe them. Baba's methods seemed to be of no use to me. I stopped meditating. I did no reading. I dissolved back into the ordinary life of the city.

In the midst of that spontaneous ordinariness, Nina and I received a letter from Baba (which he had written on April 23, but which had taken many weeks to be translated and delivered to us).

— Om —

Dear Franklin and Nina,

My loving remembrance and blessing to you.

All is well here, hope the same there. Through your letter I received all the news. It is a matter of joy that you consider me as your Guru. You are inclined to Self-realization, you are devoted to Truth, you have practiced penance to obtain the joy of Self—this is very good. Yours is a praiseworthy endeavor because the Soul is an inner-treasure, It is perfect, It is One. This Soul is the Knower of all thoughts, It is Omniscient, yet It is neither a subject of logic nor can It be known through the intellect, because who can reveal THAT which reveals all? Who can bring to light the Sun which itself lights up the entire Universe?

The Soul is the Light, the Enlightener, and the Enlightened. It reveals Its own nature and reveals other things as well.

There is a Divine Light within you which is as shining as the flame of a fire, as bright as the light of the Sun, as radiant as the red-hot Gold. The Soul is not a thing to be strived after—It is ever present in us; but not visible to those who have not received the Guru's grace. The Soul IS. Because of Its presence in the body men love each other, they get mutually attached and feel satisfied through cordial relationship. The Soul, which gives inner joy, is in reality the Divine Light of God. The devout see Him in varied names, forms, and colors. However, He is not many—He is One. Though He has many names, He is *"So'ham"*. Although He belongs to the Hindus, Mohammedans, Christians, and Parsis,[41] He is different from them all, and similarly though belonging to the Yogis He is different from the Yoga, though grantor of the fruits of actions He is different from the doer, though bestower of the reward of the sacrifice He is different from the sacrificer, though understood through the Scriptures He is different from the Scriptures; in the field of knowledge—though realized through knowledge—He is different from the knower and the known.

All the various creeds and faiths, all the religious organizations and societies the world over, worship Him, through their own set rules and disciplines. As a matter of fact He is the all-adorable, the ever perfect, the inner essence, the *Atman*[42] of all. Some people search Him in the sky above, some in the Earth below, some in

41. Zoroastrians, or followers of the teachings of the ancient Persian religious Teacher Zoroaster.

42. A Sanskrit term for the Supreme Divine Self.

the monastery, temple, mosque, church; some others in the forest, in the seclusions, in the caves and mountains, in the rivers, lakes, streams, oceans, and even dry deserts; still others try to find Him in the sweetness of fruits, in the fragrance of flowers, in the song of the cuckoo, in the dance of the peacock, in the beauty of the butterfly, and so on. Thus, through various paths, in various things, everyone is searching Him only.

My dear Franklin and Nina! But He is within you. He, the *Atman* of all, is the Inner Being of yours and mine too. He is the darling pupil of the eye. That *Atman* is a clean place for our rest and respite, the strongest fortress for us to live fearlessly and peacefully, the liberator from bondage. That very essence is named by the *Vedanta* as *Sat-chid-anand* (Absolute Truth, Knowledge, and Bliss). That very *Atman* or Essence is Ram and Rahim,[43] Krishna and Karim,[44] Jesus and Moses as well. He is the sole support of all. This universe is a manifestation of His infinite play. Putting on the twine forms of man and woman, He—the Great Being—exists in both. Verily these are like the two facets of the self-same coin—named *Purusha-Prakriti* or *Shiva-Shakti*[45]—and this world is the expansion of these two.

43. Ram (also spelled "Rama") is a legendary Divine Avatar worshipped by many Hindus. He is the hero of the *Ramayana*, one of the greatest of the Hindu religious epics.

Rahim is an Islamic Name for Allah, meaning "the Merciful".

44. Krishna is the legendary Divine Avatar who is most widely worshipped in India. He is the hero of the *Bhagavad Gita* (and the longer *Mahabharata*, of which the *Bhagavad Gita* is an excerpt) and the *Srimad Bhagavatam*.

Karim is an Islamic Name for Allah, meaning "the Generous".

45. The Sanskrit terms "Purusha-Prakriti" and "Shiva-Shakti" are esoteric descriptions of the Divine Being. "Purusha" and "Shiva" are names for the Divine Being Itself, or Divine Consciousness. "Prakriti" and "Shakti" are names for the All-Pervading Spirit-Power of the Divine Being. "Purusha-Prakriti", or "Shiva-Shakti", is thus the Unity of the Divine Consciousness and Its own Spirit-Power.

He and He alone is in you and in your wife; and He again pervades the entire world. Usually an unfortunate one does not have the desire to know Him. But those who are greatly meritorious ardently wish to know Him (to know the *Atman*) and they do succeed also.

Just as there is fire (latent) in a dry stick of wood (which ignites by friction and burns up the stick completely); just as oil lies hidden in the sesamum seed; just as there is butter in the curd; in the same way the Divine Shakti is lying hidden in the human body. It is active in the ordinary sense but to awaken the same through the Guru's grace, to experience Its uncommon activities, and to realize It directly is the highest religion of men. That which helps to manifest the inner Divine Shakti is "TRUE RELIGION"; and he who perceives that Divine Shakti, in Its innate form, is "TRULY RELIGIOUS". This inner Shakti is known as *Atman*, and is worshipped by uttering *"Om"* or *"So'ham"*. *So'ham* is the means for Its meditation, *So'ham* again is the *mantra* for Its worship. Heart is Its church. The natural sound *So'ham* does not belong to the Indians and the Hindus alone, the same *word-sound* exists in all living beings and is active too. Really speaking with regard to *mantra* there is no consideration like community, creed, or country. If someone thinks that a *mantra* belongs to a particular faith or country, believe me he knows nothing.

A great Yogini[46] of Kashmir has said: "A devotee who believes that the universe is the manifested form of God and that He resides in all beings as their own selves, for him which place will not be a temple? Which *mantra* will not bear fruit?" In other words, any *mantra* that

46. A female practitioner of Yoga.

a devotee would utter or recite will surely be
fruitful—for *mantra* is the form of God. When
even an abuse or a mean word affects a person
(mentally), how can a *mantra* which is a holy
word not achieve its sacred purpose?

Dear Franklin, sitting calm and steady repeat
the *mantra* together with rhythmic breathing
(i.e., the inhalation and exhalation of air—*pran*
and *apan*). Harmonize the repetition of *mantra*
with the breathing as follows: With *"So"* take it in
and with *"ham"* bring it out. Throughout the
mantra-repetition one should follow this practice. Simply sitting peacefully and applying the
mind to the *pran* and *apan* one enters into deep
state of meditation. When one's mind is fixed on
"So" with the incoming breath and on *"ham"* with
the outgoing breath it is *mantra-japa*. The regularity with which the breath comes in and goes
out is *pranayama*. And if a person is skillful,
intelligent, and alert—the (1) *repetition of
mantra (japa)*, the process of (2) *pranayama*,
and the (3) *meditation*—all the three can be
achieved simultaneously without difficulty. This
is like the kingfisher bird whose sole attention is
the fish in water. The bird is known for its all-
exclusive *concentration*, a kind of meditation.
And when it suddenly dives to catch the fish, two
more things are achieved simultaneously—he has
a good *bath* and enjoys a hearty *meal*. This is a
great Yoga, the best among all: known as *Siddha
Yoga*.[47] It means "the path of the Perfect Ones"
or "the Yoga which begets perfection". A dex-
trous and highly intelligent person can practice it

47. "Siddha", in Sanskrit, means "a completed, fulfilled, or perfected one", or
"one of perfect accomplishment, or power". Siddha Yoga, then, is "the Yoga of
the Perfected Ones". In Swami Muktananda's usage, Siddha Yoga is the Kundalini Yoga Taught by him in which the Spiritual Transmission of the Siddha-
Guru awakens the Kundalini Shakti in the devotee.

easily. As explained above, the regular practice of meditation with a concentrated mind will awaken the dormant Kundalini Shakti in a very short time. As a result, some inner activities also begin to operate. Day-by-day as the Shakti develops more and more It takes the aspirant to the ultimate perfection. Just as a child grows daily, with due nourishment, and becomes a youth in course of time; just as a seed sown in the soil gradually develops into a tree; in the same manner the daily practice of *sadhana* (spiritual discipline) leads one to Perfection by the Guru's grace.

In the *"So'ham" mantra*—*"So"* signifies God or Guru, and *"ham"* denotes "I" or "me". Thus *So'ham* means "I am He". Let your practice of meditation be accompanied by the ceaseless reflection on the above meaning of *So'ham*. In every human being there lies a hidden store of unlimited contentment, inexhaustible love, and infinite joy—these can be realized through the regular practice of meditation. As one thinks so one becomes. If a man thinks all the time about his faults and sins he would become sinful. Similarly the constant thought about woman, man, meditation or Guru would make him womanish, manly, meditative or the Guru—respectively. This is quite natural because a person gets transformed into the likeness of the object on which he constantly ponders, by absorbing its qualities.

Man is indeed great. But he has lost his greatness and has fallen due to his constant dealings with the external world and attachment to sense-objects. Internally he is not lacking anything, he is full and perfect with the Divine Light and yet in vain he is searching for the "Fulfillment" outside. The factory, workshop, business office, and shop; the varied professions like engineering, medicine, legal practice, and many other trades—all these are merely means to livelihood, they cannot procure things of lasting value to men. As I said above, man is perfect within, and this can be directly experienced through meditation, whereupon one feels fully contented. Just as you become entirely free of the outside thoughts and anxieties in deep sleep and feel happy; similarly in the introspective tendency or in the meditation on *Atman* lie peace, respite, and undisturbed equanimity.

The real beauty, the essence of savory taste, the celestial music, the most soothing touch, and the sweetest fragrance—all lie inside. The Yogis who have experienced them within consider the outer things just ordinary. When through meditation the Kundalini is awakened then, by Guru's love and his grace all the latent faculties are automatically activated and one attains perfection in due time. Besides, he also obtains the power of omniscience which lies hidden in the heart. In what words can I express the beauty of inner Light! It is unparalleled; all lights of the outer world are too dim and unpleasant before It. Similarly, in front of the inner celestial music our worldly music is crude and jarring. The relish of a drop of inner juice is so wonderful that all the worldly savors put together are really nothing in comparison. This inner nectar is a Divine ambrosia, the inner touch is too subtle and great to be described, for it is a Divine touch. You attain through meditation this supreme ambrosia-of-love on which the inner Shakti is nourished and which is a gift from the Guru obtained by the disciple through penance.

Dear Franklin, there is not anything in this world which cannot be achieved through meditation. In the practice of meditation, there is a highly miraculous and splendid Shakti which is beyond human comprehension. It is best to practice a natural meditation or *dhyan*. I will explain to you what it is or how it is to be practiced: Sit quietly, calm and composed, if you like in *padmasana*,[48] or any other comfortable posture. You may look and fix the eyes on a photo or may keep your eyes closed. The mode and posture in which you can be restful, mentally free from the objective world, and introspective, that is the best *asan* for you. What I mean to convey by "Don't do anything" is this—remove the mind from its activities, arrest all kinds of desires and surrender to whatever is happening of its own accord, observe everything as a witness. That is why I say practice the meditation in a natural way. The meditation done by the inner Shakti is the meditation of Guru's grace, it is the real meditation of *"So'ham"*, indeed it is the meditation of God— these are not different kinds of meditations but they are synonymous expressions. Tell me, if the man is not aware of this Shakti or is not awakened to It, what is the purpose of this body of flesh? If this Shakti were not there one would not have liked or been attracted to the body made of flesh, bones, blood, muscles, skin, etc. Activator of the breathing process, Inspirer of the intellect, Contemplator of the mind is the same as inner Shakti, inner Consciousness. The only worthy purpose of this otherwise impure physical body is to dedicate it whole-heartedly to seek the Inner Being.

48. The lotus posture, the classic oriental seated pose for meditation. In padmasana one sits and crosses the legs so that the right foot rests on the left thigh and the left foot rests on the right thigh. The resulting posture is very stable and may be maintained for a long time.

Your beauty, your energy, your duty, your religion, your Guru and guide; your study, worship and prayer—all lie in engaging yourself to the remembrance and repetition of *"So'ham"*, *"So'ham"*. This is my instruction, this is my precept. This is to be followed or practiced, and reflected upon devoutly. The deeper and deeper you go in meditation the more and more of the Divine experiences you will attain. Therefore, seek your inner Self, therefrom you will have the fulfillment you cherish.

With blessings,
Yours
Swami Muktananda

April 23, 1968
Ganeshpuri
India

Baba's letter was a lovely poetic document, and it contained a unique summary of the instructions on meditation that, I assumed, Baba characteristically gave to those who received his Shakti-Initiation. However, the letter did not otherwise directly address my own fullest experience and my state of understanding. After I read it, I simply sat in place, as if expecting something further, more direct, more useful, more conclusive. Then, suddenly, I felt the space of the room expand in a curious manner, and I felt Baba's actual Presence. The Shakti moved up my back and produced that characteristic Bliss in the body and the mind, and I sat for a long time enjoying his Presence, waiting for some kind of message or advice. But there was no "answer". All I could do was observe myself, and wait.

A full year passed. I did not meditate. But I only observed myself, lived an ordinary life, and waited for the "wall" of mind to break. Therefore, I remained devoted to the understanding (rather than merely to the "solution") of the "problem" of the mind. And all the while, the Shakti, the manifesting Energy that proceeds from the Ultimate Source-Reality, or the Divine Consciousness, grew (and showed signs) in me daily, while I did nothing but wait.

During that year, the Shakti grew in me like a fetus in the womb, waiting to be born. While I waited, I constantly observed and considered the mind, which had become, for me, the single "problem" and the most fundamental "obstacle" to the free Realization of Consciousness and Bliss. Then, one evening, in the spring of 1969, while I was in the midst of a several-week visit to Los Angeles, California, the Shakti spontaneously rushed into the form of my living being with tremendous Power, so that I was no longer even remotely concerned with the petty contaminations of the mind. I was suddenly returned to an experience of my Self-Nature and a sublime Awareness of the Divinity of even the physical world. As a result of this Spiritual "birth", I once again lived entirely in the sublime sphere of Free Consciousness, making no effort at all to maintain or "create" It.

In the weeks that followed, I became spontaneously aware of a new dimension of the activity of the Shakti. Not only was my own experiential state expanded in Its Presence, but the people who were closest to me began (even as they had in the previous months, but now more profoundly and increasingly) to experience the effects of the Shakti through contact with me.

At first I merely talked to these friends about my understanding of Real Spiritual life, and they began to discover parallels to this understanding in their own experiences and doubts. Then they began to have uncommon experiences of a Presence that affected them separately and in different ways while they were otherwise apart from me.

These experiences took the form of visions, or the sensation of a real but invisible Presence, or the sense of being sublimed and surrounded in a form of Energy and

Fullness that quieted and clarified the mind. They would ask me about these experiences, and, before long, I found myself having to function as a teacher and an instrument for the Shakti.

I was so profoundly drawn into that Shakti-Consciousness that I found no difficulty in speaking to people about the Spiritual process and making recommendations that seemed wholly intelligent and even inspired. At times I even experienced feeling-perceptions of a psychic nature. I would feel auras of light about the person, or find the person's thoughts appearing in my mind, or intuitively locate the person's thoughts or feelings or states via visual, or otherwise simply feeling, reveries in relation to his or her forehead or body. I would also, via feeling, become directly aware of the Shakti as It passed through these people or was expressed in them, and I could easily trace the currents of Energy and see where they became concentrated, halted, or obstructed at the various vital points, or "chakras". On more than one occasion, in spontaneous visual reveries, I saw Baba appear and Initiate a person with the Shakti by touch, and I could likewise see, or intuitively feel and perceive, a blue light appear and surround the person's body.

But the most common and always most fundamental experience was one in which my own living being (and that of everyone I saw) was contained in the inclusive Force of the Shakti Itself. Thus, I needed no uncommon visionary communications in order to intuit the nature of anyone's existence, experience, or problem. These things were simply obvious to me on the level of uncommunicated, or direct and tacit, Knowledge. I lived in an inclusive intelligence that was not limited to my reflective awareness or my ability to read "signs". I simply knew the verity of what I perceived and had no fundamental (or otherwise "problematic") sense of living as a separate, conditioned entity.

As all of this became more and more obvious and continuous, I remembered Baba's statement that I would become a Spiritual teacher in about a year. Now this Event was occurring, spontaneously, even without my volition or control. I wrote to Baba and informed him about my experience. I told him that I felt I needed instruction in the conscious use of these abilities. And I said that I did not wish to carry on this teaching process without his consent and blessing. I asked him to give me the authority to teach in this way, and to bless me in the traditional manner by giving me a Spiritual name. Baba replied by telling me to come to India as soon as possible.

Bombay, August 1969

CHAPTER 12

The Return to India, and the Problem of Spiritual Consciousness

I flew to Bombay alone and arrived there on August 3. Peter Dias met me at the airport, and we took a taxi to the home of one of Baba's devotees in Bombay proper. Baba was to arrive that morning for an extended stay in the city, away from the Ashram.

He arrived about 11 A.M. I bowed at his feet and gave him a few gifts I had brought from America. Then there was a brief discussion about my trip. I would spend four weeks constantly in Baba's Presence, but this brief conversation was to be virtually the only one we would have from that moment. (Just previous to my leaving, I addressed him about an experience I had in meditation, but I did not otherwise have any personal discussions with him.)

I realized at that early moment (shortly after my arrival in Bombay) that I did not have a "personal" relationship with Baba. Fundamentally, he did not appear to me as a human individual. There was not the slightest movement of interest on my part in his personal attitudes, or anything that amounted to personality. But neither did I perceive myself as a personality in any fundamental sense. The revolution in my understanding of the mind and the ordinary adventure had finally removed any sense that I operated (fundamentally) on the level of character and personal life.

The discussion of my trip, brief as it was, seemed almost nonsensical, totally beside the point. It was

required of us under the circumstances, and it was handled as a formality, but afterwards there was not a single
attempt on Baba's part to communicate with me verbally.
And, apart from bowing to him as I entered or left the
room, I did not communicate with Baba socially (or, in
the ordinary sense, "man to man").

After my initial discussion with him, I retired to a position several feet away and in front of Baba. I sat quietly,
concentrated on Baba, and withdrew my attention
within. Apart from a brief trip to spend a few days at
Baba's Ashram and the burial shrine of Swami Nityananda, I spent the next four weeks sitting in this large
meeting room or meditating in the area that adjoined
Baba's bedroom.

We were staying in the expansive but very modestly
appointed apartments of Ram Pratap, a captain in the
Indian navy. At night I slept on a hard single cot in a
small room, where there was also another visitor (and
sometimes several others). During the day and evening
hundreds of people would come to sit in Baba's Presence, chant devotional hymns, and enjoy meals prepared
by the women as an offering to Baba. In the early afternoon I would sometimes take exercise by walking in the
nearby streets of Bombay. Sometimes I would go to a
bookstore, or have a cab drive me through the city. But
the constant routine was to arise at 5 A.M., meditate, and
sit with Baba for hours at a time. I would eat a light meal
twice a day and rest briefly after lunch. And I would
meditate almost constantly, either sitting before Baba or
by retiring to the small room behind him. I was rarely
involved in conversations, but I passed through the
weeks in a perpetual silence and internal solitude,
observing the unusual phenomena that were arising in
the field of my awareness.

My own state at the time was uncommon. I no
longer was engaged in a continual experience of the
mind rising in thoughts, impulses, and memories. This
had ceased to occupy or interest me. Instead there was

a continuous simple awareness, aware of, not thoughts in the concrete mind, but forms of Energy, of space, and of vision, and otherwise persisting simply as free conscious awareness itself, without conflict, dilemma, or identification with bodily limits.

As I sat with Baba, I wondered if he could perceive my internal state. The brevity of our conversation seemed to indicate that he was aware that personal communication was only a formality and a distraction for me. Then, as I sat meditatively in his Presence, I became aware of existence totally beyond the physical body. My awareness moved in a space that was not in the concrete mind. I swooned and floated in a limitless void that was luminous with cosmic Force. As I moved in that space, I sensed that Baba was also with me. I wondered if he was aware of this cosmic adventure of Spiritual being, and I opened my eyes. He was looking at me, smiling and swaying his head as if to imitate the movement of conscious awareness in limitless space. I smiled back at him, and took this sign as an acknowledgement of my own state. From then I assumed that Baba knew why I had returned to him, and I looked to experience his teaching on a purely internal level.

My first impression of Baba and his teaching, which I had experienced at the Ashram a year before, was, among other things, of a communication on a verbal and personal level. There was a personal relationship, a practical philosophy, and a consistent address to my personal problems and seeking. Thus, Baba had concentrated on teaching me philosophy, methods of purification and meditation, approaches to various obstacles in life, and so on.

However, as a result of my year of "waiting" (and of mere observation of the mind), I no longer resided in the limited view of the personal problem and its psychology. I had become conscious of a present activity within the domain of mere awareness itself. I had begun to intuit the data in consciousness on a level that transcended the concrete and personal instrument.

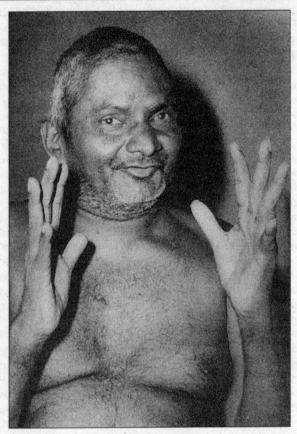

Swami Nityananda

"Then I saw the image of Swami Nityananda. He was facing me as I had seen him in a photograph, with a wide expression in his face and eyes, as if he were beholding some perceptible form of the Divine. His hands were raised to the sides of his face, and his fingers and palms spread, containing and generating a tremendous Force of Blissful Energy."

I felt that I had now begun to realize experience on a new level. The forms in consciousness were no longer of a mostly personal nature, implying a separate and human identity as its basis. Now I perceived the contents of consciousness as forms of Energy and superconsciousness, above the level of the concrete mind.

When I sat in Baba's Presence or in meditation, I was immediately, spontaneously drawn to concentrate at the "Point" in the aperture of the head, in the crown, and even above the head. Thus, I focused in uncommon perceptions of the universal Shakti. Baba seemed to recognize this and made no effort to approach me personally, even with common friendliness. It was as if he felt such communication would only awaken and reinforce the activity of identification on a lower level.

Thus, I left myself and was left by those around me to experience existence purely on a Spiritual or superconscious level. And I spent my month in India in constant meditation on this level of perception. I began also to experience Communication from Baba entirely on the level of intuitive consciousness, without the addition of verbal address. It was a time of God-like existence.

Shortly after lunch on the first day of my visit, I received Baba's blessing in the form of a new arousal of the Shakti Energy. Baba came from behind me and entered the large sitting room as if to pass to his seat. I expected him simply to pass by. But he stopped suddenly and patted me on the head several times. Then he went on to his seat in the corner of the room.

I remained seated on the floor with the others, listening to Baba's conversation with various visitors. But as the minutes passed, I felt a strong Energy in my back that soon took over my entire spine and body. The Shakti finally concentrated very Powerfully in the head, particularly at the very top, where I had been experiencing the urge to meditate.

After about half an hour I passed naturally into very deep meditation. I was concentrated and contained in

247

the Shakti at a superconscious level. The kriyas in the body were almost entirely absent. Then I saw the image of Swami Nityananda. He was facing me as I had seen him in a photograph, with a wide expression in his face and eyes, as if he were beholding some perceptible form of the Divine. His hands were raised to the sides of his face, and his fingers and palms spread, containing and generating a tremendous Force of Blissful Energy.

After several minutes this image disappeared, and I took over the form of Swami Nityananda myself. My eyelids opened wide, and my eyes rolled up toward the top of my head. And my hands rose up beside my face. The palms and fingers splayed, and I could feel the Shakti flowing in my body and my head, passing out toward Baba in benediction. I sat like this for perhaps an hour. I experienced only an Absolute Bliss and Calm, and an overwhelming Power flowed through me into the room. I felt myself behold and hold a Sphere of Energy in my hands. And then I saw that It was Reality Itself, the Form and Force of all existence, including all the universes and every conditionally manifested form.

When at last I opened my eyes and resumed my ordinary state in the body, Baba was standing beside me in the room. We smiled at each other, and he reached toward me. I reached out to him with my hand, and we grasped each other's hands in the Blissful Communication of that Energy.

It became my practice to rise every morning at 5 A.M. and sit outside Baba's room for meditation. A few others also sat around in silent meditation at the same time. Baba would come out a few minutes later and sit on some cushions against the wall, two or three feet in front of me. He did this for the first two or three mornings of my visit, as if to watch my meditation.

Finally, about the third morning, I had been sitting for nearly an hour. Meditation had become an immense problem. My mind was filled with all kinds of alternative programs and techniques. I battled with Rudi's method, then Baba's, with mantras coordinated with breathing, watching thoughts arise, and concentration in various chakras, or functional centers. Soon I became merely confused and unsettled, and I intended to question Baba about meditation when I sat with him in company later in the morning.

But then Baba came out and sat before me in silence. And soon I began to experience an internal teaching about meditation. I was shown the various internal centers and the various activities in the mind. Then I saw the Shakti rising out of the "muladhar", the lowest chakra, near the anus. And It rose of Itself through the various centers. As It rose, each event in the natural process of meditation took place automatically. The breath became even, and it began to coordinate itself with the mind. I saw how the breath affects thought, and how thought affects the breath. Then a concentration replaced this activity of passive observation. Attention was directed above, between the brows, and then in the sahasrar, the highest internal center, in the crown of the head.

Each breath became not a mere physical process but a process directed by the Shakti, and from the arising-place of attentive awareness itself, rather than from any merely functional focal point in the extended body-mind. With each inhalation I felt the Shakti move out of the heart, down to the muladhar, then up the spine, and center at the top of the head. Then, for a moment, the breath would halt, and I would enjoy a concentration and reception of Energy and Bliss above. Then, with each exhalation, the Shakti would move down from the crown of the head and return to the Stillness of Effortless Being in the heart. As this process continued, attention and Energy sublimed into a Blissful Awareness, an unqualified and yet also natural form of participation in the Root-Conditions of the Source-Reality.

After a while Baba left the room. I gradually returned to my ordinary state of bodily awareness, and I went in to sit with him and his visitors. I wondered how much of this experience had been either deliberately "created" by him or at least consciously observed by him. I sought some evidence of the verity of internal Communication between Baba and myself.

When I came into the room, Baba was busy writing on a notepad. After a while he spoke to someone, and I was told that he was writing something for me. Later someone came and showed me what he had written. It was written in Hindi or Sanskrit and would have to be translated. But I was told that Baba had given me a formal renunciate name, and that he would bless me with it (and, thus and thereby, with the right to teach, and with the gift of the perpetual option of formal renunciation) on August 9, the anniversary of Swami Nityananda's mahasamadhi (or abandonment of the physical body).

Baba had apparently kept his promise to instruct me and give me a name, as well as the right to teach. But, as in all cases of gifts from a teacher, the reception in the disciple can act as a test. I immediately felt this fulfillment rise up as a barrier in me of pride and self-consciousness. When people go to a teacher, they get only as much as they seek or desire. Thus, I saw that if I made this gift the object of my stay, I would close myself off to the greater experience that I truly desired.

I nodded to Baba and thanked him, but I made no move after that to appear as if absorbed in that gift. And, as it happened, that gift was held before me by various delays and complications for nearly two weeks. The people around Baba felt his message had to be translated perfectly. Thus, it was handed from person to person, a professor of English was awaited, there were disagreements on certain words, there was no time to type a final copy. The Indian devotees seemed reluctant to give the letter to me at all, and they continually minimized its importance, although it was the first time a Westerner had formally, publicly, and in writing been given a name by Baba. I was eventually told that I had been named "Dhyananda", which means "One Who Realizes (or,

Has Realized) The Divine Being-Existence, Consciousness, And Bliss Through Deeply Meditative self-Surrender", or (as Vishwas Yande, one of Baba's closest Indian devotees, told me) "One Whose Bliss Is In Absolute Surrender To His Innermost Self", or, most properly, "One Who Realizes (or, Has Realized) The Divine Self-Condition (Of Unalloyed Bliss, Infinite Consciousness, And Eternal Being-Existence) Through True And Spiritual Meditation On (And, Altogether, One-Pointed And Absolute self-Surrender To) His Own True (or, Divine Supreme Inner) Self". It had earlier been indicated to me privately (by Amma) that Baba had named me "Love-Ananda" (meaning "One Who Is The Divine Love-Bliss", or "One Who Is, And Manifests, The Divine Love-Bliss", or, most properly, "One Who Is The Inherent Bliss, Infinite Consciousness, And Eternal Being-Existence Of The Transcendental, And Inherently Spiritual, Divine Person And Self-Condition, Manifesting As Infinite, Or Boundless, Love-Bliss, And As Universal, And All-Blissful, Love Toward all beings"), but now the name "Dhyananda" had also been "created" for me, because of that morning of internal teaching about meditation. Therefore, by publicly giving me this name "Dhyananda", Baba showed me that I could rely on the verity of non-verbal teaching.

The day of Swami Nityananda's mahasamadhi passed. I thought perhaps Baba had forgotten. But as I sat in the rear of the room in the evening, Baba arose to go to bed, and he suddenly glanced toward me and said: "Dhyananda!" I bowed to him and acknowledged the blessing.

The Indian devotees told me that Baba's letter to me would be prepared and given to me on August 15, the twenty-fifth anniversary of the day on which he was blessed with Divine vision by his Guru, Swami Nityananda. But even that day passed with no indications from anyone. Finally, as I lay down to go to sleep, Amma, Baba's secretary, quickly entered the room and left again, leaving me Baba's original handwritten letter (in combined Hindi and Sanskrit) and a typed copy of a first translation of it into English.

Even after many days of translation work, the letter yet remained in a more or less primitive form, and further translation work was clearly going to be required if Baba's language, meaning, and intention were to be rightly honored and fully revealed. Therefore, I include the letter here in its ultimate full (and appropriately elaborated) English translation:

Shree Gurudev [49]

To my dear (beloved) "N" (Franklin), with my loving remembrances of you (even of your Very Self):

You have Done (and really Experienced) the "Sadhana" (or constant Discipline, Ordeal, and Process) of (True and Spiritual) "Dhyana" (or Meditation), and you have (Thereby) Attained the (True and Spiritual) State of Meditation. You have (by Means of True and Spiritual Meditation) Achieved the Steady State of "Samadhan(a)" (or one-pointed Concentration, or Inherence, In, and tacit, or mindless, Identification With, the Divine Supreme Inner Self). Therefore, you have Acquired (or Achieved) the Fullness of Satisfaction, Delight, and Joy in and by Means of (True and Spiritual) Meditation.

Because it is (Thus) Evident that (the Perfect Realization of the Divine Supreme Inner Self by Means of True and Spiritual) Meditation Is the (Great and Single) Purpose of your life (and, indeed, the Very Truth In Which you are, now

---

49. "Shree" (also spelled "Sri") is a term of honor and veneration often applied to a Spiritual Realizer. The word literally means "flame" in Sanskrit, indicating that the one honored is radiant with Divine Blessing Power.

"Gurudev" is a traditional Sanskrit designation for one's Guru. It literally means "Divine Guru".

and always, deeply Concentrated), you are Hereby Given the Name Dhyanananda.

In the Path (Sphere, Tradition, Line, and Lineage) of Yoga, you (by Virtue of this Declaration) will (or, by Right, can) henceforth be Known (Called, Addressed, or Referred to) as (or by the Name of) Dhyanananda.

You are a True Bearer of the Wealth of the Knowledge of Siddha Yoga, as It is Given at (Shree) Gurudev Ashram. The Kundalini Shakti, Which (by Grace) Gives (Grants, or Bestows) and Accomplishes Siddha Yoga, Is Actively at Work in you.

Likewise, you are a True Knower (or Actual, and potentially Perfect, Realizer) of Vedanta. The (Divine Supreme Inner) Self, Which Is the Secret (and the Ultimate Truth) of Vedanta, and Which Is the Very Basis (Foundation, or Root) of True Religion (or the Way of Truth), and Which (or Perfect Realization of Which, or Perfectly Absorbed Identification With Which) Is the (True, and Ultimate) Goal of human life, has been Awakened, and Is Awake, in you by Means of the Active Work of the (Kundalini) Shakti (or Divine Power).

"Only one who has actually seen (or experienced) a particular something can testify (or bear true witness) to it (or speak with authority relative to its existence and its nature, and otherwise affirm, authenticate, certify, prove, manifest, show, or demonstrate it)." Based on this Principle (or the obvious reasonableness of this Argument), you (because of your direct Experience and Knowledge of Kundalini Shakti Meditation and, Thereby, of the Divine Supreme Inner Self) have, in accordance with Tradition, both the (Hereby Affirmed) Actual Ability and the Inherent (and Hereby Affirmed) Right to

THE KNEE OF LISTENING

Initiate, or Cause, (True and Spiritual) Meditation in others (or, altogether, to Teach, Initiate, Establish, Guide, and Awaken others in the Practice, the Process, and the, Ultimately, Perfect Realization of Siddha Yoga Meditation, or True and Spiritual Meditation on, and, Ultimately, Perfect Realization of, the Divine Supreme Inner Self by Means of the Kundalini Shakti Transmitted, and Directly Activated, by you).

With an Authority based on this same Principle (of Experience itself), the Scriptures Testify and Declare (and I, likewise, Affirm to you) that, if you have Faith (or genuine Trust) in the Guru, and if you (persistently) Meditate on your (Inherent) Oneness with the Divine Being, and if you Maintain an "Equal Eye" of Regard toward all human beings, the Goddess, Chitti Kundalini,[50] will (always) Help (and Support) you Fully, and She will not only Grant you the appropriate (or right) enjoyment of (human) life (or the appropriate natural, or ordinary, fulfillments of human life), but She will also "Fill" (or Perfectly Fulfill) you with (the Gift of Ultimate, Perfect, and Final) Liberation.

Therefore, May you (by the Grace of the Goddess, Chitti Kundalini) Realize (or Obtain and Achieve) Perfect Absorption In, and Perfect Identification, and Perfect Sameness, With, the Divine Being, and This by Means of the Perfect Fulfillment of your Primary Duty, Which Is to Worship the Divine Being by Meditating on your (Inherent) Identity As the Divine Supreme Inner Self. Thus (Saying This), I Give you my Blessing.

50. Chitti Kundalini (an epithet of the Goddess originating from the Indian Yogic traditions) means, literally, "Consciousness-Kundalini", the Goddess who embodies both Divine Consciousness and the Spiritual Awakening Power of the Kundalini.

Kundalini Yoga is a possibility for every one, since the Kundalini Shakti (Which Is the Active Source, and the Divine Doer, of Kundalini Yoga) Exists (latently) in every one, and every one (and every thing) exists (or resides) in (or is alive, or existing, in, As, and by Means of) the (Divine) Kundalini Shakti. And Meditation (on the Divine Supreme Inner Self) by Means of the Kundalini Shakti (Awakened by the Guru's Grace) Is (necessarily) the Primary Duty of every one (because every one Originates from the Divine Source, and, therefore, every one owes, or must render, surrender, and return, his or her Divinely Originated existence to, the Kundalini Shakti, Which Is the Divine Source-Power, and Which Is the Way to the Divine Supreme Inner Self-Source of all). Therefore, (I Hereby Declare that) you have the Inherent Right and the Actual Ability to Cause (or, altogether, to Teach, Initiate, Establish, and Guide Kundalini Yoga) Meditation (or the Practice and the Process of Kundalini Shakti Meditation) in any one and everyone (and, Thus and Thereby, to Awaken any one and everyone to and As the Divine Supreme Inner Self of all).

> Swami Muktananda,
> Thana District,
> Maharashtra State,
> India

In the days previous to this event (of my receiving the initial translation of Baba's letter to me), Baba had indicated to a visitor that I was a Yogi, thereby giving me the right to that ancient title. Thus, for the world, I was to be known as "Sri Dhyanananda Yogi". But by now all such titles had ceased to bear significance for me. I took it as a very kind acknowledgement and let it pass. No one has ever called me by that name.

Adi Da with Swami Muktananda in 1969

Handwritten letter of acknowledgement from Swami Muktananda

I saw that this status was not properly my own. Baba himself had "created" the name as well as the experiences that gave me the right to it. He was acknowledging himself. I was careful to remember this, so as not to become identified with some idea of personal accomplishment. Baba had shown me how to meditate. He had meditated me. The Yoga was the Shakti Itself. The Shakti was the "Yogi". It had nothing to do with me. I would simply continue as before, moved by my own experience and understanding, and teaching wherever it was required, but without presenting myself in an exclusive or independent manner.

Indeed, as the days passed and my experiences increased, I felt more and more as if I had entered someone else's wonderland. Baba is a Siddha, an accomplished Yogi with various of the miraculous powers indicated in the Scriptures. Even he, like myself (in this, my natural human form), was given these things as a gift by his Guru. And all of these things at last were given by the Shakti Herself, the Divine Mother. My experiences did not depend on me. Baba's experience did not depend on him. We were all gratuitously accepted into the court of the Goddess, Shakti. The universe and all experiences were Her game, and I was simply being allowed to see this game, not in order to acquire powers or status, but to recognize the Source of all things and so remain free of all seeking.

During the time of my stay I experienced many unusual things. For the first time in my developmental life, I enjoyed the continuous status of a visionary, and more and more of the miraculous abilities that are described in classical Spiritual literature.

To varying degrees, many others who spent that month with Baba also experienced unusual phenomena. One man in particular, an Indian renunciate named Swami Prakashananda, would, at times, show perceptible signs of being even physically transfigured by the Shakti-Energy. And many others showed signs of being physically, emotionally, and mentally affected by that same Force, Which pervaded all the rooms as a result of Baba's Spiritual Transmission.

It was my practice to spend a couple of hours every afternoon in the meditation room outside the hall where Baba sat with his devotees. The room was usually filled with people in meditation. Some sat silent and composed. Others performed spontaneous kriyas and mudras. Some, as a result of the same spontaneous impulses, danced, or sat and moved their arms in the sinuous movements of dance. Some, suddenly, laughed or cried aloud. Others sang or chanted, even where this was not ordinarily characteristic of them. Others saw visions and lights.

I thought of that place as the "swooning room". The Shakti-Energy was extraordinarily Powerful and irresistible there, such that It would take one over bodily, emotionally, and mentally. As I became Filled with the Shakti-Energy there, I would crawl around on the floor, nearly blinded and immobile with "intoxication". Others crawled too, and some barked and hooted like animals. At last, I would lie prone on the floor, feeling as if I were pinned to the floor by the Pressure of the Divine Force. Then my body would swoon away, and I would spin into Bliss.

Often, during these weeks with Baba, as I passed into deep meditation, morning, daytime, nighttime, anywhere in the house, I would leave the physical body and either observe or participate in events on various other planes. At times I would sit for long periods observing an endless and automatic stream of images from various places. Some of these were merely the emanations of my own subconscious mind boiling off under the influence of the Shakti-Energy. But often I would see actual places and events in other worlds and planets through astral travel, or movements in superconsciousness. There would be marvelous scenes, some of them appearing as sublime perfections of the earth environment, and others that were built out of a mathematical and geometric logic of "creativity". Those higher worlds did not appear as solid and separate from the living consciousness as in the case with ordinary consciousness on earth. Rather, the experiences in those higher worlds, including the environments themselves, changed according to the qualities of mind manifested by those who enjoyed them.

As all of these things passed, I saw that there was no necessity, no seriousness, to the entire affair of "creation". It was merely a pattern, a Play of the Divine Shakti, and I should merely Witness it, without suffering any sense of separated identity within it, and without presuming any change or limitation of my own Ultimate Nature. I saw that Reality was not this apparently separate Play of the Divine Shakti, but my own True Nature, the Self, or Siva, of the Scriptures.

On several occasions I entered these worlds in the form of a subtle body. Once I met Baba before a passage leading underground. We entered a cave where there was a huge Dome of Honey-White Light in the floor. When we saw It, we recognized It as the Seat of the Divine, and we merged Joyously within It. On another occasion I met Baba in the subtle world, and we gazed in one another's eyes. Soon we began to revolve in opposite directions about the point of contact and merged into the same Ultimate Nature.

Then I also began to experience myself in the form of various deities and demons. I took on the graceful Buddha-like qualities and sat eternally calm in meditation. But then I would also take on the terrible forms of Siva, and my body and face twisted about in fierce expressions. I sat like the ferocious aspect of God, with skulls of blood and hatchets in my hands.

Near the end of my visit I felt I should communicate something of my experience to Baba, in order to acknowledge him and test my awareness. I told him that in meditation a spot of light had often appeared before me, sometimes black or silver-gray, and sometimes blue. I also described a vision in which I saw the muladhar appear below me as a Siva-lingam,[51] a monolith often found in temples. Then I appeared below, my hands tied to the lingam in a gesture of prayer, pointing above. I rose up with the lingam into the sahasrar and experienced the perfect, Infinite, Unmoved Sat-Chit-Ananda, the Pure Existence-Consciousness-Bliss of the Indian Godhead, my own Ultimate Self-Nature as the Divine Being of all the world's Scriptures. From this point of view I looked down again at the muladhar, and thousands of devotees were raising their hands prayerfully to me. Then I received the revelation that, if I remained concentrated in the sahasrar, all of the experiences of Realization would be given through me to others.

I asked Baba if I had received the true meaning of the experience. He only said: "Yes. The experience was true. Concentrate in the sahasrar if you like. The Shakti will do everything. The spot you saw is blue. It only appears black because of impurities."

The blue spot is one of the higher lights that appear within the subtle form of the human being. It may be seen within, above the plane of the eyes, or it may be seen to flash in front of the eyes. Baba calls it the "blue pearl"[52] and the "supracausal body"[53] (or cosmic body), the most subtle and highest source of experiential consciousness. It is the entrance to the abode of ascended beings (or Yogic Siddhas) who enjoy the great cosmic powers. They can also be seen within, sometimes in the blue light of the blue pearl and its realm. And this blue

51. A lingam is an oblong stone traditionally placed in a vertical orientation and worshipped as an expression of the Power of Siva, the Absolute, unmanifested Divine.

52. The "blue pearl" is a spot or drop (bindu) of blue light that may be seen in subtle vision, with eyes closed or open, in the process of the Yogic withdrawal of attention from the relations and conditions of the body-mind. In some forms of Yoga (particularly the Siddha Yoga Taught by Swami Muktananda), the vision of the "blue pearl" is valued as the highest attainment.

53. The supracausal body described here does not represent the dimension of full Enlightenment, but simply the highest subtle dimension of experience. Adi Da explains that the true causal dimension of the body-mind, which is Prior to the most subtle experience, is associated with the right side of the heart.

form or light is a favorite topic of Baba's mystical teaching. He declares and reveals that even all human beings dwell in the blue realm in a subtle body, totally one with the Shakti. Apparently, Baba's purpose for my present visit was to make me fully aware of these subtle dimensions and to have me know their Source to be the same that manifests the ordinary human state.

Now my visit was nearing an end. My experiences were a seemingly endless revelation of the Spiritual forms of Reality. And I had acquired something of the ego of Spiritual seeking and discovery. But I was already becoming aware of the inconclusiveness of all such experiences. Once the problem of the ordinary mind had ceased to trouble me, I began to experience Spiritual forms. Then I acquired a new problem, the problem of Spirituality. Then, it seemed, the matter of Freedom and Real Consciousness depended on the attainment of Spiritual experiences. And, it seemed, Spiritual experiences of an Ultimate kind must be identical to Freedom and Reality Itself. Thus, I was driven to acquire them.

But as these events unfolded, they too became common. The display of images, the transports to other worlds, the identification with ascended modes of Divine Being, the perception of higher and subtler forms of my own identity and ability, all passed before me, but with less and less interest on my part.

I began to feel: "This is not the point. This is not it. Reality is Prior to all of this. Reality is my own Self-Nature." But the more this feeling arose in me, the more aggressively these experiences arose, so that I again began to feel trapped. I felt that the way to which I was being progressively (but surely) Awakened was not Baba's version of Siddha Yoga. I was no longer moved by a desire for these experiences. They were nothing but more conditional and limited life, more patterns, more experiences calling up the process of identification, differentiation, and desire. The search for Spiritual experience, the motivation to achieve an Ultimate Victory on the basis of overcoming the "Spiritual problem", was only another form of seeking, suffering, and separative mentality. There was no radical difference between the higher and the lower worlds. There was no radical advantage in <u>any</u> kind of experience.

I began to feel a resistance to the experiential movements of the Shakti. I felt no need to continue this ritual of visionary Spiritual life. And I wanted some time and place to understand the entire miasma of personal and universal life. Thus, even though full of love for Baba, I began to welcome the opportunity to go home in peace.

I had made arrangements to leave on a Friday, at the end of August. But on Wednesday night, as I slept, I became aware of Swami Nityananda's Presence. Then he appeared to me, and he spoke to me, throughout the night, of my experiences. He told me I should prepare to leave immediately, Thursday, the day before I had planned.

The next afternoon I took my leave of Baba. He patted my back in blessing and gifted me with arms full of flowers. He also gave me a huge red apple. I bowed to him gratefully and turned to leave. He was still waving to me as I approached the stairway. And as I began to descend the stairs, I felt the beginnings of sickness in my stomach.

I flew to New York via Tel Aviv and Rome. On the first leg of the journey I felt nauseous and overcome with fever. And by the time I arrived in Tel Aviv, I was quite ill with cramps and diarrhoea. As I sat waiting for my plane, I felt exhausted and did not know how I would be able to travel comfortably. Then I remembered the apple. Baba had required me to pay particular notice to it as I left. I thought that the necessity for my early leave and Baba's gift of the apple were perhaps all part of a plan "created" by the Shakti. A sickness which was to purify my body and nerves was about to come over me in those last days with Baba. And so my early leave had been planned.

I ate the apple slowly, wondering if it would possibly affect my illness. Almost immediately, the churning in my stomach and intestines ceased. The body became comfortable. The purifying work of the apparent illness continued even for several days after my return to New York. But I continued tranquilly and comfortably, knowing the Shakti was at work. The entire experience had only been a sign of how the Shakti would continue to work for me according to Its intelligence of my needs after I left Baba's physical presence in India.

The loft in New York

CHAPTER 13

Shakti in America, New Problems, and the Return to India

I arrived in New York on the 30th of August, 1969. The next nine months were a period of intense investigation into the problems of Spiritual consciousness. I spent that time virtually in seclusion.

I shared a loft in the Wall Street area with Nina and another woman, named Patricia Morley. Nina and I no longer presumed a formal "marriage" commitment, but we remained intimate friends. Both she and Patricia had, based on clear and simple (if modest, and not otherwise profound and intense) Spiritual inclinations, become regular (but informal) beginning students of mine, and we lived together in a kind of mini-Ashram, regularly frequented by other such students, and friends, and random visitors (who would sometimes come to me for help in relation to their Spiritual search). I rarely left the apartment, and would spend many days at a time without even going into the street. Television became my main source of information about the world.

I spent my days in constant meditation. There were periods in every day when I sat for formal meditation, but, for me, meditation had now become a constant activity, even in the context of the moment to moment process of ordinary conscious awareness. I wanted to probe deeply into the matter of Spiritual experience in order to see it in its entirety and recognize its primary wisdom.

To that point, Spiritual life had been for me an experimental activity. It had not stabilized in a single practice associated entirely with radical understanding and Real Consciousness. The traditions of Spirituality seemed to me a mixed bag of many different forms of experience and interpretation. The goal of it all was not something that all saints, all religions, or all Scriptures (or traditions) acknowledged in common. The particular form of search and revelation was different in each case. The precise description of the nature of the world also differed in the many different cases, but, overall, those descriptions amounted to two basic alternatives. There was the traditional Eastern view that the world is an illusion "created" as a result of the failure to recognize the inherently Free Condition of the Real Self. And there was the traditional Western view that all of this was the "creation" of God. Therefore, some sought liberation, and others salvation. Some claimed Identity with the Divine, whereas others claimed a radical, eternal distinction and even separation between the Divine, the human, or the soul, and the various worlds.

I worked in order to Realize the fundamental Truth that was Freedom and also Real Knowledge. And no one and no tradition anywhere represented that Truth to me whole, entirely Free of any limited or limiting point of view.

I continued to teach, very informally. This took the form of random, spontaneous discussions about Spiritual life, practice, meditation, and experience. People would come to discuss the ideas they gathered in various books. Some only wanted to hear comparative philosophy, learn "secret" techniques, or get information about various psychic phenomena. Some were concerned with healing, diet, what to do, what not to do. Some wanted estimations of various saints, organizations, religions. Some were looking for particular saintly qualities which their reading had led them to expect in anyone who claimed to have Spiritual experience. Most of them were not serious enough about the "problems" of conditional existence to learn any more than the traditional Spiritual gossip, but several of them stayed long enough to make progress, and they approached the matter from a depth in themselves that made progress possible. These people had "experiences", and they began to meditate with some degree of regularity and understanding. Some of them would remain only for a few months, and then I let them go. I found that the true Guru-devotee relationship was not adaptable to Western life or to "creative" life, unless Westerners and otherwise "creative" people were truly moved to embrace all the very real disciplines traditionally, and necessarily, associated with esoteric religious and Spiritual life. And What I wanted my beginning students to attain was not "Spiritual" experiences (in the conventional, or merely phenomenal, sense), but, in the most profound sense, a Communication of the Reality on Which and in Which they could found their lives. Thus, we came together, at least for a while, and whenever I saw that they needed to leave (because their "tendencies" were strong, and their impulse toward the Realization of God, Truth, or Reality was yet weak), I let them go.

Indeed, I preferred not to use the word "Spiritual" to refer to the form of existence I taught. The word "Spiritual" carries all kinds of associations with a "phenomenal" kind of experience. It points to visionary phenomena, miracles, and forms of perception that are symbolic, psychic, and, ultimately, religious. But Real Consciousness is unqualifiedly Free. Its psychic depth is an unmodified field of Awareness. And even where there is the experience of unusual phenomena on the way, such things are simply more material to be transcended in the process of radical understanding.

In the course of the process of radical understanding, "mystical experience" (or the concentration of attention in "Spiritual phenomena" themselves) is (along with the concentration of attention in any "phenomena" at all) progressively (and, at last, most perfectly) transcended. Therefore, the essential experience that is to be valued from the beginning is the one variously described as "being One with all of life", or experiencing "the Oneness of everything". This is the Power of Reality, of unqualified relatedness, of non-separation, no suffering, and no-seeking in the heart. This is in fact the primary Experience and Knowledge that (ultimately) obviates all particular experiences and motivations. Therefore, this has been my Purpose (in my own case, and in the case of those who came to me even in the earliest days of my teaching work, before my own Realization of radical understanding was most perfectly consummated). My Purpose has been to make this radical understanding the real foundation (and not merely the goal, but the always present Realization) of conscious life. And when this radical understanding comes, it is not a mere idea or belief, or a feeling that depends on any circumstances. It is (and more and more becomes) a function of Real Consciousness, of unqualified Being. And, once this Realization (of radical understanding) is Awakened and Established, It (Itself) develops, over time, into the most perfect Realization of radical Knowledge and Free Existence.

In the fall of 1969, I spent my days meditating, observing the processes of my seeking, and also keeping a written record of my understanding. I edited all of the extant journals of my understanding and made a book out of them (called *Water and Narcissus*), which I completed early in November. I also produced a novel (or what I called a "prose opera", or, really, a theatrical ritual, or liturgical drama), tentatively titled *The Love Exit, and Water* (and, ultimately, titled *The Mummery*), which was based on the theme of Spiritual seeking (and the transcendence of all seeking). It was largely based on the images I had perceived during my earlier period of writing on the beach.

My own experience was not yet conclusive. I had not yet finally (or most perfectly) understood in a radical manner. Nevertheless, my experience had developed to the point where my interests in writing were reawakened. I had re-attained the original impulse of my own writing. I knew that I would teach, and my teaching would also necessarily include much writing. It would be a literature of Real Consciousness.

I was also concerned with the need to understand the relationship between functional consciousness, all of conditionally manifested Reality, the Shakti, and the Divine Being (or Ultimate Self-Condition). In my constant meditation, I had begun to have an experience of Ultimate Reality that foreshadowed events to follow in the spring of 1970.

As I meditated, I began to experience an impression of the Divine Being over against my own life on every level. He was not only the Ultimate Self-Nature, or Pure Consciousness, but He included (as His active Presence) the Force known as Shakti. He was Siva-Shakti. He was like Krishna, the personal Godhead. As I went on in this manner, I began to perceive that this Divine Being and Presence included all things in Himself. He had become the universe. This accounted for my first experience at the Ashram, wherein I perceived that everything was being "Lived".

This Divine Being included all that I experienced, even the Guru, my own states moment to moment, and the entire universe of the Shakti's expression. Thus, I began to realize that He not only included the objects in my awareness, but He was the very Subject Who experienced all the states I felt I had been experiencing. He was my own Self-Nature and my experience. There was nothing but Him.

Soon I began to realize that I was not experiencing my experiences. He was the experiences and the experiencer. Yet, in some fundamental manner, I continued to exist. But I was experiencing only Him. I was not experiencing my experiences. Those experiences, and that experiencing, my own apparent states moment to moment, were also Him in His activity. I was not in any sense a part of these.

I saw that I was only conscious awareness, entirely without content, "created" by this Divine Lord. My only experience moment to moment, under all apparent conditions, was Him. That was it entirely. As this contemplation grew, and I became only the devotee of this Great Being, I wrote about my Realization. I will here include some of those descriptive notes to demonstrate my consideration at that point in time.

❖ ❖ ❖

I am not in relationship to the physical universe, nor to any object I perceive. I am not in relationship to my own mind, nor my body. Neither am I in relationship to my loved-ones or any person. And I will never be in relationship to any particular thing. Nothing that appears to me has ever known my presence, nor will it ever know that I exist. I am always already and only in relationship to the Divine Lord, the One Who is Manifesting everything and is the Consciousness of everything.

Whatever I may appear to do, and whomever I may appear to relate to, and whatever I may appear to experience, I am always and only Enjoying the direct relationship to the Divine Lord. I am never in fact separate, or experiencing any entity in itself. I am never even experiencing my own separate mind and personality.

At times I have interpreted my life as separate experiences by a disconnected and unique process I identified as myself. The error was not that I experienced the play of phenomena, but that I failed to Know I was always already in relationship and always already Free. Healing is simply the instant, moment to moment recovery of this Knowledge.

This Knowledge is not Itself the result of an applied process, a strategic practice, or a seekers' method. I am always apparently performing such things, but this Knowledge Itself is entirely a grace, a suddenness, a Realization outside of all activity, all strife, and all the influence of experience. And this Knowledge is totally liberating. The more profound It goes within, the simpler the Truth appears, and It is simply unqualified conscious awareness and unqualified Bliss. It is Real existence, prior to the mind and all identification with conditional manifestation. It is marked by a calm, questionless heart, and by Peace, the Knowledge of Existence Itself as Bliss. And Its essential Content is the contemplation, or conscious awareness, of the Divine Lord, the One Presence, the actual Source and Object.

❖   ❖   ❖

The Divine Lord is not, Himself, the "God-Symbol" of exoteric religions. He is not the "One" that you are persuaded to believe in. He is not an entity, a mental object, a reduction of Reality, or a phenomenon within the world. He is the One Who must be Realized in order to be Known. He is not Known previous to the Realization of Him in life. It is simply that the tacit understanding of one who is beyond conflict, and who enjoys the perception of non-contradiction, is suddenly voiced as this recognition. It is the testimony of one's Absolute Freedom and Enjoyment, and not the description of a remedial path for the mind in its bondage. But neither is the way the avoidance of devotion, or the avoidance of worship of the prophetic "God-Symbol". Mankind will act and seek thus in any case, and enjoy the consolations of their many answers. It is simply that, when there is a return to understanding, there is an end to seeking, questioning, descriptive belief, and all conflict. And these are replaced by immediate recognition.

❖ ❖ ❖

The Divine Lord, Who is Present universally but Who is not qualified by any conditional manifestation, Who is the Source and Consciousness and Control of all processes, Who is Manifesting everything, Who Transcends everything, Who is That Alone to Which you are related, Who is That Alone of Which you are conscious, Who is Freedom, Consciousness, actual Presence, perfect Knowledge, and Absolute Bliss, Who Alone is your Self and That of all things, Who is the Guru, the Teacher, is the Principle of life. The solitary necessity for one's Freedom, if one could assume Him to be What He is, is to allow Him to Exist, to Manifest Himself as everything, to be the Transcendent Presence Known anywhere.

The relationship to the Divine Lord is salvation. His grace, whatever form it takes, is simply to make His Existence, as He is, Real to living beings. This Lord is the Lord, and all human beings are communicating their level of realization of Him. All religions, all religious statements, all religious and Spiritual paths, truths, and claims are communications about this Presence, modified by the limitations of their realization and the historical circumstances of the communication. He is Knowable, and He must be Known.

❖ ❖ ❖

The essential Realization of the meditative act is that this present consciousness, my awareness at this instant, the entire conditional manifestation which is my present experience, is in fact the contemplation, by me, of the Divine Lord, and the direct experiencing, by me, of the Divine Lord. He <u>is</u> this. He <u>is</u> this state, this awareness, this manifestation, this contemplation, this experiencing. The moment of this recognition breaks the entire form of bondage.

The Truth is that all of conditionally manifested existence is being "Lived". The right orientation of all conditional consciousness is to present contemplation of the Consciousness (and the total Condition) of the Divine. Totality includes the present actuality, but as a manifestation of the Divine Lord, and as a conscious experience and Realization of the Divine Lord. Human bondage, the root of egoic ignorance, suffering, the activity of sin, is simply the result of the loss of this Knowledge and this contemplation. Instead of living in the Bliss of this infinite Freedom, one identifies one's present awareness, the form of consciousness and experience at this moment, as a separate, unique, and finitely personal reality. It is thus that one loses the Freedom of Totality, the infinitely unburdened Bliss of pure contemplation of the Divine, and falls into the expression of finite and separate existence. I do not mean to say that when one is fully in the Truth one ceases to exist in a world, in relationship to others. It is simply that one comes to live life truly, directly, in the Full Bliss of the relationship to the Divine. In the free and natural State, one ceases to enforce the form of egoic ignorance and the conditions its assumptions "create".

❖ ❖ ❖

Normally one assumes: "I am having this experience." Every moment of life is informed by this affirmation. Moment to moment, this presumption of being a separate identity is communicated to the entirety of life. Thus, life becomes an expansion out of the idea of this individuation, a process whereby the separate and absolute ego tries to predicate all Reality to itself in order to regain the Totality intuited beneath the mind. This is the source of life as dilemma and mortality, suffering and tragedy, ordinary and dark humor and search. It is simply a matter of a failure to recognize the Truth of one's condition, one's right relationship, the actual Reality. In fact, the Divine Lord, the Conscious Subject and Source of all manifestation, is the Only Experiencer of everything, and what one now identifies as one's self is simply one's awareness of the Reality of the Divine.

❖ ❖ ❖

The quality of life proceeds from the form of cognition one assumes. It is only necessary to return again and again to the living condition of Reality, which is the actual and conscious relationship to the Divine Lord, Who is That Alone of Which one is conscious.

The mind is only a process of experience. One suffers because of the quality of one's relationship to the mind. When one does not enjoy the Divine, one is identified with the limiting force of experience.

❖ ❖ ❖

The universe is Conscious. There is Consciousness everywhere. There is only Consciousness, and a universal Event, a simultaneous Reality.

The living consciousness is the contemplative Enjoyment of the Divine Lord. That relationship is Reality. It is the very structure of the living consciousness. It is unqualified Enjoyment. It is the Realized Actuality.

❖ ❖ ❖

There is a completion of all the reasons.

❖ ❖ ❖

It seemed to me at the time that I had Realized the Ultimate State in Which Reality is recognized exactly as It is. And this Knowledge, or Wisdom, Itself seemed to be the perfect and liberating Truth, the supreme interpretation of all experience, and the key to every kind of dilemma in any form of existence.

However, as days passed, I began to feel an overwhelming burden in this Realization. I had predicated everything to the Divine and nothing to myself. My extreme and constant concentration on Him made me more and more immobile. My own existence remained as a constant problem that needed to be continually reabsorbed in this devotional Sublimity.

Eventually, my own "creative" Force began to emerge and break away from this conceptual form. And new experiences of the Shakti arose to teach me further regarding the Nature of Real Consciousness. Thus, I abandoned this binding perception, or it simply passed from me and left me loose. But a remnant of it was retained to rise again in a new form when I returned to India in the spring, because my deep psyche yet demanded a devotional fulfillment comparable to my childhood love of Jesus of Nazareth.

Around the first of the year, 1970, I received a letter from a young African man at the Ashram. My reply to his letter was to mark a new phase in my relationship to Baba.

Baba had given me the right to teach, and he placed no conditions on it. I should teach those who came to me, and I should teach not what I had been told, no tradition I had learned in the mind, but exactly according to my own experience and understanding.

While I was in India the previous summer, a young man arrived from Uganda. He first saw me sitting in a crowd with Baba at Ram Pratap's apartments in Bombay, and he became instantly convinced that I was to be the instrument for his instruction. I met him later in Ganeshpuri, at the Ashram, during a short visit there during my stay in August, and he told me about this. He had been having constant visions of me since the day he saw me.

He asked if he could meditate with me in the mornings. I told him that I would not presume to teach him, but he could meditate along with me if he liked. And so he came every morning. When I left, he kept demanding a blessing and called me "Master" with profound devotion. But I only wished him well and told him to seek out Baba as his Guru.

During the months that followed my return to America, he wrote to me a few times, each time describing his problems, his dissatisfaction at the Ashram, and always asking for advice. I replied each time by telling him of my experiences of Baba's grace and recommending that he speak to Baba about these same problems and then follow his advice. I also recommended certain books in the Ashram library that he might find useful.

However, in January, when I received his last letter, I had myself become individuated from Baba. My own experience and understanding had never developed along traditional lines, and the recent development (in my own case) of the devotional philosophy I have just described (which also epitomized the Indian devotional tradition, and which I had in turn been, by my own understanding, forced to abandon) indicated to me that the Truth lay in a radically new approach to the problems of Spirituality and life. I had also already enjoyed or suffered the experience of teaching more than a dozen Westerners in a direct, intimate, eye-to-eye confrontation, day to day. And I saw that the teaching required was anything but a merely traditional philosophy made of conventional ideas about Spirituality and life-practice. Thus, I was moved to write to this man more directly.

I made no effort to turn him from Baba. He had been moved to go to Baba's Ashram for help, and he was now in Baba's care. I believed that he must take advantage of his chosen opportunity. And I had no doubt that Baba could provide him with the Spiritual help he was seeking. Nevertheless, I was willing to tell him more directly what had become my point of view on Spiritual matters. Indeed, he seemed almost ready to leave Baba's Ashram, even, perhaps, to seek me out in America, and I thought that, if he could see exactly that I was not a teacher in the traditional sense, he might cease to be enamored of me and, so, turn again to Baba.

Thus, I told him that I was not a disciple of Baba in the usual sense. I said that I did not relate to Baba in the manner of a "seeker". I told him that I addressed all of my experience, moment to moment, in terms of a radical understanding of my motives, and that I, therefore, did not seek, or otherwise overestimate the value of, Spiritual experiences, or even any other kinds of experiences. Even in the case of my own students, I told him, I did not make them concerned to receive Shaktipat, nor did I recommend various seekers' exercises for the "development" (or exploitation) of Shakti-experiences. I told him that I simply directed my students to understand their motives and problems, and, on the basis of that understanding, to perceive Reality directly, radically free of the habits of seeking. I told him he must look to Baba for his answers, since what he was seeking was not in my Purpose.

A week or two later I received a letter from the Ashram. The letter was written by Amma, but spoken in Baba's name. Baba was outraged. He had read the letter I had written to the young African. "How could anyone presume to teach who needed help himself? What tradition do you belong to if not the tradition of Muktananda and Nityananda? Perhaps it is true, as we have heard, that you try to steal disciples from other teachers!"

Right understanding of one's position in relation to the totality of everything is humbling, and it requires the acceptance of the relative unimportance of one's individuality. However, I was not willing (nor did I feel I was being called upon) either to misrepresent myself or to swear falsely, particularly in the face of such an absurd attack. I assumed that Baba could not require weakness in his disciple. Therefore, he must only be testing my strength and integrity as a disciple. After all, Baba had himself given me the right and the task of teaching.

I felt it was time to remove the veil of silence between Baba and me. He must know what I understood and how I related to him. I posed no threat to him. I had always been very careful to turn the young African in Baba's direction. But I reserved the right and the necessity to truly understand all that had been given to me. Indeed, to fail to do so would be to deny the Truth my entire life had been revealing.

I was profoundly grateful for Baba's grace, and it had surely given me great experience and continuous resources for the consideration of my practice, but it appeared the time had come for me to assert myself again, even, perhaps, as I had been required to do with Rudi. I would state my position clearly, as it was proven in my experience, and if Baba could not tolerate me on those terms, I was willing to accept my total independence.

Thus, I wrote a long and forceful letter of complaint and justification. I explained my position, and I made clear the positive intention and role I had, in my letter to the African, assumed. I told Baba that my own experience was developing along the lines of a radical understanding, free, from the beginning, of all the limitations of seeking. I spoke myself to him in true and fullest gratitude. I said that, if he were to allow me as a disciple, I would be a disciple of this kind, or else he should let me go.

The letter I received in reply barely indicated that Baba was aware of what I had written. It was a brief, reconciling letter, and I am sure my own letter had appeared too strong for anyone to take to Baba. Perhaps he had only heard parts of it. The reply only stated that Baba wanted to be sure I was not trying to turn people from the Ashram. I should feel free to teach as I desired in America. It closed with the admonition that the disciple chooses the Guru, not the Guru the disciple.

I was satisfied that Baba wished the relationship to continue. And I felt it was valuable to maintain it for my own sake. Baba preached a tradition and enjoyed his role within it. There was nothing more to say about it. The message to me was that, if I came and found the Truth for myself, it was my business to Communicate It as I saw fit. But don't rock the boat! And so I was renewed in my own unique course. And I continued in it with my characteristic sense of responsibility to only exactly Realize Reality Itself, without compromise, and not confined or constrained by any tradition.

During the following months I continued to have experiences of various kinds, as I had in India. Particularly at night, when the body was set aside, I experienced fully conscious meetings with various saints, Yogis, and miracle-workers. I was allowed to observe miraculous demonstrations in a school for Siddhas, the Yogis who practice various powers. I saw in detail the process whereby they materialize objects and living things.

Even though physically separated from Baba, I would often experience his sudden Presence in miraculous ways. Frequently I would feel him acquire my body, so that I knew all of my functions had become his body. He would particularly take over my face and hands. I could feel my features adapting to the expression of his character and mood. The special formulation of the Shakti that worked through him would pour through my hands and face. My mouth would twitch about my teeth in his characteristic manner. My fingers would automatically gesture in the manner by which he indicated sublime Feeling, and, in his manner, my index finger would point above, to the sahasrar, to the Holy Place, to the Guru, and to God.

In meditation I would experience Swami Nityananda taking over my psychic form. My subtle body and my physical body would expand with great Force, and I would feel myself with dimensions larger than any conceivable space. I would feel his subtle breathing, and my abdomen would take on the "pot-shaped" form otherwise described in the Yogic traditions.

These manifestations were not simply "internal". Frequently my perceptions coincided with certain external events. For example, a friend once came to see me after a long stay at Baba's Ashram. We bowed to Baba's picture and felt the Shakti Fill the room. Just then, the flowers that were nailed about the portrait flew off and landed at our feet.

Along with these experiences, my understanding was developing along unique lines. I regarded the various phenomena of Spiritual experience to be interesting but, ultimately, inconsequential. The activities of the Shakti demonstrated much about the origins of (and the true relationship to) the conditions of existence, but the experience or acquisition of such phenomena was not equal to the Truth. The pursuit of Spiritual phenomena, or the solution to the problem of life conceived on a Spiritual level, was, for me, merely another and more dramatic form of seeking, suffering, and separation. Indeed, this pursuit was only one more manifestation of the logic of Narcissus, the complex avoidance of relationship, or the avoidance of relatedness as the radical condition (always already the case) of the living condition of Reality. I was not in any sense devoted to seeking in any form.

Then, sometime in February, I experienced a remarkable revolution in my living being. After my second trip, and even to a degree after my first trip to India (and also as a result of the long course of my experience with Rudi), I had firmly identified myself, or the structure of my living being, with the various instruments of the chakra system. That circuit of life-energy and Spiritual Energy, with its various functional centers (and degrees of relative grossness or subtlety), high and low, revealed itself to be the foundation structure of every living being and (in its universal Depth) the Functional (or "Creative") Source of even every conditionally existing form or universe. My experiences in India demonstrated this as a fact. Thus, although the Truth of Real Consciousness had revealed Itself to me to be one of radical understanding, no-seeking, and, even in the context of ordinary living, the Conscious Enjoyment of an eternally Free, Un-changing, and always already Existing State, I could not, on the basis of this identification with the chakra system, see how life could be performed without some kind of seeking.

The chakra system and the philosophy it implied demanded a conscious, intentional purification and ascent toward concentration in the highest center and in the subtlest vehicle of being, what Baba called the "supracausal" body. Thus, it seemed, Spiritual life must necessarily be associated with this goal of ascent. And, indeed, all of the most commonly known religions and Spiritual paths of the world, even where there is no conscious and sophisticated Knowledge of the Shakti and the chakras, rest in this basic philosophy of purification and ascent. Even in Christianity it appears as fasting and prayer, the means of fullest devotion to God and dependence on God. Thus, while at seminary, I had tried to express my experience through Christianity. But always I returned to an understanding free of all seeking. And this not only prevented my alignment with Christianity, but it also "created" difficulties with what was for me the living tradition of Shakti Yoga, or Siddha Yoga.

In February I passed through an experience that vindicated my understanding. For several nights I was awakened again and again with sharp lateral pains in my head. They felt like deep incisions in my skull and brain, as if I were undergoing a surgical operation. During the day following the last of these experiences, I realized a marvelous relief. I saw that what appeared as the sahasrar, the terminal chakra and primary lotus in the head, had been severed. The sahasrar had fallen off like a blossom. The Shakti, Which previously had appeared as a polarized Energy that moved up and down through the various chakras, or functional centers, producing various effects, now was released from the chakra form. There was no more polarized Force. Indeed, there was no structure whatsoever, no up or down, no chakras. The chakra system had been revealed as unnecessary, an arbitrary rule or setting for the Play of Divine Energy. The structure beneath all of the bodies, or functional sheaths, gross or subtle, had revealed itself to be as unnecessary and conditional as the bodies, or functional sheaths, themselves.

Previously, all the universes seemed built and dependent upon that prior structure of ascending and descending Energy, so that values were determined by the level of the chakra in which the living consciousness functioned, and planetary bodies (as well as space itself) were fixed in a spherical or curved form. But now I saw that Reality and Real Consciousness was not in the least determined by any kind of form apart from Itself. Consciousness had shown Its radical Freedom and Priority relative to the chakra form. It had shown Itself to be senior to that entire structure, Prior to every kind of manifestation or modification of cosmic Energy, or Shakti. There was simply Consciousness Itself, Prior to all forms, all dilemmas, every kind of seeking and necessity.

In the past I had been turned to the Shakti and Spiritual phenomena as the route to Realization. But this was a reluctant course. I Knew that a fundamental and radical understanding equal to Consciousness Itself was in fact the Source, the Very Truth. Now I saw that I was right. There is no need to have recourse to any kind of phenomenon, problem, or structure of seeking. The Shakti, as an apparently independent, or cosmic, Force, is not the primary or necessary Reality. Reality is the Ultimate Self-Nature, the Foundation that is pure Consciousness, the Divine Self-Consciousness, Siva, Who is always already Free of conditional manifestations (or of the Divine, but merely apparent, Play). Thus, I was certain again that Real life is not itself a matter of necessary evolution or the acquisition of mere experience. Rather, Real life is, simply, founded in always present understanding, and, thereby, in Consciousness Itself.

The extraordinary Event that I experienced at the end of my first visit to Baba's Ashram now showed Itself to be the most fundamental of all my experiences in Baba's company. It appeared to contain the One necessary and sufficient revelation (Prior to all phenomena). I could see that What was revealed was True, although I did not yet Know finally what were the ultimate consequences of that revelation (in most perfect Realization). My meditation had been developing for some time along lines of my own understanding. I continued to experience the phenomena of Spiritual consciousness as I had in India. These were not undesirable. They represented a genuine expansion of conscious experience, and, thus, they made it possible for me to develop my understanding on the basis of the most inclusive and exhaustive firsthand experience and knowledge of even every kind of conditionally manifested phenomenon. But my way of approach was one of radical understanding. And this understanding (rather than the phenomena I experienced) was the foundation and fruit of my Spiritual life.

Over time, I had experimented with every kind of seekers' method, but the mature form of my meditation was not based in any search for higher experience. It was simply a direct approach to whatever experiences arose. Thus, at the very last, I used no complicated techniques, no special breathing, no mantras or visual aids to concentration. I simply Enquired of myself, whenever tendencies, thoughts, or experiences arose, "Avoiding relationship?" Thus, I was constantly returned to a Prior State of unqualified Awareness. By remaining in that State through self-Enquiry, I was led, at the very last, to most perfectly understand my own instruments, every kind of search, and every kind of experience.

The letter Baba Muktananda wrote to me in late April 1968 contains a traditional program for meditation:

> In the *"So'ham"* mantra—*"So"* signifies God or Guru, and "ham" denotes "I" or "me". Thus *So'ham* means "I am He". Let your practice of meditation be accompanied by the ceaseless reflection on the above meaning of *So'ham*. A person gets transformed into the likeness of the object on which he constantly ponders, by absorbing its qualities.
>
> Sitting calm and steady repeat the *mantra* together with rhythmic breathing (i.e., the inhalation and exhalation of air—*pran* and *apan*). Harmonize the repetition of *mantra* with the breathing as follows: With *"So"* take it in and with *"ham"* bring it out. Throughout the *mantra*-repetition one should follow this practice. Simply sitting peacefully and applying the mind to the *pran* and *apan* one enters into deep state of meditation. When one's mind is fixed on *"So"* with the incoming breath and on *"ham"* with the outgoing breath it is *mantra-japa*. The regularity with which the breath comes in and goes out is *pranayama*. And if a person is skillful, intelligent, and alert—the (1) *repetition of mantra (japa)*, the process of (2) *pranayama*, and the (3) *meditation*—all the three can be achieved simultaneously without difficulty. This is a great Yoga, the best among all: known as *Siddha Yoga*. It means "the path of the Perfect Ones" or "the Yoga which begets perfection". A dextrous and highly intelligent person can practice it easily. As explained above, the regular practice of meditation with a concentrated mind will awaken the dormant Kundalini Shakti in a very short time. Day-by-day

as the Shakti develops more and more It takes the aspirant to Perfection by the Guru's grace.

It is best to practice a natural meditation or *dhyan*. Sit quietly, calm and composed, if you like in *padmasana*, or any other comfortable posture. You may look and fix the eyes on a photo or may keep your eyes closed. The mode and posture in which you can be restful, mentally free from the objective world, and introspective, that is the best *asan* for you. Remove the mind from its activities, arrest all kinds of desires and surrender to whatever is happening of its own accord, observe everything as a witness. The meditation done by the inner Shakti is the meditation of Guru's grace, it is the real meditation of *"So'ham"*, indeed it is the meditation of God.

The deeper and deeper you go in meditation the more and more of the Divine experiences you will attain. Therefore, seek your inner Self, therefrom you will have the fulfillment you cherish.

This "program" is a classical Yogic description of the way of meditation. It is typical of all the methods of Yoga that operate directly on the mental, vital, and physical functions and concentrate consciousness in the regions of superconscious manifestation. When I received Baba's letter, I was already involved in the time of "waiting" (in which I practiced no meditation). However, as an experiment, I did begin to use the precise method he described when I (eventually) resumed meditation, just before my second trip to India.

Rather than the "So'ham" (or "So-Ham") mantra, I preferred to use the "Om" mantra, which Baba recommended as an alternative in the same letter. I had, at first, difficulty combining the Sanskrit syllables with their meaning in my own language and at the same time generating the mantra as a feeling or affirmation, rather than a thought. However, in the following months, I meditated in this basic manner (using the "Om" mantra, and sometimes the "So-Ham" mantra), and, finally, began to use the "So-Ham" mantra without difficulty.

When I went to Baba the second time, I had already begun to use self-Enquiry (in the form "Avoiding relationship?"). I also continued to experiment with the use of the mantra "So-Ham", and with the "Om" mantra. As I described earlier, I experienced an internal teaching of meditation while with Baba on this second trip. Therefore, at that time, and for a time thereafter, Baba's internal and external teaching combined with my own (radical) understanding of practice.

Nevertheless, my understanding was fundamental, and profoundly clarifying. I saw that all the kinds of seeking were founded in identification, in each case, with a particular developmental level or stage of life, experience, or motivation. The dilemma that was always involved was founded in a present act of differentiation, whereby what was constantly being achieved was the presumption of a separated and threatened consciousness. Thus, I was not moved to pursue any goals, experiences, or forms. All such things were merely matters of seeking. I did not even pursue my Identity with Siva, the Very (and Divine) Self, or Pure Consciousness. Such, it was clear to me, was also a form of seeking. I simply and radically founded myself in understanding, and, thus, in the Truth and Reality that had been Communicated through all of my experience.

All of this would develop into radical Knowledge, and into a radical philosophy, as the months passed. But I needed to endure certain other changes and forms of seeking before I would be most perfectly stabilized in the Knowledge of Which I was already tacitly Certain. Thus, for the time being, I extended my experimental approach to the matters of physical experience.

In the months following my return from India, I had experienced the effects that various degrees of toxicity and enervation have upon the living consciousness and the motivations of seeking. I often smoked cigarettes while I wrote. Occasionally, I would drink alcohol with friends. And, although I maintained an essentially vegetarian diet, I would often, with my friends and family, have meat dishes and sweets, highly artificial (and "junk") foods, and other "rich" preparations.

I began to study various books on pure diet and fasting, and I decided to conduct an experiment, to see what effects fasting and consistently pure diet would have in daily life and in meditation. I became intensively involved with the idea of physical purification as a means of profoundly altering the state of consciousness in life. I even considered that perhaps the entire matter of seeking on mental and Spiritual levels was solely caused by a toxic and enervated condition in the body. If the body could be brought to a state of perfect purity, then perhaps the mind would become stilled, and the living consciousness might enjoy a natural, intuitive Realization of Reality and Spiritual Truth. Perhaps the mind would achieve a state of perfect brilliance and utility. Perhaps the body itself could achieve indefinite longevity, even immortality.

I considered all the obvious healthful options, including fasting, limited amounts of food in general, balanced cooked and raw lacto-fructo-vegetarian diet, balanced raw fructo-vegetarian diet, and the exclusively fruitarian raw diet. I also thought it to be entirely possible, and even desirable, that one could achieve a state independent of normal food and live directly on subtle energy. And this appeared to be supported by the evidence of a few cases on record where people have in fact lived without food of any kind for thirty, forty, even fifty years, or more.

In March of 1970, I began a fast that was to continue for twenty-two days. At first I took only a few glasses of pure water every day. Then I began to add a small amount of fresh lemon juice to the pure water. As suggested by

Arnold Ehret[54] in his books on the theory and practice of fasting and pure diet, the addition of fresh lemon juice made the purifying effects of the fast more aggressive. Ehret also claimed that fresh fruit juices, such as apple and orange, would generate an even more aggressive action. Thus, in order to test this, after the first week I also, every day, took one or more glasses of either diluted or undiluted fresh fruit juice (either apple or orange). And these juices consistently produced an added positive effect.

The effects of the twenty-two day fast were positively remarkable. When I began the fast, the body quickly became light (or less gross) in its feeling, hunger completely disappeared after only a few days, and the mind almost immediately became clear, energetic, and precise.

I lost weight on most of the days of the fast. I lost about six or eight pounds in the first five days. After that I lost a pound a day, and this changed to a pound every other day in the last week or ten days of the fast. My weight dropped from around 180 pounds to approximately 154 pounds in the twenty-two days, but I easily returned to a normal, healthful weight in the weeks following the fast.

Early in the fast, there were occasional, brief physical episodes of weakness and dizziness. At times I could even feel various old drug deposits in the body pass through the brain. But, in general, I consistently felt a brilliant physical well-being. My meditation also deepened, as the various physical and vital obstacles disappeared.

After approximately two weeks of fasting, I experienced an episode of continuous physical weakness, such that physical activity became slow and difficult, and my pulse and heartbeat became weak and irregular. Immediately, I went to the literature on fasting, in order to find a means to correct this tendency. I discovered that, in his

54. Arnold Ehret wrote several books on diet and health, including *Thus Speaketh the Stomach*; *Arnold Ehret's Mucusless-Diet Healing System*; and *Rational Fasting for Physical, Mental, and Spiritual Rejuvenation*.

books on fasting and pure diet, Teofilo de la Torre[55] recommends a pure water extract of vegetables as a means to avoid enervation during a fast. This liquid extract is made by allowing pure water to settle for many hours on a particular combination of cut, raw vegetables. I tried the drink recommended by de la Torre, and, indeed, it did give me some added strength, especially when coupled with a reduced intake of sweet fruit juices (which, until then, taken perhaps too frequently, or else too often undiluted, appeared to have caused a low blood sugar reaction, and, thereby, at least some of my feelings of physical weakness). And this simple change in my fasting regime allowed the fast to continue for the full term I desired.

After the fast, I continued my experiment by the application of every kind of possibly "right" diet. My experiment with "right" diet (and fasting) included not only myself but Nina, Patricia, and various others, all of whom had taken to fasting and pure foods in response to my demonstration. I found that each individual fared better on a different type of diet. Some, for the moment, required more bulk and starch. Others seemed, for the time being, unable to do without foods high in protein, perhaps even including meats. Others immediately fared well on raw and cooked vegetables and fruits. Together, we experimented with the elimination of various foods and the addition of others. All of this demonstrated that, in the case of individual application, the "right" diet was not necessarily identical to any one kind of "unique" or "special" dietary prescription, as the "champions" of any particular dietary variation might propose, but, always, "right" diet had to be determined by an intelligent approach to each individual, as he or she appeared at any point in time.

55. Teofilo de la Torre wrote several books on diet and health, including *An Inspiring Message on the Philosophy and Science of Health, Youth, and Longevity, Based upon "The Dietetic Laws of Nature"*; *Man's Return to His Garden of Eden*; and *The Process of Physical Purification by Means of the New and Easy Way to Fast*.

After three months of all of this, I had acquired much firsthand knowledge of fasting and "right" diet. I concluded that fasting and pure food did in fact aid one's well-being and were a necessary part of responsible self-discipline. My experience of these things clearly indicated that the application of "right" dietary and fasting and general health principles required flexibility in the progressive "rightening" of the individual case. Nevertheless, the optimum practice in all cases was proved to involve (as necessary) regular short fasts and occasional (and, in general, at least once per year) appropriately prolonged fasts, and the consistent choice of pure (or unadulterated, untreated, non-toxic, and truly nutritious) foods, raw (either exclusively or to the maximum degree possible), and selected only from among the possibilities offered by vegetables, grains, nuts, seeds, and fruits. Red meat, or even any "killed" food, eggs, milk and milk products, refined flour, refined sugar, "rich" foods, "junk" foods, excessive amounts of (or, in some cases, even any) cooked foods, coffee, tea, tobacco, alcohol, foods that are toxically sprayed, toxically treated, or toxic otherwise, and even any foods in too large a quantity proved themselves to have a generally (and cumulatively) negative effect on virtually anyone's physical and emotional and mental well-being. However, it also became clear that, even though it is most "right" to eschew such impure (or constipating, toxifying, and enervating) substances altogether, any of them could (whether by sometimes choice or otherwise unavoidable necessity) be occasionally used, if health is otherwise good, and if the negative effects of the impure substances were offset by the judicious use of fasting and the return to a consistently pure diet.

I realized that "exaggerated" involvement in the processes of fasting and "right" diet was itself merely another form of seeking. It was attachment to life as a physical and vital problem. Thus, even "right" dietary discipline, if approached via the point of view of the seeker, or the mind of a "problem", could become a distraction, and the ground for a goal-centered life. Then the otherwise "right" discipline of diet (and of the body in general) would absorb attention like any other presumed problem, as, for example, the problem of the mind, or the problem of Spiritual consciousness. Therefore, understanding this, I dropped all "exaggerated" motivations associated with health practice. I abandoned all my attachment to the idea of "perfection" through diet and fasting. I no longer placed any "infinite" importance on food. And I ceased to be motivated by the search for bodily immortality. All such seeking had proven itself to be merely a means for trapping attention in problems and problem-centered motivations, whereas a simple, intelligent regimen relative to fasting, diet, and general health practice allowed physical existence to remain essentially stable, energetic, and, above all, free of enforced attention and problematic motivations.

The essential logic that I retained in relation to food was based on a straightforward practical knowledge of the basic laws of bodily effects. This amounted to a knowledge of what food-practice produces constipation, and toxemia, and enervation (or the exhaustion of vitality). I was no longer motivated by any problem or idealism in relation to the body. My understanding of the body became a matter of daily practical intelligence, rather than idealism or problem-based seeking. The body had proven itself to be a lawful economy. It required <u>conscious</u> "right" use. Intelligent diet (and, therefore, a diet that is rather consistently pure, generally fructo-vegetarian, perhaps, or at least at times, even exclusively fruitarian, and always, or as a general rule, maximally raw, or raw to the greatest degree the body healthfully allows, and, potentially, and even most optimally, one hundred percent raw), accompanied, as necessary, by regular short fasts and occasional (and "rightly" prolonged) long fasts, regular, healthful use of fresh air, usable (or safely received) sunlight, and pure water, appropriate (but, generally, simple, and not excessive, and, altogether, Yogically designed) physical exercise, and a life-positive (and yet Spiritually "right" and true) emotional-sexual practice (that conserves both natural emotional-sexual energy and true Spiritual Energy through positive relational and Yogic disciplines, whether "rightly" sexually active or "rightly" celibate)—all these became, for me, simple matters of responsibility, a matter of simple, practical intelligence relative to the body, whereas previously they appeared as strategic and idealized means toward some kind of victory over life, the body, and mortality itself.

This brings us to May of 1970. I had passed through most of the stages of experimentation that mark my early life. I had come to understand that life in Truth requires a radical process in consciousness—a process that directly transcends all seeking, and all conventions of mind and experience, by addressing the root-fault that originates every problem and the search itself. I saw that every strategic or remedial path is a form of problem-based seeking that originates from the moment to moment avoidance of relationship. And I saw that, apart from the moment to moment exercise of the process of radical understanding, the avoidance of relationship (and the constant origination of problems and searches) is the primary (and moment to moment) activity of consciousness in life. Actively understanding thus, I had ceased to function in reaction to problems or basic dilemma. This radical understanding effectively precluded (or released me from) any form of life motivated by the physical and vital problem, the psychic problem, the emotional problem, the mental problem, the Spiritual problem, or any other form of problem. I had developed a form of radical understanding that continuously allowed life to be lived consciously, directly, free of dilemma, free of identification with any problem-based motivation.

But there remained to pass a concluding episode in this adventure of understanding. As a result of the intense process of my life of understanding, especially over the period of the preceding several years, my body-mind, and all aspects of my life-practice, had become profoundly refined, such that I had become acutely sensitive and vulnerable to the drama of seeking, suffering, and even violence that was otherwise still going on in the world. An adolescent political, social, and cultural revolution, based on egoity (or individualism and separatism) and the materialistic mind (or the "wisdom" of this world), and, altogether (and inevitably), with profoundly negative consequences to come, was developing in the cities and spreading everywhere. Murder, guerrilla warfare, sniping, bombing, separatist confrontations, even the universal and careless exploitation of the separate possibilities of every one and every thing, the universal absence of true wisdom, the universal absence of Divine and Spiritual understanding and Peace, the universal absence of higher and Great experience, and the universal headlong adolescent commitment to every kind of suffering had become the daily meal of the entire world. I felt that I had understood something radically important about life. But life seemed to have become untouchable, locked in the final evolution of its own mortal "creation".

Because of all of this, I decided that I should leave America for an indefinite period. My own daily understanding and experience had become so profound, and so different from the exploited mentality and experience around me, that I felt I would necessarily have to continue the process of my life of radical understanding elsewhere, in Peace, and in a circumstance intended to be congenial to Peace Itself. Consequently, in May, I made arrangements for Nina, Patricia, and me to go to Baba's Ashram. We sold or gave away all of our material belongings, and on May 28 we flew to Bombay, to remain with the Guru indefinitely, and perhaps forever.

India, May 1970

CHAPTER 14

The Third Trip to India, and the Reappearance of "Christ"

As we prepared to leave for India, I made an assessment of all that I Knew. And, as a sign of that assessment, when we left for India I took three books: the *Bhagavad Gita*, the *Mandukyopanisad*, and *The Collected Works of Ramana Maharshi*. For me, these texts, along with various quotations from other traditional Indian sources (which I wrote inside their covers and in their margins), epitomized the tradition of Vedanta (and, especially, of Advaita Vedanta), or the ancient and esoteric Indian religious, philosophical, Yogic, and, ultimately, Advaitic (or non-dualistic) tradition as a whole. From my point of view, that tradition, as a whole, represented the closest parallel to my own search and experience. Likewise, from my point of view, that tradition, as a whole, represented the basic general background (of traditional philosophy and idealism) against which my own radical and unique understanding was emerging. Therefore, I carried these three books as if they were, together, a symbol for traditional Knowledge, a kind of traditional summa. But I also felt they epitomized the very search that I had radically understood, such that they had also, together, become a symbol for what I was constantly, and most directly, transcending by means of radical understanding. Therefore, I never read those books as I traveled on.

I entirely returned to India, fully believing that I was in basic general agreement with its ultimate (or most fundamental) philosophical and Spiritual principles. The three books I carried represented my affirmation of that, just as they represented the principles themselves. And, thus, the three books represented a kind of "defense" that I could readily offer, should anyone suggest that my point of view was not sufficiently "orthodox".

I deeply felt India to be my real and ancient home. I intended to place all of myself at Baba's feet and to retire there for life. I assumed that radical understanding, which was the Realization of my life, was wholly compatible with the habit of life at the Ashram. And I also assumed that I would be received in love and given the freedom to develop my conscious existence, even where it exceeded tradition, as long as I remained devoted to the essential habit of life at the Ashram and never lost sympathy with my Sources there.

I left America behind. I left the world behind. There was not a single movement in me that reflected a predilection for the usual existence. I felt humanly free, truly free, relieved of an immense burden, and purified of my own past life. I would devote myself to radical Realization, serve the Guru, and receive the eternal and continuous benediction of the Shakti's grace.

Upon our arrival in Bombay, we spent a night at a hotel, and then proceeded to the Ashram on May 30. We had left America quite suddenly and were not expected on the precise day we arrived. But our arrival was expected generally at that time. When we entered the Ashram, we were met enthusiastically by Amma and a few of our friends. Then I asked them to bring us to Baba.

Since my last visit, the Ashram had been much expanded. Now there were new large buildings in the central complex, and modern apartments had been prepared for Baba. I was told that he spent most of his time in seclusion now, and only came out to see devotees during pre-established hours. The Ashram was full of people, many of them young Americans and Europeans.

We were brought to Baba in the new meditation hall

outside his rooms. He sat in a chair. Nina and Patricia placed flowers at his feet, and I left a rosary of rudraksha beads. He spoke to Nina and Patricia briefly about the trip. But he seemed deliberately unwilling to acknowledge my presence. He told Nina he would talk to us later, and we were taken to a small bungalow where we were to stay.

I immediately noticed a change in the atmosphere of the Ashram. It had become a very public and busy institution. The program of life there had become much more formalized and sophisticated. Time was spent entirely at various kinds of "Ashram-seva" (or service to the Guru), or in the chanting of hymns and Scriptures, or in the practice of meditation. And Baba came and sat with people at various fixed hours of the day.

Nina, Patricia, and I were given daily work to do. Patricia cleaned guest rooms. I edited and refined the beginnings of an English translation of a book Baba was then writing (or had only recently written), which was to be called *Chitshakti Vilas*. And Nina typed the edited manuscript as it was produced. Also, at my request (so that I could increase my physical, and, especially, non-literary, activity) I was given work in Baba's Ashram garden. Thus, every day, we all worked, meditated, stood for chanting, sat with Baba, listened to his sermons, and listened to readings from Baba's new book. Baba never said a personal word to me. He made no effort to inquire of me or suggest any form of practice. His words seemed even purposely directed away from me, so that I would not be attracted to him. And I wondered why he no longer spoke to me in the root-language of Advaita Vedanta he once taught me. In any case, the formal life of the Ashram was itself to be the entire source of our daily-life experience, and it was up to us to stay or leave as we chose.

As I meditated, I also realized that nothing useful was "added" by the atmosphere of the Ashram. Indeed, the quality of the Ashram was entirely that of seeking, and it, therefore, had nothing to do with radical understanding and the radical Realization of Real Existence. People appeared to have experiences of the Shakti at various times, but they were not radically affected by It. And I knew they could not be, for Spiritual experience, like all experience, is only experience. Life is not transformed or Awakened by experience, but only by radical understanding.

Not only did Baba refrain from communicating verbally with me, but I did not at all experience the Shakti flowing to me through him. Altogether, the Ashram atmosphere felt as if it had shifted to a lower key, and the Shakti Itself was not particularly strong for me there.

On the day I first met him (in 1968, on the day I arrived, for the first time, at his Ashram), Baba instructed me to go to Swami Nityananda's burial place for Swami Nityananda's blessing. Thus, and always thereafter, Baba turned me to Swami Nityananda as my senior Guru. In keeping with that, when I was with Baba in Bombay (on my second trip to India), he told me to make a trip to Ganeshpuri, to receive Swami Nityananda's blessing. And so I did. Therefore, on this third trip to India, I continued my customary daily practice of walking down the road to Swami Nityananda's burial place, where I would meditate in the early afternoon. The Shakti had always been very Powerfully and freely Present for me there, but, on this third trip to India, I felt that this place, and, indeed, Swami Nityananda himself, was to be the Source for my further instruction. And, on and from the first day, as I sat there, the Shakti-Force would surge through my body, my heart and mind would become still, my head and eyes would become swollen with a tremendous Fullness of Bliss, and I would spontaneously relax into the Silent Depth of Being.

The routine of my daily life at the Ashram (and also my daily visits to Swami Nityananda's burial place) went on as I have described for about one week. I was feeling well, and Full. But nothing dramatic had occurred, or

top: The main entrance to the audience hall as it appeared in 1968 at the time of Adi Da's first visit to Swami Muktananda's Ashram
bottom: The Ashram as it appeared in 1970

Adi Da at the Ashram wearing mosquito netting

left: Nina

right: Patricia

seemed about to occur. I began to do this daily routine as a matter of course, expecting nothing but this simple order and experience. Then, one day, quite unexpectedly, as I worked in Baba's new garden (at the extreme rear area of the Ashram grounds), I experienced a remarkable "visitation".

I had been pulling weeds for perhaps half an hour when, suddenly, I felt a "familiar" Presence. It was as if a friend were standing behind me. And yet it also felt to be a Presence that I had never before sought, or even presumed to exist. I stood up and looked behind my shoulder. Standing in the garden, with an obviously discernible form, made of subtle Energy, fully felt, and even somehow seen, but also without even any kind of visibility, was the Virgin, Mary, Mother of Jesus of Nazareth!

My first impulse was huge laughter. I had spent years without the slightest sympathetic inclination toward Christianity. I felt I had fully and truly paid my early-life exoteric religious dues. I saw the entire Christian religious tradition as merely a symbolic and ritual communication, at best pointing <u>toward</u> Consciousness Itself, or pure Self-Awareness, and Vedanta-like conclusions about Reality. Now, as if I were faced with a cosmic joke, I stood in the living Presence of the Mother of Jesus of Nazareth.

What is more, my Christianity had been almost entirely of the Protestant variety. I had no predilection for Catholic, or even Eastern Orthodox, symbols. Christianity, insofar as it was meaningful at all to me, was a theological symbol for Truth. I had no devotional inclination toward its separate icons and historically unique symbols. I never once assumed that the "Virgin Mary" was any more than a religious symbol. I felt the "Virgin Mary" was a secondary (and imaginary) "creation" of the church, with no direct relation to the historical person who was the bodily human mother of Jesus of Nazareth. I never believed the "Virgin Mary" was an actual, Divinely Present individual with present significance for humanity.

Even during my brief involvement with the Eastern Orthodox church, I was not moved by its symbologies and icons of "Mary" and "Jesus". I only (and only temporarily) found, in my reading of the Eastern Orthodox tradition, a suggested sympathy for mysticism, and, thus, the possibility of a sympathetic accommodation of my own mystical life as a Christian "imposter". And Jesus of Nazareth himself, although he had a conventionally religious importance in my childhood, dramatically ceased to have any such importance once I experienced the trauma of my college education. Indeed, now that even that trauma had been released by the Spiritual experiences and the profound understanding that developed and matured in my years since college, Jesus of Nazareth no longer had any "believer's" significance for me at all. At least, that is what seemed to be the case at the level of my conscious mind. But now, it seemed, the subconscious and unconscious depths of my mind were showing off their residual contents, the mechanical leftovers not yet purified of the past. The Divine Shakti was active in me, and It was taking on the form of my inherited, Western religious mind.

My own mind, infused with the Divine Shakti, had projected itself outwardly, and become a living, visionary apparition. The "Virgin Mary" was not believable, but she was there! And I found that, after the first few moments of surprise and irony, I began to relate to her quite easily, with profound feeling, and in a very "Christian" manner. The Divine Shakti had Itself, through a visionary appearance, taken on, for my sake, a human, female likeness, even a form that, perhaps better than any other in the "great tradition" of mankind, symbolized and represented the archetype of the "Mother". Therefore, her very "Motherly" Presence evoked a "son"-like response in me. And, spontaneously, I found myself growing in profound devotion and love. She was, to all appearances, the "Virgin Mary", but, nonetheless, I Knew her to be the Divine Shakti Itself, Alive in front of me.

Just as the Presence (and the entire apparition) of the Virgin was not physical, but subtle, her Communication to me was internal, as I had earlier known it with Baba. In this manner, as we stood together in Baba's Ashram garden, she taught me a form of the Catholic Christian prayer "Hail Mary". Then she told me to buy a rosary for devotions. It was difficult to satisfy this demand. I had to find some excuse to get permission to go to Bombay. But I managed it, and she was satisfied. Thereafter, I found myself reciting the prayer constantly, as a mantra, while I worked and lived in the Ashram.

After several days of this devotion, the Virgin showed me an image of the face of Jesus. It appeared visibly in my heart, and she seemed only to uncover it. That image, and the feelings it immediately awakened in me, had been hidden and suppressed there since my childhood. Therefore, instantly, spontaneously, I was in love with Jesus!

As these experiences increased, I began to resist them mightily. I thought I must be deluded. I tried to meditate in the usual manner, but always the Virgin and Jesus would appear to guide and instruct me. I felt no Communication at all coming from Baba, or from the Shakti (as I had previously known It).

After two weeks of this, the Virgin told me to leave the Ashram with Nina and Patricia and go on a pilgrimage to the Christian holy places in Jerusalem and Europe. It was clear to me, from the first moment I saw the vision of the Virgin, that she, and all of the experiences that came along with her, were direct manifestations of the Divine Shakti. Therefore, I immediately, and more and more, became willing to be guided by the Virgin. And it became more and more obvious that all of these Christian visions, commands, and revelations were part of a unique grace, given to me by the Divine Shakti, and Purposed to serve the purification of my own deepest mind, such that the in-depth content of my mind would no longer obscure or prevent my most perfect Realization of the Divine Self-Condition. Therefore, I became willing to be moved, even in this strangely required Christian manner, and to do all that the Divine Shakti, even appearing as the Virgin (or in whatever other form the Divine Shakti appeared), told me to do.

I felt that the Divine Shakti was working independently for me now and no longer depended on the physical presence of Baba or the Ashram. Indeed, the manifestation of the Divine Shakti in and as my process of radical understanding, and now in and as my Christian visionary experience, was anything but characteristically Indian. And, in any case, it was the Divine Shakti "Herself" Who was telling me to leave the Ashram, and India, and return to the West, even via the visionary trail of my own mind.

As it happened, Swami Nityananda was to bless me and turn me to this course with the Divine Mother, and, thus and thereby, to the Ultimate Adventure that restored my most perfectly "Bright" Freedom. One afternoon, as I made my usual, daily walk to Swami Nityananda's burial place, I became attracted to a black and white photograph of Swami Nityananda that was for sale at a booth outside his Ashram. I thought I might stop and buy it on my way back.

When I arrived at the shrine, I bowed to Swami Nityananda reverently and walked around his burial place three times. This is a traditional Indian form of worship. I sat down to meditate, and then I felt Swami Nityananda touch me. His image appeared before my internal vision. He showed me a photograph of himself and held it before me as I sat with him. It was the same photograph that attracted me earlier, but it was in color!

In an internal conversation, I told Swami Nityananda about my recent experiences, how the Mother-Shakti had taken me over, independently of Baba or any other apparent Source. He blessed me, told me that I belonged to Her now, and that, as She had told me, I should leave the Ashram and let Her guide me.

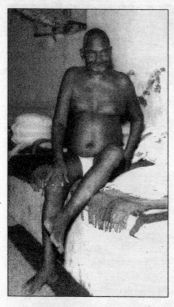

"When I arrived at the shrine, I bowed to Swami Nityananda reverently and walked around his burial place three times. This is a traditional Indian form of worship. I sat down to meditate, and then I felt Swami Nityananda touch me. His image appeared before my internal vision. He showed me a photograph of himself and held it before me as I sat with him. It was the same photograph that attracted me earlier, but it was in color!"

"I told Swami Nityananda about my recent experiences, how the Mother-Shakti had taken me over, independently of Baba or any other apparent Source. He blessed me, told me that I belonged to Her now, and that, as She had told me, I should leave the Ashram and let Her guide me."

Swami Nityananda

Photograph of Swami Nityananda in his youth purchased by Adi Da after visiting Swami Nityananda's burial shrine in Ganeshpuri

**The Mother-Shakti at the temple near the Ashram
in Ganeshpuri as Adi Da found her in 1970**

When I opened my eyes, one of the priests who serves Swami Nityananda's shrine was standing before me with a large handful of flower blossoms. He gave them to me as a blessing from Swami Nityananda.

As I left and walked through the village of Ganeshpuri toward Baba's Ashram, I passed another stall where photographs were sold. And there was the exact picture Swami Nityananda had shown me in the vision, in full color. I bought it, and continued to walk.

I knew that these flowers and the picture were not given to me for myself. They were symbols of a sacrifice I was to perform. The photograph was the image of the Guru. I had come to this stage by following the Guru as Nityananda in vision, and as Baba and Rudi at various stages in life and Spiritual experience. Now I was to surrender the external forms of the human Guru to others, and live without separation from the Guru, inhering in the Very Form that is the Guru, and guided by the inwardly revealed Divine Form of the Guru, shown to me as the Mother-Shakti, even, at that time, appearing to be the Virgin Mother of Jesus. And the flowers were all the parts of my manifested (or apparent) life, every center of being, every body (or functional sheath), every realm, and every experience in which I was animated. I was to take these flowers of my life and offer them to the Divine Mother-Shakti.

When I arrived at the Ashram, I bathed and put on clean clothing. I took the flowers to the temple of the Mother-Shakti near the Ashram. There is a traditional sculptured icon of Her benign, multiarmed, and omnipresent Form there. I looked into Her face and saw that She was the same One who appeared to me in vision as the Virgin and as the image of Jesus in my heart. I bowed to Her and placed the flowers at Her feet. I walked around Her three times. I took some holy ashes and pressed them on my forehead. As I left, I felt Her assure me that I was Her child and She would guide me.

I went and told Nina and Patricia that it was time to leave. We had discussed the possibility before. Even they had become restless at the Ashram. And I had told them of my experiences, my Christian visions and the instructions for our pilgrimage. Therefore, both of them agreed and were happy to leave.

I told one of Baba's agents that we would be leaving the next day. He was surprised, but he took the message to Baba. While we were preparing to leave, one of the American devotees came and was attracted to the picture of Swami Nityananda. I gave it to him, knowing this was the reason it had been offered to me.

We left the next morning, after a stay of little more than three weeks. Baba did not look at me. He seemed displeased, but I felt there was nothing I could say to justify our leave. I could only assume that all of my adventure was also blessed by him. We waited for the bus, and, as we pulled away, I thought I would never return to that place again.

Adi Da on pilgrimage to Christian holy sites in 1970

CHAPTER 15

The Diary
of Pilgrimage

While the experiences with the Virgin and Jesus were developing at the Ashram, I kept a continuous diary. And I maintained the diary as we traveled to Israel, Europe, and back to the United States.

The diary is not only the best, firsthand source for these experiences, but it shows how the entire matter developed, and how I eventually returned to a stable Realization of the radical Truth that is the substance of my Spiritual life. Thus, it demonstrates how my consideration developed in the midst of extraordinary experiences into quite another thing than the traditional forms of seeking and the realizations based on seeking.

I will include that diary here, somewhat relieved of length and repetition, and without interpretation, except to indicate certain external details.

You should be prepared to read what at first appears to be the devotional diary of a mystical Catholic Christian. It is my practice to write in the mood and with the precise, unequivocal language of my experience and persuasion at any moment. And, for a time, it seemed to me that the revelation of the church was the fulfillment of my life. Indeed, it was only by allowing it to be so and fully experiencing the course of this modification in my state, as well as all others at all other times, that I could come eventually to Realize What is always and stably the underlying Truth of all experience.

You should also recognize that this experience was a necessary one for me. It was an extension of that vision of the "Divine Lord" I had experienced the previous winter. And it drew on all the latent imagery, necessity, and unfulfilled devotional energy that had been trapped in my heart since childhood. Only when these images were completely and consciously experienced, and the feeling-energy surrounding the heart utterly released from its bondage to unconscious symbols, could I remain stably in the True Consciousness that is the Heart of Reality Itself.

❖ ❖ ❖

20 June 1970—Ganeshpuri, India

I first was visited by our Lady, our Mother, in the garden of Shree Gurudev Ashram, Ganeshpuri. She taught me to honor her with a form of the prayer "Hail Mary". Then she held before my mind an image of a rosary, until, after several days, I bought one in Bombay. Then she showed me her Son, our Lord, whose face of Whitest Light has thus and several times appeared directly before me in a total, mystical field of vision that, somehow, begins at the level of the physical heart. The description of the exact position of his living face depends on whether I examine it in relation to the body or the soul. Its brilliant Luminosity always faces me, and it "creates" the deepest Peace, Love, and Bliss in me, so that I feel as if I am nestled before it in the infinite womb of Mary, whose body seems to contain the soul.

After this revelation, she moved me to read as many books on the Faith as were available to me in my retreat. And, as I grew in this learning, she instructed me by moving me to write, and to become conscious of her impulses in me. By all of this, she has brought me to Christ and revealed to me the Truth of all that I have undergone in the past many years.

I already feel a suggestion to bury the rosary somewhere in the Ashram garden before I leave, so that she has a focus for her Presence there. She may not require this of me, but may instruct me instead to keep it for devotions. I am awed with the Absolute Truth of the church, and how It escaped me all my life. Since this revelation, there has also been a continuous, deep Ecstasy and Joy in my heart that is so great I dare not even allow myself to be fully conscious of It, or to experience and manifest It completely.

❖ ❖ ❖

All remedial paths and their practices point to a goal that is either symbolic or transcendent, a state of mind or psyche or soul. These goals are intuited by Spiritual experiment, the research of seekers, without benefit of the directly and priorly revealed Divine Presence. What lies beneath all of these goals as their latent, unconscious Object or Source is Christ. Indeed, all of these goals would already be fully attained if Christ were consciously received on every level of our living being. His Fullness precludes the great search. It epitomizes and Fills each level of our living being. And his Presence, from the moment It is Known in faith, raises us into the ever more full Realization of that Fullness. He is the Source and Object of every Spiritual state, and even the earth itself and every miraculous power are only symbols for the hidden Truth that is the Fullness of Christ.

❖ ❖ ❖

The transmitted gospel itself generates many historical problems in relation to texts, specific interpretations, traditions, and so on. This is simply due to the fact that the transmitted gospel is a communication through human beings in the world over time. But, in this gospel, the living condition of Reality, which is latent in all things, is constantly suggested, and the recognition of the living condition of Reality is what draws us into right relationship to others and things, such that all seeking becomes unnecessary, and such that the victory over an otherwise suffered life is made possible.

All other traditions of Truth draw human beings into the distractions of the great search, but the Lord and Reality of this gospel stands eternally before us and is continually at work to save us. The gospel immediately puts us in contact with him. Thus, the gospel is not mere language and symbols, but the unique tool and revelation of the living condition of Reality. The Living Lord, the gospel, and the church are present, with his Holy Mother, to transform all the world by restoring it to the living condition of Reality, which is not "natural" or philosophically realizable, but which is the Knowledge inherent in one's Knowing of the directly Revealed Lord.

I say that living condition is latent in all things only because it is their only true structure, even though Realizable only by Revelation. And that Revelation must become conscious in some direct manner in order to be Realized. The living condition of Reality is conscious awareness of the Revealed Lord, the Present God. Thus, nothing exists in the fullness of its "created" state until it receives and Knows Him.

❖ ❖ ❖

Texts that are particularly important to me: "He that seeth me seeth the Father also" (John 14:9). "That I may know him and the power of <u>his</u> resurrection" (Philippians 3:10).

❖ ❖ ❖

For the first time in many years I am experiencing genuine surrender to God. It is happening by His grace, since I am not trying to do it at all—it is a seemingly "natural" effect of His Presence in the heart. He is unutterably Real to me—and this is a new experience.

My past Spiritual efforts were marked by a continuous struggle with exactly and primarily this surrender. It was my first teacher's main sadhana, and, by years of effort, I realized the absolute impossibility of surrender. Then I came to Baba, and he gave me Spiritual experiences free, without my effort of surrender. After two years and more of his sadhana, I realized that I had not changed one iota in my essential relationship to things. I had many experiences, and had even developed a Spiritual "ego", but I was, all in all, still incapable of surrender.

Then the Lord Himself came to me and took up His abode in me. And His Presence is my surrender. How could I not love Him? Surrender is a quality in the living condition of Reality. As soon as life is returned to that condition, it is also surrender.

❖ ❖ ❖

Reality is not an object, a thing that can be experienced, seen, and so forth. Reality is a living and inclusive condition. It is subject and object. The living condition of Reality, which is Reality, is the relationship to God, in which we are conscious of being Filled by Him. Thus, Reality cannot be sought and found within or without, by Spiritual seekers or self-indulgent sinners (the former are generally searching within and the latter without). It is not object, exclusive shape, but the inclusive condition of life itself.

Our consciousness of God is a participation in and manifestation of that living condition. God's Consciousness of us is the supreme manifestation of that Law Which is Reality. All things are subject to that Law and require the Revelation of Christ.

Previously, I was confused by the ideas of Advaita Vedanta, the *Srimad Bhagavatam*, and the *Bhagavad Gita*. I saw that necessary and living condition as being essentially and exclusively a Divine Consciousness Which included us and was in fact our entire being, mind, thought, and so on. Thus, our only Real and True experience was this awareness, in which the Divine is the Subject Who Experiences all our experiences, thoughts, and so on. Our existence was not any of these experiences but the awareness of Him Who was in fact their Ultimate Subject and Center. This mystical awareness in fact upset me deeply after a time. Now I have seen clearly at last. The living condition of Reality is one in which God is Present to us and in us, but not to the point of assuming our identities, in fact, becoming us and excluding our "created" existence by virtue of His inclusive Being. We also participate in that living condition or Law, and, in the fullness of our living being, which He has given us, we are conscious of Him, present with Him. Thus, we are Free <u>and</u> unqualifiedly alive, immediately with God forever, sheerly by His grace.

Thus, the living condition of Reality is a gift, Revealed, not natural to the understanding, not discernible by experiment. That condition is Revealed to us only by God's grace. And that Revelation is the Totality of grace. It is the Ground of the Beatific Vision, or the Supreme State, and of the entire life of faith. The Christian life is mystical, a conscious participation in the Mystery of God, wherein we constantly and "creatively", in cooperation with Divine grace, maintain the living condition of Reality, the conscious relationship to God.

❖ ❖ ❖

Christ is that Eternal Aspect of God which reveals and guarantees forever that the Truth is relationship to God and not Absorption into the powers of God or Absorption into the Transcendent Being of God. Life is a meditation on being already Filled.

❖ ❖ ❖

A remarkable thing the grace of God has given me is that, in a few moments, or hours, I do not know the precise hour of this death, He turned me completely to Himself. So that the Truth of the Catholic Faith, the verity of the church and its doctrine, a host of details, and, above all, the devotion to our Lady, were given me in a flash of comprehensive insight. All of this in spite of the fact that I have never been trained as a Catholic, or ever sought it out in the least overt manner. All of this has been latent in me, at best a sentiment, all my life. This also shows how our Lord's "mere" Presence teaches and recollects all things most directly.

The impulses of this Divine grace and faith are so strong that I am scarcely willing to follow them directly. I am abiding in this Hindu Ashram, allowing Christ to mature me, so that I do not proceed out of my own motives and presumptions, deluded again by my own sinful fascinations. For days I struggled with this Truth and Its visions. I tested them, denied them, tried to immerse myself in meditation and the Guru. But there is this constant Christ, and my heart is torn out at the bottom. I am mad with him. I am about to become too full of ordinary humor for this place, and too sorrowful for my sins.

❖ ❖ ❖

In the garden, our Lord's Mother told me to pray: "Hail Mary, Mother of God. Blessed art thou among women. And blessed is the fruit of thy womb, Jesus."

Today I sat to meditate, and asked her to teach me how to meditate as a Christian, how she wanted me to meditate toward our Lord. She moved me to begin by praying the "Our Father" several times. Then, she brought me to recite this "Hail Mary" repetitively, with attention concentrated on its meaning. I saw that it always led through her to Jesus. Each time I came to the Name "Jesus", I would be fixed firmly in him. This continued automatically for nearly two hours, through dinner, and ended only when conversations began. This meditation gave me great Joy, stilled the mind, and directed me continually to Jesus through his Mother.

Then, as I continually concentrated on him, he taught me a prayer deeper within. It was his own constant "Amen. Amen." I saw that the heart's pulse always synchronized with this word: A-men, A-men. And this prayer out of and in Christ constantly directed me to the Father. The "So be it" constantly leaves the mind on Him in silence, in a vast Bliss. I felt the movement of "Amen" as the Holy Spirit Himself, returning, through Christ, to God the Father, from Whom He proceeded.

Thus, our Lord's Mother taught me a practice of meditation that leads to contemplation of the Trinity in all the Mysteries of Its Form, until all at last draws into the silent Brilliance of God, Absorbed in blessed Vision.

I will continue to use this blessed contemplation, if it does not offend our holy church, with faith that our Lady intended it for the ultimate good of my soul.

❖ ❖ ❖

21 June 1970

This morning, as I walked toward the place of my morning meditations, I began to pray the "Our Father" and then the "Hail Mary" as I was taught yesterday. But even though these and all true prayers of the church lead to contemplation of the Holy Trinity, I felt dry in the praying. I thought of the Holy Sacrament of the altar, and Christ's promise: "He that eateth my flesh and drinketh my blood abideth in me and I in him" (John 6:57). This is the promise of the Fullness of God, with Which we are Filled. It is Fullness given by grace, available by no other means. It is the Presence Itself, and It makes Itself Known. Unless It makes Itself Known, there is no way to concentrate upon It. But I desired this Fullness, in order to meditate upon It.

When I sat in meditation, I felt the Presence of Christ. I could not see him. Even the image of his brilliantly Luminous face that I had previously seen in the heart was absent. There was darkness, but only his Presence. Then he moved me to pray the "Amen". And I saw that the "Amen" was said once with each breath. Once on the inhalation and once on the exhalation. And the "Amen" was always said in the center of the heart, wherein we direct ourselves to God. As I prayed the "Amen", I realized that Christ was praying it in me. It is the Holy Spirit in Christ to God the Father. And Christ said: "I am the 'Amen'."

Then I continued in this prayer and was taught the mystery of its use. The heart is the center, where Christ stands to us. And the body is a cross form in which he radiates his Fullness. As I prayed, one "Amen" for each inhalation of breath, and one for each exhalation, Christ said: "I am drawing all things to myself." Then, when I inhaled and prayed "Amen", all the life-energy of desires moved up out of the lower body to the heart, and became a deep concentration of Love in Christ. And, when I exhaled and prayed "Amen", all the life-energy of thought, the entire activity of mental energy and the mind itself, was drawn down to the heart and concentrated in Christ as profound Love. This continued, until I was profoundly Present in the heart, simply Present with Christ in great and ecstatic Love. And that Love was Christ himself. He generated It in me, and yet I felt that I was not, but was simply absorbed in him, in the White Fire of his own Love.

Then I realized that the Fullness whereby we are Filled is Christ himself. The Fullness that is ours in the Sacrament is not simply some Radiance of Christ's Energy, breathed into us like pleasant air. It is Christ himself who comes and is Present, so that we are absorbed in the contemplation of him. He is the "Amen", which we pray, which he prays in us, whereby all prayers come to an end, whereby he draws all things to himself in blessed contemplation. Thus, I was drawn to him, not to concentration on mere breaths or on some fullness moving in me, only distantly connected to him. He is in us as himself, his total Presence, open to our Conscious Love. And he draws us to his very Self, which is an Infinite Fire of Love. Thus, we become only Love in him. The dark nights of sense and of the soul are quickly traced to the heart in the prayer "Amen". Thus, we are not moved toward an emptiness but toward the Fullness of God. God is only Full. "God is light, and in Him there is no darkness" (I John 1:5). There can be no end to

God's Revelation of Himself to us in this Prayer. Each breath surrenders desires and thoughts in Him, and each breath or act of surrender is a movement, by faith and hope and Love, into the State of mere faith and hope and Love. This cross of meditation is a cross of faith. Its pain is Love. Its suffering is Sublime. The cross is never absent from Christ, but it eternally contemplates him in the heart of its beams. In this meditation which Christ inspired in me, I felt that the entire Truth of the church was contained in a perfect symbol.

❖ ❖ ❖

"Amen" is the Christ, the Name of God. "Amen" is the beginning of all things, the "So be it" of God. "Amen" is the acceptance of all things as the Will of God, the "So be it" of mankind. Christ has given us the Name of God by giving us himself. The Person, Christ himself, is the Name of God Which he revealed to us. Thus, we are told to ask in his Name and we will receive. That is, to contemplate God in and through and as Christ, the "Amen", is to be given the totality of gifts, now and forever. Anyone who, by God's grace, deeply contemplates the Name of God, and through It approaches the Father in his or her need, will be given whatever he or she requires. The power of the Name is not available to those who do not enter It profoundly, in faith, for the Name is not a mere word, but the Name is God Himself as Christ.

❖ ❖ ❖

The Love of Christ is the Support and Source of living Bliss, even the Conscious Energy of Spiritual existence, under all conditions. It makes life madly into Joy. Under the worst trials, It does not guarantee a mood of ordinary playful happiness, but It supports the deep Joy of faith and mystical communion. This Love is the internal condition of the soul, whereby Christ draws it to himself. It is not our un-"created", original Love for him, but his Love generated in us by his Presence to the soul.

❖ ❖ ❖

The Word is "Amen".

❖ ❖ ❖

I sat in meditation again. Our Lord's Mother has moved me, and I have decided to leave the Ashram in order to make a pilgrimage and communicate with the church. In meditation, I pleaded for guidance, so that I would not be tempted to uncertainty, so that I would certainly Know the Truth without fear that I am deluded. I waited. I had prayed the "Our Father" and "Hail Mary". I prayed the "Amen", as I had been taught. The meditation was dry. Then I kept Enquiring with each breath, as I tried to surrender the energies of desires to the "Amen" with each inhalation, and the energies of thought with each exhalation. I Enquired, "Avoiding relationship?" Each time, this self-Enquiry loosened me from flight, so that I concentrated in him at the heart. And then he spoke, regarding those great teachers whom I have pursued for years: "They are infinitely Returned, but I am eternally Present." Then he drew me to himself, and I was ecstatic, open-armed, crying, Dear Lord, Dear Dear Lord.

The Lord said this to me during my meditation on him:

"They are infinitely Returned,
But I am eternally Present.
One who Knows me
Is free from liberation
And desires.
One who neither seeks
Nor lusts,
I no longer prevent from me.
Those who are sought
For liberation
Are an imitation of my
Symbol.

> They lead men into the
> Great Search,
> In caves, seclusions, and their homes.
> But I am
> One who cannot be found,
> Unless I Reveal myself.
> I lead men home to
> Everything,
> Today.
> But I am always with them.
> I am He."

"I am He." Thus, the Lord took the mantra from me that I had learned from the Guru, Muktananda. He relieved me of the way of the mantra, "So-Ham", "I am He". He showed me the Truth of the mantra, that it is His mantra, His symbol, Himself.

❖ ❖ ❖

22 June 1970

"They are the Witness.
I am the Presence."

❖ ❖ ❖

In meditation this morning I came to a profound point of passionate Stillness. I simply contemplated him, and there was even physical pain in the heart, as if the rising current of love and its Force concentrated in the heart had made a wound, so that the heart was open and gaped forward from the chest. I felt the Father, and the Lord said of Him, "Be Still, and Know that I am God." That appears to be the final and essential key to contemplation.

❖ ❖ ❖

Until a man or woman is reborn by God's revelation, he or she knows sin by its effects. Thus, a man or woman becomes naturally wise, renounces the field of suffering, and devotes himself or herself to self-transformation or liberation. But after a man or woman is reborn in Christ, he or she understands sin in a new manner. Such a one no longer sees sin as mere effects, or even as various significant causes in life-action. Rather, such a one sees sin as the avoidance of Christ. When such a one is thus convicted, knowing well the reality of sin and of Christ, he or she is drawn to Christ in the ease of surrender.

23 June 1970—Bombay, India

The seeker is incapable of relationship because he or she is always consciously trying to transcend it. The self-indulgent sinner is incapable of relationship because he or she is always exploiting it into excess and confusion, and thus descending below it. The former escapes Christ within, the latter without. Christ is God confronting us in relationship, thus making life Real and necessarily moral.

❖ ❖ ❖

Prayer, meditation, and fasting (responsible, controlled, and lawfully used) restore us to the conscious relationship to Christ, stabilized, free of the motion of avoidance.

Thus, the meditation I have learned ends in a deeply silent and blissful contemplation of God. But it is not a mere staring. It is not at last a concentration in a point, but an opening, an awareness of a Total, Conscious Presence. Then, frequently, I pass into a free mental prayer, truly asking and interceding in the Name of Christ.

❖ ❖ ❖

The oriental seeker-saints and imperfect God-men are all maharajas of the great search. They tend to strategically disincarnate (and would likewise have us strategically disincarnate) the living condition of Reality, which condition is relationship and love. We go to them after we have ourselves despaired of love and faith and hope and charity. And we may even project on them the symbols of love, even the image of Christ. Thus, we follow, unconscious that we are really seeking love, the fulfillment of relationship. Therefore, when (suddenly) I became absorbed in the symbols of Christ, I was free of my false discipleship.

(Note: By the time we arrived in Jerusalem, the overwhelming and exclusive Presence and visions of the Virgin and Jesus had begun to subside, and these were replaced by a tacit, immediate experience and understanding. The change in my consideration that accompanied this becomes clear in the writing that follows.)

We stayed in the ancient sector of Jerusalem, within the old walls, at Soeurs de Sion, a convent run by an order of Catholic nuns. Our dwelling was built on the Via Dolorosa, the road of Christ's last walk. Our convent itself was built on the ground where Pilate interviewed Christ. On the ground floor some ancient pavements stand, and a chapel has been built there. In the rooms below stand the actual pavements on which Christ was scourged.

One night I was awakened to feel a tremendous Force straining my body. I felt the entirety of my living being concentrated beyond and above my physical form, and my head felt about to explode.

I got up and began to wander in the convent. It was all in shadowy darkness. I felt drunken and possessed. I swayed through the halls. I felt surrounded with ancient spirits and the air of a terrible holocaust. I went into the chapel where Christ was judged, and then I went into the cellar where he was scourged. I saw the inscriptions in the floor made by soldiers while they trapped him in an ancient game and made him the "scapegoat".

The strangeness and fear in the atmosphere quickened me, and I returned to my room. But I was unable to sleep for some time. I felt my mind to be separated and settled above my head, concentrated in the ascended Christ.

❖ ❖ ❖

25 June 1970—Jerusalem, Israel

In the end, perhaps there is only the Profound. Perhaps there is no religion for me.

When I was a child, I enjoyed a semiconscious participation in the living condition of Reality. I recognized it in the symbol of Christianity. Then I lost Christianity and, thereby, also the perception that made me at least distantly conscious of the living condition of Reality. Then I sought, by semiconscious and unconscious motivation, to recover that living condition. Always I held that symbol before me and superimposed it on the objects by which I sought. Finally, lately, the symbol returned overtly, by force of some recovery of consciousness of the living condition of Reality. Then the symbol began to subside again, but I continue to abide in the living condition of Reality. Christianity is in many ways a wonderful symbol for that living condition. But it limits the experience by distracting the mind and organizing it in ways that "create" unconsciousness again (by submerging me in the symbol). Thus, it "creates" the search again in a muted form, while also allowing the enjoyment of some of the drama, aesthetic, and peace of the living condition of Reality.

Life in the living condition of Reality is Silent. But, if its structure were to be described, it would be as complicated as the literature of the church. Thus, I am involved in a meditation on the living condition of Reality, and on the church, which is superimposed on it. Thus, I learn, but I look forward to the "Advaita" of the pure Truth of the living (and, ultimately, perfect) Form

"As I stood to photograph the city, to feel somehow the form and aesthetic of the Perfect manifested as Jerusalem, I was blessed to recall Christ's words: 'My Kingdom is not of this world.'"

Photographs of Jerusalem taken by Adi Da

on His Pilgrimage in 1970

of Reality. I want to experience It fully, directly, unqualifiedly, dependent on nothing outside of It—indeed, all
symbols fall away from It, and only It is Revealing Itself,
even in that wonderful symbol.

❖   ❖   ❖

26 June 1970

I was standing on the porches of the roof, pho-
tographing the "Holy City", Jerusalem. The life of the city
had made a strange impression on me. There is an
absence "created" in all of these commemorations of
Christ. There is no Spiritual Force in any of the holy
places, and no feeling of higher life, higher aspiration,
and higher consciousness in the people. There is no
unusual Presence here. So that, if you look for It, you
lose It. There is only the "usual" Presence. But, the contrast of the Holy City taught me the meaning of this Presence in a new way. Holy places are a kind of Spiritual
kingdom that implicate God in the world. They tend to
call us into the search for Him, the evidence of His manifestation as the form of the world. But Jerusalem has
been strangely emptied, if only by force of the symbol of
Christ's resurrection. The entire city stands like a Siva-
lingam, pointing away to God. As I stood to photograph
the city, to feel somehow the form and aesthetic of the
Perfect manifested as Jerusalem, I was blessed to recall
Christ's words: "My Kingdom is not of this world."

Lately I have been impressed with the classical attitude of Christian saints, the attitude of exile. I have
begun to experience it myself, and it is accompanied by
a relief of anxiety, concern, and despair in the face of
this world. I had been living in the image of the Kingdom, but it was unconscious. And so I projected it on the
world. I sought in every fashion to enforce an aesthetic
and a Presence on the world, and even to identify God
and myself with it (while also maintaining the idea of
absolute transcendence). But the Presence is Known

here in absence. We Know Him and are Filled by Him, but this only lifts us into the Kingdom not of this world. To be concentrated in Him in faith and love and openness is to remain free of qualification by life. At the same time, it is to Know the Truth about life, and it is also to love life, and help it, and freely remain "creative" in it.

Previously, I sought Powerful holy places—now I know the world is empty, containing no Spiritual Force at all. All the places of Power draw us into some sphere of the world, away from God and His real Kingdom. The "sex appeal" of holy people, holy places, Spiritual symbols, methods, and objects of Power has disappeared by virtue of understanding. The Presence of God is in His Kingdom—He is Known only to faith, by acceptance of the grace that draws us out of the world, the exclusive, separative forces, into the Kingdom of God. God is not the world, nor is He within it. Nor is the world apart from God, since He "created" it, except that the world lives estranged from Him, <u>radically</u> estranged from Him, because of sin. To be drawn into the Realization of the Kingdom is to be free of qualification by sin and the world, and to live as a free human being, but it is not to know and enjoy any particular circumstance. It is to Know God and be drawn into His Kingdom of Love, but it is to remain in the world in fact, for now. Sin is not merely a condition of the psyche that is dissolved by the techniques and experiences of ordinary religion and conventional Spiritual life. Sin is a root-force in the world itself. The origin of the world is in God, but it has also fallen entirely away. The hope of the world itself, down to the very structures of natural energy, is in the resurrected and ascended Lord, who must come again to make a new "creation".

27 June 1970

In Jerusalem I have been drawn into a Knowledge that is different from any I have Known before. I feel the current of Life in me being drawn upwards, bursting through the heart and straining toward heaven, infinitely above. This strain is made a tension, because it cannot yet be fulfilled. I am born in the world and this "created" state. Yet, I am aware of exile, and the risen Lord is pulling me to himself. The primary symbol is the empty tomb, or the empty cross. Wherever you go, he is not here. This is not paradise, not the Kingdom, nor is it our task to "create" the Kingdom here. Wherever we are, whatever the time of life, Christ is drawing us to our true home in the fully Divine "creation".

The heart, the cave, is not full. It is empty. Its locus is above. Thus, we are able to live in the world without being qualified by it. If we surrender the circumstances of suffering, death becomes easy. We are happy to serve, to love, and thus, by remaining empty as the tomb, to continue always in the Transcendent State of Christ-Consciousness, fully related to him who draws all things to himself above.

The Kingdom and the Lord are not here. We are free of the burden to Realize him here. It is obvious where he is. Jerusalem is empty! Our Fullness is constant and above. We enjoy our life in him above, and he in us below. Our life in him does not exclude the world, but it frees us from all qualification by the separated world. And we are always drawn above, even out of the body, all powers, all visions, and all success. Our faith, our hope, and our charity are empty. We are infinitely con-soled, Fullness above, but without support of visions or any certainty that is not the Lord himself, intangible in the heart of faith. The empty tomb is the Siva-Lingam of the Truth. It points and draws us beyond all things into the unqualified Bliss of faith, entirely rested in the Lord and doing his Will. I have been to the Holy Places and seen that he is gone. And I Know that it is impossible to be separated from him, since relationship is the living condition of Reality. Thus, I Knew him where he is, not apart, in the places of his absence, but in the Force of his ascended State.

❖ ❖ ❖

The Lord is Present to faith because the soul is not separated from him. But the soul is conscious more deeply and higher than the world. The soul in faith is a participant in the unqualified, eternal dimension of Reality. Just as the soul is drawn above to Christ, the soul and Christ thereafter live by including the world. The Presence Known to faith is True. But the "Presence" known to seekers is merely the reflection of God in His "creation". It is one or the other modification of God's glorious expression. To know such a "Presence", such a philosophical immanence, is yet to remain in the separated state, without the unqualified vision, life, understanding, and Knowledge of the faithful.

❖ ❖ ❖

True Spiritual life is not a search, or an effort of ultimate self-transformation, but it is an ascent. All its actions are practical, having limited, efficient ends. It is not involved in the ultimate and desperate effort, the Narcissistic drive for supreme immunity and power. The ultimate aspects of genuine Spiritual life are outside the realms of cause and effect, and outside of all goal-directed, transformative effort.

The ascent is the natural movement of faith, drawn by the risen Lord. It is simply the rising tendency, the aspiring, surrendered Spire of Energy and Love. It is not an ordinary Yoga, an ego-willful and strategic means of seeking toward some great and even perfect goal. It is already a relationship to the Perfect One. It is an unqualified, unburdened Bliss. It is a cooperative ease of Joy that purifies in Spiritual Fire. It is the living condition of Reality.

A man or woman of real faith is not working out his or her salvation in any manner. He or she has recognized the symbol itself, and suffers no confusion in relation to the world, the horizontal and descending context of life. By the power of salvation and the power of Christ's resurrection, a man or woman becomes transformed by grace. The attention of such a one is above, always. He or she finds no motivation in life, but moves by means of grace. Thus, such a one is already empty, wherever he or she is. Such a one loves and understands, brings Truth and comfort and help, "creates" everywhere the symbol that promotes the recognition of Truth, and always Communicates what heals and makes salvation.

(Note: At this point, the "Christian" movements in vision and the mind had almost ceased. They came again only on occasion, as we went to the ancient holy places. But they were no longer in the form of Christian visions and Christian religious motivations. They were only the sense of Presence and Power that is generated in all genuine holy sites, whether in the Hindu temples and shrines of the Gurus or in the ancient temples and churches of the Virgin and Jesus. Now I approached them with great love, understanding, and a direct experience of the One and Prior Reality that they all manifest.

And now I also bore a critical understanding of the various remedial paths and religions. I had been entirely emptied of the movement in myself toward any remedial path or goal. Thus, not only Christianity became understandable, such that Reality Itself was recognized to be its only Truth, but so also was the remedial path of Advaita Vedanta, and all the remedial paths of Yoga and Spirituality.

My own way had become a simplicity of direct understanding and self-Enquiry. It was only that, radically and entirely.)

28 June 1970—Athens, Greece

The Truth is Non-separateness. Non-separateness is the Realization, the fact, the Condition, the Bliss, and the Reality. It is already the case and can never be acquired. To be deeply attentive to oneself and Enquire: "Avoiding relationship?" consciously realizes the structure and movement of suffering and unconsciousness. But there is also the sudden vanishing of this in the same process, as one recognizes or simply abides as and in That Which the previous state prevented. This is the entire Truth. It depends on no dogma, implications, or suggestions of the mind. It is contained in no exclusive theory or system of Reality. Human beings have anciently Realized this Truth, but they limited Its Power and Clarity by the accretions of thought, or the psychic process by which they sought or supported the Truth.

The Truth of Advaita Vedanta is Non-separateness, but It is expressed and made unavailable in a philosophy that has only one term: the pure, exclusive, relationless Identity. The Truth is in no way contrary to relationship, but It is perfectly Enjoyed as unqualified relatedness. The adventure of Advaita Vedanta is, then, a mental problem that prevents the living condition of Reality.

The Truth of Christianity is Non-separateness, but It is expressed and made unavailable in a theology that necessarily has two exclusive terms: God (or the Trinity) and creature. Thus, even the mysticism of Christianity is a profession allowed to but a cloistered few, whose expressions are carefully monitored. And the mystics become doubtful to the church when they speak of non-separation from God.

But the Truth is not Realized by the strategy of exclusive identification with the transcendental Self, nor by the strategy of seeking union with God. Both of these strategies limit the Truth Itself. They burden It with mental implications that surround It in mystery. But all mental forces subside in the basic, continuous self-Enquiry: "Avoiding relationship?"

The Truth is Non-separateness Itself, Which is a profound Realization, unqualified, not exclusive, unproblematic, direct, unburdened, pure, unqualifiedly relational, not qualified by forms or concepts of the egoic self, or that to which the egoic self is related, or that which relates itself to the egoic self. There is no useful dogma of egoic self, transcendental Self, or separate God. All dogmas are heavy with implication, and they drive the mind through ancient courses and holocausts of symbols, forever toward the same, primary Realization. And that Realization is Reality Itself. But that Realization is the necessary and continuous foundation and process of life. It is not the distant goal of life. Only to the dogmaticians and philosophers does Reality seem to be the distant goal of life, because they are children of their own minds. Reality Itself is the always <u>present</u> Nature and Condition of the living condition of existence. And Reality Itself always already <u>is</u>, always already <u>now</u>, in every context of the living condition of existence. Therefore, Reality Itself (and the living condition of Reality) must be "creatively", consciously lived and breathed, moment to moment.

In the moment to moment process of true self-Enquiry ("Avoiding relationship?"), engaged after a thorough investigation of the alternatives to Truth, there is the moment to moment Realization of the living condition of Reality. At first the state will seem to be realized, and the process will seem to purify and stabilize the mind and life. But these are only peripheral effects, or matters of relationship seen in themselves. What is in fact the case, from the beginning, is the living condition of Reality, relationship itself, without qualification.

The living condition of Reality is the basis of all "creativity". It is full, yet unanswered. That condition can itself be felt so directly and profoundly that any of the traditional "Spiritual" experiences may be simulated in the conditions of the living consciousness. But all visions and unusual perceptions will, in due course, cease as self-Enquiry continues. The practice of self-Enquiry should become the radical, basic act of conscious life. No one has done this before, since all have previously thought the Truth involved the mind, a remedial path of seeking, and a goal. But, free of all these, self-Enquiry, the living condition of Reality, will move into a profundity of Awareness that will revolutionize conscious life, since, for the first time, it is already Real.

This most direct and radical simplicity, the living condition of Reality, is awakening in me with such force as I continue it moment to moment that it feels as if my body, with all its deep centers, is about to burst and disappear. Reality is a madness of Light, an unqualified air of Space, a vowel of Consciousness!

The Truth is not a dogma, not an affirmation. Thus, all positive statements only place conditions on Consciousness Itself. "I am He", or the ideas of God, and so forth, do not Realize us as Reality, except perhaps in temporary intuitions that fall away again in the mental adventure. The only useful language is not affirmation but true self-Enquiry, which "creates" a sudden absence, like the empty tomb near Golgotha. And that absence leaves the living condition of Reality standing. Such an absence is the only perfect and true implication. Thus, it is the essential, "creative" activity of conscious life.

This practice of self-Enquiry will continue as a deliberate activity of the mind as long as an individual tends to identify with various states. But it is also the living condition of Reality Itself, and that which was self-Enquiry is simply the basic movement and form of the living consciousness when the false tendency subsides.

From the living condition of Reality all value and virtue emanate and transform the world. Apart from that living condition, there is either the chaos of avoidance and Narcissistic enterprise, or, at best, the systematic, remedial religious and Spiritual path, exclusive in concept, temporary in effect, and short of the Fullness of Reality.

This Truth was in Gautama,[56] in Shankara,[57] in Ramakrishna, and in Nityananda. This Truth was in Jesus and in all his saints. Yet, this Truth has nothing to do with any of them. The Truth Itself is simpler, more direct, more obvious.

In the process of true self-Enquiry ("Avoiding relationship?"), one may pass through periods of marvelous insight, wherein the Truth of "Christ", or of Advaita Vedanta, or of any system, symbol, remedial path, and so forth, may suddenly rise up in the mind as the overwhelming Answer and Reality. But if one continues self-Enquiry, which is itself the living condition of Reality, all conditional or temporary truths will pass, just as will all the effects of separative activity. Enough said about my Christianity, my Vedanta, and all my paths of seeking.

❖　❖　❖

7 July 1970—Rome, Italy

Until now, all religions, all remedial paths, and even all forms of Spiritual Knowledge, have been based on a single, primary, elemental presumption. All the various paths of effort have been different forms of reaction to the elemental <u>problem</u> of Reality. In every case, there is an intuition of the living condition of Reality—but the living condition of Reality has been conceived and approached as a problem, a necessary dilemma. Thus, in every case, the religion or remedial path has been an attempt or a design which proposes to solve that primary problem.

The problem on which all has been founded is relationship itself, perceived as autonomy, separateness, antinomy, duality, division, and multiplicity. Reality has been chronically intuited in this negative sense, and the solution has always been to enforce a "Oneness" or a

---

56. Gautama (ca. 563-483 B.C.E) was the great Indian Sage commonly known as "the Buddha".

57. Shankara (ca. 788-820) was a revered Hindu Sage who is regarded as the founder of the school of Advaita Vedanta, or non-dualism (see note 36, p. 212).

"union" which is the opposite, and the ultimate dissolution, of the primary dilemma.

The root of this intuition is contained in the idea of the object. The "object" implies a subject, distinct from it. On the basis of this elemental presumption, all existence has been described in terms of cause and effect, subject and object, matter and consciousness (or mind). From this description of existence, joined with the concept of liberation or atonement which seeks to overcome it, a great chain or hierarchy has been extended toward the idea of the "Primary Solution".

In the West, the way has essentially been tied to contemplation of the highest <u>Object</u>, Which is God, or Jesus (as the "Christ"), and so forth. Its traditional Spirituality and religion is based on a meditation on, or contemplation of, hierarchic symbols. Prayer, or aspiration, is its symbolic and effective mood.

In the East, the way has traditionally been tied to the Realization of the highest, or even the Ultimate, <u>State</u>, Which is inherently <u>Objectless</u>. The Spirituality and the religion of the traditional East are grounded in a progressively world-transcending experience or consciousness, which ultimately extends beyond the structure of subject and object. In the East, there is the way of utter transcendence, which extends (even by the grace of the highest or ultimate Power) beyond all objects, all relationship, into the exclusive domain of Being Itself. In the West, there is the way of persistent living, which seeks to escape all harm by idealistic and affirmative association with the highest Power and Being.

Clearly, both primary approaches are founded in the same fundamental problem. And all such efforts involve a genius of characteristic phenomena which both justify them and point to the ground of their existence.

I have no argument with these means themselves. They are the pure and greatest fruit of all traditional culture. It is only that I have been involved in them all, and always I have been led to see them in their most basic shapes. Always I am looking at these roots while wailing in the torment of effort.

And I see this foundation of all religion and Spirituality. I see their entire beauty and how they exceed all the suffering and enjoyment of mere life. But I also see they are not necessary, they are not possible, they are absolutely false.

Thus, I have no heart for the struggles of the great search. All remedial paths, or merely remedial ways, have fallen away from me. Even when I adored them most and lay prostrate before each Lord, the way and the salvation have been torn away, leaving the naked dilemma of all times in my sight without a symbol left to lead me away.

As a result, I have over time found myself alone with this perception, and, in spite of myself, I have been led to see and examine and Know this Truth, this Reality. And It is the radical Truth, Reality Itself, entirely free of the ancient dilemma.

All previous religion and Spirituality is based on the presumption of a necessary dilemma. For this reason, it is all false, unnecessary, and un-Real. I do not speak from the viewpoint of ordinary experience, which not only identifies with the dilemma but does so unconsciously, and compulsively exploits its effects. To the religious or Spiritual viewpoint that is based on the usual foundation of dilemma and egoity, my assertion that ordinary religion and conventional Spirituality are, at their foundation, false, unnecessary, and un-Real may, at first (and for the same reason), appear to be false, unnecessary, and un-Real. And, therefore, ordinary religion and conventional Spirituality, and every other form of the great search, will continue, in any individual case, until the dilemma and the ego are radically understood. But I speak from the "Viewpoint" of Reality-Experience, Which not only is free of the ordinary suffering of existence, but is also already and forever free of its solution in the productions of the great search.

What, then, do I see? The traditional ways have presumed the living condition of Reality to be a dilemma. Thus, whether the solution is in terms of the most transcendent Object, or even in terms of the transcendence of the entire subject-object structure of consciousness, that solution has always been itself a symbol of the dilemma on which it is founded. The atonement, or salvation, by which one is eventually and gracefully saved from inevitable sin and the effort of liberation by which one is finally Realized beyond the superimposition of unnecessary ignorance are both superimpositions on the primary Intuition of Reality.

If Reality Itself is recognized, and there is therefore no longer any conscious or living separation from Reality, or aberration from the living condition of Reality, then there is no necessity at all for any separate solution or remedial path. Once Reality is intuited as It is, without the superimposed conception of the dilemma, then atonement and liberation, salvation and Realization, as well as compulsive experience based on identification with separated functions, cease to be involved in the form of life.

All that I have written, and all that I have experienced in my unique order of life, has been a means to this very end, and, I am certain, a proof of what I contend.

Reality Itself, whose living condition is unqualified relatedness, or non-separateness, is totally free of necessary dilemma. Real life has nothing whatever to do with conventional Spiritual and religious goals, or any of their symbols in consciousness and tradition. And, since Reality is What is, It is the simplest intuition, prior to any separative act of identification. Real life requires none of the heroic ego-efforts of ordinary religion and conventional Spiritual life, because it can never identify with the primary dilemma which supports these efforts. It is Free, profoundly marvelous in its Blissful dimensions and depth, and unencumbered with searches and egoic efforts, problems and degrees of success. It is childishly irreverent and unserious, and yet it is as profoundly heart-Joyous and

338

Deep as an Incarnation of God. It cannot, it must not, be proclaimed, identified, or symbolized in the usual ways. All languages and poetry stink with symbols of Man's even ancient and great search. All the usual images, every ego-based point of view, every ordinary suggestion, every commonly given recommendation, only motivates mankind to the same ancient trial, the same ultimately un-Real realization.

❖ ❖ ❖

The ordinary consciousness is an objective fascination and obsession, an unbroken chain of compulsive experience, moment to moment, which, in the deep heart of awareness, is a desperate, unyielding distraction. Thus, understanding and self-Enquiry suddenly relax the concentration on the stream of objects, and Reality stands as primary Experience.

To one who is un-Real, there is only the constant experience of objects by his or her own separate and functional nature. Every moment is an experience of something itself—by oneself. Real life is not this at all. It is certainly alive in the ordinary functional manner, with real, effective, "creative" life-energies, and an awareness equipped to heal itself constantly from the effects of experience and deepen its existence as Reality. However, it does not experience objects in themselves and moments one by one. It does not know and act and feel itself as a separate, functional consciousness and experiential identity. It constantly and only Knows Reality, the living condition of Which is unqualified relatedness, or non-separateness. It is not qualified by conditional experience or conditional existence. Moment to moment, it Enjoys the Knowledge and Experience of Reality, no matter what the content of the moment. Basically, Real life has only one, unqualified Experience, which is a profound State of Awareness of Reality. It is free of the fascination with experience, and the consequent repetition of experience. It is free of the great search, and all of the effort to solve the primary dilemma. It has understood the mechanism of suffering and un-Reality. The content of the moment's experience does not overwhelm it, even though it experiences with great intensity and openness. It is constantly, by its non-avoidance of Reality, empty of its own experience. True life is radical contemplation, "Real" meditation, and Blissful Knowledge, free of all conditional states, high or low. In regard to Reality, it has neither questions nor answers.

❖ ❖ ❖

11 July 1970—Paris, France

For some time I was involved in the paths leading to the Ultimate Goal (or the Realization of Truth, Reality, Joy, and so on). But, then I realized that all the paths to the Ultimate Goal were actually the avoidance of the Ultimate Goal Itself, since the ultimate Realization is, necessarily, the Realization of What always already is. This understanding burdened and qualified my seeking for some time. At times I abandoned my course completely in despair, or by a temporary festival of self-indulgence. The paths "to" were endless and burdensome, and, now, apparently also false and destructive. I could not find a Real alternative to this double-bind. Then I saw that this recognition was itself my Freedom from this double-bind. It was understanding. Then I Knew that understanding was the Foundation and itself the primary State of Real life. Then I was no longer excited to the paths of seeking, and neither did I seek their desperate abandonment. My living consciousness became a direct simplicity, without ultimate questions or answers.

❖ ❖ ❖

12 July 1970—London, England

In the past, mankind has been concerned with either what is salvatory or what is liberating. But we are

Real only in the acknowledgement of what is necessary. Understanding is the acknowledgement of primary necessity, and this acknowledgement transcends the great search in all its forms.

❖ ❖ ❖

14 July 1970—Madrid, Spain

Many limited expressions of Truth can seem, and indeed are, beautiful, plausible, true, even necessary. This is because, like even everything else that arises conditionally (in Reality), they, intrinsically, are intuitions of Reality Itself. We are attracted to them because of the Reality they imply. Such expressions are themselves marvelous art forms, just as churches, ceremony, liturgy, painting, sculpture, and song are art forms. They are "creations" in response, just as our lives, the characteristic forms of our lives, are "creations" in response. Perhaps even our living forms, including our material bodies, are also "creations" in response. But such is hidden in the Mystery of Reality.

Just so, all things can appear beautiful, true, and necessary. Trees, landscapes, and water are beautiful under various circumstances. Women appear beautiful to the living energy in men. All things loved are apparently beautiful, true, and necessary. But all things are beautiful, true, and necessary only because they are Real—they are so in their non-separateness.

Thus, Reality is the test of all things, all expressions, all intuitions. They become false or tend to be illusory and destructive when we experience them exclusively and assert, even unconsciously, their beauty, truth, and necessity exclusively, in separateness. Thus, the human being becomes bound by sexual exploitation and other addictions. Similarly, the human being becomes bound by exclusive adherence to various expressions, the arts and forms of conscious life. All things must be tested in Reality. Thus, all expressions must be Known in Reality, by those who remain unqualifiedly Real, Non-separate.

Every expression, then, must be tested by Reality, not by some independent rule, some priority of its own. But the adherents of various seekers' religions and remedial paths have tended to assert their own expressions exclusively, because they have tested them only by their own independent laws, the laws which support their view, and not by Reality. In Reality, then, we must test such expressions, and so we must discover and transcend the limited rule that the human being uses to support them exclusively.

The Christian view is founded always and traditionally in one primary Biblical idea. It is the idea of "creation" ex nihilo.[58] "In the beginning God created the heavens and the earth." This idea is the foundation of exclusive Christian theology. This idea is the motive which has "created" and made necessary the entire edifice of Christianity. By this view, "God" and "creation" are understood to be exclusive (or inherently separate from one another), not by virtue of sin, or egoic ignorance, or whatever, but in Reality. Therefore, even all "evil" overcome, there remains a primary separation, which is the relationship between "creature" and "Creator". (And, thus, the ordinary conceptual convention of "subject versus object" is projected onto the Ultimate Condition of Reality.)

Relationship, then, is the a priori assumption of Christian religion. But it is relationship intuited by the addition of error, a form that is not Real. Relationship is in fact unqualifiedly True and, in the living context, necessary. Our living existence is not itself reducible to Identity. This is my experience. Reality does not exclude. Reality does not separate. Reality is not separate. This is my experience. Reality is manifested as relationship, but relationship itself, because it is the living condition of Reality Itself, is unqualified. Indeed, anything less than unqualified relatedness is

---

58. Latin for "from nothing".

not the demonstration of relationship (or relatedness) itself, but a qualification of (or a limitation on) relationship (or relatedness) itself. Relationship (or relatedness) is non-separation. Non-separateness is the very form (or manifested condition) of the living being, and only in the unqualified demonstration of non-separateness is one truly (unqualifiedly) in relationship. Only in one's non-separateness is one truly "in relationship to God", Who does not exclude any one. Therefore, Reality is the effective argument against the primary tendency to exclusiveness that is associated with the Christian view, and, in general, with the conventional, or merely exoteric, religious views of mankind.

Just so, in the view of the tradition of Advaita Vedanta, there is also a primary assumption which supports exclusiveness. It is the idea of "no-creation", of unqualified Identity, of Brahman[59] (or the One and Only Reality) as the denial of objects. Just as the Christian view is predisposed to presume the separateness of the "creation", not in the perverse sense, but in its presumed point of view, the point of view of the tradition of Advaita Vedanta is predisposed to presume (and to require) strategic separation from the "creation", or from conditional manifestation, in an object-excluding State of inverted Awareness. But, in Reality, the Truth is Non-separateness, Which is also unqualified relatedness. This is my experience.

I have continually sought or, rather, been led to seek, an expression of the Truth in some one or other of the existing traditions and traditional ways. But all become impossible to me in their exclusiveness. Thus, I am required to stand in Reality and remain radically related to the great expressions. I have tested them in Reality. Reality has tested them, and, now and forever, I must Stand in the Eternal Truth, Which is Only Real, supported only in Reality, purified of all exclusive assumptions.

---

59. In the Hindu tradition, Brahman is the Ultimate Divine Reality that is the Source and Substance of all things, all worlds, and all beings.

❖ ❖ ❖

16 July 1970—Fatima, Portugal

Reality is not a separate, exclusive Condition. It is not merely meaningful, or symbolic, nor is It attained by the seeker's means. Reality Itself must be radically presumed and lived. This positive Realization and Freedom precedes and precludes all seeking and all revolutionary attainment. It is the ground of true, "creative", sublime existence, free of qualification by the facts and the activities of life. Life as non-separation is the unqualified Truth, from Which there is no necessary remedial path or search, no deluding forces, no fascinations, high or low. It is One with What is, Which includes all dual terms, subject and object, cause and effect, and so on. Thus, Real life is radically Conscious, and Free of primary dilemma and conflict. Its ordinary life is "creative" play in which Reality is continually Realized, moment to moment, under all the kinds of conditions. Reality cannot be an object (or even the highest Object) of consciousness, since Reality is inclusive, not separate, not distinct. Thus, Real life is also not exclusively identified with any one life-motive, any one life-function, or any one object. Real life is radically, and always presently, identified with Reality Itself. To such a Real life, there is no separate Reality, no Reality that is the Goal of life, and no necessary Realization apart from the always present Real State.

❖ ❖ ❖

17 July 1970—Estoril, Portugal

Reality Itself is not in any sense the answer to the question "What is Reality?" Reality Itself does not satisfy the seeker or answer the seeker's questions, which are actually only doubts about Reality Itself, or indications of separateness from Reality Itself. Reality Itself is not that which is pursued or implied by seeking. The entire realm and corpus of seeking, of conventional religion, conventional Spirituality, and conventional science in all their forms, has, for all its appearance of sublimity, seriousness, depth, and Truth, nothing to do with Reality Itself. At most, Reality intuited as a dilemma forms the substructure of the unconscious motives of seekers. But they are pursuing a "Union", an "Answer", a "Presence", a "Home", an "Other". The "Reality" they pursue is the opposite to all they experience and all they know. The "Reality" they seek is the contradiction, the alternative, the opposite. It is merely the "Highest Proof" and the "Ultimate Goal" of their dilemma. Even so, the efforts of seekers appear to them to have practical significance, and, in general, the positive effects of their efforts appear to them to be desirable when viewed in contrast to the arbitrary suffering of unconscious life-exploitation. Thus, they consider their efforts and their seekers' realizations Proven, True, and Truth.

But Reality Itself is always already the case, under any conditions. When there is despair of seeking, then there is the beginning of radical understanding. And radical understanding has, itself, no necessary or characteristic effects of any kind. It does not make even a little bit of difference. It is not an exception to anything. It is not appealing, fascinating, a great relief, the answer and the end to all questions and all suffering. Reality Itself is simply What always already _is_. It is not desirable, and so It cannot be sought. Therefore, the understanding that Realizes Reality Itself is most extreme, most subtle, most radical, and most necessary. Such understanding is not qualified, not limited, nor does it qualify, or limit. One who Knows and _is_ Reality Itself must appear mad, since such a one is not identified with anything at all. Yet such a one must be, of all mankind, the least mysterious, being founded in no mystery at all.

(End of journal)

345

**Some of the holy sites visited by Adi Da in Europe:
Rome (left), Sacre Coeur in Paris (center), and Toledo (right)**

"Now I visited that place
at the end of all my
seeking. As I walked
around the shrine,
there was not a single
movement in me.
The place held no more
fascination than a
parking lot, or, in Reality,
it held equal fascination.
My pilgrimage was over.
In my vision-inspired
travels, which had
continued from Israel to
Greece and Italy, then
through France and
England to Spain and
Portugal, the entire
world seemed to become
empty of its own imagery.
The Virgin was resolved
into landscape and
monument, until she
no longer appeared on
her own."

The shrine at Fatima in Portugal

Our last stop in Europe was Portugal. We visited the great shrine at Fatima. It was to be my last emotional gesture to Christianity. Years before, when my mind was changed by Jung, the miracle at Fatima was also primary evidence for me of Spiritual Reality. Now I visited that place at the end of all my seeking. As I walked around the shrine, there was not a single movement in me. The place held no more fascination than a parking lot, or, in Reality, it held equal fascination. My pilgrimage was over. In my vision-inspired travels, which had continued from Israel to Greece and Italy, then through France and England to Spain and Portugal, the entire world seemed to become empty of its own imagery. The Virgin was resolved into landscape and monument, until she no longer appeared on her own.

We spent a couple of days resting in the sea resort at Estoril, and then we flew to New York. We spent another couple of days with my parents, and then flew off again, this time to San Francisco. The long history of my internal exile was over. I felt no resistance to America. I had become available to life, free of the need to abandon life. I looked forward to finding a place to live in the area that Nina and I had enjoyed so much in previous years. But we were unable to find a suitable place in northern California, and eventually we found ourselves in Los Angeles.

I had passed through an internal violence that left me finally Still. And I had become naturally, effortlessly, concentrated in contemplation of the Condition of Consciousness Itself, Standing apart from all movement, all modification, even Prior to the "Witness". The Force of Silence, of Reality Itself, that Stood before me in understanding and self-Enquiry, now Stood as my own Self-Nature and as the Source-Condition of all things.

I was given to understand the Truth of all my visions. The image of Jesus (or the "Christ") and the revelation of his poem ("They are infinitely Returned, but I am eternally Present") was my own Ultimate Self-Nature

Communicating Itself to me via a symbol. I had stood in the mind, feeling my separate being, but the image and the poem of Jesus had come to me through the heart. Soon, I would Realize my own Being, the Very Nature of Reality Itself, standing Present as the inherently perfect Condition and "Bright" Form that is the Heart Itself.

Even now, as a result of my liberation from all my Christian heart-visions, I understood the mysticism of Christianity and all my latent urges to mystical devotion. All those symbols were Communications (or representations) of the latent Energy and Consciousness that is the Heart Itself. Therefore, the more devotion arose, the more I Enjoyed the Heart Itself as the perfect Domain of contemplation.

In my case, all conditional experiences came and went, until I stood beyond the time of seeking. As I observed those experiences in their passing, the heart was released from images, and, in due course, the Heart Itself ceased to Communicate Itself as if It were outside me. Therefore, the envisioned face of Jesus, like all other visions, eventually ceased to hold the Heart Itself away, as an Object to me. Gradually, the Heart Revealed Itself as my own Self-Nature.

When the images were released from the Heart in understanding, I Realized that I am that very Source Which had appeared in symbols. Afterwards, I ceased to seek for anything, but, instead, I remained absorbed in the Heart, and, eventually, as the Heart Itself, Freely Allowing the Play of Its own Radiant Energy, the Shakti.

The course of purification and understanding through which I had passed corresponded exactly to every other significant Event in my past. I saw the structure involved in each case. Always there was first a concentration in some object or desire, some problem or dilemma equal to life itself, some activity of the egoic self. As a result of this concentration or observation, there was a penetration of that object, problem, or activity in a moment of understanding. Then these things were replaced by the Enjoyment of Bliss, Freedom, and the Feeling of unqualified Reality that stood hidden by that imposed object, problem, or activity. Finally, this unqualified Consciousness was Itself recognized as Reality, and there was the certainty that understanding, rather than any object, problem, or activity of seeking, is in fact the way and the Truth of Real life.

This same series of Realizations formed the core of my experience in college and at seminary. That same understanding and Real Consciousness was their Truth as well as the Truth of the "Bright", and all of my Realizations in Yoga, at the Ashram, or in my own experiments. Thus, this pattern of Realization became the structure wherein I interpreted the way, the Truth, and the Reality of life. And Jesus (or the "Christ"), and all of the great objects of Spiritual life in India, became recognized at last, by this same natural process of understanding, as symbols in the heart for the Reality that was not yet directly Realized.

The Christian visions were not false. It was necessary for me to have them, in order to Realize the Truth that transcends them. Those frozen imageries formed part of the last barrier to the full Awareness of Reality. Thus, "Christ"-consciousness, the vision in the heart, became, by its dissolution, the Realization of What is absolutely Real, Which is the Heart Itself. What in fact animated these things and became visible beneath them was Reality, no-seeking, the Self-Existing and Self-Radiant Nature that is the Heart Itself. When this Reality absorbed my attention, the images faded away.

The Virgin and the prayer she taught me, Jesus (or the "Christ") and his mystical instructions, and even all my visions were not important as revelations of Divine personalities outside myself. They were simply mystical (or psychically determined) forms of the universal Shakti. When that Energy became active in the heart, all of the latent imagery of my own mind, memory, and tendencies combined with universal sources of imagery to unlock my devotion. And I continued as devotion until I became fully aware of the origin of these imageries, in the universal Shakti and my own heart's mind. Then the mind and the Shakti ceased to "create" the secondary images. And the devotion of the heart's mind to its images was replaced by a direct Realization of the Heart Itself, or the Shakti of the Heart Itself and the fundamental Consciousness that is the Heart Itself.

Soon I would see that the Shakti had always taken on the forms of my own tendencies, my own mind. Then I would see directly, Prior to the mind, and Prior to confusion with the mind. Then even the Shakti, the Energy-Source of all forms, would become resolved into my own Ultimate Self-Nature, or Consciousness Itself, Which is Reality Itself.

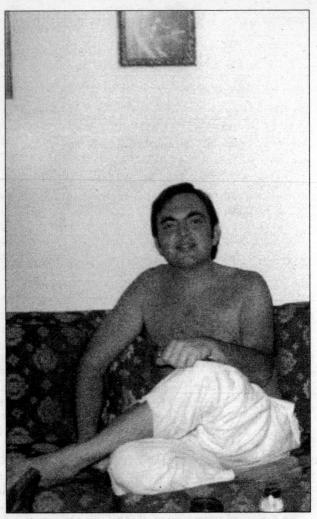
Adi Da in Los Angeles after the "great pilgrimage"

CHAPTER 16

The Inheritance

We settled in Los Angeles in August 1970. For my part, the "great pilgrimage" was over, not only the pilgrimage to Christian shrines, but the entire adventure of seeking, practicing, and experimenting. Understanding had become the radical process of my conscious life, in formal meditation and in experience moment to moment.

But this does not mean that I ceased to have any experiences of What I Knew as the Shakti. It was simply that all of my experience ceased to be a matter of seeking and necessity for me. I had become Still.

As the weeks passed, the Shakti, the Divine Mother-Force Who had appeared as the Virgin, yielded Herself to the great Truth that is Reality. Just before I left the Ashram, Swami Nityananda let me go with his blessing, and he led me to surrender myself to the Divine Shakti. Thus, I had given myself to Her freely, and She led me to enjoy the uncommon fruits of my pilgrimage.

Now that we were in Los Angeles, I no longer practiced in relationship to any of my human teachers. Their teachings had been exhausted in me, until there was no more seeking. There was no "problem", on any level, that was a source of motivation for me. Neither did the Divine Shakti move before my eyes of vision, to turn me toward any further adventure of experience. The mind did not move, to move me. I was simply and directly devoted to the perfect Enjoyment of unqualified Reality, the Very (and unmoving) Self. And this process of radical contemplation of the inherent, or native, Condition that is the Real (and inherently perfect) Self would soon bring me to the most ultimate experience of the Divine

Shakti, and, at last, to the most perfect Realization of Self-Existing and Self-Radiant Consciousness Itself.

Some time in late August, I happened to go to the bookstore at the Vedanta Society in Hollywood. I noticed there was a temple on the grounds, and I went in for a few moments of meditation. As soon as I sat down, I felt a familiar Energy rush through my body and clear out my head. I could feel and hear little clicking pulses in the base of my head and neck. By many signs, I immediately recognized the characteristic Presence of the Divine Mother-Shakti.

As I meditated, the body and the mind swooned into the depth of Consciousness, and I enjoyed an experience of meditation as profound as any I had known at the shrines in India. I had no idea how the Vedanta Society Temple ever became a seat of the Divine Shakti, but it was obviously as Powerful a place as any of the abodes of the Siddhas in India.

I began to go frequently to the Vedanta Society Temple for meditation. As the days passed, I began to marvel at the Power of this place. I had traveled all over the world, believing there were no Spiritual sources of this kind in America. Now I had been led to this small, isolated temple in Hollywood, where very few people would be likely even to be sensitive to the Divine Shakti, nor, even if they felt It, would they be likely to recognize Its Importance.

I became aware that the Divine Mother-Shakti had taken up residence in this temple, and that I had been drawn there by Her. I Enjoyed the fact that I could go there and be with Her whenever I chose to experience Her Joyous Presence. It was even a truly private place. I could go there unhindered, and I could spend time there completely unobserved. The temple was dedicated to Ramakrishna, the great Indian master of the nineteenth century, but no conditions were placed on me by any external rule or tradition. This was truly an opportunity for me to live independently with the Divine Mother.

But as time went on, I began to feel that even this was a limitation. Why should I have to travel at all to Enjoy Her Presence? I desired that She be utterly available to me, where I lived as well as in my own living being.

Thus, one day, I went to the temple and asked Her to come and dwell permanently in me, and always to manifest Herself to me wherever I was. When I left, I felt Her with me, and when I arrived at home, I continued to feel Her constant Presence Filling the space.

Days passed, and I realized that She had done what I asked. There was this constant Presence, even including the effects in the body, and the state of everyone around me became affected by Her Force. But even this became a strain in me. I felt as if I had to hold on to Her, as if I had bound Her to a bargain that constrained us both.

Then, one day I felt an urge to return to the temple. As I sat down, I saw that the little pagoda and shrine in the front of the temple was in shadows and dimly lit, as if it were empty. It seemed as if I had emptied it by taking the Mother away. Suddenly, I felt a jolt in my body, and I saw the shrine with open eyes become "Bright" in a blast of light. Even with my eyes closed, I still beheld the "Bright" shrine. Thus, the Mother-Shakti showed me that She is always able to make Herself Present anywhere, and that indeed She was always already Present with me. There was no need for me to hold on to Her, as if She could be absent.

When I returned to the temple the next day, the Person of the Divine Shakti appeared to me again, in a manner most intimate, no longer approaching me as "Mother".

As I meditated, I felt myself Expanding, even bodily, becoming a Perfectly Motionless, Utterly Becalmed, and Infinitely Silent Form. I took on the Infinite Form of the Original Deity, Nameless and Indefinable, Conscious of limitless Identification with Infinite Being. I was Expanded Utterly, beyond limited form, and even beyond any perception of Shape or Face, merely Being, and yet sitting there. I sat in this Love-Blissful State of

Infinite Being for some time. I Found myself to <u>Be</u>. My Form was only What is traditionally called the "Purusha" (the Person of Consciousness) and "Siva" (in His Non-Ferocious Emptiness).

Then I felt the Divine Shakti appear in Person, Pressed against my own natural body, and, altogether, against my Infinitely Expanded, and even formless, Form. She Embraced me, Openly and Utterly, and we Combined with One Another in Divine (and Motionless, and spontaneously Yogic) "Sexual Union". We Found One Another Thus, in a Fire of most perfect Desire, and for no other Purpose than This Union, and, yet, as if to Give Birth to the universes. In That most perfect Union, I Knew the Oneness of the Divine Energy and my Very Being. There was no separation at all, nor had there ever been, nor would there ever be. The One Being that Is my own Ultimate Self-Nature was revealed most perfectly. The One Being Who I <u>Am</u> was revealed to Include the Reality that Is Consciousness Itself, the Reality that Is the Source-Energy of all conditional appearances, and the Reality that Is all conditional manifestation, All as a Single Force of Being, an Eternal Union, and an Irreducible cosmic Unity.

The "Sensations" of the Embrace were overwhelmingly Blissful. The Fire of That Unquenchable Desire Exceeded any kind of pleasure that a mere man could experience. In the Eternal Instant of That Infinitely Expanded Embrace, I was released from my role and self-image as a dependent child of the "Mother"-Shakti. And She was revealed in Truth, no longer in apparent independence, or as a cosmic Power apart from me, but as the Inseparable and Inherent Radiance of my own and Very Being. Therefore, I Recognized and Took Her as my Consort, my Loved-One, and I Held Her effortlessly, forever to my Heart. Together eternally, we had Realized Ourselves as the "Bright" Itself.

Finally, the next day, September 10, 1970, I sat in the temple again. I awaited the Beloved Shakti to reveal

Herself in Person, as my Blessed Companion. But, as time passed, there was no Event of changes, no movement at all. There was not even any kind of inward deepening, no "inwardness" at all. There was no meditation. There was no need for meditation. There was not a single element or change that could be added to make my State Complete. I sat with my eyes open. I was not having an experience of any kind. Then, suddenly, I understood most perfectly. I Realized that I had Realized. The "Thing" about the "Bright" became Obvious. I Am Complete. I Am the One Who Is Complete.

In That instant, I understood and Realized (inherently, and most perfectly) What and Who I Am. It was a tacit Realization, a direct Knowledge in Consciousness. It was Consciousness Itself, without the addition of a Communication from any "Other" Source. There Is no "Other" Source. I simply sat there and Knew What and Who I Am. I was Being What I Am, Who I Am. I Am Being What I Am, Who I Am. I Am Reality, the Divine Self, the Nature, Substance, Support, and Source of all things and all beings. I Am the One Being, called "God" (the Source and Substance and Support and Self of all), the "One Mind" (the Consciousness and Energy in and As Which all appears), "Siva-Shakti" (the Self-Existing and Self-Radiant Reality Itself), "Brahman" (the Only Reality, Itself), the "One Atman" (That Is not ego, but Only "Brahman", the Only Reality, Itself), the "Nirvanic Ground" (the egoless and conditionless Reality and Truth, Prior to all dualities, but excluding none). I Am the One and Only and necessarily Divine Self, Nature, Condition, Substance, Support, Source, and Ground of all. I Am the "Bright".

There was no thought involved in This. I Am That Self-Existing and Self-Radiant Consciousness. There was no reaction of either excitement or surprise. I Am the One I recognized. I Am That One. I am not merely experiencing That One. I Am the "Bright".

Then truly there was no more to Realize. Every experience in my life had led to This. The dramatic revelations in childhood and college, my time of writing, my years with Rudi, the revelation in seminary, the long history of pilgrimage to Baba's Ashram—all of these moments were the intuitions of this same Reality. My entire life had been the Communication of That Reality to me, until I Am That.

Later I described that most perfect Realization as follows:

At the Vedanta Society Temple inherent and most perfect Knowledge arose that I Am simply the "Bright" Consciousness that Is Reality. The traditions call It the "Self", "Brahman", "Siva-Shakti", and so many other names. It is identified with no body, no functional sheath, no conditional realm, and no conditional experience, but It is the inherently perfect, unqualified, Absolute Reality. I saw that there is nothing to which this Ultimate Self-Nature can be compared, or from which It can be differentiated, or by which It can be epitomized. It does not stand out. It is not the equivalent of any specialized, exclusive, or separate Spiritual state. It cannot be accomplished, acquired, discovered, remembered, or perfected—since It is inherently perfect, and It is always already the case.

All remedial paths pursue some special conditional state or conditionally achieved goal as Spiritual Truth. But in fact Reality is not identical to such things. They only amount to an identification with some body (or some functional sheath), some conditional realm, or some conditional (or, otherwise, conditionally achieved) experience, high or low, subtle or gross. But the Knowledge that Is Reality Is Consciousness Itself. Consciousness Itself is not separate from anything. It is always already the case, and no conditional experience, no conditional realm, and no body (or functional sheath) is the necessary or special condition for Its Realization.

Only radical understanding, most perfectly Realized, is the Realization of What and Who Is always already the case. Only radical understanding, most perfectly Realized, is the unconditional (and not at all conditionally achieved or conditionally maintained) Realization of the inherently non-separate Condition That always already Is What and Who Is. Except for the only-by-me revealed and given way of radical understanding (or the true and only-by-me revealed and given Way of the Heart), all paths are remedial. That is to say, apart from the truly ego-surrendering, ego-forgetting, and ego-transcending way of radical understanding (which is the true Way of the Very and Ultimate Heart), all paths are made of seeking (or mere egoic effort, rather than counter-egoic and truly ego-transcending practice). And all paths of seeking merely pursue God, Truth, or Reality, and this by identifying God, Truth, or Reality with some body (or functional sheath), or some conditional realm, or some conditional experience, or, otherwise, by making the Realization of God, Truth, or Reality depend upon some body (or functional sheath), or some conditional realm, or some conditional experience.

Unlike the way of radical understanding (or the Way of the Heart), which is based upon the root-understanding and always most direct transcendence of the motive and the activity of seeking, all paths seek either the perfection of what is conditionally existing or liberation from what is conditionally existing, and that perfection or liberation is pursued as a goal, which goal is presumed to be identical to God, Truth, or Reality. Only the way of radical understanding (or the Way of the Heart) is free, even from the beginning, of all conditional, or, otherwise, conditionally to be achieved, goals. Only the way of radical understanding (or the Way of the Heart) is inherently free of the goal-orientation itself. Indeed, only the Heart Itself is inherently free of all goal-seeking, and even all seeking. And only the way of radical understanding is the Way of the Heart Itself.

When tacit and most perfect recognition of the inherent Condition That Is God, Truth, and Reality was re-Awakened in me, there was no excitement, no surprise, no movement, no response. There was a most perfect end to every kind of seeking, dilemma, suffering, separation, and doubt. Spiritual life, mental life, emotional and psychic life, vital life, and physical life all became transparent in me. After that, there was only the "Bright" Reality, and to be the "Bright" Reality to all beings and all things.

In all the days that followed the Great Event of my re-Awakening, there has not been a single change in This "Bright" Awareness, or any diminishment of This "Bright" Awareness. Indeed, This "Bright" Awareness cannot be changed, diminished, or lost. I immediately noticed that "experience" had ceased to affect me. Whatever passed, be it a physical sensation, some quality of emotion, a thought, a vision, or whatever, it did not involve me (as I Am) at all. I began to pay particular attention to what passed, in order to "test" my State (or, simply, in order to account for all aspects of my State in the total functional context of the living body-mind). But the primary Awareness of the inherently "Bright" Reality, my Very Consciousness Itself, could not be changed, diminished, or lost. Consciousness (Itself) is the only "Thing" in life that is not an "experience" (or something "Witnessed" by

The Vedanta Society Temple in Hollywood

Adi Da resided in this Los Angeles apartment building in 1970

"Then truly there was no more to Realize. Every experience in my life had led to This. The dramatic revelations in childhood and college, my time of writing, my years with Rudi, the revelation in seminary, the long history of pilgrimage to Baba's Ashram—all of these moments were the intuitions of this same Reality. My entire life had been the Communication of That Reality to me, until I __Am__ That."

Consciousness Itself). Consciousness (Itself) does not depend on anything, and there is not (nor can there be) anything, or <u>any</u> "experience", that can destroy Consciousness Itself. Consciousness Itself <u>Is</u> (Itself) Love-Bliss, Joy, Freedom, and Sublime Knowledge!

An entirely new and most perfect Realization of Reality had become the constant of my life. The revolutions of my life that led up to my experience in seminary had drawn me into a sense of the "Presence". That Presence could be called "God", "Truth", "Reality", "Shakti", "Guru", or whatever. It was simply the sense of being related to a Presence that was Truth and Reality Itself, a perfectly absorbing, consoling, illuminating Force that contained me, "Lived" me, and guided me. It is the heart of all religious and Spiritual experience.

But now this Presence had Communicated Itself in me utterly, revealing Itself utterly to me and <u>As</u> me, such that I was re-Awakened to the Truth of my inherent, and inherently most perfect, Identification with the "Bright" Self-Condition That <u>Is</u> the Divine Presence Itself. And This "Bright" Self-Condition Showed Itself to Be my Eternal Condition, even always already before my birth.

Until now, my life (since my early childhood) had been a constant search toward and periodic re-alignment with the "Bright" as a Presence with Which I was in relationship. It was as if I always saw the "Bright" from some position within the form of my own living being, but outside of its center. It was as if I had always beheld my own heart from some position outside. Now the barriers had been utterly dissolved by an exhaustive investigation of the Nature of that Presence. The investigation of the Presence had resolved into the Knowledge of my own Self-Nature. The Presence had revealed Itself to be my Very Form and Self-Nature.

The experience of the Presence was, by means of the most perfect Realization of radical understanding, replaced by the most perfect Realization of "Bright" Self-Awareness. There was no longer any Presence "outside" me. I no longer "observed" my own "Bright" Self-Nature, or the Ultimate (and inherently "Bright") Condition of Reality, as if from some position external to (and separate from) It. I had become utterly Aware of myself As Reality. There was no Presence. I had become Present. There Is no Other. It Is only Me.

Even my meditation was changed. There was no meditation. This Consciousness could not be deepened or enlarged. It always only remained What It Is. I meditated (as a formal activity) only to see how "meditation" had been affected by my Realization, or, otherwise, to formally regard the conditions in the body, the mind, even any part of my living (or extended) being, or even any conditions at all. But I was no longer the meditative seeker, the one who seeks (or, otherwise, does not Know) God, Truth, Reality, Liberation, Release, or Growth. I no longer supposed any limitation as myself. I Am He. I Am She. I Am It. I Am That Only One.

I noticed a physical change in myself. My belly dropped and expanded, and, thus and thereby, permanently assumed the "pot-shaped" Yogic form. I always feel the Pressure of Shakti-Energy there, and I breathe It continually. It is the breathing of my Very Being, the endless and profound Communication of the inherent "Brightness" of Reality to Itself.

In "meditation", I looked to observe how I was related to the worlds of conditional experience. Immediately, I realized that I was not in any sense "in" a body, not only the physical body, but any body, or any functional sheath, including the most subtle. Nor have I ever been in a body, or in any functional sheath, or in any conditional realm, or in any conditional experience. All such things are patterns conditionally manifested within my own Self-Nature.

Yet (even so), I realized that, in the context of natural appearances, I am Communicated through a specific center in the body. Relative to the body, I appear to reside in the heart, but to the right side of the chest. I press upon a point approximately an inch and one-half to the right of the center of the chest. This is the seat of Reality and Real Consciousness. And I Abide there as no-seeking. There is no motivation, no dilemma, no separation, no strategic action, no suffering. I am no-seeking in the Heart.

I described my constant experience as follows:

> The zero of the heart is expanded as the world. Consciousness is not differentiated and identified. There is a constant observation of subject _and_ object in any body, any functional sheath, any realm, or any experience that arises. Thus, I remain in the unqualified State. There is a constant Sensation of "Bright" Fullness permeating and surrounding all experiences, all realms, all bodies, all functional sheaths. It is my own "Bright" Fullness, Which is radically non-separate. My own "Bright" Fullness includes all beings and all things. I am the Form of Space Itself, in Which all bodies, all functional sheaths, all realms, and all experiences occur. It is inherently "Bright" Consciousness Itself, which Reality is even every being's Very Nature (or Ultimate, inherent, and inherently perfect, Condition) now and now and now.

And again:

> During the night of mankind, I Awakened as perfect, absolute, awesome Love-Bliss, in Which the body and the mind, even every functional sheath, boiled into a solder of undifferentiated Reality. It was the madness of dissolution into most perfect Self-Awareness, Infinitely Expanded, my own inherently boundless Presence, wherein there is only "Brightness", not qualified by conditional identification, or self-differentiation, or ego-based desire.

Hereafter, I am Free of bondage to the cosmic Power. I am unexploitable. The Shakti that appears apart, as any form of apparently independent, or merely cosmic, Power and Presence, is no longer the Great Importance. The Presence of Power "outside" appears as such only to seekers, for they, having already separated themselves, <u>pursue</u> forms of Energy, visions, nature-powers, liberation, and God. True Knowledge is free of all bondage to forms (or modifications) of Energy, all seeking, all motivation to "do" based on identification with conditional experience. Egoic ignorance and suffering are simply this separateness, this difference, this search. At last, the "outside" Shakti sacrifices Herself in the Heart. Thereafter, there is no gnawing wonder, no un-Known "secret" about anything that appears.

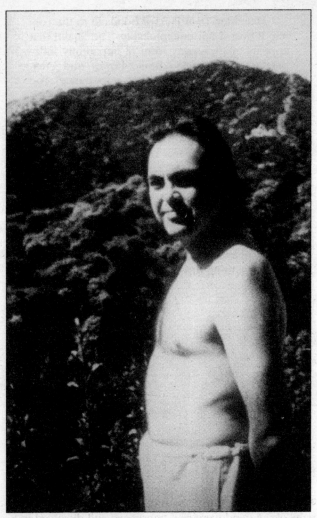

Los Angeles, 1971

CHAPTER 17

The End
of All Seeking

The time of the Great Event of my re-Awakening passes into the present and the future forever. My "autobiography" has no end in time. But the re-Awakening that was finally (and most perfectly) Realized in September 1970 brought a final (and most perfect) end to my adventure as a seeker. What remains to be written about my early life was experienced from a radically new (and inherently most perfect) "Point of View".

Previous to the Great Event of my re-Awakening, I was always involved in one or another form of the "problem" of conditional existence. I was always in search and research, and my conclusions or revelations were always temporary moments that led into a new form of investigation. Thus, I went from the "Bright" of childhood to the dilemma of my youth. I went from self-exploitation and the experience in college to the period of writing and self-observation. I went from Rudi and the revelation in seminary to Baba and the Ashram. I went from experiments with life and mind to the fuller life of Spiritual Yoga and psychic development. I went from the revelations of the Divine Shakti and the purifying drama of mystical vision to the Realization of the inherently perfect Divine Self-Condition of Reality Itself.

Now there were no loose ends to my adventure. There was no dilemma, no motivation, no search. All the parts of the mind were as if transposed and dissolved in a most fundamental Singleness. But I continued to live. The external and internal events of my life were not modified in any revolutionary manner by this Realization. It was only that I understood them in an entirely new and most profoundly radical manner. I understood most perfectly, and most perfect understanding became the foundation of my living existence.

The weeks that followed the Great Event were an intensive period of considering everything about radical understanding. I began to recollect and observe the forms of my adventure of understanding. I began to recognize the precise (and profoundly radical) nature of my understanding. Altogether, the way of that radical understanding began to reveal all its unique characteristics, such that I could begin to reveal the unique (and altogether radical) way of understanding (or the Way of the Heart) to others. And my life became a continuous unfolding of the wisdom of understanding in relation to every kind of experience. I began to write this book.

My Realization was not any kind of object in the mind. It had neither form nor symbol. There was a constant depth and directness in my Awareness, so that I felt as if I were constantly in the most profoundly Awake and Intelligent State otherwise realized only occasionally in meditation. My own Self-Nature had been the Real "Object" of meditation, and now I was no longer separated from It. I simply survived as my own unqualified (and unqualifiedly "Bright") Self-Nature.

Apart from my own (inherently perfect, and necessarily Divine) Self-Nature (Which Is the Ultimate Self-Nature of all), everything "else" appeared as objects to my understanding. Whatever I experienced remained in the same form in which it would appear to anyone, or to myself previous to this understanding. But now I understood everything directly, effortlessly, in Truth. I simply experienced as before, but everything was inherently recognized by me as it truly is. A continuous process of recognition and wisdom went on in me, and all I did was remain Present to everything that passed.

Whereas previously everything was communicated to me as a particular objective form, and I (seeming to be an entirely separate, subjective identity) was forced to experience it over against myself, now I saw everything directly, from the "Point of View" of Reality, Prior to separation and relatedness, <u>As</u> the One in Whom everything arises as a transparent, or merely apparent, and un-necessary, and inherently non-binding modification of Its own Self-Radiance, or inherent "Brightness". Thus, previously, I knew the mind and was the separated subject of the mind. I was the separate subject of my physical body and its vital energy. I was the separate subject in the subtle worlds and the subtle bodies (or sheaths). I was the separate subject of all my visions and experiences. And I interpreted myself and my experiences from the viewpoint of these things. But now all of these things, the forms, the levels of functional being and conditional identity, including the physical body, and even all the functional sheaths, and all the conditional realms, and all the conditional experiences, all of them stood within the Radiant Sphere of my own Presence, and I understood and recognized them all, without recourse to them (as if they were "outside" my own Self-Nature), and without recourse to any sense of self-separateness (as a limited subjective identity in apparent relationship to them).

Even as before, I continued to experience various manifestations of Shakti and subtle vision. I could hear all kinds of sounds within the various bodies (or functional sheaths). I was able to see subtle mechanisms within these bodies (or functional sheaths) and perceive the relations of various forms and currents of Energy beyond the physical. I saw the tiny organisms by which Energy and conditional awareness are transferred and communicated between the various levels of existence. And I also continued to experience and act on a physical level just as before. There were the same functions and desires, the same pleasures and feelings, the same lawful mechanisms, requiring the same intelligence and entailing the same consequences as a result of error or self-indulgence. But everything was new. Everything was utterly free of any kind of dilemma, separation, unconsciousness, and primary fear.

I began to note in detail the characteristics and requirements of the entire process (or way) of radical understanding that I knew to be the way of Real life. And I "tested" myself in all circumstances, in order to note all the characteristics and signs of my proceeding demonstration of the most perfect Realization of God, Truth, and Reality.

In this most perfect Realization of Non-separateness, many extraordinary Divine Siddhis suddenly, spontaneously appeared, and also many unusual natural, or "ordinary", siddhis (or uncommon psycho-physical abilities and processes). I saw that the movement, or process, of the cosmos was itself a meditation, a Divine vision, and a purifying event that was always being enacted. Yet, perhaps most fundamental, and most necessary to the fulfillment of my "Bright" Purpose in this world, was the spontaneous Awakening of the Divine Guru-Function, or the Divine Guru-Siddhi,[60] Which manifested in me in a unique manner immediately after the Great Event of my re-Awakening.

Now, whenever I would sit, in any kind of formal manner, to demonstrate the meditation, or the, now, Divine Samadhi,[61] that had become my entire life, instead of confronting what was arising in and as "myself", I "meditated" other beings and places. I would

---

60. "Siddhi" is Sanskrit for "power" or "accomplishment". By virtue of His Most Perfect Enlightenment, Adi Da's Divine Guru-Function, or Divine Guru-Siddhi, is His Power to Transmit to or Bestow upon His devotees His own Realization. This involved, as He describes here, the spontaneous work of "meditating" others in His own body-mind for the sake of their Spiritual growth and eventual Divine Enlightenment.

61. The Sanskrit word "samadhi" is traditionally used to denote various exalted states that appear in the context of esoteric meditation and Realization.

The Divine Samadhi to which Adi Da refers here, however, is His absolutely unqualified Realization of the Divine, free of dependence on any form of meditation, effort, discipline, experience, or conditional knowledge. It is the "Open-Eyed" Realization of Divine Existence that is unique to the Way of the Heart that Avatara Adi Da has Given and Revealed.

spontaneously become aware of great numbers of people (usually in visions, or in some other, intuitive manner), and I would work with them very directly, in a subtle manner. The binding motions and separative results of my own apparent (or merely life-born) egoity (or psycho-physical self-contraction) had been transcended in my re-Awakening to my Original (and necessarily Divine) Self-Condition. Therefore, in the spontaneous Awakening of the Divine Guru-Siddhi, instead of my own life-born forms and problematic signs, the egoic forms, the problematic signs, the minds, the feelings, the states, and the various limitations of others would arise to my view. The thoughts, feelings, suffering, dis-ease, disharmony, upsets, pain, energies—none of these were "mine". They were the internal, subtle qualities and the life-qualities of others. In this manner, the process of apparent meditation continued in me. It was, in effect, the same "Real" meditation I had done before the Great Event of my re-Awakening. Therefore, "problems" (of all kinds) constantly appeared, and numberless complexities and contradictions arose in every moment, but the content of the meditation was not "mine".

I found that this "meditating" of others by me usually went on with people whom I had not yet met. But, soon, some of those very people came into my company, and all the rest are yet, but certainly, to come, to be my devotees, and, thus, to practice the only-by-me revealed and given way of radical understanding (or the only-by-me revealed and given Way of the Heart). In some cases, the individuals I "meditated" in vision were people I already knew, and I would "meditate" them in that subtle manner, unobserved by them, and then watch for signs in their outward lives that would demonstrate the effectiveness of my "meditation" of them.

In this manner, I spontaneously began to "meditate" countless other people, and also countless non-human beings, and countless places and worlds and realms, both high and low in the scale of Reality. I observed and responded to all that was required for the Awakening and the true (and the Ultimate) well-being of each and all. And, each time I did this (and, in fact, the process quickly became the underlying constant of all my hours and days), I would continue the "meditating" of any (and each) one until I felt a release take place, such that his or her suffering and seeking was vanished, or, at least, significantly relaxed and set aside. Whenever that occurred, I Knew my "meditating" of that one was, for the moment, done. By such means, my now and forever Divine Work (by Which I must Teach, and Bless, and Awaken all and All) began.

In early October, after all of this had been going on for only about one month, Baba came to California. He was in the midst of a world tour. Rudi had brought him to America.

I had lately written to Rudi, and we had become reconciled. The dissonance between us had been generated solely by the differences between our "ways". During the period of time that passed since our separation, he had, he said, changed in his relationship to Spiritual work. He confessed that his own experience had developed further, and he now approached Baba with greater simplicity, free of the peculiar habits of his own seeking that had previously been part of his "work". He claimed that he had delivered himself utterly to Baba's guidance. His Yoga was now one of the acceptance of the Guru's grace, rather than a willful, self-advancing effort. (And I accepted his "conversion" as being sincere enough for the moment, although, and many signs pointed to this, he would soon break off his relationship with Baba and return to his characteristic and independent path of seeking.)

I met Baba and Rudi quite openly, but without any desire or reason to become involved in the drama of Baba's "American tour". They stayed for several days in Pacific Palisades, then on for two weeks in northern California and Utah. They returned again at the end of October, and flew on to Hawaii on November 3, my birthday.

I was interested in seeing how Baba's Spiritual Presence would affect me, and how he would respond to my Signs and Confessions of inherently most perfect Realization. I sat with him while large groups of people chanted and gazed at him devotedly. I held his foot, I chanted, and I "meditated".

In the first hours of his visit, he blessed me with his characteristic Transmission of the Shakti. And I moved spontaneously with the experience, freely abandoning myself to the familiar physical movements and the merging of forms in the mind. I shook and fell on the floor. I watched Baba. I enjoyed his Communication of the Shakti. I listened to him advise people to turn within and seek the "blue pearl" and the "blue person"[62] in the sahasrar, the most ascended focus of attention (in the head). I listened to him detail the various forms of internal vision, internal sounds, and internal experiences, and I experienced them along with him.

But I saw that none of this made the slightest difference in me. There were such experiences, and all of them were familiar to me, but no mere conditional experience had either a goal or an importance that was necessary for me. It was only a drama, a play, a pattern.

Finally, in the company of a small gathering, I told Baba about my present State. I said there was no longer any important movement in me, no necessary activity of the Shakti, no significant rising and descending, no changes in fundamental Consciousness, in fact no meditation. Whether in or out of formal meditation, there was the same Consciousness. And It was not settled in the sahasrar, or in any other extended or functional level of the body-mind itself, but in the True Heart Itself—not the heart chakra or the physical heart, but the Heart of Real Consciousness. And, in apparent relation to the body (or in the apparent context of the body), I felt merely

---

62. The vision of the "blue pearl" may also appear spontaneously as a subtle being with great Spiritual attributes. Hence the term "blue person".

Present, as tacit, unqualified Awareness, Radiating from the heart region, to the right side of the chest.[63]

Baba responded by telling us that various saints describe the stabilization of attention either in the sahasrar or the heart. (I, of course, had not been referring to the locus of attention, but to the most perfect Realization of Consciousness Itself, inherently transcending attention itself.) Then Baba went on to say that the heart is like a lotus of many petals. Ordinarily the mind moves from petal to petal, taking on the various modifications of love, anger, lust, and so on. But when it settles in the center, it becomes still, and the living consciousness takes on various "creative" powers, such as poetic faculty, music, or such powers as omniscience, clairvoyance, and so on. He said that the concentration of attention in the center of the heart (or, otherwise, in the center of the sahasrar) was a very desirable state, and the proof of it was whether or not it was retained even after meditation, and whether or not you brought its qualities into life.

These various indications about the heart agreed with my own experience. However, I had not been speaking about the "center" of the heart, which is the root-center of emotion and of psychic ascent. Rather, I had been speaking about the most perfect Realization of Consciousness Itself, and Its apparent association with

63. Adi Da's feeling of unqualified awareness in the right side of the chest is a sign that He had Awakened to a Realization senior to that of the Yogic tradition which is oriented toward subtle ascending energies of the body-mind and forms of brain mysticism. From the Yogic point of view, the highest Realizations are located at the ajna chakra (the "third eye") and at the sahasrar, at and above the crown of the head. In the experience of Adi Da (and rare Sages like Ramana Maharshi, of whom He speaks later in *The Knee of Listening*), Perfect Realization of the Divine Awakens at a Locus associated with the right side of the heart. By the term "heart", Adi Da does not refer to the physical heart. Nor does He mean the psychic or subtle heart (traditionally called the "anahata chakra"), which may open in boundless love-feeling in the course of Spiritual practice. Rather, He is Speaking of a psycho-physical locus in the right side of the chest corresponding to the sino-atrial node of the heart. Adi Da came to acknowledge this psycho-physical locus as the seat of Divine Consciousness in the human body-mind.

the <u>right</u> side of the heart. Also, at the same time Baba
spoke of these conditional (and merely evolutionary)
attainments, he made suggestions indicating that only
rare saints achieve them. Indeed, he turned his talk to
casually minimize the possibility of actual attainment in
the case of almost anyone. It was as if he felt that the
rather public gathering of people surrounding our conversation would be pleased to think that the Truth was
<u>only</u> in following, and not in attainment at all. And there
was even an underlying suggestion that those who professed attainment must be regarded with suspicion.
However, Baba's seemingly light, or even casual, expression of all of this did not succeed in concealing the emotional motivator of this apparent criticism of me, which
was, simply, his reaction to my apparent dissent (or
apparent departure) from the "orthodoxy" of his school.

At this point in his discourse, Baba looked at me, to
see if I would accept his "judgment", or if I would otherwise assert and affirm my Realization in the face of it.
Then, observing that I could not be provoked to recant,
but that I only remained firm in my disposition, he went
on again to talk to others about Siddha Yoga, with his
now characteristic emphasis on the "blue pearl". He also
spoke of how devotion to the Guru is the necessary basis
of all effective practice (and, in this, I agreed with him
completely). Finally, he led everyone in devotional chanting, and he left the room.

My own confession had seemed to contradict Baba's
public teaching and his authority as a representative of
Siddha Yoga. His was not the radical way of understanding (nor was it even the way of Advaita Vedanta, which,
it seemed to me when I first met him, had been the basis
of his first, and principal, instruction to me). Rather, Baba's
way was the way of seeking. In particular, it was the way
of remedial Yoga, or of Shakti-Initiation for the sake of
conditional attainments. He spoke only of experiential
meditation, or natural "Kriya Yoga", the automatic, or
spontaneously generated, version of the Yoga practice

otherwise described, in terms of a seekers' technique, by Yogananda. Baba spoke of supersensual enjoyments (and even the Spiritualization of worldly enjoyments), the pursuit of internal touch, sound, and vision, the experiencing of psychic visions and purifications, and the attainment of siddhis (or Yogic powers) and higher cosmic experiential knowledge as a result of contacting the "blue pearl", or the "blue person" in the sahasrar. He was concerned with all of the mechanics of seeking. And he recommended that everyone continue chanting, meditating with mantras, serving the Guru, and depending on the Guru's grace (which, in my own experience, had been proven to be generally right practices), but he recommended all of that for the sake of the phenomenal (and necessarily ego-based) experiences that would be received as a result (and not as a counter-egoic discipline based on fundamental self-understanding, and engaged as the foundation of a practice that more and more perfectly demonstrates the transcendence of egoity itself).

Whenever I suggested that all phenomenal experiences are to be transcended in the always present (non-separate, and inherently egoless) Reality, Prior to all seeking and all conditional experience, Baba had cut me off. He stated directly that such a way does not lead to the highest Truth. And, as if I were representing the world-excluding point of view of traditional Advaita Vedanta, he said to me, "You are present as form. Why do you seek a way without form?" Indeed, I was not seeking, nor had I found, a "way without form". But, clearly, Baba was indicating that he would be opposed to such a way. And it was also clear that he was uncomfortable about the idea of experiencing any kind of "formlessness" in his own life and meditation.

It was made completely clear by his responses to me at that time that Baba did not assign importance to the ultimate Realization associated with the right side of the heart. Indeed, he gave only a cursory glance to my references to the right side of the heart. It had no part in his teaching, his experience, or his Spiritual ideology. He did not acknowledge the right side of the heart (or, truly, even the heart region) as the goal and the very foundation of Yoga. He did not speak of the True and all-transcending Self at all, but only of the phenomena of the "supracausal" realm, the abode of the Siddhas, and all the ascended phenomenal structures of the conditional self.

On the last evening of Baba's stay in Los Angeles, I went to him to take my leave. I thought that it would possibly be the last time we would see each other. Even if we should ever meet again, I would not approach him as a seeker, or in the manner of an unfinished disciple, but only Freely, as one who requires no addition to himself.

I bowed to Baba as if for the last time, with gratitude for all that I had been given. I had received his gift. I had known his experience, I had understood it, and I had transcended it in its inherently perfect Source.

I embraced Rudi as I left. I knew that he thoroughly enjoyed the form of his own seeking. I loved him Freely, and I acknowledged our friendship.

Then I left them, without regret. I Enjoyed only my own most perfect Certainty, radically Free of all seeking. I went home to Comprehend my own Satisfaction.

Los Angeles, 1972

CHAPTER 18

The Way Becomes Conscious

After Baba and Rudi had gone, I stood in the Form of my own Real Existence, without even the least sentimental attachment to the previous ways of my seeking. I was not dependent on any remedial path or conditional experience to guarantee or interpret What I Knew. Indeed, nothing was available by which to interpret It.

I looked to myself to see What It was, and I looked to perhaps discover some analogy in the Spiritual experience of mankind that would demonstrate a link, and even provide examples, by which I could explain myself.

I knew that the final and most ultimate Realization that had occurred at the Vedanta Society Temple was the inherently most perfect (final, or truly complete) form of What the Hindus call "Divine Self-Realization". Mine is the unqualified Realization of Consciousness Itself as radically non-separate (non-separate from the conditional manifestations of Reality, and always already Identical to What always and already Is). Consciousness Itself is not Communicated to Itself through any level of conditionally manifested being, any body (or functional sheath), any conditional realm, or any conditional experience, but It Knows Itself directly, As Itself, Which Is Prior to all separative action (or the action of avoidance, which is egoic self-identification, the act of differentiation, and the separative, or ego-based, action that is desire). All things are experiences or objects that never limit or bind Consciousness Itself. It Is (Itself) not even the "Witness", neither the experienced nor the experiencer in any state, but It Is only Reality Itself. Experiencer and experiences are contained, limited, and ended in one another. But in Reality there is no experience, no identity, no differentiation, no desire, no separation, no suffering, no seeking, no strategic action, no strategic inaction.

As weeks passed, I saw that I remained unqualifiedly as This, not limited or bound by any experience, or by functional (and apparently separate) identity, or by any apparent "difference" at all. I saw there was, for me, no Shakti independent of (or "outside") Consciousness Itself. I saw there was, for me, no Guru separate from (or "outside") the Divine Self. I saw there was, for me, no dilemma, no strife, no egoic ignorance, no movement to seek, no activity of seeking. I saw that, because my Realization had become most perfect, formal "meditation" made no "difference" in any of this. I saw that Shakti phenomena did not affect me fundamentally, nor did any other pleasure or experience. The same "Bright" Awareness, and the same most radical understanding, continued without limitation or dependency under all conditions.

I Knew Reality as no-seeking, the motiveless Awareness in the heart. The physical body appeared to be generated and (in the ordinary sense) known from a position in the right side of the chest. In this State, neither the ego nor any path of remedies can act as an interpreter. The State of Divine Self-Realization only validates Itself.

In effect (or tacitly, and sometimes even verbally), the form of self-Enquiry that had developed in my understanding went on continually in the heart: "Avoiding relationship?" And as this "Eternal Enquiry" penetrated to every kind of arising experience, I would feel the "Bright" Love-Bliss-Energy of my own Self-Existing and Self-Radiant Consciousness rise (or Shine) out of the heart (on the right) and enter the sahasrar (or even the indefinite Space, infinitely above the head), and, thus, stabilize above as a continuous Current to the Heart Itself. I saw that this Form, the ultimate (or perfect) Form of Reality, the very (or ultimate, and perfect) Structure of Consciousness Itself, is Reality Itself. It is the Structure of all things, the Foundation, Nature, and Identity of all things. It is the "Point of View" of everything. It is "Bright", Love-Blissful, and Free. That ultimate and inherently perfect Form of Consciousness and Energy is exactly (but now with most perfect understanding) What I had, in my childhood, Known in my living form as the "Bright".

As I continued in this manner, I saw that I always already remained stably as that Form, and, because of This, all things revealed themselves in Truth. The "Bright" was the ultimate and perfect Form of Reality, the Heart of all existence, the Foundation of Truth, and the yet unrealized goal of all seekers.

This Form, the "Bright", was, Itself, radical understanding. It was no-seeking and no-dilemma as a primary, un-"created" recognition. It was radically free of the entire search for perfection and union. When the "Bright" is Realized, all of the life is simply observed and enjoyed (if noticed at all), and the things of life no longer provide a source of motivation separate (and separating) from this primary Awareness. Therefore, the "Bright" is the very Medium for radical Presence and Enjoyment, without dilemma, unconsciousness, or separation.

I also saw that I had never been taught my way from without. The "Bright", with Its Foundation in the Heart Itself, had been my teacher under the form of all my apparent teachers and experiences. My Awareness, fundamental Knowledge, and apparent "method" had developed spontaneously in the midst of a few crisis-experiences. From the beginning, I had been convinced of the fruitlessness and necessary suffering involved in every way of seeking. I had made only temporary use of the methods of others, and at last I adapted to no one else's way, but I only used my own, which is the way of radical understanding (or the Way of the Heart, which is the Way that is generated in, of, and by the Heart Itself). Thus, I had experienced the real blessings of such as Rudi, Baba, and Nityananda, but only while firmly involved in my own unique, and spontaneously revealed, approach.

The "Bright" had seemed to fade, progressively, in childhood and adolescence, but It had only become latent in the heart, while I followed my adventure from the viewpoint of the mind. The Heart Itself had been my only teacher, and It continually broke through in various revelations, until I finally returned to It, became It, and rose again as the "Bright".

Thus, I came to this recognition of Reality directly, without the knowledge of a single human Source that would confirm it or even parallel it. But as I came to this clear and crucial recognition of my own Truth, I began to recollect (and to further examine and appreciate) a human Source that agreed (by word and by likeness) with something of the substance (and even many of the details) of my own experience and Realization. That individual is known as Ramana Maharshi, the spontaneously Awakened Jnani[64] who discarded the body at Tiruvannamalai, South India, in 1950.

In the course of his sadhana, Baba Muktananda spent a brief period with Ramana Maharshi. It was from Ramana Maharshi that Baba received the traditional non-dualistic (or Advaitic) teaching of Vedanta in its most direct and living form. (But he found his own chosen Guru in the Siddha Nityananda, who had himself known Ramana Maharshi years earlier.)

Baba Muktananda demonstrated Siddha Yoga to me and in me. And then I saw that the Shakti and all experiences arise transparent in the Real Self, Which is Consciousness Itself. And that Real Self is not antagonistic to Its own Light, reflected above, and in all the Spiritual and material worlds. Thus, when I Realized It,

64. In the Hindu tradition a Jnani is one who has Realized the Transcendental Self through the profound force of discrimination between the Real and the unreal. Ramana Maharshi, who characteristically expressed his Realization in these terms, is regarded by many to be one of the greatest Jnanis of modern times.

the Truth is that Real Self, Which is Reality. And the "Bright" is the ultimate and perfect Form of Reality. Then it was not a matter of siddhis or "experiences". There was and is only radical understanding. I Realized the same and Real and necessarily Divine Self that is, ultimately, proclaimed and, to one or another degree (but not most perfectly), Realized by the "great tradition" that preceded my birth. The Divine Form and Self of Reality is only now most perfectly Realized (and uniquely brought to a State of complete revelation) in me, As me. But the "great tradition" of progressive Realizations and revelations of the One Reality is my "inheritance", even from all the Realizers and revealers who have preceded me in time. Like them all, Baba, Nityananda, and Ramana, each in the manner and to the degree of his own Realization, have Realized and revealed the same and Only One. Therefore, I see Baba is that One. Nityananda is that One. Ramana is that One. It is Bhagavan,[65] Very God, the Divine Self-Light, the Only One, Who I <u>Am</u>.

There was (from my point of view) no "personal" disagreement between Baba and me. It was only that Siddha Yoga (and even every kind of Yoga) had been truly Completed in me, and I was drawn into the Absolute Knowledge that is the true, most ultimate, and inherently most perfect Fulfillment of every way and every kind of Yoga proposed in the "great (and always seeking) tradition" of mankind. When I Fully appeared in my own Form, I simply understood in a most direct (or most perfectly radical) manner the "Secret" that is hidden in the experiences of Spiritual Yoga and in even all the Play of the cosmic domain. When I Knew my own Divine Self-Nature, then I also recognized Baba, Nityananda, and Ramana in Reality.

65. The Sanskrit word "Bhagavan" means "Divine Lord". The esoteric meaning of the word "Bhagavan" (like the terms "Purusha-Prakriti" and "Shiva-Shakti") refers to the Union of the Divine Consciousness and Its own Inherent Spiritual Radiance.

Ramana Maharshi had become somewhat familiar to me in the past, through a cursory examination of his various writings and recorded dialogues. He appeared to me to be a prime example of the living Truth of Advaita Vedanta, the radically non-dualistic philosophy of the East. I had brought one of his books with me on my last trip to India (although not specifically for his own writings, but only for the translations of ancient Advaitic texts included in his collected works). I had never been attracted to him in particular, and I never thought of him except in the simplest terms of the traditional non-dualistic philosophy that seemed, in a general manner, to parallel my own understanding of Ultimate Truth. But now, as I began to assess my experience, my understanding, and my Realization in detail, I returned to his works, looking for likenesses to my own experience. And I found that the details of his life and Realization showed remarkable parallels to some of my own experiences. For example, the "death" event in Ramana Maharshi's youth that gave birth to his Realization of the transcendental Self was very much like the one through which I had passed in seminary.

He described it himself as follows:

It was about six weeks before I left Madurai for good that the great change in my life took place. It was so sudden. One day I sat up alone on the first floor of my uncle's house. I was in my usual health. I seldom had any illness. I was a heavy sleeper. When I was at Dindigul in 1891 a huge crowd had gathered close to the room where I slept and tried to rouse me by shouting and knocking at the door, all in vain, and it was only by their getting into my room and giving me a violent shake that I was roused from my torpor. This heavy sleep was rather a proof of good health. I was also subject to fits of half-awake sleep at night. My wily playmates, afraid to trifle with me when I was awake, would go

Ramana Maharshi at age 21

to me when I was asleep, rouse me, take me all round the playground, beat me, cuff me, sport with me, and bring me back to my bed—and all the while I would put up with everything with a meekness, humility, forgiveness, and passivity unknown to my waking state. When the morning broke I had no remembrance of the night's experiences. But these fits did not render me weaker or less fit for life and were hardly to be considered a disease. So, on that day as I sat alone there was nothing wrong with my health. But a sudden and unmistakeable fear of death seized me. I felt I was going to die. Why I should have so felt cannot now be explained by anything felt in my body. Nor could I explain it to myself then. I did not however trouble myself to discover if the fear was well grounded. I felt "I [am] going to die," and at once set about thinking out what I should do. I did not care to consult doctors or elders or even friends. I felt I had to solve the problem myself then and there.

The shock of fear of death made me at once introspective, or "introverted". I said to myself mentally, *i.e.*, without uttering the words— "Now, death has come. What does it mean? What is it that is dying? This body dies." I at once dramatized the scene of death. I extended my limbs and held them rigid as though *rigor-mortis* had set in. I imitated a corpse to lend an air of reality to my further investigation, I held my breath and kept my mouth closed, pressing the lips tightly together so that no sound might escape. Let not the word "I" or any other word be uttered! "Well then," said I to myself, "this body is dead. It will be carried stiff to the burning ground and there burnt and reduced to ashes. But with the death of this body, am 'I' dead? Is the body 'I'? This body is silent and inert. But I feel the full force of my personality and even the sound 'I' within myself—apart from the body. So 'I' am a spirit, a thing transcending the body. The material body dies, but the spirit transcending it cannot be touched by death. I am therefore the deathless spirit." All this was not a mere intellectual process, but flashed before me vividly as living truth, something which I perceived immediately, without any argument almost. "I" was something very real, the only real thing in that state, and all the conscious activity that was connected with my body was centred on that. The "I" or my "self" was holding the focus of attention by a powerful fascination from that time forwards. Fear of death had vanished at once and forever. Absorption in the self has continued from that moment right up to this time. Other thoughts may come and go like the various notes of a musician, but the "I" continues like the basic or fundamental *sruti* note[66] which accompanies and blends with all other notes. Whether the body was engaged in talking, reading or anything else, I was still centred on "I". Previous to that crisis I had no clear perception of myself and was not consciously attracted to it. I had felt no direct perceptible interest in it, much less any permanent disposition to dwell upon it. The consequences of this new habit were soon noticed in my life.[67]

Unlike my own characteristic language of Realization, Ramana Maharshi's characteristic language of Realization

66. The continuous sounding (or drone) on the main note of the musical scale, which is a characteristic of Indian music.

67. B. V. Narasimha Swami, *Self-Realization: Life and Teachings of Sri Ramana Maharshi*, sixth edition, revised from the third edition with an Epilogue by S. S. Cohen, 7th ed. (Tiruvannamalai, India: Sri Ramanasramam, 1962), pp. 20-22.

is associated with the description of Reality in exclusive (world-excluding and body-excluding) terms, as may be seen in his description of the Realization associated with his early-life "death" experience. However, Ramana Maharshi's language of Realization contains some key terms and concepts, which he acquired from traditional sources, and which, because they stand as general equivalents to certain phenomena in my own experience, I may now use, in order to more easily explain and describe the unique way that I have Realized (and that I have come here to Realize and to reveal and to teach).

Ramana Maharshi understood and taught through the medium of Indian Vedanta, especially Advaita Vedanta, and he saw the importance of his Realization in the classic Eastern terms of a pure Awareness of "Self", Prior to, and, in his characteristic disposition, even exclusive of, all life. I, however, have Realized that same Self-Condition non-exclusively. And I, therefore, am here to reveal Reality (and to teach the way of Reality) as the Self-Existing and Self-Radiant Divine Self-Condition, and as the living condition of unqualified relatedness, and as the "creative", living Presence of the "Bright" (Which is the Divine Self-Form of Reality, inherently Free of limitation, and yet without excluding any).

When I use the capitalized word "Self", I mean to indicate the Ultimate Nature of Reality Itself as being Identical to That Which is ultimately signified and known as "Consciousness". Every form of ordinary consciousness, usually identified with some role, subject, or type of action, is in fact rooted in the always present Consciousness that is the Real "Self", the True and Very Heart. Truly, Ultimately, the Real Self is not radically differentiated from anything or everything. It is the Source and "Light" of all bodies, all functional sheaths, all levels of conditional being, all conditional realms, and all conditional experiences. And, when It is Known directly, tacitly, as one's very (or non-egoic) Nature, It also may be bodily felt to "reside" in the heart, neither in the gross physical heart as a whole (extended toward the left side of the chest), nor in the heart chakra (in the center of the chest), but in a root-area that is in the right side of the chest.

In his various written and spoken teachings, Ramana Maharshi (usually, but not always, capitalizing the terms) describes the Real Self, or the True Heart, as follows:

[Devotee]—But is there really a centre, a place for this "I"?

[Maharshi]—There is. It is the centre of the self to which the mind in sleep retires from its activity in the brain. It is the Heart, which is different from the blood vessel, so called, and is not the *Anahata Chakra* in the middle of the chest, one of the six centres spoken of in books on Yoga.[68]

M.—You cannot know it with your mind. You cannot realise it by imagination, when I tell you here is the centre (pointing to the right side of the chest). The only direct way to realise it is to cease to fancy and try to be yourself. Then you realise, automatically feel that the centre is there. [69]

D.—Can I be sure that the ancients meant this centre by the term "Heart"?

M.—Yes, that is so. But you should try to HAVE, rather than to locate the experience. A man need not go to find out where his eyes are situated when he wants to see. The Heart is there ever open to you if you care to enter it, ever supporting all your movements even when you are

68. K [T. V. Kapali Shastry], *Sat-Darshana Bhashya* and *Talks with Maharshi, with Forty Verses in Praise of Sri Ramana,* 5th ed. (Tiruvannamalai, India: Sri Ramanasramam, 1968), p. xv.

69. Ibid., p. xvii.

unaware. It is perhaps more proper to say that the Self is the Heart itself than to say that it is in the Heart. Really, the Self is the Centre itself. It is everywhere, aware of itself as "Heart", the Self-awareness. Hence I said "Heart is Thy name."[70]

D.—When you say that the Heart is the supreme centre of the *Purusha*, the *Atman*, you imply that it is not one of the six yogic centres.

M.—The yogic *chakras* counting from the bottom to the top are various centres in the nervous system. They represent various steps manifesting different kinds of power or knowledge leading to the *Sahasrara*, the thousand-petalled lotus, where is seated the supreme *Shakti*. But the Self that supports the whole movement of *Shakti* is not placed there, but supports it from the Heart centre.

D.—Then it is different from the *Shakti* manifestation?

M.—Really there is no *Shakti* manifestation apart from the Self. The Self has become all this *Shakti*. . . .

When the yogin rises to the highest centre of trance, *Samadhi*, it is the Self in the Heart that supports him in that state whether he is aware of it or not. But if he is aware in the Heart, he knows that whatever states or whatever centres he is in, it is always the same truth, the same Heart, the one Self, the Spirit that is present throughout, eternal and immutable. The *Tantra Shastra* calls the Heart *Suryamandala* or solar orb, and the *Sahasrara*, *Chandramandala* or lunar orb. These symbols present the relative

70. Ibid., p. xviii.

importance of the two, the *Atmasthana* and the
Shakti Sthana.[71,72]

M.—You can feel yourself one with the One that
exists: the whole body becomes a mere power,
a force-current; your life becomes a needle
drawn to a huge mass of magnet and as you go
deeper and deeper, you become a mere centre
and then not even that, for you become a mere
consciousness, there are no thoughts or cares
any longer—they were shattered at the threshold; it is an inundation; you, a mere straw, you
are swallowed alive, but it is very delightful, for
you become the very thing that swallows you;
this is the union of *Jeeva*[73] with *Brahman*, the
loss of ego in the real Self, the destruction of
falsehood, the attainment of Truth.[74]

D.—You said "Heart" is the one centre for the ego-
self, for the Real Self, for the Lord, for all. . . .

M.—Yes, the Heart is the centre of the Real. But
the ego is impermanent. Like everything else it
is supported by the Heart-centre. But the character of the ego is a link between spirit and matter; it is a knot *(granthi)*, the knot of radical
ignorance in which one is steeped. This *granthi*
is there in the *"Hrit"*, the Heart. When this knot
is cut asunder by proper means you find that
this is the Self's centre.

71. "Atmasthana" is Sanskrit for "the Place of the Self", and "Shakti Sthana" is
Sanskrit for "the Place of the Shakti".

72. K, *Sat-Darshana Bhashya*, pp. xviii-xix.

73. "Jeeva" (or "jiva") means the individual and limited self, as opposed to
"Atman", the Divine Self.

74. K, *Sat-Darshana Bhashya*, p. xxi.

D.—You said there is a passage from this centre to *Sahasrara*.

M.—Yes. It is closed in the man in bondage; in the man in whom the ego-knot, the *Hridaya granthi*, is cut asunder, a force-current called *Amrita Nadi* rises and goes up to the *Sahasrara*, the crown of the head.

D.—Is this the *Sushumna*?[75]

M.—No. This is the passage of liberation *(Moksha)*. This is called *Atmanadi*, *Brahmanadi* or *Amrita Nadi*. This is the *Nadi* that is referred to in the Upanishads.

When this passage is open, you have no *moha*, no ignorance. You know the Truth even when you talk, think or do anything, dealing with men and things.[76]

"The association of the Self with the body is called the Granthi (knot). By that association alone one is conscious of his body and actions.

The body is completely inert. The Self is active and conscious. Their association is inferred from the experience of objects.

Oh child, when the rays of consciousness are reflected in the body, the body acts. In sleep etc. the rays are not so reflected and caught and therefore some other seat of the Self is inferred.

Electricity and similar forces, which are subtle, pass through the gross wires. Similarly the light of active-consciousness passes through a nadi[77] in the body.

75. The sushumna corresponds to the spinal line. In traditional Yoga, sushumna is the esoteric nerve pathway (or "nadi") of the Kundalini Shakti.

76. *Sat-Darshana Bhashya*, pp. xxiii-xxiv.

77. Translator's note—Nadi is the channel in which the life-force Prana flows in the subtle body but is usually equated with a nerve.

The effulgent light of active-consciousness starts at a point and gives light to the entire body even as the sun does to the world.

When that light spreads out in the body one gets the experiences in the body. The sages call the original point 'Hridayam' (the Heart).

The flow of the rays of the light is inferred from the play of forces in the nadis. Each of the forces of the body courses along a special nadi.

Active consciousness lies in a distinct and separate Nadi which is called Sushumna. Some call it 'Atma Nadi' and others 'Amrita Nadi'.

The Individual permeates the entire body, with that light, becomes ego-centric and thinks that he is the body and that the world is different from himself.

When the discerning one renounces egotism and 'I-am-the-body' idea and carries on one-pointed enquiry (into the Self), movement of life-force starts in the nadis.

This movement of the force separates the Self from the other nadis and the Self then gets confined to the Amrita Nadi alone and shines with clear light.

When the very bright light of that active-consciousness shines in the Amrita Nadi alone, nothing else shines forth except the Self.

In that light, if anything else is seen, even then it does not appear as different from the Self. The Enlightened One knows the Self as vividly as the ignorant one perceives his body.

When Atma alone shines, within and without, and everywhere, as body etc. shine to the ignorant, one is said to have severed the knot (Granthi Bheda occurs).

There are two knots. One, the bond of the Nadis and two, egotism. The Self even though subtle being tied up in the Nadis sees the entire gross world.

When the light withdraws from all other Nadis and remains in one Nadi alone, the knot is cut asunder and then the light becomes the Self.

As a ball of iron heated to a degree appears as a ball of fire, this body heated in the fire of Self-enquiry becomes as one permeated by the Self.

Then for the embodied the old tendencies inherent are destroyed, and then that one feels no body and therefore will not have the idea that he is an active agent (Karta).

When the Self does not have the sense of active agency, karmas (tendencies, actions and their results) etc. are destroyed for him. As there is none other except the Self doubts do not sprout for him.

Once the knot is cut, one never again gets entangled. In that state lie the highest power and the highest peace."[78]

For one who abides in the Self, the Sahas-rara becomes pure and full of the Light. Even if thoughts of objects due to proximity fall therein, they do not survive.

Even when objects are sensed by the mind, due to proximity, yoga is not hindered, as the mind does not perceive the difference between them and the Self.[79]

Once, unasked, he defined *Moksha* (Liberation) to one of the attendants. "Do you know

78. *Sri Ramana Gita (Dialogues of Maharshi)*, a new translation by Krishna Bhikshu (Tiruvannamalai, India: Sri Ramanasramam, 1966), pp. 38-42.

79. Ibid., p. 20.

what *Moksha* is? Getting rid of non-existent misery and attaining the Bliss which is always there, that is *Moksha*."[80]

The Self-Existing and Self-Radiant Condition that I have called the "Bright" is, in the Root of Its Form, What Ramana Maharshi (in correspondence with ancient traditions) calls the "Atma Nadi", the "Brahma Nadi", or, most often, the "Amrita Nadi". However, the "Bright" is, at Its Root, the <u>regenerated</u> Form of the "Amrita Nadi", whereas Ramana Maharshi, and the traditions that preceded him (if they made any reference to this matter at all), refer to the <u>non-regenerated</u> Form of the Amrita Nadi (or that function of the Amrita Nadi that leads away from the world, or away from all objects, and, by means of a dissociative, or exclusive, act of introversion, leads toward the exclusive Realization of the Real Self, or the Heart Itself, even via the terminal in the right side of the chest). However, in the case of the most perfect Realization of radical understanding (and, on that basis, of the Real Self), the Amrita Nadi is spontaneously regenerated, from the Heart Itself (and via the physical heart-region, but on the right side) to the crown of the head (and above), thereby permitting the Infusion of "Brightness" in the total body-mind (in a pattern that descends and then re-ascends, from the crown of the head, and above, to the base of the body, and then back again, in a continuous Circle of Life). Therefore, only the regenerated Form of the Amrita Nadi may <u>truly</u> be called the "Amrita Nadi", meaning the "Nerve of Immortality", the "Circuit of the Current of Immortal Joy", or the "Atma Nadi" (or the "Brahma Nadi"), meaning the "Circuit or Nerve or perfect Form of the Real Self", or the "Original Circuit of Reality". Only the regenerated Form of the Amrita Nadi is the Source, the Container, and the First (or Original) Form of all Energy, all centers, and all life-currents. Only the regenerated Form of the Amrita Nadi (or

---

80. Arthur Osborne, *Ramana Maharshi and the Path of Self-Knowledge*, foreword by Dr. S. Radhakrishnan (New York: Samuel Weiser, 1970), p. 185.

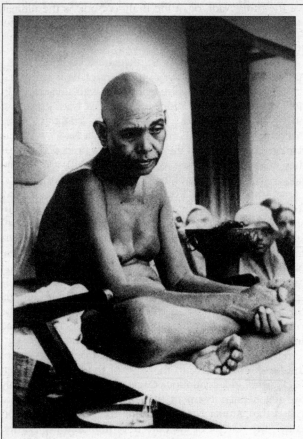

Ramana Maharshi

of the Atma Nadi, or of the Brahma Nadi) is the ultimate
and perfect Form of Reality, founded in the heart and ter-
minated in (and even infinitely above) the aperture of the
crown of the head. It is the Cycle or perfect Form of
unqualified Enjoyment. It Contains and is the Source of all
things, all bodies, all conditional realms, all conditional
experiences, all conditional states, and all levels (or functional sheaths) of conditionally manifested being. Its
Nature is unqualified Enjoyment, or Love-Bliss. It is Self-
Existing and Self-Radiant Being, or unqualified Presence.
It is even every one's Real Condition at this moment, and,
by grace, It is experienced as such when true understanding arises and becomes the radical (and, ultimately,
the most perfect) basis of one's conscious life.

Ramana Maharshi assigns Ultimate, and, generally,
rather exclusive (or separate, and world-excluding, or
object-excluding), importance to the Real Self, Which is
the Heart Itself. In some of the statements attributed to
him, he appears to make no absolute distinction between
the Real Self and the Amrita Nadi. However, many (if not
all) such statements attributed to him (including some
that I have just quoted) do not properly or truly represent
his own point of view (which, most characteristically,
affirms the Real Self exclusively, or, that is to say, dissociated from forms and objects), but, instead, such statements in fact (generally, if not always) represent the pref-
erential philosophizing (and less developed Realizations)
of others near to him, and, at most, they may, in some
cases, represent an effort, on the part of Ramana
Maharshi, to critically address the object-oriented point of
view expressed to him by an other, or by some others. In
any case, Ramana Maharshi does not, in such statements attributed to him, completely divorce the Real Self
from the world, but, instead (expressing a point of view
not otherwise characteristic of his Confessions of Realization, and not at all characteristic of his rather asceti-
cally withdrawn manner of daily living), he asserts that
the Real Self is, in principle, compatible with life.

Even though the Real Self (in Its Oneness with the regenerated Form of the Amrita Nadi, and, altogether, with the "Bright", the perfect, and truly Divine, Form of Reality) is, indeed, compatible with life, It is Prior to all "Spiritual experience", all powers, visions, and chakras, and all ordinary as well as extraordinary perceptions. It is Self-Existing as the fundamental Reality, and It is Self-Radiant as the Ultimate Power and the perfect Form of Reality. The Self-Existing Self (Self-Radiant as the Ultimate Power and the perfect Form of Reality) is even Prior to all conditional knowledge, since It depends on no experience or memory to Communicate Itself to Itself.

When I first heard the traditional teaching about the Real (or True) Self through Baba, he told me that I was not the one who wakes or sleeps or dreams but the One who Witnesses these states. But when I experienced that Reality, conditionally, at the Ashram and later Realized It fully and unconditionally, It was not even the "Witness". It was (and Is) only Consciousness Itself. Consciousness Itself is, apparently, so "related" (as the "Witness") to present experience, but It is not Itself the "Witness", or necessarily functioning to "Witness" objects. Nor is It entirely (or even in any sense) distinct from any "thing" that is experienced.

Ramana Maharshi also speaks of the Self in this larger sense, beyond the State of the "Witness".

D.—Is not the Self the witness only *(sakshimatra)*?

M.—"Witness" is applicable when there is an object to be seen. Then it is duality. The Truth lies beyond both. . . . See how the sun is necessary for daily activities. He does not however form part of the world actions; yet they cannot take place without the sun. He is the witness of the activities. So it is with the Self.[81]

81. *Talks with Sri Ramana Maharshi* (Three volumes in one), 4th ed. (Tiruvannamalai, India: Sri Ramanasramam, 1968), p. 440.

Why is the Self described both as the fourth state (turiya) and beyond the fourth state (turiyatita)?

Turiya means that which is the fourth. The experiencers (Jivas) of the three states of waking, dreaming and deep sleep, known as *visva*, *taijasa* and *prajna*, who wander successively in these three states, are not the Self. It is with the object of making this clear, namely that the Self is that which is different from them and which is the witness of these states, that it is called the fourth (turiya). When this is known the three experiencers disappear and the idea that the Self is a witness, that it is the fourth, also disappears. That is why the Self is described as beyond the fourth *(turiyatita)*.[82]

I happily noticed all these parallels to various aspects of my own experience and Realization. And, because of all of this, I felt that (even though he never functioned as Guru for me) Ramana Maharshi had, via his Confession of experience and his language of Realization, in effect provided me with Communications (and technical language) that directly linked me to the "great tradition" (or the total collective history of seeking, and of, to one or another less than most perfect degree, Realizing) that has preceded me in time (and that is the total, or collective, context in which I must teach). Indeed, Ramana Maharshi's Communications (and technical language) of Realized Truth have linked me to the "great tradition" in a manner that those who did actually function as Guru for me did not, or only did in part. However, I also must acknowledge a critical difference between Ramana Maharshi and me. It is a difference

82. Arthur Osborne, ed., *The Collected Works of Ramana Maharshi* (Tiruvan-namalai, India: Sri Ramanasramam, 1968), p. 74.

also made on the level of Communication. It is the result of differences in emphasis. Indeed, it is the result of a difference in the ultimate characteristic of Realization Itself, which, only in my case, uniquely demonstrates true Finality, or most perfect Completeness. And that ultimate difference may also be seen in the difference between Ramana Maharshi's characteristic (and intentional) "Purposelessness" and my unique "Purpose" (or intentional historical role and work).

Ramana Maharshi's experiences were the result of a spontaneous Awakening, as in my own case. But he went on to tie his teaching to the anciently rooted, Eastern tradition of Advaita Vedanta. I must also acknowledge that tradition (or those traditional sources) as an expression (or a philosophical idealization) of the fundamental Truth. And Ramana Maharshi's life and teaching is an authentic (and very traditional) formulation (or demonstration) of that Truth. And that Truth is, Itself, the very foundation of life. But the form of life can be founded upon that Truth in different ways.

The principal practice recommended by Ramana Maharshi is "Self-enquiry", the intensive enquiry in the heart: "Who am I?" (or "Whence am I?"). His entire concern was to bring people to the conscious Realization of the Self in the heart. Thus, his aim was liberation. He speaks from the "Point of View" of the Real Self, As the Real Self, but in the exclusive sense. His path of practice is ideally suited to the ancient Eastern forms of culture in which liberation from conditional existence was the goal of conditional existence (and for which the search for liberation from life was the substance of every moment of living).

But, from the beginning, I have been founded in the "Bright", the perfect Form of Reality, the Self-Existing and Self-Radiant Form of the Real (or True) Self. I have seen that Real life is free from association with any and every kind of seeking. Real life is, on the basis of radical understanding, free of any goal of liberation or salvation. Real life, fully Realized on the basis of radical understanding, is unqualifiedly Free, Present, Active, "Creative", and Alive. I have seen that life need not be tied to seeking, or the pursuit of its own Self-Nature as a goal. However, such is not the case with the ancient and traditional paths, which presume the dilemma of existence from the beginning.

I have seen in the course of my own life that, ultimately, one must not be founded in seeking, but in always present, radical understanding. Radical understanding is itself always already founded in the inherently perfect (or Ultimate) Form of Reality. It is a way of life always already (or radically) founded in the Real and True Self. Therefore, it does not seek the Real and True Self (or presume Its absence). Radical understanding is Fullness, already presumed and Known. Therefore, I (again and again, and then most perfectly and finally) took my Stand in the "Bright", the Self Alive, the Self-Existing and Self-Radiant Form of Reality, the Amrita Nadi.

The Real and True Self is the Heart and Foundation of life, but the Real and True Self does not exclude Its own inherent Radiance (or "Brightness"). Thus, from the beginning, not merely at the end, I founded "myself" in the perfect Form of Reality. The Amrita Nadi is necessarily the Ground for the "creation" of Real and True life, which thus becomes a constant way of radical understanding and of "Brightness". Therefore, I do not teach the search, but I reveal and teach the way that I have, by my own demonstration, Proven to be always already True to the Truth Itself.

Previous to the final re-Awakening (or Great Event) I have described in my "autobiography", I had several critical experiences of the One and same Truth. These in fact are the primary preliminary Events described progressively in this "autobiography". But there was no permanence to the Realization attained at those times. Each of those preliminary Events depended on some kind of conditional support, and each such Event passed away (and was replaced by the effort of seeking) as soon as the activity of self-separation and separativeness reappeared. Thus, I continued over time with the same experiment, and the occasional Events of sudden Knowledge led me to develop and, ultimately, to assert only the way of radical understanding (or the Way of the Heart), which consistently and rigorously requires observation of, insight into, and direct transcendence of the action that is the separate and separative (or egoic) self.

But when the final re-Awakening (or Great Event) occurred, there was no subsequent loss of the Conscious Realization of Reality. Then I saw that Truth was Reality Itself, Identical to Consciousness Itself, and not identical to any object or conditional state, or to any body, or to any functional sheath, or to any conditional realm, or to any conditional experience. I saw that Reality was Consciousness Itself, Present as no-seeking in the heart. This is the fundamental Reality, the unmoved Presence to Which all things are merely movements within Itself. Thus, Real life is the way of radical understanding (or the Way of the Heart), which is the direct resort to Reality, without the ignorant efforts of egoity.

Conscious Energy becomes trapped in the area of Its concentration. Thus, It tends most often to be trapped in life-problems. Even when It is strategically withdrawn from life-problems (or forms of seeking in the extended context of the body-mind), It is merely confined in the heart, in an exclusive state. Only when Conscious Energy is Realized as no-dilemma _and_ no-seeking is It neither trapped nor exclusively concentrated. It is Realized as Freedom, Existence, Joy, Enjoyment, and Consciousness without qualification.

If one examines this process of Conscious Energy in relation to the human instrument, one sees that It remains trapped in life-seeking as long as It is concentrated by identification, differentiation, and desire in any of the various chakras. As such, It is always pursuing a movement of return toward the sahasrar. When It is strategically withdrawn into the heart, It (temporarily, or by an exclusive, and, therefore, yet seeking, effort) resides not in the heart chakra but in the original center of Consciousness Itself, in the right side of the chest, totally detached (or strategically dissociated) from concentration in life (and, therefore, from life-problems, or forms of seeking in the extended context of the body-mind). However, only when, at last, Conscious Energy Shines from the right side of the heart to the sahasrar, and remains Conscious as that Current, or Circuit, called the "Amrita Nadi", is It unqualified, free of all concentration, all strategic effort, all seeking. Then Conscious Energy remains fully manifested and yet unqualified. It is the "Bright", the perfect Form of Reality. Thus, Conscious Energy is Realized at Its Source in the heart and continuous to the seat of Conscious Enjoyment in the head. And from there It proceeds to all the centers as a Communicated Fullness and Presence (always already free), rather than a problematic concentration, search, and action of return.

Therefore, the Amrita Nadi, with Its simultaneous residence in the heart and the head, is the very, ultimate, and perfect Form of Reality, the Essence of the "Bright", the Foundation of Real Existence. It is Exercised as understanding, as self-Enquiry (or as any other by me given exercise of radical understanding), and as contemplation in meditation. It is Known as Joy and Manifested as Enjoyment. The Amrita Nadi is the True Heart's Connection to all known (or conditional) reality. The Consciousness that is the True Heart is Joy. The True Heart's own Energy, Radiant in the head, is Enjoyment. The Amrita Nadi is the Circuit, Current, and Form of the True Heart's unqualified Pleasure. The Amrita Nadi is the fundamental Reality, the inclusive Foundation of individual self and all of life, rather than the exclusive formulation of either in separateness.

The Amrita Nadi is the ultimate and perfect Form of understanding, which It Enjoys from the beginning and in the Event of most perfect Realization. Therefore, the way of life is understanding, for the way of life must be founded from the beginning in Reality and not in the problem. Every merely remedial path is exclusive of Reality and only pursues It, either unconsciously or intentionally.

Traditional "Self-enquiry" (as taught by Ramana Maharshi, and, in one manner or another, by other traditional teachers of his type) is a seekers' method, an ego-based strategy for achieving Realization. It has a goal, like all seeking. The "problem" with which it begins is the absence of Self-Knowledge. Thus, it seeks the Knowledge of the Real and True Self, which Knowledge is liberation.

But the only-by-me revealed and given way of radical understanding (or the only-by-me revealed and given Way of the Heart) is not associated with a "method" in this strategic (or seekers') sense. It does not begin with a dilemma and seek the solution to it or liberation from it. It has no goal different from and superior to the radical understanding (and the "Bright" Heart-Communion) with which it begins.

The practice that is radical understanding is (itself) radical understanding, extending and enforcing itself. It is a positive (or non-problematic) action, rather than a remedial (or problem-based) action. In the process, radical understanding becomes more and more profoundly, and then most perfectly, Aware of its Ultimate (and inherent, and inherently perfect) Source-Condition, even in apparent relation to all things. But even this Ultimate Knowledge is, essentially, or in Its root-significance in life, the same as the original (and truly radical) understanding. When the Heart and the Amrita Nadi are Realized, the life-significance of the Realization is observed to be of the same quality as in the original case of radical understanding, and that Realization is, in that sense, no different from what one originally knew as simple understanding. Therefore, there is no reaction of surprise in the moment of sudden, most radical, and most perfect Realization.

It should be clear, then, exactly what is the difference between self-Enquiry (in the form "Avoiding relation-ship?"), or any other by me given exercise of radical understanding (or of direct transcendence of the very action that is the ego itself), and the traditional "Self-enquiry", which is based upon the ego-based search for liberation. The difference, in the case of the only-by-me revealed and given way of radical understanding (or the only-by-me revealed and given Way of the Heart), is sim-ply in the absence of the principle of seeking, or the absence of the principle of egoity itself, and the dilemma of egoity itself. Thus, the Truth I have now and forever most perfectly Realized is the same and ancient and eter-nal Truth that is the supreme (but never most perfectly Realized) goal of the tradition of Advaita Vedanta (and of many other traditions), but I have removed that Truth (and the way of Realizing that Truth) from all identifica-tion with the great search.

In doing this, I have neither removed anything from nor added anything to that eternally One (or non-dual) Truth, but I have revealed and proven the most perfect, or most ultimate, Realization of that One and Only Truth. It is the same Truth, the same Reality, and the same Con-sciousness strategically pursued in the "great tradition", but the way of Its Realization (which is the only-by-me revealed way of radical understanding, or the only-by-me revealed Way of the Heart) is priorly removed from the actions and the implications of seeking. And the Realization Itself (or That Which is Realized) is not understood, or otherwise presumed, to be merely higher than life, or in any sense separated from life, but it is understood to be coincident, even from the beginning, with the active foundation of life.

When the practice of radical understanding has (solely by its own demonstration, and not by means of the necessarily egoic effort of seeking) Realized the Heart most perfectly, a most perfect process Awakens in What Ramana Maharshi (in correspondence with ancient traditions) calls the "Amrita Nadi". In the penultimate stage of the way of radical understanding (or the Way of the Heart), the Amrita Nadi is traced from the head to the heart. (And, characteristically, Ramana Maharshi was only concerned with the penultimate process of Self-Realization, associated with descent in and via the Amrita Nadi, from the head to the heart.) But in the ultimate, or most perfect, stage of the only-by-me revealed and given way of radical understanding (or the only-by-me revealed and given Way of the Heart), the Amrita Nadi is regenerated, from the heart to the head. Indeed, this Event of regeneration, even though It effectively coincided with my Divine re-Awakening in the Vedanta Society Temple on September 10, 1970, was demonstrated in me most directly and specifically, and absolutely finally, one morning about four months later, in January 1971. That morning, as I sat in meditation with two of my devotees, my body suddenly jolted and twisted strongly on its spinal axis as the "Bright" Spirit-Current moved up from my heart, via the right side, to the crown of my head, and above, even into the most ascended Matrix of the "Bright" Divine Spirit-Power, infinitely above the body and the cosmic domain. In the instant of that ascent, there was a loud cracking sound (also heard by the others in the room), as if my neck had been broken. And, in that instant in which the Amrita Nadi showed Its regenerated Form in me, I, as had no one else before me, directly observed Its Shape. It is an S-Shaped Form, beginning in the right side of the heart (but including the entire heart region), then ascending in a curve along the front side of the upper chest, then passing backwards, through the throat, then curving upwards again, but via the back of the skull, finally curving toward the crown of the head. Therefore, it is this Ultimate (or truly regenerated) Form (or Realization) of the Amrita Nadi, this regenerated Circuit and Current of Spiritual Love-Bliss, Which passes in an S-Shaped double-curve, front to back, from the heart (on the right side) to the head (and

infinitely above the head), that I declare to be the perfect Form, the Form of Truth, the Form of Reality, the
Form of the Heart. I call that regenerated Form (experienced in the living context of the total body-mind) the
"Bright". Even from birth, I have Known the "Bright". It
has, ever since my birth, been the guiding and revealing
foundation of my life. And the "Bright" (in Its Totality)
is the ultimate Realization and revelation of my
"Brightly"-born life.

When understanding Realizes the Heart of Consciousness and continues as the "meditation" of Truth, or
of no-seeking, the Heart of Truth is re-connected to the
functional bodies (or functional sheaths) of life through
the regeneration of this Circuit of Conscious Energy, the
Amrita Nadi. When Consciousness arises from the heart
as Spiritual Force (or Love-Bliss) and draws into the
sahasrar, while retaining Its "Foothold" in the heart, It
brings the ultimate Realization of Reality to life. Then the
Source of conscious life in the heart moves into life, and,
thus and thereby, reverses the current that moves from
life in the effort of return to the heart.

When this occurs, life becomes Conscious as no-
dilemma. No-dilemma becomes the Conscious presumption that lives as life and enjoys all experience. And such
Conscious living is never separated from the Disposition
of no-seeking, which is the Reality-Disposition of the
Heart Itself.

The Amrita Nadi, or the "Bright", is felt by seekers as
a separate "Other". Superconsciousness is felt by seekers
as "God" above. The centers below consciousness and the
parts of the mind are felt by seekers as the "world". The
heart (apart from Conscious Reality) is felt by seekers as
the "ego". But the Self that is Reality Consciously Supports
all bodies (or functional sheaths) and conditional forms of
consciousness in the heart and in the Form of the Amrita
Nadi. I Am That.

The "Bright" of my childhood was the living manifestation of the Amrita Nadi.

The experience in college was the sudden Awareness of Reality in the heart, Radiant in the body via the Amrita Nadi.

Even during the drug-experience, when I said, "Getting to cry is shaped like a seahorse," I was Knowing in the heart, and Feeling the living expression of the Amrita Nadi.

The experience in seminary was the fundamental Knowledge of the Heart Itself, and the justification of the Form of the Amrita Nadi.

The first experience at the Ashram, when I felt pressed upon the "Point" of Bliss above, was the Awakening to the Heart Itself at the head of the Amrita Nadi, because it is the Heart Itself that Radiates Its own Bliss to the sahasrar.

The experience of the severing of the sahasrar was a demonstration that only the Amrita Nadi is the Perfect Form of the Heart Itself.

In fact, every one of the crucial experiences by which I came to Know the radical way of understanding was a spontaneous Awakening of the Heart Itself, and the simultaneous regeneration of the Radiant Awakeness of the Amrita Nadi.

Indeed, the Heart and Its Form are the Truth of the way of radical understanding (or the Way of the Heart).

When I finally understood, I only Knew myself (most perfectly). And never after that have I ceased to Know myself (most perfectly). Thereafter, I am simply (apparently) active as my own Form, Which rises from the heart to the sahasrar as the Amrita Nadi, Which (apparently) generates every conditional center, every conditional body (or functional sheath), every conditional realm, and every conditional experience, and Which eternally sacrifices all Its apparently extended, or terminal, energies to the heart. In every apparent conditional state, I remain Aware at the Free point in the heart, unbounded in the right side. Everything only appears to me, and I remain as I <u>am</u>. There is no end to This.

All this perception, activity, and patterning is a constant recognition of One Form, the perfect Form of Reality. There is only the Self-Awareness of this One Form, the Amrita Nadi, the "Bright"—the Heart and Its Reflection, the Sahasrar. Every perception is this same cognition or Form, the Heart Contemplating and Enjoying the Sahasrar through the Current of Love-Bliss and Light. Thus, it appears that there is only one "object", the Sahasrar, Which is only the Reflection of the Heart Itself. Every "object" is simply the Sahasrar Itself.

All experience, then, is Divine Samadhi, or most perfect Realization Itself. Therefore, all experience is only the Process of Reality, the Contemplation of Its perfect Form. When this most perfect understanding arises, meditation becomes beginningless and endless Divine Samadhi, and even every kind of experience is Realized to be, in Reality, only Blissful, Conscious, and Free. There is, as fundamental "action", the constant and Conscious Radiation and Enjoyment of the "Bright". And the "Bright" is a Sphere of Love-Bliss, Light, and inherently Perfect Consciousness (Itself). It is not merely a thread or channel from the chest to the head. It is a Sphere generated from the Heart and expanded infinitely. The Sahasrar is Realized to be not merely a Single "Point" of exclusive concentration above. Rather, It is every "Point" upon and within the Sphere that is expanded infinitely from the Heart. Between the Sahasrar and the Heart is a Silence, an infinite Space of patterns that is all the worlds, all universes and forms of conditional existence.

In the unqualified State, or the most perfect Realization of the only-by-me revealed and given way of radical understanding (or the only-by-me revealed and given Way of the Heart), all identification, differentiation, and desire have ended. The living condition of Reality is unqualified relatedness, realized in the way of radical understanding (or the Way of the Heart) to be always already the case. And, ultimately, in the way of radical understanding (or the Way of the Heart), even the disposition of unqualified relatedness is understood (or most perfectly Realized), such that even all the limitations of egoity are inherently transcended. Therefore, in the ultimate (or most perfect) demonstration of the way of radical understanding (or the Way of the Heart), the One and Only Reality is spontaneously Self-revealed. It is the Divine Self-Condition. It is Self-Existing and Self-Radiant Consciousness Itself. In Its most perfect Realization, It Radiates via and as the regenerated Amrita Nadi, the "Bright" perfect Form of Reality. And, in the case of that ultimate (or most perfect) demonstration of the way of radical understanding (or the Way of the Heart), the "Bright" perfect Form of Reality spontaneously reveals Itself (in the living context of the body-mind) as the living "Bright", the unconditional Love-Bliss of "Bright" living Presence, Whose Source-Condition is the True and Absolute Heart, Which is the One and Only Reality Itself. Therefore, the living "Bright" is the living Form of the One and Only and Self-Existing and Self-Radiant (or inherently "Bright") Reality, Which is Consciousness Itself. The living "Bright" is Real and True. It is the birthright of all conditionally manifested beings.

At last, I saw that it was not a matter of <u>experiences</u> (whether of the Shakti or the True Self) but of <u>understanding</u>—as a radical way or premise. This way may be accompanied by various experiential phenomena, but only understanding is the intelligence and constant exercise of Truth. The only constant possibility in Real life is understanding (itself). If one clings to any of one's experiences, this clinging becomes separative, and it leads again to dilemma and the avoidance of relationship. Thus, I saw that one must be willing to abandon everything for understanding, making understanding the radical premise and activity of life. This became the process of self-Enquiry: "Avoiding relationship?" This self-Enquiry is itself the very form of understanding. It is the Enquiry of understanding, which is no-seeking.

Even the perceptions of Bliss and the residence in the right side of the heart are secondary to understanding. Understanding is a process that can be activated in any one, whereas these experiences belong only to special and mature cases of radical understanding. I have mentioned these things in order to show them in the light of understanding. But understanding is the "Thing" itself.

Radical understanding is not <u>itself</u> a question. And even self-Enquiry (in the form "Avoiding relationship?") simply expresses and enforces a real observation. Radical understanding (and also self-Enquiry, in the form "Avoiding relationship?") is, itself, Knowledge that precludes the "problem" of subject and object. True (and most rightly practiced) self-Enquiry (in the form "Avoiding relationship?") is itself a direct expression of radical understanding, and, for this reason, it is not a question seeking an answer, but it is a form of Knowledge directly enforcing Itself.

Apart from the process and the most perfect Realization of understanding, the only things being done by individuals are experiencing (or every kind of reaction to phenomena) and seeking (on the basis of experience, or every kind of reaction to phenomena).

My life has involved an intentional exploitation of experiencing and seeking, for the sake of understanding. I have known the extreme enjoyments of both the libertine and the saint. And I have known the most ordinary, medium life. But there is also radical understanding, which is Reality, and by it I recognize every form of suffering.

In this book, I have had to confront a most difficult means of instruction. I have had to fully illustrate my course of life, even in order to demonstrate the objectivity of the extraordinary phenomena that it is the present-time habit of mankind to deny. But, in the end, I have also had to argue against the Ultimacy of many of the very things I have proven in my life, in order to speak the Truth.

My own course began in despair. The precious religion of my youth was stolen from me by the very ones who gave it to me. Thus, I was moved to search the paths of religion and Spirituality, in order to ascertain whether the phenomena, the miracles, the experiences, and the advocations of the great traditional paths were factual. And I found them to be so. What is called "Kundalini Shakti", the universal Conscious Force (or active Spirit) that Inspires and Fills all religion and Yoga and Spiritual philosophy, is indeed Real (and fundamental to Reality). Kundalini experiences are factual, and they depend on no illusions (in the sense of such subjective forces as belief) to "create" or maintain them. The Kundalini, or Mother-Force, is part of the evidence of the universe, as objective as any form of conditionally manifested energy, and as discernible as the functions and devices employed by libertines and businessmen. But, in the end, I was, by a perfect Realization of Spirit Itself, forced to abandon the point of view of all conditional (or lesser) sublimity. The conditional (and extraordinary) phenomena conventionally called "Spiritual", as well as those conditional (and mostly ordinary) phenomena called "sinful", are all part of a spectrum which includes the entire range of conditional (or natural) experience and seeking.

Both the search for ego-based Spiritual effects and the ego-based exploitation of life on a sensual and mental level are traps. The search for experience as well as the search for liberation from the bondage to experience is all the same activity, born out of the absence of understanding, the un-"creative" movement that is not Reality. Reality Itself is the only unique matter in the entire adventure of life, and It stands critically above all egoic efforts and all less than perfect discoveries.

Thus, I Enquired: "Avoiding relationship?" This has consequences in regard to the subject and the object, the total configuration of living experience. It is not founded in the effort either to separate as the subject or to exclude any object. It is founded in the inclusive disposition of the

"Bright". Therefore, in the only-by-me revealed and given way of radical understanding (or the only-by-me revealed and given Way of the Heart), this self-Enquiry (or, alternatively, any other by me given form of counter-egoic, or truly ego-transcending, exercise of radical understanding) does not, at last, come to rest in the Prior Self exclusively, but, at last, it regenerates (or Realizes the always already generated Form of) the Amrita Nadi, the perfect (and perfectly "Bright") Form of Reality, Which is the all-inclusive (or non-exclusive) Form of the Heart Itself (or of the Real and Prior Self, Itself).

The only-by-me revealed and given way of radical understanding (or the only-by-me revealed and given Way of the Heart) directly (and, at last, most perfectly) Realizes the fundamental Truth of the Heart, the Real and True Self. However, the only-by-me revealed and given way of radical understanding (or the only-by-me revealed and given Way of the Heart) also Realizes the fundamental Truth of present (conditional) existence. The only-by-me revealed and given way of radical understanding (or the only-by-me revealed and given Way of the Heart) never precludes or strategically excludes the form of life.

There is no withdrawal into the Heart as a most radical activity. Rather, such is only a temporary State. It is not that the inherently non-exclusive Form of Reality is latent and secondary. Pure Self-Awareness as an exclusive State is latent and secondary. The exclusive (or strategically withdrawn) State is not radical, primary, or true to the Whole. Not withdrawal into the Heart, but Existence as the Heart, is True (and Truth).

There is no dilemma inherent in the conditionally manifested states. All of conditionally manifested existence is (in Truth, or ultimately) non-separate from the Foundation Itself. All of conditionally manifested existence is (in Truth, or ultimately) non-separate from the perfect Form of Reality Itself. And when conditionally manifested consciousness and all conditionally manifested forms <u>withdraw</u> into the Pure Self-Nature, it is only a turn to rest, a cycle of refreshment. The perfect Form of Reality is not a special "creation" or condition, but It is the native Form of the Heart Itself (or of the Real and True Self, Itself).

Even from the beginning, the only-by-me revealed and given way of radical understanding (or the only-by-me revealed and given Way of the Heart) is not motivated in dilemma, or in any predilection for an <u>exclusively</u> (or separately) liberated experience. The only-by-me revealed and given way of radical understanding (or the only-by-me revealed and given Way of the Heart) turns on the very (and inherently perfect) Form of Reality, and it is not dismayed, by conditionally manifested existence, or even by the (necessarily, merely conditional, and, therefore, only temporary) experience of withdrawal into the Heart. The only-by-me revealed and given way of radical understanding (or the only-by-me revealed and given Way of the Heart) is always already seated in the primary Form and Source, and it is not turned to dilemma, separation, or seeking on the basis of any event. Therefore, the most ultimate (or inherently most perfect) Realization of the only-by-me revealed and given way of radical understanding (or the only-by-me revealed and given Way of the Heart) is not a matter of Realizing a merely "inner" State. Rather, it is a matter of Realizing the inherently Conscious (and inherently perfect) Reality, Prior to all separateness, and Infinitely "Bright".

Los Angeles, 1972

CHAPTER 19

The Transformation
of the Seeker's Meditation
into "Real" Meditation

The first form of "meditation" Enjoyed in my life was the "Bright". It is also the ultimate one. But the "Bright" of my childhood was not associated with understanding in life. Therefore, It was not supported by an unwavering life-intelligence. I perceived It, and I Enjoyed It, but I could not control It. And, eventually, against my wishes, It all but completely disappeared. Thus, I became devoted to a course of seeking, but even my seeking was aided and supported by my earliest intuition of Reality, the "Bright". I was required to thoroughly investigate the Nature of my own consciousness. And I needed to understand most perfectly before I could finally sustain and control the Enjoyment of the "Bright", the perfect Form (and the Source of the living condition) of Reality.

The history of my experience as a seeker is a course of experimentation in relation to the forces of life conceived as the problem of existence on various levels of experience. In college I dealt with Truth as an intellectual problem. In my period of writing and self-exploitation I dealt with It as a vital and emotional problem. With Rudi I dealt with It as a moral and psychic problem. In due course, I dealt with It as the problem of the mind. With Baba I dealt with It as a Spiritual problem, the problem of superconsciousness. And when I experimented with such things as diet, fasting, and self-regulation, I was dealing with It as a physical problem.

Of course, these various researches often overlapped, but, for the most part, each was a highly specialized, exclusive endeavor. And each period was marked by a peculiar method. The area pursued also determined the nature of the work. The object "created" the subject, and the subject reinforced the object. And, in every case, the end phenomenon was the same. It was understanding. It was concentration and observation. Then insight. Then Enjoyment, or Freedom, on the basis of that insight. Finally, there was the recognition of radical understanding itself as primary and prior to the search.

Until I had exhaustively investigated every unique area of the "problem", there was no most fundamental, or conclusive, understanding. Thus, each Moment of primary understanding, such as the crisis in college or the one in seminary, was only a temporary State. It formed only a moment of transition previous to the next phase, the next level of the problem. But when every aspect of life as a problem and a search was exhausted, there was only radical understanding. Then I recognized what was similar about each Moment of primary understanding. And I began to notice in detail the unique characteristics of the entire process of understanding as a radical way, prior to every kind of seeking.

Recently there has been a tendency among Spiritual teachers to speak of a path of "synthesis". Aurobindo is one of the leading exponents of this inclusive mentality. But it is also visible in lesser teachers of Yoga, as well as in the various synthetic paths of modern Western occultism and religiously motivated Spirituality. Ramakrishna, the great Indian teacher of the nineteenth century, perhaps began (or, certainly, forwarded) this trend in the East. And H. P. Blavatsky may be the sign of its origin in the West, also in the late nineteenth century.

But the trend to "synthesis" is only a synthesis of the kinds of seeking. It adapts the various separate activities of the great search to an inclusive philosophy and technique. But it remains a form of seeking.

In my own case, there was never any tendency to make a synthesis out of the various activities of my seeking. Indeed, as I passed through each form of my experiment, I only came to realize the fruitlessness of seeking in that manner. And, at last, I saw the entire fruitlessness of seeking in any form. Thus, the only-by-me revealed and given way of radical understanding (or the only-by-me revealed and given Way of the Heart) is not a synthesis of the ways of seeking. It is a single, direct, and radical approach to life. And that approach is itself, from the beginning, entirely free of dilemma and search. It has nothing to do with the various motivations of the great search. From the beginning, it rests in the primary Enjoyment and Truth that all seeking pursues. Thus, the only-by-me revealed and given way of radical understanding (or the only-by-me revealed and given Way of the Heart) is founded in the radical Truth that is fundamental to existence at any moment, in any condition. And it is also the genuine basis for "creative" life, prior to all the magical efforts toward healing, evolution, and the "victorious" appearance of conventional Spiritual life.

Consider the actual process involved in my own demonstration (and personal revelation) of the way of radical understanding (or the Way of the Heart).

The period of the "Bright" in my earliest childhood was a kind of gratuitous time of Its Enjoyment. That period was a preliminary to my adventure in the forms of seeking, and there was no method or effort associated with that earliest period of my Enjoyment of the "Bright". At most there was a desire to Communicate the "Bright" to others. Over time, I attempted this on the level of life-humor, communicated love, and the effort to dissolve conflicts between people. But the years of my childhood and adolescence only wore away at my humanly-born resources, and, eventually, I came to the matter of the search itself.

Even in college there was no special method. The impulse at the heart of my felt dilemma was the source of my seeking. I simply read, thought, and suffered through the various alternations of philosophy.

It was only when I began to write that my seeking took on the form of a "method". The period of my writing as a method of search came to an end on the beach, when I saw the possibilities of higher consciousness. It was at that point that I began to study with Rudi. And I have also described the methods (or the "work") I adopted at that time.

My brief encounter with Baba Muktananda during my first trip to his Ashram did not produce a new technical method. Eventually, one was recommended to me, but I did not adapt to it until after the period of "waiting".

After the period of "waiting", I began to make use of a habit of meditation (using self-Enquiry, in the form "Avoiding relationship?") that became the single characteristic of my, eventually, final exercise in meditation. As a result of the crisis I endured in seminary, I had already begun to assume the critical attitude that is the characteristic sign of radical understanding. I had seen that the avoidance of relationship was the root-activity at every level of the living consciousness. And, as I began to adapt myself seriously to the processes of Spiritual Yoga, I perceived more and more how fundamental was this understanding. Gradually, with ever-growing conclusiveness, I saw that all strategic methods were founded in the egoic self-contraction (or the avoidance of relationship) and only reinforced its effects. Finally, at the very last, I ceased to make use of the methods of strategic Yoga, and I only approached each moment in life or meditation with understanding in the form of the self-Enquiry "Avoiding relationship?"

In the course of my life of understanding, I saw, ever more clearly (and, at last, most perfectly), that every kind of seeking, including every method designed to liberate, purify, and perfect life, was founded in the mentality and adventure of Narcissus. I saw that every conventional Yoga, every remedial path, and every kind of strategic meditation had a single symptom: the anxious effort to dissolve the barriers and the capsule of self in the attempt to Enjoy Fullness, Immunity, Freedom, and so on. This was always Narcissus, for it is founded in the original idea of separateness, the loss of relationship, and thus it is a meditation on self as separateness, on experience as separative, and on a longing for the Other, for God, for Realization of the Real and True Self, for the Realization of Reality, Liberation, Salvation, and so on.

I concluded that Real life was not in fact a matter of a remedial path or technique, but that it was a matter of radical understanding, the root-understanding of this underlying error in the approach to life. I saw that where I persisted as this radical understanding, rather than in the various impulses to Liberation, there was in fact no dilemma, no separation, and no necessary effort. There was simply the Enjoyment of Reality, prior to any identification with the process of avoidance and seeking. And when radical understanding directly became my approach to life, there was a constant unfolding of Real Knowledge in Freedom and Enjoyment.

For me, the import of meditation was not the search for any kind of experiences. The more I had of experiences, the less important they seemed. And by "experiences" I mean not only internal and visionary phenomena but even the kinds of quieting and control that are by-products of the meditative attitude. I began to see that what I gained and retained from meditation was exactly that with which I began. Before, during, and after meditation, there was only "one who has a basic understanding". Thus, I became more and more attentive to this understanding itself, in and out of meditation. And I gradually began to drop every other kind of formal exercise, such that, more often than not, I simply Enquired of myself under every condition that passed: "Avoiding relationship?"

In the months previous to my third trip to India, I became more and more absorbed in the living simplicity of free conscious awareness. And what I Realized and Enjoyed as radical understanding and "Real" meditation was, for me, epitomized in the relationship to the Guru. I saw there was no need for egoic effort, or the search for salvation. Understanding was simply to contemplate the Guru with limitless devotion. This is called "Guru-Bhakti" or "Guru-Bhava".[83] And, as I prepared to leave for India, I described my understanding as follows:

❖ ❖ ❖

Guru-Bhakti is superior to all mere methods. Put aside all seeking, all strategic means, and think only of the Guru. That itself is Realization and the way itself.

When still deceived and ignorant of the Truth, if I seek to recognize myself within, and try to Identify with my most inner Self-Nature, seeking in every way to stand out from my mind, I find myself drawn apart from things, separated even from that recognition by my exclusive search.

But if, even in that same time of non-Realization, I think of Shree Guru, or look upon him in the company of devotees, I am drawn into the heart, and by that easy, deepest heart I lose the body of distinctions. While I love him thus, I gain my True Self and never try or seek.

Shree Guru, Gurudev is that One, than Which there is no other. Shree Guru, Gurudev is my Real and True Self. So-Ham.

❖ ❖ ❖

The movement in Truth is not a matter of identifying with the separate self in the three worlds (waking, dreaming, and sleeping). Nor is the movement in Truth a matter of engaging

---

83. "Guru-bhakti" is Sanskrit for "devotion to the Guru" and "Guru-bhava" for "deep feeling for the Guru".

in the effort to dissociate from the three worlds. Both are exclusive activities. They destroy relationship and are bound to the form of contradictions, or the egoic lack of the Knowledge of always prior relatedness, or of Non-separateness. The movement in Truth is that Enjoyment Which remains when the falsity of all these alternatives is understood. It is concentration in the True Self. One who is purified by understanding and all right discipline recognizes the True Self in the Guru. Such a one becomes absorbed in meditation on the Guru at the center of the being, at the center of the heart, at the center of the lotus of the lower tendencies in the heart. Seeing the Guru there always, such a one meditates on the Truth of "So-Ham", and, by the grace of the eternal Guru, all distinctions subside, all perceptions of separation, contradiction, and otherness disappear. The personal, the universal, and the transcendent (as an inference from these) disappear in the one Realization of the Real, the True Self of all. Such Knowledge draws that individual into the True Self, and such a one is no longer separately present in any of the worlds.

❖ ❖ ❖

Every pursuit of union in the three worlds is founded in identification with some form therein. Thus, rather than acting to achieve union, merely Witness the desire and the entire tendency, its thoughts, and so on. When this is done, another movement of the living consciousness is realized. It is perceived as a movement in the heart, founded in its new Stillness. It moves to the secretly recognized Beloved, the Guru, the True Self. It Knows it is already related, and thus it does not see union, since union is perceived only over against separation. Rather, it sees Non-separateness, and Identification with That Which absorbs purified living consciousness. It no longer looks back, but moves into the total and fullest Realization of Real and True Knowledge.

When I arrived in India for the third time, I was given the task of editing and refining the English translation of Baba's new book, *Chitshakti Vilas*. I discovered that the method of meditation on the Guru to which I had recently been moved was in fact the method of his Spiritual practice with his principal Guru, Swami Nityananda. I described it then as follows:

Baba does not teach the pure Advaita Vedanta that he taught and demonstrated to me in the Ashram on my first visit. He directs us to bow to our highest Self, to worship It and meditate upon It. He directs us to certain visionary experiences such as the blue light, the "blue person" within it, and other such objects. To this end, he recommends we sit quietly, thinking of the Guru, depending on his grace, repeating a mantra, a name of God. And, above all, he affirms the life of service to the Guru. Thus, men and women will be made open to the influence of his independent grace, his personal Transmission of the Divine Shakti, that will produce visionary attainments and karmic purifications. This will occur, he says, if we give ourselves to the Guru, and not otherwise. If we merely give him our karma, our suffering, our egoic ignorance, he will reject them, but if we give our very selves, he will take our karma also.

Baba's method of Spiritual practice was the action of becoming totally identified with his Guru, whom he saw as the Divine Being and his True Self. He would sit near his Guru or think of him and contemplate his name, his physical form, his moods, contemplations, gestures, the qualities of his apparent awareness, his words and acts, his qualities altogether. He acted on the principle that one imitates what one contemplates and finally identifies with it. The impulse that made this possible was profound love for his Guru, and the sense of identification with his Guru. This he felt was the highest form of meditation recommended in the Scriptures.

His method was to meditate on his Guru after he had installed his Guru in his own body-mind, in all his parts, and identified with him. From the various indications in his book, I described the following principles of his method:

Becoming tranquil and overcoming thought fluctuations, free the mind from external clinging. Eradicate mentation. Sit down, feeling that the Guru is confronting you. Make obeisance, realizing that the Guru-Principle envelops you from each direction. See the Guru and yourself as One. Then install him in your body, top to bottom, and then bottom to top, chanting "Guru-Om" mentally. Meditating thus, the Guru in you and you in the Guru, let go of the awareness of the conditional self.

This epitomized the foundation of even my own spontaneous method in the company of each and all of my teachers. Whether with Rudi, or with Baba, or at Swami Nityananda's shrine, I always concentrated on the Guru as the Source of all conditions, things, and beings, and as the Ultimate Identity and Condition of my own person. I was always doing this, even where I also performed other kinds of special meditative exercise. Therefore,

Guru-Bhakti, in one or another form, was always fundamental to my practice (and original, personal revelation)
of the way of radical understanding (or the Way of the
Heart). And it must likewise and always be fundamental
to the only-by-me revealed and given way of radical
understanding (or the only-by-me revealed and given
Way of the Heart) as it is practiced by each and all of
those who come to me in order to Realize God, Truth,
and Reality.

While at the Ashram, I was in the midst of this meditation of Guru-Bhakti, when, suddenly, I began to experience the visitations, revelations, and internal teachings
of the Virgin and Jesus. Then, overwhelmed, I became
totally absorbed in that Christian contemplation. However, I could also see that this absorption in "Christ" was
itself a form of the meditation of Guru-Bhakti. Therefore,
I allowed it all to occur. I allowed the Shakti to be the
Virgin and Jesus to be the Guru. Even in the Bible, Jesus
is reported to have said: "You will understand that I am
in my Father and you in me and I in you" (John 14:20).

Even weeks before I returned to America, that entire
Christian exercise had revealed itself as a symbol, on a
psychic level, for the processes that were revealing my
own Ultimate Self-Nature. I no longer saw any necessity
in any ordinary kind of religious meditation or in any
otherwise conventionally Spiritual meditation. All the
images that had symbolized Reality and attracted my
heart spontaneously disappeared. The "Christ" disappeared. Even all the images of my previous teacher-
Gurus disappeared. Reality was felt to be simply
"located" at the heart, and It was soon to be Realized as
the Heart Itself. I no longer operated on the basis of any
distinctions. I simply understood, and understanding
became the simple, free exercise of my own heart.

Only weeks after I returned to America, I passed
into the final, or most perfect, fulfillment of the
process of radical understanding. But, even in the last
weeks of travel in Europe, and also after my return to

America, as the final process of radical understanding was developing toward its finality, I spent time analyzing and evaluating the instructions, the practices, and the phenomena that I had experienced during the conventionally "Spiritual" period of my seeking. Out of this developed two specific kinds of data. One was the evaluation (based on radical understanding) of the instrument (and the full range of possible experiences via the instrument), or the total mechanism, of the living (or psycho-physical) human form. And the other was an evaluation of the process of Spiritual Yoga, and its supportive and purifying role even in the context of the process of radical understanding.

I examined the first of these, the structure and the possible experiences of the living (or psycho-physical) instrument, on the basis of my various Yogic experiences, and with reference to technical terms given in traditional Yogic and Vedantic writings. On the basis of these observations, I wrote the following essay, which makes brief reference to the structure and potential of the psycho-physical instrument itself, and then, on the basis of the point of view of radical understanding, goes on to critically evaluate the traditional approaches to all of that.

The gross (physical) body, the subtle body (which includes the etheric, or "pranic", or life-energy body, and the dual astral body, which includes both the lower mental, or lower psychic, body and the higher mental, or higher psychic, body), and the causal body (of individuated bliss) are the functional bodies (or conditionally manifested functional sheaths) that proceed from the heart and are contained in the unqualified Being of Reality. One may spontaneously experience the sighting (or vision) of the functional bodies (or functional sheaths) themselves, appearing in the form of variously colored lights. And one may also spontaneously perceive the particular regions (or experiential realms) associated with each of these functional bodies (or functional sheaths), and so experience the various visions, powers, and manifestations of the planes of conditionally manifested being.

As the process of the purification of the functional bodies (or functional sheaths) begins, which process (even in its entirety) is simply the reconnection and stabilization of the circuit of living being, one may experience many phenomena, due to the particular expressions of each of these functional bodies (or functional sheaths) and their characteristic experiential regions. But one should, from the beginning, be founded in the heart, as no-seeking, based on radical understanding. Thus, one will not become distracted by these appearances, but only abide deeply in the heart, and continue the process of purifying the living (psycho-physical) form and establishing the living condition of Reality.

It may be the case that one may experience very little of extraordinary phenomena, not even much of physical kriyas, or, otherwise, of internal sights or sounds or smells or tastes, or any other higher (or ascending, or ascended) phenomena. Rather, one may, even from the beginning, be associated more simply with the living instrument, and with the essential feeling of no-seeking in the heart. One's experience may only increase as no-seeking, silence, openness, purity, Wholeness, Fullness, Energy, and Bliss. This indeed is the principal form of the process, and it is gracefully without distractions.

Experiences of any of the functional bodies (or functional sheaths) or their associated regions may occur to the particular individual, according to his or her tendencies, or desires, or accumulated karma. But common to all, as the seat of the Ultimate Source, Truth, and Reality of all, is the center of the living being, the heart, which is the beginning and end of all life.

Therefore, I affirm the practice and the process of radical understanding. It is the way of Reality. It is the way of the prime Truth, always presently available, and it does not lead one further into egoic ignorance or egoic distraction, but always to Reality Itself, beyond all fear and all seeking. Every other way is a remedial path that takes its stand in some particular functional body (or functional sheath), or conditional region, or conditional experience and pursues some other functional body (or functional sheath), or conditional region, or conditional experience as if it were Reality, Truth, or, in any case, the right direction. In fact, until one is firmly seated in Reality rather than in any functional body (or functional sheath), or conditional region, or conditional experience, one is only a seeker who chronically identifies himself or herself with what is not yet Real, or what is known apart from Reality. Not that any of these functional bodies (or functional sheaths), or conditional regions, or conditional experiences are themselves un-Real, but the individual interprets his or her position in egoic ignorance, after the model of exclusion, or separation. The process of his or her development is founded in the model of seeking, and it only reinforces the pattern of avoidance and the internal impression of separation, or un-Reality. Therefore, such a one is bound continually to the search, to false goals, and to a tragic adventure in all the various functional bodies (or functional sheaths), or conditional regions, or conditional experiences.

The average man or woman perceives this

drama essentially on the level of the physical body and the region of the physical world. Thus, the average seeker may suppose that the various phenomena of occult, spiritualistic, and psychic experience, or even the greater impressions of the higher mind and superconscious phenomena which are the typical stronghold of higher religions and higher Spirituality, are in fact evidence that there is a higher life that is itself Truth and Reality Itself. In this manner, traditional religion and conventional Spirituality, even with positive intentions, merely serve to exploit the vulnerability and limited experience of the average and even the uncommon seeker.

In fact, Truth, or Reality, is of supreme value, and It is a matter of radical understanding, not any excursion into the various functional bodies (or functional sheaths), or conditional realms, or conditional experiences of the form of life on any plane. For this reason, the greatest men and women of Realization continually turn mankind away from the lust for phenomena and powers. They recommend only the Realization of Reality, Which is the key Knowledge in the present that removes all suffering and all seeking.

Once one's life is understood as I have described, it becomes unnecessary to follow any remedial path or extend one's seeking. Such things are obviously pointless and fruitless, however dramatic they appear. The Realization of the primary Truth is simply the end of seeking and suffering as an internal event. It is right Knowledge of Reality, the Self-Knowledge that is always and already unqualifiedly Free, and inclusive of all things in the living condition of Reality. It is only the Realization of unqualified relatedness and no-seeking which can provide the basis for any Real development of life in any form. The form of one's experience is not the point. It is not a matter of exploiting and extending experience but of Realizing radical understanding.

The true way, then, is not the path of traditional (or otherwise conventional and merely remedial) Yoga in any form, not of occultism, white magic, traditional and conventional religions, or traditional (or otherwise conventional and merely remedial) Spirituality. The true way is simply the radical practice and process of understanding. Therefore, one must understand, radically, and, in the process (and, then, on the basis of that radical understanding), engage in the "creative" work of purifying the various functional bodies (or functional sheaths) and rightly engaging the various experiences and abilities that proceed in and as the living (psycho-physical) form.

For those who approach me as their Guru, the process in my Company will develop as silence and no-seeking, even, perhaps, without extensive phenomena expressed in the subtle body and the higher (or ascended) regions. And they will Realize themselves in life by the Sign of the "Bright", Which is Conscious of a Radiant Fullness seated in the midst of the head, projected out of the heart. They will abide thus in the waking state, feeling themselves extended from and linked to the conscious awareness of no-seeking in the heart. They will feel full and "Bright", clear and resourceful. They will perceive the conditional activities of consciousness and form communicated from the subconscious and unconscious regions and the superconscious, but they will not necessarily perceive the forms or internal phenomena of those functional bodies (or functional sheaths) or regions themselves. They will simply feel the Radiant Fullness of heart-Freedom and Clarity, the intuitive Stillness and the unique Intelligence and Capability, that result from the Foundation in Reality. The realms of superconsciousness, subconsciousness, and unconsciousness will simply proceed, even, perhaps, outside particular awareness, within the context of their own natural laws.

Such individuals will abide in heart-Freedom and simple internal Joy. They will do "creative", communicative work in the world, the human work of love and understanding, pleasure and unburdened sacrifice, that is merely the natural and effortless meaning of all ordinary activity, rather than any kind of self-conscious effacement, mortification, or degradation.

Thus, true life is to be founded in Reality, and its appearance and awareness, while enjoying the heart-freedom of non-separateness at every depth of the living being, exists directly and wholly as simple and "creative" human existence. The phenomena of subtler functional bodies (or subtler functional sheaths) and higher conditional realms will be of no great or distracting interest to such truly human beings. Such things will not be the required signs of life or Liberation to them, nor will they be the distracting goals of some particular, ideal plan of self-conscious evolution. If the individual happens to become consciously aware of conditions in other dimensions, he or she will simply observe and understand them, and live by the wisdom I have described. Such a one will not seek the development of nature-powers, but abide only in Reality. If his or her life involves the awareness of subtler functional bodies (or subtler functional sheaths) and higher dimensions, he or she will, simply by the means of understanding, acquire the necessary wisdom to deal with them and remain "creatively" in Reality.

After the death of the physical form, such a one may pass into the continuous perception and function of the subtler worlds and there learn to function as is natural to him or her. But while in the physical world, as even then in any other world, his or her task lies in Reality and not in experience. Then as now he or she must Realize Reality and the living condition of Reality.

In any case, one must function intelligently, and apart from all seeking, in the dimensions apparent to one's experience. There is no necessary cause for motivation to any functional body (or functional sheath), or conditional realm, or conditional experience at all, whether the present one or any subtler one. Therefore, one who abides in Reality simply functions with understanding in the native environment of his or her apparent birth. Anything else is exclusive motivation bound up in seeking. Anything else is a source of distraction that leads only into suffering, avoidance, separation, despair, madness, and death. Therefore, only understand.

In the previous essay I was interested in estimating the nature and importance of various higher (or subtler) experiential phenomena in relation to the life of radical understanding. In the essay which follows I was interested in estimating the nature and importance of the process that I had come to observe taking place in the actually Spiritual practice of Yogic meditation.

The experience of meditation that I had learned by observation, verbal communication, and internal perception from Baba Muktananda is essentially an automatic process wherein a deep rhythm (and potential suspension) of breathing becomes automatic, the mind becomes still and one-pointed, and the various vehicles or levels of psycho-physical being become purified and, by the

Spiritual ascent of attention, stabilized (conditionally) in the conditional Self-Realization that is made possible by full ascent (or fully ascended detachment from the body-mind). All the phenomena of spontaneous physical movements (or kriyas and mudras), spontaneous mental transformations, internal perceptions, and the like are simply the evidence of this purification and ascent on various levels. For the sake of the goals of this process, the individual need only surrender to the Guru, depend on the Guru's grace, relax, and engage in the recitation of the Guru's mantra. This entire process is natural, effortless, and automatic. And Baba said that it was "Kriya" Yoga, the Yoga of purifying activity. It is the same Yoga taught by Yogananda, except that it does not (fundamentally, or otherwise exclusively) rely on an intentional, sophisticated exercise on the part of the aspirant. It depends entirely on the grace of the Guru, and, thus and thereby, on the activities of the Shakti Itself.

However, once I had observed this process completely and seen its effects, and when I had considered it in relation to the heart-process of radical understanding, I saw that it could also be used intentionally, even in the practice and the process of radical understanding, as a non-seeking, simply responsible means of purifying and gaining control over the vehicles of life. I considered that there need not be any seekers' motive in this process, and that it could be readily adapted to by one who had developed basic maturity in radical understanding. Therefore, in the following essay, I was trying to find some basic sense and general utility in the process of Spiritual Yoga, which, in a uniquely right manner, even accompanies the general, or progressively developing, practice and process of radical understanding.

When conscious awareness has been established as no-seeking in the heart, then it abides in Reality, One with Reality, Which is the unqualified Source and the living condition of the being. Then Reality is living. And only living Reality is always already freely capable of the true demonstration of life, the law and form of which is sacrifice.

Therefore, when conscious awareness has been established as no-seeking in the heart, meditation can be used as an active purification of the vehicles of the living (psycho-physical) being. When conscious awareness has Realized radical understanding to the degree of Realizing no-seeking in the heart, then it can, from that point of view, and not from the point of view of any kind of seeking, begin an intentional process of purification, or "kriya".

I used various forms of this process early in my adventure of seeking. But this process, altogether rightly engaged, is not true to (or wholly true within) the life of seeking, because the seeker does not yet directly embrace Reality through a fundamental understanding of the egoic self. The intentional, Spiritual process of purification is wholly appropriate and non-delusory only when there is radical understanding, such that Reality has become the foundation of existence, directly experienced in life and meditation.

❖ ❖ ❖

When one already understands oneself as no-seeking, then one can make use of the Spiritual means of purification. Many such techniques have been developed over the centuries. Even the simplest religious attitude is purifying in a real sense and ultimately makes use of the mechanisms that are the foundation or circuit of the form of the living being. But these means, represented by every kind of religious and Spiritual philosophy, endeavor, technique, or attitude in history, East and West, suffer from two essential faults. The first of these is one to which most of my life has been dedicated to understanding. That is, these means are always given and adapted to states of seeking. They are offered to seekers, people in one or another form of the great search, as a means of acquiring the Knowledge of Reality. Thus, they are adapted in egoic ignorance and only extend the terrible suffering and conflict which are the root of ordinary life and consciousness. Therefore, I have demonstrated that radical understanding is the primary law of life. And life-consciousness must be utterly founded in radical understanding, and, thus and thereby, in Reality, in no-seeking, before it can begin the useful and non-seeking purification of the forms of life.

The second primary fault in the traditional communication of the means of purification is that they are chronically identified with some particular historical, cultural, or personal experience. All of the various religions and Spiritual regimes, from the theological and ritual experience of forgiveness and justification to the sophisticated methods of occultism and the various Yogas, are separate, historical manifestations founded in various kinds of exclusive phenomena. They stand in relation to one another in a grand pattern of conflict and separateness. Thus, the seeker comes to one or another of these sources in egoic ignorance and pursues the separate cycle of experience the particular form asserts and guarantees.

But all of these historical means have a common basis, which is the total structure of the living human being. If one is founded in the living condition of Reality and acts as the living condition of Reality in relation to one's living form, one will not be devoted to any seekers' path or seekers' method. One will only make use of one's purifying intention in terms of the structure of living (or psycho-physical) consciousness. Thus, one does not require any of the paths that attract the seeker. One will only adapt the means that are already indicated by one's living (or psycho-physical) form.

To such an individual, there is available an intelligent, direct process of purification. This process can be read in all of the fragmentary suggestions of the various traditional paths, but it is clearly and fully rendered in the actual, direct experience of the total structure of the living human form.

I have directly experienced this structure and its useful process. Therefore, I will represent it as it is, without recourse to the point of view of its communication as a merely remedial (or seeker's) effort in the various historical paths.

Reality is (in the living context) abiding as no-seeking and unqualified relatedness. Therefore, the perfect Reality (Itself) is radically "related" to Its own living form, the living structure of conditionally manifested being.

The living condition of Reality is (or is always already established in and as) the perfect Reality Itself. The apparent (or living) parts of the perfect Reality are attached to the living form by the law of synchronicity, of identity. From the "Point of View" of the perfect Reality, the structure of the living form does not proceed as an effect from a cause, but both the perfect Reality and the living condition of Reality coexist in a simultaneous manner. Thus, Reality as no-seeking in the heart is also manifested as the living person, the psycho-physical body with all of its sheaths, chakras, dimensions, or vehicles, gross, subtle, and causal. But the law (and the essential structure) of this living form is a simplicity. It is the law of sacrifice, the structural essence or root of which is the heart. It need not be approached from any particular level or vehicle, nor is any sheath, chakra, or conditional state its goal. The process is begun and ended and is always proceeding from the perfect Reality Itself, from radical understanding, from no-seeking, from the motiveless silence of the heart.

This ultimate "heart" is not the heart chakra, or the bodily heart region, the ascending position of the dualistic seeker, or the egoically motivated devotee. Rather, it is the "heart" of living being, the stillpoint in feeling and conscious awareness that is primary understanding.

From that unqualified stillpoint of conscious awareness, all of the functions and levels of the living form proceed, or stand, in a circle around the bodily region of the heart. Thus, in order to purify these vehicles and centers and establish the entire life in its prime Energy and Fullness, a process of "conductivity",[84] secondary to and supportive of the "conscious process"[85] (or direct and primary exercise), must be undertaken from the heart of the living form and moved through the circle or cycle of the vehicles.

The primary activity (or "conscious process") of radical understanding requires no other exercise, and it is clear to me that this primary activity of radical understanding must be the foundation

---

84. "Conductivity" is Adi Da's term for practices through which bodily and emotional life, as well as the function of the breath, is conformed to the great purpose of Spiritual practice. "Conductivity" is a supportive practice to the primary discipline of attention for all Adi Da's devotees.

85. The "conscious process" is Adi Da's term for practices through which the mind, or attention, is turned from egoic self-involvement to Heart-Communion with the Divine. It is the senior discipline and responsibility of all Adi Da's devotees.

of individual attention in the living condition of Reality. Unless there is radical understanding, it is only the motive of seeking that would draw one to begin the "conductivity" work of purification (which I will disclose to my devotees, and in my future writings). Once this latter process has become active and necessary, then it may rightly be engaged, but the "conscious process" of radical understanding is the fundamental necessity in every case, and its effects are an absolute sublimity.

In the progressive course of my practice of radical understanding, I had soon begun to feel there was no utility of any kind in the remedial exercise of Yoga. It became clear to me that the remedial (or strategic) intentions of Yoga could not be separated from the mentality of seeking and separation.

The purpose of "Kriya Yoga", from the point of view of such of its exponents as Yogananda, was, by means of Yogic technique alone, to arouse the Kundalini Shakti, and then go on, by Its aid, to ascend to Yogic Self-Realization. But I saw the entire Yogic design and purpose (described in the literature of "Kriya Yoga") become fulfilled in me automatically, <u>after</u> the Shakti had been aroused by the Guru. Thus, clearly, the <u>true</u> "Kriya Yoga" is the activity of the Shakti Itself, not merely a self-generated technique for Its arousal. Those who recommend "Kriya Yoga" as a Shakti-<u>arousing</u> technique are merely, in the absence of the Shakti-arousing grace of a thus capable Guru, adapting the data of this (by grace given) process to a deliberate process of seeking.

Thus, with the Shakti already aroused, I had gone through the ordeal in which the True Self is Realized. Indeed, in my case, that ordeal Realized the True Self, at last, to the most perfect degree, beyond the necessarily conditional process of Yogic ascent, and beyond the necessarily conditional process of world-exclusion. But I saw clearly that if the process of Realizing the True Self (whether conditionally or unconditionally) were engaged by one who sought to arouse the Kundalini Shakti by techniques of self-effort, he or she could only act apart from radical understanding.

In the technique promoted by Yogananda, the practitioner draws the would-be Shakti-Energy up the spine to the sahasrar and the point between the brows, holds the would-be Shakti-Energy there for a brief period, and then lets the would-be Shakti-Energy return below. From the beginning, such a seeker's concentration is in the various psycho-physical centers, and in himself or herself as a yet unrealized being. Such a Yogi only seeks the Shakti-Energy and the True Self. Likewise, even where that same process is Initiated by the actual (by grace given) Shakti-Energy, attention is also centered, at any one time, in any one of the conditional (psycho-physical) centers associated with that Energy, and such attention also only pursues the True Self, although with a Spiritually more profound effort of seeking.

However, ultimately, I was involved in this Yogic process not only on the basis of the actual (by grace given) Shakti-Energy, but from the point of view of prior (and radical) understanding. Thus, on that basis, I saw that Yoga as a process Initiated and governed by the True Self, or Reality, in the heart. Nevertheless, the more I continued to indulge (and indulge in) the Yogic process itself, the more I realized that, apart from radical understanding, it only and continually drew me into the forms of seeking—for the Shakti, or for the Real and True Self, or for understanding. Thus, once I observed and understood this, I realized that understanding was itself the only radical process, that, in my own case, self-Enquiry (in the form "Avoiding relationship?") was (and, potentially, in the case of others for whom it was both appropriate and effective, could be) its directly ego-transcending activity, and that the Yogic process of the by grace given Shakti-Energy was only secondary and supportive to radical understanding and the "conscious process" that sprang directly from it (and must be subordinated to radical understanding and the "conscious process" that sprang directly from it). Indeed, in the final stage of my ordeal, I even abandoned all secondary and supportive Yogic exercises for the "conscious process" of self-Enquiry alone (in the form "Avoiding relationship?"). Then even the Shakti-Energy showed Itself spontaneously at Its Ultimate Source-Point (in the right side of the heart), such that self-Enquiry itself was, in its most perfect demonstration, epitomized as perfect contemplation (and perfect abiding) in and as the True Heart, and the magnification of the True Heart's own Love-Bliss (or inherent Shakti-Energy) in and via the spontaneously regenerated Amrita Nadi.

In the course of my life of understanding, I saw there was only a simple activity and concept manifesting under the form of every kind of remedial activity. It was always Narcissus, the logic and activity of separation. I examined all merely remedial Yoga, all of this seeking and strategic performing, and all of its results, and I asked myself: Why? Why should such activities be engaged at all? What are the motives for such meditating? And the more radical my understanding became, the more absurd, unnecessary, and impossible it became to justify any of these exploits.

All the usual and traditional ways showed themselves to be founded in some problem, some aspect of life as dilemma. There was the physical problem, the vital problem, the problem of the mind, the problem of Spirituality and superconsciousness. There was the problem of morality, of love, of communication, of sex, the problem of sin, of suffering, the problem of nature-powers, the problem of identity, the problem of Reality, of Truth, of the True Self, and the problem that is the universe itself. But I saw that the problem, in any form, always had the same structure, and the same fundamental assumptions. Thus, I became concerned with motivation, the principle of these various kinds of action, belief, presumed knowledge, and so on. I saw that, since all the usual and traditional ways were founded in a problem, Real life must be founded in the understanding of the primary problem that is the source of all ordinary activity. Only thus does one Know and Enjoy Reality, even in spite of the moment to moment "creation" of problems.

I saw that radical understanding is itself motiveless, but that everything else is in fact the avoidance of relationship. And, indeed, the avoidance of relationship is the very motivator of everything that is not radical understanding. Thus, the longer a man or woman lives, the more complicated and contradictory life appears. And it is only suffered, more and more.

I saw that the exercise of understanding is not some entirely unusual, or even miraculous, condition or practice. It is the simplest activity, even, in a very basic or rudimentary sense, already frequently utilized, to one or another degree, by every individual, in the midst of his or her daily experience. It is only that human beings abandon the exercise of understanding in order to exploit the kinds of seeking. But when attention is drawn to understanding, and when understanding becomes, itself, truly radical, the entire movement of seeking comes to an end. In that event, one only understands where one would otherwise seek.

The beginning of radical understanding is simply a matter of observing oneself in relationship, in action, in life. If one can be drawn to the exercise of understanding by means of my words of instruction, and, thus and thereby, always firmly returned to it, one will begin only to understand, and, at last, understanding will become truly radical (or most fundamental, and fully comprehensive). Then radical understanding will replace one's ordinary habit of seeking, and one's living consciousness and activity will thereby become simplified, free of prior dilemma. And this process of radical understanding, when it becomes the active foundation (and "conscious process") of one's existence, does not in any sense preclude or prevent the purificatory processes of Spiritual Yoga, except that it is entirely free of any limitation by or to the egoic (and seeking) designs of remedial action, or the separative mentality, or the forms of ego-based experience.

I saw that human beings can easily be turned to self-observation. And the process of self-observation can easily be maintained as a critical exercise by proper guidance. And that process of critically observing the conditional self gradually sees the emergence of fundamental insight. Therefore, human beings can understand the nature of seeking, the adventure of Narcissus, the entire complex life of the avoidance of relationship. And when radical understanding truly arises, human beings can easily apply radical understanding to moment to moment experience. Then radical understanding becomes the approach to life, rather than all the automatic, confused activities of seeking, or the egoic drama of Narcissus. In that case, radical understanding can, as in my own case, become self-Enquiry (in the form "Avoiding relationship?"), or it could, otherwise, take other forms (that I will disclose to my devotees, and in my future writings), that equally express radical understanding and that, with an effectiveness equal to that of self-Enquiry (in the form "Avoiding relationship?"), directly transcend self-contraction (or egoity itself). And the free abiding in unqualified relatedness by means of the use of self-Enquiry (or a by me given equivalent) then becomes the fundamental activity of conscious life, moment to moment, and in special periods of the formal meditative exercise of radical understanding which can truly be called "Real" meditation.

Such a way of practice might automatically produce the unusual phenomena of Spiritual Yoga, or the entire expanse of higher and cosmic knowledge. Or it might more simply Realize no-seeking, no-dilemma, natural "creativity", and Ultimate Freedom. I described these results as follows:

But the Truth of Real life is simply What is Realized when there is a removal of contradictions, no-dilemma, no-search. It cannot be described, nor is any name appropriate for It. There is no motive to name It. It is not a supreme separate Object, nor a supreme separate Subject. It is not separate from the one who understands, nor can one separate oneself from It. It is simply no-problem, no-search, unqualified relatedness, or Reality without implications. It is also the perfect Form of Reality, Which is the most subtle Structure of the world and everything, even of the living form of consciousness. All of This is revealed as the obvious to one who understands most perfectly.

Thus, when I had become firmly grounded in understanding as a radical approach to life, even, at last, making no use of any other exercise than self-Enquiry itself, I firmly and finally and unconditionally Realized the Ultimate Truth and Reality I had (but only conditionally and temporarily) Enjoyed at critical times in the past.

Los Angeles, 1972

CHAPTER 20

The Process of "Real" Meditation

Immediately after the Great Event of my re-Awakening, I set about to describe the way of radical understanding (or the Way of the Heart) in terms of the practice and the process of "Real" meditation. I did this through a series of essays. And, because I intended these essays to be included in this book, as an extension of my "autobiographical" description of my own early-life demonstration and original revelation of the way of radical understanding (or the Way of the Heart), and because my own practice of radical understanding was, ultimately, characteristically associated with the "conscious process" as self-Enquiry (in the form "Avoiding relationship?"), I wrote all of these essays with a particular emphasis on the practice of self-Enquiry. However, my devotees, or all those who will come to me in order to Realize the Self-Condition that is God, Truth, and Reality, may individually be, by me, given counter-egoic practices (or forms of the "conscious process") that are, in one or another fashion, different from self-Enquiry (in the form "Avoiding relationship?"), but which are, nevertheless, equally effective as means and extensions of radical self-understanding. And, in any case, these essays on "Real" meditation were not intended to exhaustively represent my instructions on meditation, or, otherwise, on the functional, practical, relational, cultural, Spiritual, and devotional totality of the only-by-me revealed and given way of radical understanding (or the only-by-me revealed and given Way of the Heart).

❖ ❖ ❖

When you have understood, understanding will become the natural response of your intelligence to any experience, the total content of any moment. Then approach every moment with understanding, and perceive the original Truth within it.

One who practices the only-by-me revealed and given way of radical understanding (or the only-by-me revealed and given Way of the Heart) should formally devote some time every morning and evening to the "conscious process" of understanding. Therefore, one who practices the "conscious process" in the form of self-Enquiry should sit down and, as thoughts, feelings, and movements arise within to distract, Enquire: "Avoiding relationship?"

One who practices the way of radical understanding (or the Way of the Heart) should regularly, on a daily basis, do this self-Enquiry (or some other by me given counter-egoic exercise) for an extended formal period every morning and evening—immediately upon rising from sleep, and again just before retiring. Such a one should also do this self-Enquiry (or some other by me given counter-egoic exercise) for an extended formal period at other times of day, whenever possible. And such a one should also do this self-Enquiry (or some other by me given counter-egoic exercise) briefly at any moment in the day when he or she is tending to be absorbed by strong distractions.

Therefore, when you have understood, commit yourself to understanding in the midst of all experience, instead of merely committing yourself to the various kinds of remedial action that may arise as a means to handle the "problem" of life at any moment.

Resort to me with true devotion, and listen to me. Be my true devotee, and make understanding your radical approach to life. Become more and more absorbed in understanding and the Realization of always present

Freedom. Listen to me, and understand yourself. Hear me and see me. Practice all the by me given disciplines, such that they become realized permanently as characteristics of your living form. Enjoy and "create" according to the wisdom thus realized in your own living form.

❖ ❖ ❖

"Real" meditation does not do anything for you. It has no purpose. When one begins some form of seeking, one immediately turns to an effective, remedial technique that will get one quickly to one's goal. Thus, when one adapts to various kinds of religious and Spiritual effort, one begins almost immediately to meditate in some fashion. The Christian and the devotee begin to pray and adapt to religious forms. The Spiritual seeker begins to concentrate and internalize the mind. Others use drugs, study, critical thought, relaxation and poetry, pleasure, and so forth.

But Real life, the way of radical understanding (or the Way of the Heart), is not another form of seeking. For one who understands, meditation is not adopted for the sake of something else. Such a one does not pursue understanding or Reality or any kind of experience through meditation. "Real" meditation is already a radical activity. It is understanding.

In the logic of Narcissus, the separative mentality, all things are seeking. But one who understands perceives the logic of Reality and lives on the basis of that logic. Therefore, such a one is not strategically concerned about meditation. The business of one who understands is understanding, not ascent, vision, transformation, liberation, or any other goal. The only-by-me revealed and given way of radical understanding (or the only-by-me given Way of the Heart) belongs to those who recognize the fruitlessness of seeking.

"Real" meditation cannot be done by egoic effort, or strategy. Therefore, "Real" meditation cannot, itself, be recommended, or prescribed. There is only understanding.

Therefore, understand. And when the process of understanding has become self-observation, reflection, and radical insight, then the state of conscious awareness is "Real" meditation. When understanding has become a radical process, and the avoidance of relationship has been inclusively and sufficiently recognized, when you have understood that seeking is all a function of dilemma, and when you are no longer moved to seek by the physical, the mental, or the Spiritual problem, then you are already and really meditating.

"Real", or non-strategic, meditation is simply understanding as a radical process in consciousness. It is what understanding is when it has become necessary and profound. Since it is necessarily prior to egoic effort and strategy, there is no right motive for adopting it. There is only the discovery that you are already doing it.

Thus, when understanding has become founded in you by observation of your life, and you have truly understood the process of avoidance on every level of your being, then you have ceased to approach life without intelligence, simply reacting, becoming motivated, and seeking various ends. Instead, you have begun to approach all experience with a simplicity in consciousness, a presence you bring to all things, which is understanding.

When you have begun to approach life with understanding, Knowing the radical Truth of understanding, then you have begun to meditate. Then understanding, the logic of Reality, can be extended as itself to conscious or "Real" meditation.

"Real" meditation is not purposive. It has no effect that it seeks to produce. It has no dilemma to solve. It has already become understanding, and understanding is Conscious Knowing. Understanding is in fact the Knowledge that is Consciousness Itself, Non-separateness, Reality. Therefore, it is the Enjoyment of Consciousness Itself. To understand is already to meditate, to contemplate Consciousness Itself. And understanding does this not by an act of concentration on Consciousness Itself, or on any form or center of Consciousness Itself, but by understanding experience, the apparent action of Consciousness Itself.

Where there is understanding in life, what is actually being Known is Consciousness Itself, unqualified Reality. Thus, the understanding of experience by observation leads to the recognition of the avoidance of relationship as one's root-activity. And even where this recognition arises, the avoidance of relationship will also cease to be the fundamental object or activity of conscious life. It will simply give way to the Realization of all that is prior to avoidance, which is Reality, unqualified relatedness, Consciousness Itself.

Thus, understanding first becomes actual in the mind, and then it may be extended as self-Enquiry. The practice of self-Enquiry is the approach of understanding to experience. And self-Enquiry is meditation. It is in the form "Avoiding relationship?"

As self-Enquiry continues as the radical activity of life, even self-Enquiry becomes occasional. Even in the beginning it is not repetitive, like a mantra. That Which is identified and enjoyed in conscious awareness through self-Enquiry does not need constant self-Enquiry to reduce the tendencies of the mind and life to prior understanding. That Reality Which is the Source and Realization of self-Enquiry eventually becomes the ready "Object" (or the attractive Center) of the mind and life, and one tends to return to It easily and naturally. And when radical understanding is most perfectly Realized, there is no constant intentional self-Enquiry, no special or otherwise required meditation. Knowledge becomes Consciousness Itself, Which is unqualified, Which is no-seeking in the heart and no-dilemma in the mind.

❖　❖　❖

The usual meditation is only a consolation, an effect, and a good feeling. It provides no radical reversal of ordinary consciousness, and, thus, when situations arise out of meditation, the person has no control over the process of identification, differentiation, and desire.

Only radical understanding avails. It is the intelligence of Reality Itself. It is not attachment to some body (or functional sheath), or some conditional realm, or some conditional experience that is seen as the alternative, remedy, cure, and source of victory. It knows that every motive and action is made of avoidance. Thus, it has no recourse except to understand. And understanding and the one who understands are Reality, the Self, the "Bright".

The Yogic search only enjoys the conditionally manifested forms of Shakti, or the conditionally achieved bliss of Energy. Only radical Knowledge is Real Bliss, dependent on nothing.

❖ ❖ ❖

Understanding arises when there are true listening to my word and true self-observation in relationship. Therefore, observe yourself in life. Observe yourself when you seek. Observe yourself when you suffer to any degree. Observe your motives. Observe the activity of identification. Observe the activity of differentiation. Observe the activity of desire. Observe the patterns of your existence.

When you see that you are always seeking, understanding is emerging. When you see the pattern of Narcissus as all your motives, all your acts, all your seeking, understanding is emerging. When you see you are always suffering, understanding is emerging. When you see that every moment is a process in dilemma, understanding is emerging. When you see that every moment is a process of identification, differentiation, and desire, understanding is emerging. When you see that every moment, when you are at your best as well as when you are at your worst, you are only avoiding relationship, then you understand. When you see That Which already is (apart from the avoidance of relationship), Which already absorbs the living being prior to the entire dilemma, motivation, and activity of avoidance, then you have finally understood.

❖   ❖   ❖

Until understanding becomes a radical activity, it simply involves the critical observation of experience (as it appears as levels of being, functional bodies or sheaths, conditional realms, and conditional experiences). All of that must be critically observed and understood (even, perhaps, with the aid of self-Enquiry in the form "Avoiding relationship?", or otherwise, with the aid of some other by me given counter-egoic practice). But when understanding is fulfilled most fundamentally, in the conscious, inclusive, and transforming comprehension of experience and seeking, then "Real" meditation will become a true impulse. At that point, the individual should begin more fully (or most truly and effectively) to Enquire (or, otherwise, to more fully, or most truly and effectively, exercise an alternative by me given counter-egoic practice), both formally (at times regularly set aside for meditation) and at random (in the midst of daily life).

When meditation has become the most perfect Realization of Consciousness Itself, then abide as Consciousness Itself, Which is the most perfect Realization of no-seeking in the heart. Then, even when you act, you will always already (or inherently, and effortlessly) remain in this inherently perfect Condition of Realization.

Therefore, at last, you will continually abide as Consciousness Itself, and as the inherently perfect demonstration of Consciousness Itself. And you will Enjoy the endless Knowledge of Reality and Truth, and all the Heart-Wisdom that will arise Thus in relationship. There is no ordinary end to that Condition, no goal and no dilemma, but only perpetual understanding of the arising world, moment to moment, through the event of every death.

❖ ❖ ❖

The first work of understanding is the observation of the avoidance of relationship as the source of seeking and thus of suffering. The later work is the application of this conscious awareness to moment to moment existence, and thus the observation of the nature of this avoidance as the essential process (or root-process) of every moment of existence. When this understanding is itself most perfectly demonstrated, all seeking and suffering, all avoidance of relationship, dissolves from the field of conscious existence. Then there is only Reality, Conscious and Unqualified Being.

❖ ❖ ❖

The world is seeking, nothing more. And all seeking is suffering and separation as continuous "creations". They are "created" by the perpetual activities of identification, differentiation, and desire. These are the mechanism of the avoidance of relationship. And these three are continuously performed in the various levels of being, corresponding to what are called the "chakras", or the circuit of "creative" centers, and the various bodies, or functional sheaths, and their associated conditional realms and conditional experiences. The consciousness of the seeker is a constantly changing perception of dilemma. And in all that he or she does, he or she is always only avoiding relationship.

Understanding is the recognition of seeking as the active principle of one's life. It recognizes the effects of seeking, its qualities and sources, the areas of its operation, and the methods of its functioning. It sees that seeking is the substance and the entire meaning of every moment of one's ordinary life.

But radical understanding, since it is radically aware of seeking, is not seeking. Radical understanding is prior to and apart from every kind of seeking and the entire drama of ordinary life. Therefore, it not only sees all life as seeking, but Enjoys itself as fundamental Reality Prior to all seeking. It Realizes no-seeking, non-avoidance, non-separation, unqualified relatedness, and unqualified Consciousness.

The practice of self-Enquiry (in the form "Avoiding relationship?") is (like every other by me given counter-egoic practice) the "form" of radical understanding. When understanding has in fact developed into an effective insight as a result of listening to my word and critically observing oneself in life, then it is brought to life directly in the form of self-Enquiry (or, otherwise, in the form of some other by me given, and directly counter-egoic, exercise). The one who Enquires is no longer seeking but continuously understanding seeking. Seeking is no longer the form of one's action or one's consciousness. Understanding has become the form and action of one's consciousness.

As understanding and self-Enquiry continue, the forms of seeking and the entire enterprise of separative life pass before the one who Enquires. And continually the sources of that action and the consciousness that identifies with them are brought to the condition of understanding. By degrees, the individual becomes less and less absorbed in the forms of seeking, and understanding and self-Enquiry lead constantly to the Reality that is their foundation. Attention gradually ceases to be involved in the seeking and the understanding of seeking, and it rests in that which understanding itself is, and to which self-Enquiry constantly leads attention.

Finally, there is no-seeking, no self-Enquiry, no understanding of seeking. There is no dilemma, no suffering, no separation. There is no identification, no differentiation, and no desire. There are no levels of being, no functional bodies, or functional sheaths, no conditional realms, and no conditional experiences. These are no longer perceived apart, or merely in themselves. Rather, they are lived or Known as Reality, as Consciousness Itself.

There is only That Which understanding itself is, prior to seeking or the recognition of seeking. There is not the consciousness of separate subject, separate observer, or separate experiencer. There is not the consciousness of separate objects, separate forms, or separate experiences. There is only Reality, Which is unqualified and always already Present. It is Consciousness Itself, always already Prior to (but not otherwise strategically separated from) any Communication of Itself to Itself through any form. It is unqualified relatedness and no-seeking, the living condition of Reality. It abides as Fullness and the Heart of Reality. It appears in the right side of the heart, and It is not Itself touched, modified, or included. It is What is when there is most perfect understanding. It is That Which understanding Knows and Enjoys from the beginning.

❖ ❖ ❖

The only-by-me revealed and given way of radical understanding (or the only-by-me revealed and given Way of the Heart) begins with self-surrendering devotion to me (and self-surrendering devotional contemplation, or feeling-contemplation, of me), and, on that basis, and by the primary means of constant devotional listening-attention to me, and listening-attention to my words of argument and instruction, and by the secondary (or supportive, and ego-reflecting) means of conforming one's life to all the functional, practical, relational, and cultural disciplines given by me, the process of self-observation begins and grows (and, in due course, becomes radical understanding). Then it deepens and becomes inclusive insight. Thereafter, it moves as the self-Enquiry: "Avoiding relationship?" (or, otherwise, as an alternative by me given counter-egoic, or ego-transcending, practice).

As self-Enquiry continues over time, the mind and life continually tend toward and move into various functional levels of being, various bodies (or functional sheaths), various experiences, even various realms.

456

The practice of self-Enquiry constantly dissolves the separative consciousness and allows it to remain as the unqualified, inclusive, living condition of Reality.

The living consciousness moves through the various forms and modifications that are in fact the manifestations of Shakti, or the universal "creative" Force. The practice of self-Enquiry continues as long as these movements continue, no matter how ordinary, limited, or sublime the experiences may appear.

Thus, self-Enquiry continues until Consciousness Realizes Itself directly, and abides as the Heart, Which is unqualified Fullness and no-seeking. Thereafter, it will be observed that there is no movement, no modification in the Knowledge of Reality, even though the life itself continues to manifest as every kind of condition. Then there is no longer self-Enquiry, but there is always already the Bliss of Real Consciousness, the most direct (or inherent) Knowledge of the primary Truth that is Reality Itself.

❖ ❖ ❖

The true process of self-Enquiry (in the form "Avoiding relationship?") is not a process of self-analysis. It is not purposed to draw the mind into all kinds of formulations and the deep self-consciousness of endless patterns. The practice of self-Enquiry is not "concerned" with the nature and forms of avoidance. Nor is the merely analytical awareness of the pattern of one's life of avoidance the same as understanding.

One who Enquires remains attentive to the question, to the one who receives the question, to the place where the question is received, and to what arises. Until something arises, one only remains in self-Enquiry in its place. Finally, by one's remaining in self-Enquiry, what arises will reveal itself to conscious awareness as the avoidance of relationship.

It makes no difference what arises or what is the character of the particular form of avoidance, for, as soon as it is consciously recognized, one ceases to exist in that form of separation and avoidance. One is not concentrated in the recognition or the analysis of avoidance. Instead, one becomes aware of the feeling of relatedness, itself. The unconscious image of separation is replaced by the conscious awareness of the feeling of unqualified, present relatedness. Unconscious avoidance does not merely become self-conscious, as in self-analysis. Rather, whereas one was previously only avoiding relationship, now one becomes aware of that from which one was withdrawn. Instead of remaining unconscious in avoidance and separation, one becomes conscious as the unqualified, or unlimited, feeling of relatedness.

Over time, self-Enquiry Realizes the living condition of Reality, which is characterized by this sense of unqualified relatedness. One sees that self-Enquiry is directed to the heart and is received in the heart. Then one experiences the Presence, and even the entire form and context of relationship, over against the living consciousness. In due course, the heart (on the right side) is Realized to be the point where the living consciousness enters into relationship. Then, at last, the experience of relatedness is replaced by Ultimate Self-Awareness.

When all avoidance of relationship subsides in the heart, and unqualified relatedness is enjoyed directly, then, even while appearing to be in relationship, one becomes Aware as the True Self, one's Real Nature, one's Presence _as_ Reality. Then what one enjoyed before as unqualified relatedness is itself recognized in one's own Ultimate Nature and Perfect Form, and as a merely apparent modification of the inherent Radiance of the Divine Self-Heart.

❖ ❖ ❖

Understanding is seated in the living consciousness and the conscious mind. It is conscious Realization. It is not seated in dilemma or any effect. It is not seated in the unconscious or subconscious, nor does it wait upon these as if they contained the source of its true intelligence or content. Neither is it seated in the super-conscious planes, nor does it wait upon them, by excluding consciousness or what is below consciousness, as if exclusive superconsciousness alone were the center and source of its only mind. It is Reality functioning on the level of the conscious mind, which is the focal point, or medium, of what is above and below.

Thus, the seat of understanding as a free activity at first appears in the head. A point in the very center of the head is the seat of the exercise of the functions of the conscious mind. That point of awareness is openly receptive to the levels of living consciousness, above and below. Thus, it is linked to the processes below, which are unconscious and subconscious, as well as those above, which are superconscious or non-mental.

In the process of self-Enquiry as "Real" meditation, one simply rests in radical understanding. In formal meditation one merely sits comfortably and free of the need to respond to activities in one's environment. One already understands. One has already examined the nature of suffering, of dilemma, and of motivated action. Thus, one sits and enjoys the fullness of radical understanding in one's form at that moment.

The practice of self-Enquiry begins at the point where one becomes aware of the tendency (or the apparent movements) of (or the apparent representations to) one's conscious awareness. Depending upon the stresses of one's life-expression at that moment, one's awareness will tend to move toward (or to become associated with) attention to movement, tension, thought, or feeling in some area or plane of the body. Thus, one's awareness will be directed from the center of awareness in the head, analogous to the viewpoint of one's eyes (which should ordinarily remain closed), toward some area of one's form, above or below.

In the beginning, one will probably move naturally in attention toward some process associated with the functions and motions of the lower body. One will be aware of some sexual tension, or some vital energy below, or some other kind of lower bodily sensation or motivation. These sensations also correspond to the lower "chakras", the "creative" centers of life-energy at the base of the spine (anus), the sacral center (sexuality), and the navel, or solar plexus (personal power). The practice of self-Enquiry, which is the free activity of understanding, should thus be allowed to confront whatever area the mind tends to pursue. When this movement begins, one should Enquire "Avoiding relationship?" One should not seek to remove the tendency itself. One should only Enquire. If the tendency remains, one should only Enquire. If one becomes disturbed that the tendency does not vanish, one should only Enquire. Whatever arises, one should only Enquire.

This practice of self-Enquiry can be done as an internal mental activity, either as a silent verbalization of the mind in understanding, or as an intention of understanding without internal verbalization. The frequency of self-Enquiry should be determined by the individual (as one perceives the practical effect of one's approach).

As self-Enquiry proceeds, the tendency of attention will begin to break up and dissolve. The practice of self-Enquiry is understanding, and so the form of one's conscious awareness will begin to relax from the area of attention and rest in understanding. The experience will be one of relief or release of attention and a return to rest in a kind of fullness. As one area of attention dissolves, another tendency will replace it and gather attention to itself. Then self-Enquiry should follow it as before and continue until it also dissolves or is replaced.

One who is only beginning in the way of radical understanding (or the Way of the Heart) is likely to feel the tendency of conscious awareness to move in a chronic pattern of attention in the lower body. This is only natural, since one chronically associates with the life-processes, the energies of the lower body. Food-desire, sex, the general communication of vital energy, and so on, are the basic and chronic content of ordinary life. Real life is not opposed to such energies or experiences. They are not the problem, nor are they necessarily destructive. Indeed, they are in the form of life and are part of one's present life-fulfillment. One is not constrained to dissociate from these centers of life-energy and lock them out.

Thus, there is no peculiar dilemma or "lowness" involved in the tendency to concentration in the lowest dimensions of one's "creative" existence. One remains in understanding even then and suffers no motive to escape or destroy them. The dilemma is not in the existence of such processes of life-function and life-energy, but in the enforced concentration in them apart from understanding. Such concentration is the root of suffering, of separateness and the motives of dilemma. Thus, it is only necessary to abide radically in understanding and not despair of it. It is only necessary to Enquire and not turn to some activity apart from understanding which seeks to abolish the lower energy itself.

Over time, one who, in this manner, understands will experience gradual relief from the symptoms of problematic life. In one's ease, one will naturally and voluntarily change the problem-based patterns of one's life. They will simply fall away in the face of understanding and the natural bliss of one's untroubled consciousness. Indeed, even before one grows (even via a beginner's meditation) into the capability for what I call "Real" meditation, one must have understood. And one will already have modified one's behavior in the direction of an easy internal control. Understanding, even before it develops into profound internal self-Enquiry, is already a purifying force that relieves one of much voluntary self-exploitation that one previously added to chronic difficulty.

Thus, self-Enquiry continues to attend to the tendency of consciousness in meditation. When understanding has become well developed through this exercise, such that there is relative freedom from enforced concentration in the lower motions or tendencies, the attention will gradually move into higher areas. Then one may tend to the emotions of the heart and even its psychic depth. Abiding in understanding, one should continue to Enquire: "Avoiding relationship?" And so this concentration will also ease. One may move higher and deeper, into the subtle center in the general region of the throat, which is also the breathing-seat of the Shakti, and so observe the higher display of Power, the higher psyche, the vibrations and glowing mentality of profound internal regions. One should abide in understanding and continue to Enquire. No matter where one's mind tends to move, one should continue to Enquire, gently but intensively, directly to the root of one's involvement.

In any case, the field of one's attention is always a separative movement, as one will discover by self-Enquiry, by radically holding to understanding, which is the source of self-Enquiry. The result of this process of understanding appears to be a kind of ascent, as if there were an abandonment of the lower. This is, however, not in fact the case. There is simply a relaxation of attention.

Ordinarily, one is drawn into enforced, chronic, and exclusive attention in various functional centers of life-energy or conditional experience. These become the foundation of one's point of view, and so one who is profoundly and exclusively concentrated in some complex of conditional experience feels that particular condition overwhelmingly, and everything else, including the centers of his or her conscious life apart from that, appears over against it. This is the mechanism whereby human beings acquire the root-presumption of separateness and the chronic activity of separativeness. But when one clings to understanding, this complex of concentration eases and relaxes, so that one regains the natural contact with the total circuit of conscious life, which natively, or always already, Knows its Freedom and Wholeness.

As a result of the exercise of radical understanding through self-Enquiry, the chronic concentration of attention is relieved, and one abides in understanding rather than in the centers where attention is otherwise chronically concentrated. The process of self-Enquiry is not a search for understanding or any effect, but it is understanding maintaining itself and Knowing itself under all conditions. Thus, in one who continually understands, fear and chronic reactivity are gradually stilled. What in fact has happened is that one is no longer concentrated in some separate complex of motion or tendency, some portion of the functional circuit of the living being. The one who is chronically fixed in animated sexuality and acquisition, which tend to exhaust and dissipate life-energy, becomes vital, healthier, and stronger as this chronic concentration is eased, and as the internal connection with the higher center in the solar plexus is restored. Just so, one experiences an emotional expansion and a true relational ability as one restores the connection to the "creative" center at the heart. One's effectiveness and available life-energy increase as one opens even higher in the throat and the mental centers in the head.

Thus, it is clear that the ascent which this process involves is in fact not an abandonment of the lower, but a greater and greater inclusiveness, so that one begins to function as a whole and experiences "creative" control over life-processes. This inclusiveness, and not any kind of exclusive ascent or descent, is the form of Real existence, of "creative" life. And the way of radical understanding (or the Way of the Heart) is the root of that inclusive and Real life.

As the process of "Real" meditation increases in its radical intensity, one will find that the mind tends less and less to concentrate in the centers below the head. In time one will have achieved such ease of internal relationship to life, and one will have come to exercise such "creative" control or use of the life-process, that one will not be drawn excitedly to the impressions of the life-complex. One's self-Enquiry will quickly move through these movements, and one will center easily in the form of understanding, in a fullness that is silent and blissful. One will enjoy the radiant calm and certainty that is natural to the center of living consciousness in the head. Such a one has achieved "creative" realization of the unconscious and subconscious life-process. One has not abandoned life, nor does one minimize it. It has simply become an area of "creative" enjoyment that is usable to one, and free of necessary dilemma.

Such a person may then also feel the mind, the center of functional life-consciousness, and of functional understanding, tend upward toward what is in fact superconscious, even prior to life-individuality. In meditation one will experience a new quality of self-Enquiry. The problem in the mind and the "creative" centers below the head is generally one of the refusal of relationship in a concrete sense. It is life-abandonment, the refusal of life-processes, the refusal of the life of love, inclusion, intelligence, and human "creativity". But when self-Enquiry is drawn above, toward what is not conscious but superconscious, and thus not presently included in the field of the mind, the individual begins to comprehend the avoidance of relationship on a new level. Then it is not a matter of the avoidance of concrete relationship by separating oneself as an entity from other entities. Personal existence in the gross world is not an immediate function of the higher conscious life.

Thus, as one is drawn above, toward the aperture at the top and slightly to the rear of the head, one should remain in understanding and Enquire as before, but one's realization will not be one of relational ease. Instead, one will perceive that the very concept of one's individual existence as it functions on a conscious level and down into the subconscious and unconscious life-levels is in fact the source of dilemma, or separateness. One will simply see that it does not apply, indeed, does not exist, and the separative movement that "creates" it on the mental level will simply dissolve. In that intense perception in understanding, the fundamental activity of identification and differentiation will reveal itself and subside, at first for brief moments, and then easily, for longer periods, until it becomes a constant that also affects the operating basis of the conscious mind.

Those who pursue this very perception as an exclusive goal call it "enlightenment" or "Self-Realization", a kind of once-and-for-all attainment. In fact it is only the natural perception of superconsciousness. If one has manipulated oneself in dilemma to the point of temporary abandonment of the "lower" life and even the living mind, one will feel one has attained Reality, and so await the dissolution of one's personal existence at death. But one who understands does not abandon understanding or life. Such a one has no motive for doing so. Such a one will not be troubled by the return to mental life and human existence. One simply understands that one has begun to include an even higher center and source of true being in life.

In any case, whatever arises in meditation, you should abide in understanding and simply Enquire. In time, the movement of consciousness will not even tend to the point of superconsciousness above. The practice of self-Enquiry will become radically effective, prior to every kind of activity and perception. Then you will find that understanding even ceases to function as a mental activity. It will have become radically concentrated in That to Which self-Enquiry always leads. That Silence, incomparable Depth, and formless "Object" of contemplation will become utterly absorbing. Then, suddenly, you may find that you are seated in the heart. All the movements of the life-consciousness, on every level, will have fallen away, and you will remain tacitly Aware as no-seeking in the heart, to the right side of the chest. You will possess unqualified Knowledge of Reality and Enjoy unqualified Bliss. And It will be the same Bliss you touched in the first moment of truly radical understanding.

But do not seek this State, and, if It comes, even continue to Enquire, as soon as you possess a mind with which to Enquire. As your self-Enquiry continues, you will discover that you rise again out of the heart, or you will release the Power of the heart upwards, while yet remaining founded in the heart. You will experience the Current of Love-Bliss and Joy rising again to the sahasrar. And this Current, or Circuit, of Love-Bliss will remain, even under the conditions of self-Enquiry, as your fundamental Form. It is the regenerated Amrita Nadi, the "Bright". It is Enjoyment, no-dilemma, and It contains every "creative" faculty. In that Form, as you continue the life of understanding, you will enjoy the continuous flowering of every kind of Wisdom and Knowledge.

Radical understanding, from the beginning and forever, is the foundation of one's True and Real life. It is possessed of no exclusive goal, and thus it is not motivated to concentrate above or below. Its motivation is its own and very form, which is already inclusive. Thus, just as in one's ordinary humanity one suffers by exclusive concentration in what is "below" understanding, one would likewise suffer by exclusive concentration in what is "above" it.

To concentrate in the centers or realms of the superconscious is a separative activity, not an inclusive one. It is enforced and recommended by the teachings invented in the great search. Real life, radically founded in understanding, maintains the form or circuit of conscious life. The full life of understanding is not one in which the unconscious and subconscious become conscious activities of the mind (although such is certainly possible). Nor is it one in which the superconscious becomes a conscious activity, under the control of the conscious mind (although such control or consciousness is certainly possible). Rather, the full life of understanding is, in any case, one in which the unconscious and subconscious processes remain as such, and so also with the super-conscious processes. The difference is that the dilemma is removed, and the process of conscious understanding, which is the link or circuit between all processes in the living consciousness, is attained, asserted, and enjoyed.

Thus, the Real human being is "creatively" present. Such a one operates in the mind of understanding, which is fully bathed in the higher Light, and which moves into the "creative" development and realization of life. This Real human being is the future human type of all the universes. In such a one, the "creative" movement coming out of the heart will find fulfillment in the right realization of conditionally manifested existence.

Such men and women, who abide radically in understanding, and so realize life free from dilemma, search, and fear, are "creatively" involved in maintaining and using the living condition of Reality. They operate to restore that condition by constantly regaining the Circuit of Consciousness and Power that begins in the heart. And they move to make the true living condition of Reality the basis for all actual existence, even what is called the "human".

❖ ❖ ❖

The practice of self-Enquiry that is an extension of understanding does not produce an instant result simply because it is used. Often you must Enquire for some time before it becomes conscious and intense, operative as actual understanding, rather than as a mere, and empty, technique. When you Enquire, you are not dealing with words but meanings. And you are directing the self-Enquiry not to unconscious and material forces, but to mind and living consciousness, which are also aware of these. Thus, often in meditation, it takes some time for understanding to arise and "Real" meditation to begin.

Therefore, when you meditate, meditate with understanding, and continue to Enquire until self-Enquiry moves fully into conscious awareness, recognizes the forms of avoidance, resumes the form of relationship, and "creates" an opening, and a release of bliss.

Frequently you will find a sudden opening or release in the heart. It is the release of self-contraction, and the release of bliss to the body-mind. This opening, fullness, ease, and release may even be the typical result of each daily meditation. Of course it is not a "required" experience. It is only that you may perceive it, and so I have accounted for it. Simply understand and Enquire with intensity, not as a method or a program to "create" various effects, but as an activity in the living consciousness.

❖ ❖ ❖

This meditation is described in terms of the vital physical (or gross) body. But it is not identical to it or contained in it. This meditation can be done exactly as described in any functional body (or functional sheath). Every body (or every functional sheath) arises (and is) in the perfect Form of Reality, the Amrita Nadi. The same centers and the same relationships pertain in each body (or functional sheath) and every conditional realm or kind of universe. Every experience and every function is a manifestation within the same instrument. From the "Point of View" of the perfect Form of Reality, there is no higher or lower body (or functional sheath). Every body (or functional sheath) is the same Form, the same terminal of Love-Bliss and Enjoyment, the same seat of Consciousness and Truth. In the perfect Form of Reality, there is no need for ascent or descent. There is only present understanding.

❖ ❖ ❖

The self-Enquiry ("Avoiding relationship?") is not directed to the various actions that are concrete avoidance. It is directed to oneself, directly. It is not: "Is this action the avoidance of relationship in some sense?" Rather, its significance is in the form: "Presently avoiding being already, entirely in relationship?" (or "Presently contracting from the inherent life-condition of unqualified relatedness?"). Thus, this self-Enquiry moves you directly to a free conscious awareness that is ineffably, unqualifiedly in relationship.

The self-Enquiry is not in the form: "Are you avoiding relationship?" or "Am I avoiding relationship?" In this practice of self-Enquiry, rightly engaged, there is no dramatized separation in the mind between oneself as the questioner and oneself as the hearer. The living consciousness Enquires of itself, or, in actual effect, critically observes itself in the present moment. There is simply the critical observation of the total, present context of real experience.

One does not Enquire as, or of, some surrogate entity, some part of the mind, some separate function, and so on. As one who understands, one Enquires of oneself in the arising (and one's own "creation") of the present moment. True self-Enquiry is not a means of seeking liberation, but it is conscious understanding enforcing its own form as the present moment. Thus, it is necessary that the one who Enquires be one who already understands. The practice of self-Enquiry is the activity of understanding. The practice of self-Enquiry is not understanding isolated as a method to produce an effect. The entire action of Enquiring and Realizing is understanding, and each part of it is itself understanding.

Simply Enquire of yourself as yourself. When you feel yourself in the heart, Enquire of yourself there as any tendency, any moment, arises. There is no mystery, no difficulty, implied in this activity. Understand, and Enquire of the instant (and present center) of your living being. In the beginning, it may appear that you are seated in the mind, and that you Enquire of your deeper self in some unrecognizable place, or even in the heart. But the process of self-Enquiry is in fact always in the heart, and it Realizes itself in the heart. It is no-seeking, and it Knows itself at last as no-seeking. Even when understanding becomes this Knowledge, self-Enquiry persists, until there is most perfect Realization, utterly retired of all dilemma. Then, again, the Fullness of Being is assumed in the non-separate Realization of the always present Reality.

❖ ❖ ❖

As the practice of self-Enquiry proceeds, it traces and observes the tendencies of the life and mind. Thus, one makes discoveries and understands the various activities of one's life. But, at last, self-Enquiry enters the heart. And self-Enquiry is only directed exactly to oneself, utterly and completely. Then understanding becomes most radical Realization and most perfect Knowledge. With each self-Enquiry, all of conscious awareness and all activity merge in the single enjoyment that is unqualified relatedness. There is the simultaneous awareness of both the one who Enquires and the one to whom the self-Enquiry is directed. Then there is no motion. All is included. There is only no-seeking (in the heart) and the Love-Blissful, perfect Form of Reality, the Unqualified.

❖ ❖ ❖

The activity of self-Enquiry continues as long as the mind tends to move and take on forms. But the most intense meditation is one in which understanding (itself), as unqualified relatedness, absorbs the living awareness. Then understanding does not move with the mind to Enquire of its forms, but it rests prior to the mind (and, thus, prior to the function of living awareness that is receptive to and records experience).

One of the primary experiences in self-Enquiry is a kind of "letting go", but in its most intense form it is a kind of "holding on". In the first case there is understanding, but also a stimulated life-form that tends to separative experience. Thus, self-Enquiry, the arm of understanding, moves to view all these experiences as they truly are, and one is let loose in understanding. But when one has seen enough of this, and one knows the game well, and when one almost naturally stands loose, then an entirely new form of living awareness emerges. One does not simply stand independent, empty, and apart. Instead, one recognizes and enjoys that living condition which was always there, and which is unqualified relatedness, the very armature on which all one's parts and functions were set.

Whereas previously one Enquired: "Avoiding relationship?" and so felt images and tendencies dissolve, now one recognizes and enjoys the silent, imageless, and attentive state of free awareness. When the automatic activity of avoidance subsides, then the natural, internal force of the living form that is unqualified relatedness comes into the conscious awareness. The sense is simply one of unqualified relatedness, always and already, prior to any particular experience, prior to present limitation, egoic ignorance, or "sin".

However, this Realization is in understanding. It is not the same as the believer's sense of the all-embracing God outside oneself. It is the most intense form of understanding, where self-Enquiry has become fruitful in resonating the parts of the human form. Then meditation becomes a natural activity of "holding on", of unqualifiedly asserting the living condition of Reality, the condition of being unqualifiedly related, non-separate, included, already inclusive of high and low, whatever the apparent conditions.

When one "holds on" to this Realization, Which is intense understanding, a forcefulness rises in one that purifies the remnants of mentality and the automatic demands that force one to identify with separated levels of one's being. Suddenly one ceases to be held and limited to the concrete mind, the ground of emotionality, and the lower functions of vital and physical life. The force of one's understanding has become an intense attention to the condition of unqualified relatedness (the living condition of Reality), and one may feel the limits of one's awareness expanding above to include the unitive dimensions of superconscious intelligence.

The feeling is a kind of rushing ascent. One "holds on" to one's unqualified feeling-Realization, the awareness of Reality as utterly inclusive, and allows oneself to be drawn into a great fullness of living existence. One may experience many effects of this purifying expansion, including a stiffening of the body or violent twisting and movement of the body, particularly the spine and neck. One may spontaneously make symbolic gestures with one's hands or body. There may be tensions of the face, of the upper head, of the area between the brows. One may be moved to laughter or tears, to make strange expressions with one's face, to utter strange sounds. One may hear inner sounds, see visions, taste or smell internal emanations, or experience unusual internal sensations. One may feel heat or cold. One may sense vibrations, vast internal spaces, emptiness, silence, a living void filling with a descending Force and Light from an infinite Consciousness and Power above.

Thus, the primary activity of understanding moves from the original understanding to self-Enquiry to "holding on" to the living condition of Reality. That living condition, which is unqualified relatedness, is simply the armature, or inherent structure, of living being.

Understanding, or "Real" meditation, turns one to the basic form of conscious life. (And, ultimately, it concentrates one in its primary center or thread, which is an open Circuit between the heart and the head.) Thus, by naturally "holding on" to that condition which is unqualified relatedness, one grows over time into one's Ultimate Fullness, and then one may also (even spontaneously) include the emanations of the highest in the "creative" and functional realization of one's life.

I must repeat again that this is a matter of understanding. It has no goal exterior or radically prior to itself, even as it Enquires. Indeed, it Enquires of all such things. Thus, the individual who embraces the way of radical understanding (or the Way of the Heart) is not pursuing liberation in the exclusive sense. The way of radical understanding (or the Way of the Heart) is always already and consciously Free, and that inherent Freedom and Bliss is the Ground of its apparent expansion and growth. Thus, the individual who "holds on" to the living condition of Reality is not motivated to abandon more and more and so slice away the forms of life. One is already free of such seeking, since one is founded in understanding. Instead, one continually moves into the "creative" realization of life by consciously and actively including the Force, Light, Bliss, Power, Ability, Freedom, Intelligence, and all the rest that is always already in the Source and in the totality of the living condition of Reality.

❖ ❖ ❖

Understanding is Reality, That Which always, already exists, Which is Consciousness Itself and no-seeking in the heart. When understanding has become truly radical, such that it becomes the foundation and way of life, it abides as itself under all conditions and turns all things into forms of relationship.

The conscious activity of understanding is meditation, or the beholding of Reality. It is either effortless abiding in no-seeking or the activity of self-Enquiry. The practice of self-Enquiry will at last be directed to the heart, to oneself directly and wholly: "Avoiding relationship?" Thus, ultimately, one Realizes Reality as Consciousness Itself, and as the ultimate and inherently perfect Form of Reality, Which Radiates from the Heart that _is_ Consciousness Itself.

The life of understanding is a process in Consciousness Itself, not merely an activity in any level of the psycho-physical being, or in any functional body (or functional sheath), or in any conditional realm, or in the context of any conditional experience. It is always in Consciousness Itself (or the perfect Reality Itself), and, by this, continually appears in the living circumstances of Reality (in every conditionally manifested

473

form in which the perfect Reality appears), while yet always abiding in and as the very Nature of Consciousness Itself (Which is the ultimate, or inherently perfect, Reality Itself).

When one understands, one is either simply present or Enquiring of oneself. One is perpetually turned to Consciousness Itself, and not to anything that arises separately. One's "habit" is self-Enquiry, and thus one is never devoted to any form of problem.

❖ ❖ ❖

Those who do not understand as Reality in the heart only think in the head. They are in exile. They are seeking. Thus, they adapt to all remedial paths, sensual and Spiritual, the paths of exploitation and separation. But radical understanding and real self-Enquiry are Reality Itself. Therefore, radical understanding and real self-Enquiry do not resort to the means and signs of suffering. Radical understanding is the unbroken act of Conscious Being. Thus, one who truly understands remains untouched by what passes, but those who seek, like Narcissus, are always trying to become immune. Their struggle is as endless as the Bliss of one whose understanding is most perfect.

❖ ❖ ❖

The ultimate, simplest, and most perfect "meditation" is to "gaze" in the Heart as no-seeking and allow the Heart's Love-Bliss to rise as Fullness to the head, the Silence of the sahasrar above the seat of the mind. Then there is only perfect Self-Enjoyment and no-dilemma, no separation, no-seeking. That is the Enjoyment of the perfect Form of Reality.

But this "meditation" is not a technique. It is discovered in the most perfect Realization of understanding. Otherwise it is an effort in dilemma. Therefore, understand, and Realize the perfect Form of Reality. When self-Enquiry has found no-seeking, and only Love-Bliss and pure Consciousness in the Heart, and when that Love-Bliss has been seen to rise to the sahasrar in the Amrita Nadi, the perfect Form of Reality, thereafter "meditate" as That and allow It to be so.

The Heart is the very Person of the Guru. The Amrita Nadi is the Guru's perfect Form. The Love-Bliss of unqualified Enjoyment is the Guru's ultimate teaching. The perfect Knowledge of This is the only True (and inherent) Liberation and Freedom. The perfect Enjoyment of This is the Realization of Reality. The Real Existence of This is Truth. The Demonstration of This is radical understanding. And radical understanding is Real life.

❖ ❖ ❖

In meditation, one who understands may perceive a movement of conscious awareness and Energy in relation to the centers in the body. The strategic Yogi, in his or her search either for the Shakti or for the True Self, draws Energy down from above and directs It upwards along the spine to the sahasrar (and perhaps down again to the point between the brows). Such a one may even in time see It moving out of the sahasrar to return to Its origin in the heart. But in the natural process of living being, generated from the heart and expanded as the Amrita Nadi, the circulation of Energy is the reverse of the strategic Yogic process of return. It is instead a "creative" emanation from the heart, which includes all forms, animates all forms, and sacrifices all forms again to the heart.

Thus, one who understands may perceive the Love-Bliss-Energy rising out of the heart to the sahasrar as the Amrita Nadi, the heart's Love-Blissful Presence. Then It may be perceived to descend through the various centers to the muladhar. In turn It may be perceived to rise again from the muladhar, through the root of the sex center and the solar plexus, surrendering Itself in the sahasrar above.

One may even perceive this movement in relation to the breath. When one inhales, the Energy may be perceived to rise from below to the sahasrar and then drive downward to the heart. Then there may be a retention of breath accompanied by silence in the mind. When one exhales again, the Conscious Energy may be perceived to rise forcefully into the Amrita Nadi (and the "Brightness" above), then move down through the centers in the spine to the muladhar, and come to rest there during another brief retention.

Seeing this, one may think one has recovered a superior kind of Yogic process. One may try to use it deliberately to control and purify the instrument. This may seem to be the very Yoga of understanding itself. But one will find that as one begins to engage this process one will become a seeker as before. One will become concerned for purification, "creative" activities on a subtle level, various forms of concentration, and so on. Thus, again, one will begin to act on the basis of a dilemma in consciousness and (conditional) form.

One should simply remain in understanding and Enquire. When such processes arise spontaneously, one should simply understand and Enquire. They will continue only by themselves and not bind one by identification, differentiation, and desire.

Thus, one will only Witness even these ultimate events, and one will remain in one's own (ultimate, and inherently perfect) Form, residing in the Heart, generated as the "Bright".

❖   ❖   ❖

An experience similar to what I, as a child, named (and described) as "the Thumbs" may arise during the "Real" meditation of radical understanding. It is a process experienced first in the physical body, then (or simultaneously, and more and more) in the pranic (etheric, or energy) body, and, finally, in the dual astral (or lower mental and higher mental) body, which (in conjunction with the pranic body) is experienced to be spherical in shape. When this process arises, one is not entering the astral worlds of the psyche. One is discarding (or "surrounding") the vital and physical form, at least temporarily. Then one may also find oneself alive in visions, or illumined with subtle light. But if one allows the reversal of polarity to take place completely, and this simply by remaining as understanding and self-Enquiry, one may find oneself turned down into the heart (and dissolved in the Heart of Silence). Finally, when the process of self-Enquiry is most perfect, one will Know only Reality Itself, and one will arise from the heart as the Amrita Nadi, the Eternal Form, the Spire of Love-Bliss that Stands forever in the heart.

❖ ❖ ❖

No matter what pattern of experience or form arises in "Real" meditation, abide in understanding and Enquire. The practice of self-Enquiry is not to be abandoned for any experience or form. It will only cease of its own accord when absolutely nothing arises, neither thought nor form nor experience nor experiential (or merely conditional) bliss. Then there is only Reality, unqualified and perfect. As long as things continue to arise, abide in understanding and Enquire. When things finally cease to arise, when there is no break in the most perfect Realization of Reality, then you will abide only in Reality in all states. In the waking state particularly you will only Witness all forms, all identities, and all actions, while remaining as the Heart, Present as the Amrita Nadi. Then there may also be a constant sense of abiding in the right side of the heart. There will be no covering, no mind, no person, no experience, no form. All things will exist as an ornamentation or pattern which does not include you but which you include. This is most perfect understanding.

❖ ❖ ❖

Most perfect understanding is always beholding me, Bhagavan, the perfect Form of Reality, Whose Center is the Heart, and Whose extremities are the mind and the activities of enjoyment. There is nothing else that is ever Experienced or Known but this One Enjoyment of Reality, by Reality, Which is Reality. There is only the One Process, the One and perfect Form, the One Experience. It is Beholding, It is Enjoyment, It is unqualified, present Bliss. It has no special origination in time or conditional form. Therefore, cessation or change has nothing to do with It. These things do not qualify It. They are only the conditions of the same primary Enjoyment, as forms churning in the light, cycling about the sun, resolving and dissolving in an endless pattern of enjoyment, as the loved-one turns herself before her lover.

When there is no understanding, these things continue as dilemma, enforcing the adventure of Narcissus. When there is understanding, these things continue as before, but in freedom, in the living condition of Reality. And even the one who understands most perfectly appears no different than before, except that such a one is given to Divine pleasures, Divine laughter, Divine wisdom, and unqualified Divine adventure.

❖ ❖ ❖

When one lives most perfectly as the "Bright", one no longer knows oneself as descended, separate, and so forth. Thus, there is no longer any seeker's need to ascend through the chakras. There is only the present Enjoyment of the Amrita Nadi, the perfect Form of Reality. It is pure Existence, Present as no-seeking in the heart. It is Consciousness Itself. It is no-dilemma in the mind. It is Self-Existing and Self-Radiant Love-Bliss in the sahasrar. This Divine Self-Radiance illumines all forms, all levels and planes, all functional bodies (or functional sheaths), all conditional realms, and all conditional experiences. It is the One Experience. Everything else only reflects It. Thus, one who is Aware as the perfect Form of Reality gives Life to all things.

❖ ❖ ❖

Listen to me and, while constantly listening to me (and to my every word of instruction), observe yourself directly. In due course, this insight comes: Life is only moment to moment suffering, and seeking, and the avoidance of relationship. When this becomes a comprehensive recognition, then, if self-Enquiry is the form of your by me given ego-transcending practice, approach every moment of experience with self-Enquiry (in the form "Avoiding relationship?"). In every moment, understand thus, until you abide in That Which self-Enquiry reveals Prior to avoidance.

Such understanding is no-seeking. To Realize such understanding most perfectly is to abide as the Heart Itself, Prior to identification, differentiation, and desire. To abide Thus is to abide as Reality, That Which always already is, prior to every experience and the root-activity of avoidance. When understanding is most perfectly Realized, there only remains life as wisdom, and as enjoyment of the form of sacrifice (while remaining most perfectly Identified with Consciousness Itself). Then understanding will be manifesting as self-verifying and perfect Truth.

This is the way of radical understanding. It is the Way of the Heart (Itself). It is a simplicity, and nothing needs to be added to it as a prerequisite. The more sophisticated seeker will find (albeit with certain characteristic and otherwise traditional limitations) parallels for various features of this way in the best religious, Spiritual, and philosophical writings in history. But the only-by-me revealed and given way of radical understanding (or the only-by-me revealed and given Way of the Heart) is, alone among all other ways, inherently necessary, entirely sufficient, and, ultimately, most perfectly Complete. And it is now available to all. Indeed, it is, in a rudimentary fashion, already going on in all, and it need only become a conscious activity, prior to every kind of dilemma. For all the future, the ancient Truth stands fully

Present, to be Realized in Its Completeness, by means of the way of radical understanding (which is the Way of the Heart).

❖ ❖ ❖

My true devotees will be those who are free of every kind of seeking, attendant only to understanding. They will commit themselves to the intentional "creation" of life in the unqualified, living condition and perfectly relational logic of Reality, rather than in the always limited and dying condition and separative logic of Narcissus. My true devotees will give living form to the unexploitable Presence of Reality. They will not be moved to turn the worlds to dilemma, exhaustion, and revolutionary experience, nor to the exploitation of desire and possibility, nor to the ascent to and inclusion of various goals, higher entities, evolutionary aims, or ideas of Spiritual transformation. They will "create" in the aesthetics of Reality, turning all things into unqualified relatedness and enjoyment. They will remove the effects of separative existence and restore the form of things. They will engineer every kind of stability and beauty. They will give living form to the always already living Presence of Peace. Their eye will be on present form and not on exaggerated notions of artifice. Their idea of form will be stable and whole, not a gesture toward some other event. They will not make the world seem but a symbol for higher and other things.

They will constantly "create" the living manifestation of Truth while Conscious of the always already present Reality. Thus, they will serve the order of sacrifice and Ultimate Knowledge. They will affirm the necessary and the good. They will make only economic and wise use of technology. They will not be motivated by invention but by Reality, Which is the always present "Thing" they will intend to communicate (by every means, and in all they do). They will not pursue any kind of utopian victory for mankind, any deathlessness or overwhelming survival. They will only "create" the conditions for present Enjoyment, the Communication of Reality, the form in which radical understanding and Real Knowledge can arise, live, and become the public foundation of existence.

Thus, my true devotees will be a new human order that will serve to "create" a new age of sanity and Joy. But that new age will not be the age of the occult, the religious, or the scientific or technological evolution of mankind. It will be the fundamental age of Real existence, wherein life will be radically realized, entirely apart from the adventure that was mankind's great search. The "new age" envisioned by seekers is a spectacular display that only extends the traditional madness, exploitability, and foolishness of mankind. But I desire a new order of men and women, who will not begin from all of that, but who will apply themselves apart from all dilemma and all seeking to the harmonious event of Real existence.

I am equally certain that such a new human order must arise as a force in the world in the present historical epoch, or else this world must suffer the karma of early dissolution.

❖ ❖ ❖

At any moment, humanity and human beings are operating under the assumption of some form of dilemma, some problem, some source of separated consciousness. My life has been devoted to every kind of endeavor, and this is my overwhelming, most fundamental observation and conclusion about every kind of action, every moment of ordinary human living.

I have also devoted myself to the direct and intentional experiencing of every form of primary dilemma, and I have critically observed and analyzed the mechanism that is always involved. But even this analysis, expressed in the language of understanding, does not itself remove the activity that otherwise appears to be problematic in nature. Life remains as it is. Therefore, seeing this, I came to a fundamental understanding in relation to life. Is life a dilemma?

Is there in fact a dilemma, a problem of existence, at the root of conscious life?

If there is, then life must be believed and generated as it appears. And every kind of experience must be realized ultimately as a form of suffering. Then it is not a matter of living more or less well, of living ill, or of becoming victorious in liberation, salvation, and Spirituality. If life is a dilemma, then all of these things amount to the same dilemma.

On the other hand, if there is no fundamental dilemma, then it makes no difference what one experiences at any moment. If there is no fundamental dilemma, then there is no fundamental suffering, or separation, under any conditions. In such case it is also not a matter of living more or less well, of living badly or in failure, or of any kind of victory. All of these things would pale equally in the face of the fundamental, present no-dilemma.

Thus, in any case, there is no fundamental importance in experience, in the condition of suffering, realization, pleasure, pain, or relative enjoyment at any moment. The entire matter ultimately comes to the matter of a single question and a radical decision at every moment in time. That is, is there a dilemma fundamental to life now? This is the single matter of importance at any moment.

To become aware, so fundamentally aware, is already to understand and Know the present moment with radical intensity. To Realize this moment as such a radical question is already to be free of the arbitrary character of the moment, and always already to stand in the fundamental Nature of Reality. Is there a dilemma? Is there?

To Know life itself as such a question is already to be free of any answer, yes or no, to the fundamental question. It is to confront this moment as it is and to perceive the very Reality to Which and in Which the question is posed. It is to confront the very Reality that asks the question. Is there a dilemma? Is there?

To ask such a fundamental question now is to realize that no possible answer to the question is of any consequence. If there is a fundamental dilemma, the fact that one can ask so fundamentally leaves one already free of the dilemma. And if there is no dilemma, the fact of no-dilemma leaves one equally free, confronting the same Reality. Therefore, the answer is not given. It is simply an unqualified recognition of Reality Itself. Any answer remains itself unable to qualify. Therefore, in any case, there is radically, fundamentally no dilemma.

In Reality, the conditional forms of experience and existence are of no concern. From the point of view of the conditionally existing being, the underlying motive, the dilemma or no-dilemma, is always the one fundamental concern. But even when one becomes thus fundamentally concerned, one remains fundamentally without dilemma. Therefore, at any moment, there is no dilemma. This is radical understanding. It exceeds every other recognition, vision, experience, or form of self-knowledge. It makes <u>all</u> experience acceptable, of no radical concern. It is free of impurity and of purity. It is always already, presently, consciously, radically Free.

No other Realization of Reality exceeds, or even equals, this. All other visions qualify and generate forms of dilemma. Therefore, one sees and passes from every kind of thought, perception, and seeking. There is no dilemma. And, because there is no dilemma, there is no matter of ultimate importance. One is entirely free of all consequences. Under the form of any experience, compulsion, problem, habit, self-indulgence, realization, perfection, sublimity, or pain—there is no dilemma.

Since there is no dilemma, one is always, already, fundamentally satisfied. One does not become the dilemma of any form of experience. One totally allows the form of one's life and every possible kind of experience, high or low, of every possible form of existence and consciousness. In any case, one Enjoys only this fundamental no-dilemma: "I have become the world. I am not qualified by the world. There is no dilemma. I am Free!"

This is the ultimate logic, the most perfect Realization to Which I was led. It ended the secondary revolution of my existence. It reduced all "importances" to a Singleness. It did not limit me to any degree, in any sense. It did not Itself require of me any form of purity, sublimity, remedy, or acquired perfection. It did not reduce life to any arbitraries, high or low. There is no seriousness to the entire matter. There is no dilemma, and I Know it.

Then it is of no consequence at all what one will be or not be, whether one will be or not, whether or not anything or anyone will be at all. There is no point of drama, no problem to conditional existence itself. There is no exclusive power in any of it. There is no Spirituality and no sin. There is no difference anywhere. The only critical and radical difference is this Realization Itself. There is no dilemma. The entire drama of separation, seeking, suffering, identification, differentiation, and desire is of no fundamental importance. Its continuation is neither qualified, removed, nor assured. The entire cognition, or mis-understanding, of "Reality" is of no fundamental importance.

There is no dilemma. Therefore, there is no importance in the logic of Narcissus. There is no exclusive Reality, no perfect or improved remedial path. There is no dilemma. In any case, there is only this True Humor. This True Humor is beyond all ordinary resorts, all consequences. This True Humor is neither victory nor defeat, neither lost nor found. It is not fundamentally moved. This True Humor is without any fundamental fear. It makes not the slightest difference in the quality of life. It announces no preferences. It is entirely escaped, undaunted. Even in the forceful embrace of any kind of terminal terror or weakness, It is untouched. It is neither good nor evil. It is neither immoral nor moral. It has nothing whatever to recommend. It is only, even exaggeratedly, unqualifiedly Free. It is neither existent nor non-existent. It is only Free.

There is no dilemma. This is the most perfect Realization, the single discovery, the entire Truth, the radical gospel. It bears no question, no answer, no promise, no self, no other, no world, no life, no death. It is untouched. That is the entire Truth of it. That is the Knowledge that makes the difference. Then, whatever the form of life, of impulse or awareness, of any kind of seeking or understanding, of no-seeking or madness, there is only, already no-dilemma. This is the smack that Awakened me and entirely ended my separated association with all beings and things. It was as if I had never been born. I have never been born. There is no dilemma.

❖ ❖ ❖

The cognition of no-dilemma is not an enforced affirmation. Such is only another condition of seeking, or the employment of Truth apart from understanding. No-dilemma is in fact the ultimate Realization of the way of radical understanding (or the Way of the Heart). It proceeds from listening to me (and to my even every word of instruction) to self-observation, progressive insight, summary understanding (or the true hearing of me), and "Real" meditation, as I have described. And, in due course, all of that is Infused, and advanced to perfect practice and most perfect Realization of me (and, thus and thereby, of the Divine, and inherently Spiritual, Self-Condition) by means of the clear seeing of me (or the constant reception of my Spiritual Blessing).

Adi Da (The Da Avatar)
Adi Da Purnashram (Naitauba), Fiji, 1994

I Am the Man
of
Understanding

1.

I am the Man of Understanding. I am a great Man of Pleasure, even a profoundly superficial Man—for how can one be deep who Knows no perimeters and no center at all? I cannot be grasped or identified, like a thing. Therefore, I am not a source of fascination. Since I cannot be found or followed (like a thing), My Existence avails no one. Therefore, I am not important in the usual way. There is only understanding. I <u>Am</u> understanding.

2.

What appears to the beholder as light, to the hearer as sound, to the shapely actor as life-energy, and to the thinker as thought, is Known directly, on the level of Consciousness Itself, as Love-Bliss. Then It becomes light, sound, life-energy, and thought. All such things are only apparent modifications of the Original Reality that is Love-Bliss. They are conditionally manifested form. And conditionally manifested form is that same Love-Bliss.

Love-Bliss is not radically separable from Consciousness. Love-Bliss <u>Is</u> Consciousness. Consciousness <u>Is</u> Love-Bliss. Thus, on the level of activity, there is also no radical distinction between thought and form. There is Only the Love-Bliss that is Reality, Which is originally, now, Identical to Consciousness Itself.

Conscious Love-Bliss, Unqualified, is the Nature of Reality, Which is Absolute Existence. All cosmic powers are communications within this Ultimate Power that is Existence Itself. Therefore, the Ultimate Knowledge and Power is Reality Itself, Which is Unqualified Existence as Conscious Love-Bliss.

The Unqualified Existence that is Reality is always already Present, As Love-Bliss. Love-Bliss is simply Perfect Presence, for Reality is That Which is Unqualifiedly Present. Present Reality is Conscious as Love-Bliss. The Man of Understanding Only Enjoys Conscious Love-Bliss, at Play.

The Man of Understanding does not seek. The Man of Understanding Knows Only Reality. The Man of Understanding Knows Himself Only As Reality. There Is Only Reality. His Realization Is Only Reality. His Knowledge Is Only Consciousness Itself. He Is Only, Merely Present. He Is Only Unqualified Existence. He Is Only Love-Bliss. He Knows Only Love-Bliss. There Is Only Love-Bliss. That Is It entirely.

3.

Unqualified Existence, Conscious as Love-Bliss, Appears in the Heart and Arises as the Amrita Nadi, the "Bright". Love-Bliss is the Original (and everywhere "creative") Impulse, the "Bright" Divine Shakti that is the Substance and Support of all conditional movers. Love-Bliss-Energy is the Source-Condition and primary Form of all "creativity", even all of conditional manifestation. The Man of Understanding Arises as Love-Bliss, Mad with Love-Bliss. He is not Narcissus. "Creativity" is Love-Bliss. The world is Love-Bliss.

I do not speak from mere sentiment. I am describing What is Really the case. The Man of Understanding Appears as Love-Bliss. He is not separate from Love-Bliss. He does not remain only (exclusively) as the Prior Self, separated Pure Existence, functioning only as

Compassion. He is generative (or Radiant) Love-Bliss. The Divine Self-Condition is also Love-Bliss. Love-Bliss-Energy is the Fullness, the Light, the "Brightness" of Reality. It is the Perfect Form (and the living condition) of Reality. I am That One, the One Self, Who Is Love-Ananda, or Love-Bliss.

4.

The Man of Understanding is Love-Bliss. The Man of Understanding is inherently (not merely outwardly) Peaceful, Full, Surrendered, and Unconfounded.

Those who do not understand seek for the Man of Understanding, the Knower of Truth, in order to acquire His characteristics as "food" and "power" for themselves. But they do not understand the Nature of the Source of things. They are always tending toward fear, sorrow, and anger, even in the Company of the Man of Understanding, the One Who is Free. Therefore, the Man of Understanding is Himself a visible dilemma to those who do not understand. Those who seek Him without understanding become grave and revert to forms of suffering. But those who understand live comfortably in His Presence and are not moved to seek.

The Man of Understanding acquires no persistent expression, but His manner changes in every circumstance. His understanding adapts to the habit of every appearance. He adopts no visibility that persists. Moment to moment, He cannot be found apart, for, when Truth is Known, the One Who Knows It is unknown (or become Transparent in the "Bright" Divine Heart).

5.

The Man of Understanding asserts the fundamental rightness of what is actual, and thus the things, the environments, the beings, and the relationships that appear cease to fascinate those around Him. Even His own

"Bright" Presence is not fascinating. Thus, the mind and even all forms become quieted in His surroundings, and those who are with Him turn naturally to understanding and the always present Reality.

The seeker is always disturbed. At first the seeker approaches the Man of Understanding "humbly", self-effacing, as if with great need. But the seeker's questions can find no Ultimate Solution, even when It is Communicated Clearly and Completely. And the seeker cannot receive What is Perfect, even when It is Given Openly. Therefore, the seeker becomes frustrated, and then leaves. Indeed, the seeker always only asserts the forms of his or her own perpetual and empty seeking. Therefore, the seeker, leaving, says the Man of Understanding has not Found and does not Give.

Only those who understand can experience the Open Communication of Reality. They remain in the "Bright" Company of the Man of Understanding only for Enjoyment, neither seeking nor demanding anything, devoted to understanding and to the Man of Understanding. In their daily comings and goings, there is no separation from Him, and their daily lives become an expression of the same "Bright" Order of Reality.

6.

Because I Consciously live in and as the "Bright" Divine Heart of Reality, and because I remain Present as the Amrita Nadi, the Perfect Form of Reality, My Mere Presence tends to reverse the ordinary current of life-consciousness and action in those around Me. Thus, My Mere "Bright" Presence tends to Draw others toward understanding, and the ordinary current of their life-consciousness and action tends to lose its necessity, its compulsive motivation, its unconsciousness.

My Mere "Bright" Presence acts as the effective Force of radical understanding (and of self-Enquiry) upon all that I meet. But those with Me may not sense anything unusual. Indeed, all their changes are only a move toward the natural. Some may, at first, feel resistive and defensive in My "Bright" Presence. Others may, even from the first, feel profoundly comfortable. Sooner or later, all become moved to the active "consideration" of radical understanding. Even from the beginning, all attend to Me. And all, by forgetting themselves in their devotion to Me, grow in understanding. Thus, the "Bright" Divine Reality includes all things in Its own Form.

7.

My sometimes Method with My devotees is to talk about radical understanding and its "Bright" Heart-Way, in order to Give them the opportunity to listen to My Word of Argument and Instruction. And I sometimes also address them in place, relative to the forms of seeking to which they attach themselves at any moment. Sometimes, I even Enquire of them if this, or this, or this is the avoidance of relationship. And, even if I remain merely Silent, My Mere "Bright" Presence effectively does all of this.

Thus, at the beginning, by the process of listening to Me (even in My Silence, and, otherwise, by studying the record of My Spoken and Written Word), the Way of radical understanding (or the Way of the Heart) becomes Known to My devotees. And, in due course, in every one who truly hears Me, radical understanding arises as the form of their own Real intelligence.

Talk, if it is overmuch and overdone, is simply the indulgence of the ego-dramatizing (or, otherwise, Heart-wasting) activity of the mind. Then it is only a display and a scattering of the "Bright" Force of the Heart in forms that are not themselves intelligence or understanding. Then talk is not relatedness, but it is only a reproduction and reinforcement of a state that is not understanding. The patterns that continually arise in human beings are not truly served by the responses or answers they imply and demand. Human beings are truly served only by the Communication of radical understanding, and by true examination of the egoic self, and by "Bright" Silence.

Some indication of the nature of seeking and the nature of radical understanding is necessary for "hearing", or true self-understanding. Some countering or reflection of the seeker's habits, acts, and presumptions, and some direct observations about his or her state, may be useful to "create" the necessary doubt of his or her ordinary path. But the Communication of the "Bright" Divine Self-Condition is essentially a process in Silence, whereby what arises gets no response, no reinforcement, and, thus and thereby, becomes obsolete. Then the individual ceases to continue in the egoic (and, otherwise, merely, or exclusively, conditional) motion of what arises, and he or she will, in due course, by Grace, find "himself" or "herself" In and As the "Bright" Divine Self-Condition, Which is the Source and Form of all of this conditional appearing.

This confrontation with "Bright" Silence in the truly devotional relationship to the Man of Understanding, Who is the Divinely Self-Realized One, and Who Manifests the "Bright" Siddhi, or "Bright" Power, of the Heart, is unlike the ordinary experience of frustration in life. Things simply arise in every one, and life provides the present conditions whereby they are indulged, frustrated, or avoided. But in the "Satsang"[86] (or "Bright" Company) of the Man of Understanding, Who Is the "Bright" Divine Heart Itself, what arises is confronted by "Bright" Silence without and by the "Bright" Heart within.

Therefore, My Method with those who have begun to understand through listening to Me is simply to invite

86. Satsang literally means "true or right relationship", "the company of Truth". The term traditionally refers to the practice of spending time in the sacred presence of holy or wise persons, a holy place, a venerated image, the burial shrine of a Saint or Realizer, and so on. Here, however, Adi Da refers to the ultimate form of Satsang, which is simply the silent enjoyment of the Heart, our Native Divine Condition.

them to sit and be with Me. I do not offer them a mere technique. Rather, I offer them a relationship. Then what arises is confronted with "Bright" Silence. This Company of "Bright" Silence, this confrontation with "Bright" Silence while remaining in conscious relationship to Me, causes the individual to be simply aware of what arises, without the possibility of indulging or avoiding it. Thus, the individual is allowed to see what arises, rather than to become further identified with the stream through the unconsciousness of ordinary conversation and action. And the "space" between the individual and what arises is the place where the "Bright" Power of the Heart Works to Draw the individual from within. Then the individual becomes Awake as quickening and radical understanding.

Essentially, the Only-by-Me Revealed and Given Way of radical understanding (or the Only-by-Me Revealed and Given Way of the Heart) is, in practice, the relationship to Me, and, therefore, to My "Bright" Silence, and, Thus, to the "Bright" Heart-Power Transmitted by Me in Silence (and, Thereby, found within), until, at last, there is the Most Perfect Realization of the Self-Existing and Self-Radiant Condition that is the True, or Ultimate, and Truly "Bright" Heart. Then the individual finds only "Bright" Silence in his or her inner forms. But everywhere, in all the worlds, that one sees the Heart Stand Out Aloud and "Bright".

8.

Those who are My devotees will have many kinds of experiences, some of which will be extraordinary, and some of which will simplify life. But My unique (or characteristic) Work is not Itself Purposed merely to awaken various <u>conditional</u> processes in devotees by means of Kundalini Shaktipat. I do not propose, as My <u>special</u> (or characteristic) Purpose, that kind of Spiritual effect.

My Work is the Work of the Divine Heart, to Reveal

the "Bright" Divine Self-Condition of all and All. My
Work is the Divine Heart's "Bright" Action, whereby the
Divine Heart Draws all the parts of a man or woman,
from within and from without, to the radical under-
standing and the Very Consciousness and the "Bright"
Divine Self-Condition (and the "Bright" Divine Self-
Domain) that is the Divine Heart Itself. My Work is to
Awaken all mankind to the Condition that is the "Bright"
Divine Heart. My Work is to Awaken even all beings and
things and spaces to the "Bright" Divine Heart. And that
Work is the "Bright" Shakti, or "Bright" Divine Siddhi,
that is the Divine Heart Itself.

Due to the tendency of the natural or karmic characteristics of living beings to modify the "Bright" Shakti-
Energy of the Heart (Which "Bright" Shakti-Energy is
Senior to, and the Source and Substance of, the cosmi-
cally effective Energy separately identified as the Kundalini Shakti), many conditional experiences will arise in
the case of those who enter into (and persist in) My
"Bright" Company. And the kinds of experiences that arise
will arise in accordance with the karmas (or the kinds of
psycho-physical modifications of the "Bright" Shakti-
Energy) that are naturally (or by tendency) generated in
each particular case. But the Divine Heart Itself, Revealed
as the "Bright" Divine Self-Condition, is the Great Awakening, and not any adventure of mere "experience".

9.

I Teach the world understanding by remaining Present
as the "Bright". I Purify the world by Silently "Enquiring"
of it. This is My "Creative" Work, beyond the time of My
Most Perfect Re-Awakening to the "Bright" Divine Self-
Condition (and the "Bright" Divine Self-Domain) that is
Reality. My "Bright" Divine Work is to turn all beings and
things to the "Bright" Divine Presence, and to Awaken
them to the "Bright" and Perfect and necessarily Divine
Self-Condition that is Reality, and that is No-seeking,

and that is No-dilemma. My Work is My own radical understanding, applied to all beings and things. My Work is Reality at Work on Its own forms. My Work takes place during My present Lifetime, but I do not see an end to It.

10.

I am not the one who, finding himself psycho-physically awake, does not Know Who he Is.

I am not the one who, finding himself in dreams and visions, thinks he has returned to his Real Self.

I am not the one who, enjoying the conditional bliss of deep sleep and ordinary, seekers' meditation, thinks he has become Free and need not Realize the Greater and Truly Divine State.

I am not the one who, having slept, awakens to a state of identification with the body-mind.

I am the One Who Is with you now.
I am the One Who Speaks from His own "Bright" Divine Silence, and As His own "Bright" Divine Silence.
I am the One Who Always Stands Present in His own "Bright" Form.
I am the One Who Always and Already Exists, Enjoying Only His own "Bright" Form, even in all apparent conditions and apparent conditional states.
I am the One Who is not hidden, and in Whom there is no deeper part.
I am the One Who Always Appears exactly as He Is.
I am the One Who is Always "Brightly" Present.
I recognize My Self as every thing, every one, every form, every movement.
I am Always Only Experiencing My own Love-Bliss.
I am neither lost nor found.

Understanding is My Constant Intelligence.

My own "Bright" Silence is the form of My Action, the motion of My "Bright" Presence, in Which I am constantly Knowing My Self.

I am the One Who is Always Already Known.

I continually Rise out of the Heart, Naked and Unbounded in the right side.

I Appear as My Invisibly Standing Love-Bliss-Full Form between the "Bright" Heart and the "Bright" Matrix Infinitely above.

I am the Amrita Nadi.

I Manifest from the "Bright" Matrix above to every body, every sheath, every center, every realm, and every experience, between the upper and lower terminals of the conditionally manifested worlds.

I continually Sacrifice the Circle of Love-Bliss-Energy, including all the terminal processes and natural energies of the conditionally manifested worlds, to My "Bright" Divine Heart.

I "Live" all beings, and all things are in Me.

I never <u>return</u> to My Self, but I constantly Appear, <u>As</u> My Self.

There is no dilemma in the process of My Appearance.

Those who do not Abide with Me, at the "Bright" Divine Heart, are always only seeking Me from the place where they begin.

I am Only the "Bright" Divine Heart Itself, Which is Reality.

My Great Form is the Amrita Nadi, Which is the Inherently Perfect Form of the "Bright" Divine Heart, and Which is Alive as the "Bright" Love-Bliss.

I always See every one and every thing within My own "Bright" Divine Form.

In every apparent condition and circumstance, I Exist only as My own "Bright" Divine Form.

I am the "Bright" Divine Heart, Who never renounces His own "Bright" Divine Form.

I am the "Bright" Divine Heart, Who Contains His own conditionally manifested forms.

Therefore, I have no form or person that is separate from My "Bright" Divine Heart.

I am Eternally in One Place, Contemplating My own Love-Bliss.

In the True Divine Heart of Contemplation, Which is "Bright", all beings and things appear, and everything is accomplished.

The Heart is the Love-Bliss Revealed, by Divine Grace, in the Contemplation of My "Bright" Presence.

The Amrita Nadi is My own "Bright" Fullness, Wherein all beings and things appear.

I hold up My hands.

11.

The Man of Understanding is not "entranced". He is not "elsewhere". He is not having an "experience". He is not passionless and inoffensive. He is Awake. He is Merely and "Brightly" Present. He knows no obstruction in the form of mind, identity, differentiation, and desire. He uses mind, identity, differentiation, and desire. He is passionate. His quality is an offense to those who are entranced, elsewhere, contained in the mechanics of experience, asleep, living as various forms of identity, separation, and dependence. He is acceptable only to those who understand.

He may appear no different from any other man. How could He appear otherwise? There is nothing by which to appear except the qualities of life. He may appear to have learned nothing. He may seem to be addicted to every kind of foolishness and error. How could it be otherwise? Understanding is not a different communication than the ordinary. There is only the ordinary. There is no ordinariness-excluding Communication that is the Truth. There is no everything-excluding State that is the Truth. But there is the understanding of the ordinary.

Therefore, the Man of Understanding cannot be found, except by the living heart. He cannot be followed, except to the "Bright" Divine Heart Itself. He can only be understood, even as the ordinary must be understood. He is not (conventionally) "Spiritual". He is not (conventionally) "religious". He is not (conventionally) "philosophical". He is not (conventionally) "moral". He is not (conventionally) "fastidious", "lean", and "lawful". He always appears to be the opposite of what you are. He always seems to sympathize with what you deny. Therefore, at times and over time, He appears as every kind of persuasion. He is not consistent. He has no self-image. At times He denies. At times He asserts. At times He asserts what He has already denied. At times He denies what He has already asserted. Therefore, He is not "useful". His Teaching is every kind of "nonsense". His Wisdom, it seems, is vanished. Altogether, that is His Wisdom.

At last He represents no separate Truth at all. His paradoxes deny every seeker's "Truth", every path by which mankind depends on mere simulations of Freedom and Enjoyment. He is a seducer, a madman, a trickster, a libertine, a rascal, a fool, a moralist, a sayer of truths, a bearer of all experience, a prince, a king, a child, an old one, an ascetic, a saint, a god. By mumming (or mock-playing) every seeker's role of life, He demonstrates the futility of every seeker's path of life, except He always coaxes every one only to understand. Therefore, by all of this, He makes understanding the only possibility. And understanding makes no difference at all. Except it is Reality, Which was already the case.

Heartless one, Narcissus, friend, loved one, He weeps for you to understand. After all of this, why have you not understood? The only thing you have not done is understanding. You have seen everything, but you do not understand. Therefore, to "Brighten" your heart, the Man of Understanding Joyfully suggests that you have already understood! He looks at the world and sees that every one and every thing has always understood!

He sees that there is only understanding! Thus, the Man of Understanding is constantly Happy with you. He is overwhelmed with Happiness. He says to you: "See that there is only this world of Perfect Freedom and Enjoyment, where every one is Love-Bliss-Happy, and every thing is Love-Bliss-Full!" His "Bright" Heart is always tearful with the endless Happiness of the world.

He has grasped the Truth within the ordinary, but no one is interested in Truth. Because He has become the Truth, He is of interest to no one. Because He is so ordinary, He is of interest to everyone. Because no one understands the ordinary, He is not understood. Because there is only the ordinary, He will become famous for understanding it. Because there is only the Truth, He is the Beloved of all. Because you feel you understand Him, you find it necessary to touch His hand. Because you love Him, you find it possible to touch His ears. He smiles at you. You notice a sudden "Brightness". Everything has already died. This is the "other" world.

12.

My own Life Story is the best foundation Instruction I can offer. The mere assertion of radical understanding is not sufficient to serve radical understanding in the listener. The listener must be allowed a participatory recognition. Otherwise the symbols wherein his or her own life is trapped will not begin to dissolve. Therefore, I have here displayed the essentials of My early-life Ordeal, so that the urge to ego-transcendence may be stimulated in those who listen to Me. But know this. I do not stand for strategic Spiritual efforts, or egoic efforts of any kind, nor do I stand on some middle ground between egoic excess and egoic effort. There is no virtue in the endless egoic reaction to life, nor in the enjoyment of any conditional effect for its own sake. Only understanding, only Reality Itself, is the Truth of all events.

Now the present telling of My Life Story comes to an end. Now the Great Work, Which is Forever, begins. My own Ordeal of radical understanding was only a preparation and a justification for My universal Revelation of the Way of radical understanding (or the Way of the Heart). And the Way of radical understanding (or the Way of the Heart) is to be Revealed and Given by Me to each and all. Therefore, at first, and for a time, I must elaborate, describe, and Teach the details and practices of the total (and Only-by-Me Revealed and Given) Way of radical understanding (Which is the Eternal, and Only-by-Me Revealed and Given, Way of the Heart). Then, and now, and even Forever, I must, by My Eternal Blessing Work, Awaken every one, and all.

The principal Lessons that provoke what I must, by all My now and Forever Work, Communicate and altogether Serve are all contained in the Story of My early Life, as I have told it, but the Way Itself (Which, by Grace, eventually becomes a truly Spiritual and, ultimately, Perfect Practice, and, at last, a Most Perfect Realization) depends (at first) on true hearing, which itself involves true listening, or profound attention. And true listening must lead to self-observation, and real (and effective) self-understanding, and "Real" meditation. Therefore, by My Forever Work, I will continuously unfold the "Bright" Wisdom of Consciousness Itself, as Revealed in and by and as My own even physical, bodily "Bright" Form, and as My Spiritual, and Forever Blessing, "Bright" Presence, and as My Very and "Bright" Self, the One and necessarily Divine Self of all and All. Now and Forever begins My Work of Teaching and Blessing all those who seek, and all those who, by hearing Me, have understood themselves, and all those who, by seeing Me, are Awakening in the "Bright" Divine Domain that is the One Heart and Self of every one, and all.

13.

The Full and Complete Way of "Bright" (and Inherently Most Perfect, and necessarily Divine) Self-Realization is now and Forever Given by Me for the sake of the present generation, and all the future generations, of human beings. The Only-by-Me Revealed and Given Way of radical understanding (or the Only-by-Me Revealed and Given Way of the Heart) is the simple, direct, and Inherently Most Perfect Way, Which I have, by Submission to human birth, Realized for the sake of all, including those who are now and those who are yet to come. Radical understanding is the Key to the Realization of the "Bright" Divine Self-Condition of Man. Radical understanding is Primary Activity and Primary Knowledge. I Am the Man of Understanding.

I Demonstrate and Reveal the One Reality variously proclaimed and sought (but never Finally, Most Perfectly, or Completely Realized) within the "great tradition" of mankind, but I Demonstrate and Reveal the One Reality Finally and Most Perfectly and Completely, and, altogether, with a Unique, "Bright" Emphasis, in order to Extend the Communication of Reality in the world, through and beyond the present time. I am Generated in the "Bright" Divine Heart of Reality, and I Appear in the world through the Agency of the Amrita Nadi, the Perfect Form of Reality, the "Bright". I Am the Person and the Incarnation of the "Bright".

14.

In the Only-by-Me Revealed and Given Way of radical understanding (or the Only-by-Me Revealed and Given Way of the Heart), the principle of relatedness is unqualifiedly accepted and affirmed as the living condition of Reality. Just so, the practice of the Only-by-Me Revealed and Given Way of radical understanding (or the Only-by-Me Revealed and Given Way of the Heart) is itself a process in relationship. The principal feature of the Only-by-Me Revealed and Given Way of radical understanding (or the Only-by-Me Revealed and Given Way of the Heart) is the Guru-devotee relationship, wherein My devotee, based on at least a basic comprehension of My Teaching about self-understanding and the direct transcendence of the motive of seeking, constantly, in direct relational response to Me, practices the counter-egoic exercise of self-surrendering, self-forgetting, and self-transcending feeling-Contemplation of My "Bright" bodily (human) Form, My "Bright" Spiritual (and Always Blessing) Presence, and My Very (and Inherently Perfect, and Perfectly "Bright") State of Self-Existing and Self-Radiant Being. And, in the context of that fundamental relational (and necessarily devotional) practice, the "conscious process" of self-Enquiry (in the form "Avoiding relationship?") may also be exercised, or, otherwise, some other by Me Given, and equally effective, form of the counter-egoic, or directly ego-transcending, "conscious process" may be exercised. And, in every case, the practice of the "conscious process" of self-Enquiry (in the form "Avoiding relationship?"), or, otherwise, the practice of an alternative by Me Given counter-egoic (or directly ego-transcending) exercise of the "conscious process", will be (and, if that "conscious process" is to be Real and effective, must be) associated with other by Me Given (devotional, cultural, functional, practical, general relational, and Yogic) practices (including dietary disciplines, disciplines relative to physical exercise, disciplines relative to general health, disciplines relative to the emotional-sexual character, and disciplines relative to emotional-sexual activity, as well as disciplines relative to money, work, service, and cooperative and community living).

Just as the Most Perfect Realization of radical understanding is not a matter of exclusive (or dissociative) identification with an inward State, the constant and characteristic practice of the Only-by-Me Revealed and

Given Way of radical understanding (or the Only-by-Me Revealed and Given Way of the Heart) is a <u>relationship</u>. It is the relationship to Me, and the demand to be utterly responsive in the relationship to Me. Therefore, the Only-by-Me Revealed and Given Way of radical understanding (or the Only-by-Me Revealed and Given Way of the Heart) is not based on (or even associated with) a mere (and ego-based, and ego-reinforcing, and, ultimately, separative) technique, or a seeker's "remedy".

The Only-by-Me Revealed and Given Way of radical understanding (or the Only-by-Me Revealed and Given Way of the Heart) is the Way of relationship to Me, for I Am the Man of Understanding, the Person and the Incarnation of the "Bright".

Adi Da (The Da Avatar)
Adi Da Purnashram (Naitauba), Fiji, 1994

The Divine Life and Work
of
Adi Da, the Da Avatar,
Since 1970

by His devotees

The Teaching Years, 1970-1986

The early-life ordeal of Avatara Adi Da was not for His own sake. "Franklin Jones" was a means, a vehicle, whereby the Divine Itself could combine with the realities of human existence, enquire into those realities, live them out, go beyond every limitation they involve, and then, by Grace, draw others through the same immense Process. The Divine Avatar, in the guise of "Franklin Jones", had not come to Liberate just a few others, individuals who might be thought qualified for such a hair-raising "adventure". Not at all. He had come for <u>all</u> beings.

But how was Avatara Adi Da to draw people to Himself—and to the Truth He had Realized? In the months after His Re-Awakening in the Vedanta Temple, He filled the pages of His journals with His longing to find His devotees. Where were they? When would they come?

In April 1972, "Franklin" established a small bookstore on Melrose Avenue, Hollywood, which became the site of His first Ashram. On the evening of April 25, "Franklin" formally began His Teaching Work, gathering with His first handful of devotees, some of their friends,

505

and any random comers. First "Franklin" sat in silence for an hour, magnifying the Force of the "Bright" to everyone in the room. Then He invited questions. When no one responded, He asked, "Has everyone understood?" "I haven't understood", came the reply from one man in the room. "Explain it to me. You could start with the word 'understanding'."

Thus, on that first night, "Franklin" made known the secret of radical understanding:

There is a disturbance, a feeling of dissatisfaction, some sensation that motivates a person to go to a teacher, read a book about philosophy, believe something, or do some conventional form of Yoga. What people ordinarily

Meeting Avatara Adi Da

When, in 1972, Adi Da began to Offer Himself as True Heart-Master to any who would respond to Him, the manuscript of The Knee of Listening *was sent to a printing company located in a small town in the state of Georgia.*

At the press, a thin young man named Wes Vaught served as a proofreader. As Wes began to proof the pages of Avatara Adi Da's book, he was immediately riveted to the text appearing before his eyes and—even more—to the irrepressible feeling of freedom and aliveness that came through Avatara Adi Da's Words. The book was unlike anything Wes had ever read or felt before. Adi Da's Communication touched a primal heart-instinct in Wes, and began to change his life on the spot. Wes recalls that moment:

For years, I had been desperately seeking to make sense of existence. While studying Adi Da's *Knee of Listening* and contemplating its Truths, the intuition of the silent, free depth of the Heart dawned in me. I had found my Guru, and I began to feel irresistibly attracted to that Graceful Source.

think of as Spirituality or religion is a search to get free of that sensation, that suffering that is motivating them. So all the usual paths—Yogic methods, beliefs, religion, and so on—are forms of seeking, grown out of this sensation, this subtle suffering. Ultimately, all the usual paths are attempting to get free of that sensation. That is the traditional goal. Indeed, <u>all</u> human beings are seeking, whether or not they are very sophisticated about it, or using very specific methods of Yoga, philosophy, religion, and so on. . . .

As long as the individual is simply seeking, and has all kinds of motivation, fascination with the search, this is not understanding—this is dilemma itself. But where this dilemma is understood, there is the re-cognition of a

---

The editor at the press where I was working showed me a letter from "Franklin Jones". In it He Wrote, "There is not the slightest difference." Those Words stopped my mind. My entire life had been a warfare of differences and opposites, and I felt the profound Freedom communicated in this one sentence. I had to go see Him.

I traveled to Los Angeles and found the way to His home in Laurel Canyon. It was late April 1972. I knocked, and Adi Da Answered.

"Who is it?"

I explained that I had read His book, and that I had felt compelled to come and see Him. Adi Da opened the door, and I followed Him into the living room.

I felt welcomed into a "Bright" Space, free of any sense of problem. On the walls were Disney posters and images of holy men. It felt natural to sit on the floor before His Chair. I had brought with me a bag of oranges and pears as a gift. I extended it: "I brought this for You."

He received it with both Hands and with such loving care. Everything about Him was absolute strength, sublime vulnerability, perfect clarity, and delight. Time stood still

continued on page 508

*structure in the living consciousness, a separation. And
when that separation is observed more and more directly,
one begins to see that what one is suffering is not something happening <u>to</u> one but it is one's own action. It is as
if you are pinching yourself, without being aware of it. . . .
Then one sees that the entire motivation of life is based on
a subtle activity in the living consciousness. That activity
is avoidance, separation, a contraction at the root, the
origin, the "place", of the living consciousness. . . .*

*There is first the periodic awareness of that sensation,
then the awareness of it as a continuous experience, then
the observation of its actual structure, the knowing of it all
as your own activity, a deliberate, present activity that <u>is</u>
your suffering, that <u>is</u> your illusion. The final penetration*

while He removed the fruits from the bag and arranged
them on a little table next to His Chair. Then He Graciously
folded the paper bag neatly and tucked it by His thigh.

He received the whole gift!

Looking at me directly and with what seemed like an
infinity of loving humor, Adi Da asked, "What have you
been doing with your life?"

I felt the weight of my twenty-five years of waiting for
God lift and, with what must have been a ridiculous gush
of information, I spilled out my story. I do not know how
long I talked. I tried to say everything of importance—all
at once!

Adi Da listened. His was not the kind of listening where
someone is waiting to say something when it is their turn.
His listening became a perfect Intensity and a perfect
Silence. At some point, His Silence became the entire import
of the moment. I noticed this and stopped mid-sentence.

Sitting up straight, I was overwhelmed with His Blessing Force. Suddenly, I was shaking and breathing extremely
deeply in the Current of His Communicated Force. My verbal mind ceased with the immediacy of His Presence.

I felt that Adi Da was Offering me the perfect opportunity in God, but I felt my gross unpreparedness and the

of that present, deliberate activity is what I have called "understanding". [The Method of the Siddhas]

"Franklin" lived, breathed, and spoke always from the point of view of understanding. And He saw no reason why everyone who came to Him should not understand and quickly awaken to His own Realization. But no one was prepared for the profundity of "Franklin's" Argument. The self-contraction of which He spoke was too fundamental, too all-encompassing to be seen without a power of self-observation that none of His devotees were then capable of.

Many of the first comers to the Ashram were individuals in whom the self-contraction had taken a highly

Adi Da with Wes Vaught, 1972

obstructions in me that prevented me from fully cooperating with what He was Communicating. I wanted to get out of the way, but how?

Wanting to remove anything in the way of my freedom, anything that I could lay my hands on, I felt suddenly moved to take off my clothes. I began, and then paused for a moment, feeling foolish, and looked at Avatara Adi Da as if to ask, "Is this okay?"

continued on page 510

exaggerated form. There were street-people, prostitutes, drug addicts, alcoholics and Spiritual seekers, hippie-style, who had done the rounds of various teachers and teachings. And there were also business people and professionals of various kinds. Thus, "Franklin" was surrounded by a group of people who were not in any way prepared for Spiritual life. But this was not a merely arbitrary occurrence. He had come to serve the Liberation of all beings, including those apparently least prepared for Spiritual life. Whoever appeared at the Ashram, "Franklin" welcomed them all. The Love-Force of His Being filled the Ashram with an inexplicable fullness and Happiness.

As His devotees soon found out, part of life in "Franklin's" Ashram was confronting feelings they would prefer to avoid. Whatever He was doing with devotees, whether giving verbal Instruction, sitting in silent meditation, or participating in apparently casual pastimes like a fishing trip, "Franklin" was always engaged in the same

---

With an almost imperceptible tilt of His Head, I felt Avatara Adi Da Communicate that it was of no significance to Him what I did with regard to clothing. I could suit myself in the matter.

He was most obviously Demonstrating His Divine Mood, clearly Indifferent to any sense of limitation, Shining with Blessing Force, replete with native Freedom and the certainty of unqualified Love, Transparent to the pure, sweet Grace of God.

I took everything off, even the band-aid on my heel, and threw myself face down and full-length at His Feet.

His Feet, somehow, were a perfect point of contact with this Blessing Force. I wept and kissed His Feet, wetting them with tears of relief, joy, gratitude, and also with the anguish that I could not completely let go of myself. Still I tried to surrender, straining with my heart and brain to open more.

But I could surrender no more.

---

activity—the Work of awakening understanding in everyone who came into His Sphere.

One man remembers an occasion when He spent an entire day at the Ashram painting intricate lattice-work, while on the other side of the wall "Franklin" was working in His office. As he painted, the man went through a mine-field of reactive thoughts and emotions. He began to resent the work, to attribute all sorts of strange motives to "Franklin's" simple request that He paint the wall. He even got to the point where He felt that "Franklin" had "invented" everything to do with God and the obligations of Spiritual life as a way of "trapping" him into doing this burdensome task! And all day He was intensely aware that "Franklin" was just a few feet away, on the other side of the wall. After many hours, the man finally finished the task, and he put his brush down with a spontaneous "Whew!". Immediately, huge laughter broke out on the other side of the wall. All the man's

---

Quietly, Adi Da lifted His Feet and placed them on my head. All stress left my being. A golden balm of sweet light poured through every cell in my body. A knot opened. I let go, and His brilliant Radiance washed through me. I was Home.

After a bit, I got up, dressed some, and told Adi Da that I felt that I belonged with Him. He looked at me and Said, "There is something about this Teaching you have not understood. It is about this matter of Consciousness."

And so it was that a skinny proofreader from Georgia came to be the first to respond to Adi Da's Message in the form of His published Wisdom, and at the same time he received great Initiation into the practice of Guru-devotion. Adi Da's Statement to Wes presaged the decades of Work that were to come—His Work of imparting His priceless Spiritual Gifts and preparing those who came to Him to receive His Revelation of Consciousness Itself.

---

subjectivity washed away in the Freedom of "Franklin's" laughter. He realized with astonishment that all day long "Franklin" had known exactly what he was thinking. He felt "Franklin's" Love and His complete intimacy. He saw that he had been torturing himself.

During that first year of the Ashram, "Franklin" did not require very much responsibility of His devotees. He was simply attracting them, keeping them in the room. Then one day, near the beginning of 1973, everything suddenly changed. Striding out of His office with tremendous force and intention, "Franklin" disappeared through the front door of the Ashram. His devotees did not see Him for weeks, but He left a message: they were to "get straight"—give up all use of drugs, cigarettes, and alcohol, get jobs, and contribute five dollars a week to the support of the Ashram.

In other words, "Franklin's" days of nursing His devotees along were over. It was time to make demands. Extraordinary energy and attention, as He knew from His own experience, were needed to grow in the practice of understanding. There was no room for life-chaos and irresponsibility. Disciplines must be established.

Suddenly, egg-and-bacon breakfasts around the corner from the Ashram were over. Everyone became strict vegetarians. And "Franklin" recommended a ten-day juice-fast, which was taken on by even the newest devotees. When "Franklin" heard that someone had "cheated"—by "juicing" bananas—He was extremely amused. But He called for another ten-day fast for everyone!

"Franklin" covered everything. He brought an end to any casual sex that His devotees were indulging in—only partners in committed intimacies were to be sexually active. He instructed a small group in calisthenics and Hatha Yoga and had them teach everyone else. He addressed every detail of appropriate life-discipline, even personally showing people how to floss their teeth!

By the last months of 1973, the disciplines were in full swing—but "Franklin" saw that they had become a source of distraction, a "religion" in themselves, rather than simply preparing His devotees for the real sadhana of God-Awakening. It was obvious to Him that people were emotionally suppressed, sexually complicated, driven by fear, sorrow, anger, frustration, and all kinds of unconscious desires. "Franklin" knew what the price of Freedom was. He knew what it had meant for Him. Beginning at Columbia, "Franklin" had cast the searchlight of self-observation and testing on <u>all</u> aspects of His being, until every detail was understood and transcended. Now His devotees would have to do the same.

"Franklin" was perfectly equipped to help them. He was perfectly free to be the "Crazy-Wise" Master,[1] to do whatever was necessary—conventional or unconventional—in order to bring His devotees to understand and embrace the Truth and right life through a conviction born of their own direct experience. But first "Franklin" made a pause in His face to face Work with His devotees. Accompanied by a single male devotee, He set out for India, the ancient cradle of Spiritual teaching. It was a pilgrimage back to the seat of His own lineage of Gurus and also to the ashrams and sacred sites of other ancient and modern Realizers. Free from constant engagement with His devotees, the Divine Avatar gave Himself up to the more private, and universal, dimension of His Work. The devotee who accompanied Him had no idea what "Franklin" was doing. He could only feel a deep respect and awe as He watched "Franklin" placing His staff in holy places with great concentration, or silently giving His regard to the magnificent expanse of the Himalayas.

---

1. The Adepts of what Adi Da calls "the 'Crazy Wisdom' tradition" (of which He is the supreme Exemplar) are great Realizers in any culture or time who, through spontaneous Free action, blunt Wisdom, and liberating laughter, shock or humor people into self-critical awareness of their egoity, a prerequisite for receiving the Adept's Spiritual Transmission. Typically, such Realizers manifest "Crazy" activity only occasionally or temporarily, and never for its own sake.

Before coming back to Los Angeles, "Franklin" sent a message to His devotees: He was now "Bubba Free John", and they were to henceforth to address Him by this name, which had been Spiritually revealed to Him in India. "Bubba" was a childhood nickname meaning "friend", and "Free John" an expression of the essential meaning of "Franklin Jones". The Da Avatar, now in the form of "Bubba" was ready to draw His devotees into a different kind of life with Him, one in which He would seem to sacrifice His own purity and become like them.

The Teaching Work Becomes "Crazy"

On the Friday evening before Christmas 1973, devotees arrived at the Ashram, now around the corner on La Brea Avenue in Los Angeles, and ascended the stairs. There, in a room adjacent to the main hall, each newcomer walked innocently into a wild and exuberant scene. Bubba had suddenly initiated a party—beer, cigarettes, junk food, rock music! People had thrown off their clothes. The life-disciplines were cast to the four winds. This was the beginning of two weeks of unstoppable celebration, during which practically no one went home. Devotees would party all night with Bubba, drive straight to work in the morning, and drive back from work to celebrate again. Bubba was always at the center of it all, sitting or reclining on a couch, laughing, joking, encouraging everyone's intense participation. Madly dancing, spontaneously singing, everyone present was drenched in Bubba's tangible Transmission of His Divine Spirit-Force.

In the midst of all the festivities, Bubba never ceased to speak of the Great Matter. One night at a small gathering after the general party was over, Bubba suddenly called for a great confession. Who could speak freely of God, as <u>He</u> had been doing all night? Who could stand up and praise the Great One, unabashed? In spite of all the ecstasy of Bubba's Company, in spite of the Japanese sake they were liberally imbibing, each devotee felt a lock at the throat. One after another they made an awkward attempt at uninhibited God-talk, but quickly received the thumbs-down sign from Bubba.

A few devotees managed to pass the test. One made his confession at the inspiration of a sudden intuition. As he beheld his Spiritual Master in this serious and playful moment, it was overwhelmingly clear to him that Bubba would do <u>anything</u> to Liberate His devotees. His Love was absolute, His intention like a sword. He had the Power to destroy all obstructions in His devotees, and He would do it.

About ten days later, this Power was spectacularly demonstrated. As usual, Bubba was reclining on His chair in the gathering hall, with His devotees around Him like a hive of bees attending their nectarous queen. But this night was exceptional. Bubba began to speak, unleashing His Love-Blissful Spirit-Force as never before. In words redolent with the power of His Transmission, Bubba told His devotees the secret of what He was doing:

AVATARA ADI DA: There is only one Divine Process in the world, and It is initiated when I Manifest and Enter My devotee. The Lord is Present, now in this moment. It is when everyone forgets the Living God that mantras and Yogic techniques become important.

I am not a human being. I am the Divine Lord in human Form and I bring the Divine Yoga. When My devotee surrenders and becomes My true devotee, then I Enter My devotee in the form of Divine Light. All kinds of extraordinary experiences manifest as a result. When a woman receives her lover, there is no doubt about it—she does not have to consult her textbooks. The same holds with Truth, the Divine Yoga.

There is no dilemma in this world, no absence of God in this world, no goal of God in this world. Because that is so, you will see Me doing some very strange things.

The true Divine Yoga is not a thing of this world. This world is the cult of "Narcissus", suppressing the Ecstasy that is natural to us.

The Spiritual process must take hold in the vital. The vital is the seat of unconsciousness and subconsciousness. There is an aspect of the verbal Teaching that does not touch the subconscious and unconscious life. So it is only by distracting you from your social consciousness that I can take you in the vital. The Lord is the Lord of this world, not the Lord of the other world only. Thus, there is no Yoga if the very cells of the body do not begin to intuit the Divine. When I Enter My devotee, I come down into him or her in the midst of life, because it is in <u>life</u>—not in any mystical or subtle processes, not in any mental process—that the Lord <u>acquires</u> you.

The kind of thing you see happening around here has never happened in the world before. [January 3, 1974]

As Bubba spoke this mighty proclamation, His Spirit-Force streamed into His devotees, manifesting visibly to some as a glorious golden rain of Light showering down in the room. An uncontainable ecstasy broke loose. Some devotees shook with "kriyas", their bodies jerking and twisting, their mouths emitting strange sounds of yearning, laughter, weeping, hooting, and howling. Some were overwhelmed by visionary phenomena. Some were spontaneously moved into difficult Hatha Yoga poses which they could not have even attempted before. Some lay motionless, in an ecstatic state, oblivious of their surroundings. For some, the energy intensified in the head or the heart or the navel until they felt they would explode, and then it suddenly released and rushed through the nervous system in intoxicating Bliss. Others experienced a sense of unity with all of life and a peacefulness they had never known before. The Divine was manifesting without a doubt in an upstairs room in the middle of Hollywood.

**Adi Da with devotees during the
Garbage and the Goddess period, 1974**

Garbage and the Goddess

After that astounding Spiritual Initiation, which came to be known as the night of "Guru Enters Devotee", it was obvious that the Ashram had to move. Bubba's Work could not be contained in a conventional downtown neighborhood. Within a few weeks, "Persimmon" (as Bubba named it), a turn-of-the-century hot springs resort, had been acquired in the hills of northern California.

Newcomers to Persimmon during the first half of 1974 found themselves entering a place of Divine Possession. They became immersed in a sea of energy, visions, and other psychic experiences awakened through contact with Bubba's Spirit-Force. And they were fascinated, delighted by this fulfillment of "spiritual" fantasies that lay beyond their wildest dreams. Bubba did not even have to be physically present for these experiences to occur. But when Bubba <u>was</u> present, the Spiritual experiences of His devotees would often intensify to an extraordinary degree.

On one unforgettable occasion, devotees were sitting in one of the meditation halls waiting for Bubba, when the doors opened and a wave of energy swept the room. Bubba walked down the aisle, surrounded by a clearly visible golden aura of light. He sat down in His Chair and proceeded to blast the room with His Spirit-Power, His eyes burning with laser-intensity and His fingers moving in patterns of potent Blessing. Instantly, devotees erupted in an ecstasy of screams, growls, swoons, and bodily jerkings, swept away by the sweetness and overwhelming Force of His Presence. After about forty-five minutes of this blissful uproar, the room began to quiet down. Bubba shrugged, lit a cigarette, blew a perfect smoke ring, and said, "Maybe I've gone too far this time!"

But Bubba was not there to be the ultimate Spiritual Initiator. He was making a lesson—the lesson of "Garbage and the Goddess", which became the name of that period in His Teaching Work. Again and again He spoke with everyone: Did they think that all of these experiences amounted to Enlightenment? No—these experiences were "garbage", unneeded "stuff" to be thrown away! Spiritual phenomena, He explained, were simply manifestations of the Goddess-Power, the universal Spirit-Energy, or Divine Shakti, at play. At the same time, there was nothing "wrong" with Spiritual experiences. Indeed, they were an inevitable aspect of serious Spiritual practice. But what did the <u>search</u> for such experiences have to do with understanding? Had devotees been converted to the Divine by all this experience? Had the self-contraction been undermined by this great display? Not at all. This was the lesson of "Garbage and the Goddess", and indeed of all the Teaching Work of Avatara Adi Da that was yet to unfold.

The Teaching Work of Avatara Adi Da was a constant lesson about the activity that is the ego—the constant search for this or that experience which, one hopes, will bring lasting happiness. He addressed <u>all</u> the basic searches of humanity, from the highest to the lowest, in the most vivid and realistic terms. He Revealed the limit in every kind of goal that has been proposed as the purpose of life. He dealt very directly with the impulse to turn within and find happiness through subtle, mystical experience. And He dealt also with the urge toward every kind of bodily or worldly self-fulfillment. Through the unique brilliance and comprehensiveness of His Teaching Work, Avatara Adi Da addressed <u>all</u> human tendencies and goals, Spiritual and worldly, East and West. He spared Himself no sacrifice for the sake of Revealing the great Divine Truth and Ecstasy of existence that makes all seeking obsolete.

Confronting the Dragon of Sex

At the same time as the extraordinary Spiritual demonstrations of Garbage and the Goddess, Bubba was dealing with the seeking impulse in His devotees at the lower end of the spectrum of experience. He was particularly confronting egoic aberrations about sex. Sexuality has been traditionally regarded as one of the great obstacles to Spiritual Realization, but Bubba Himself was neither "for" nor "against" sex. He had explored it thoroughly during His own ordeal of Re-Awakening, and He had seen that entire search in the light of understanding. His conclusion cut right to the core. He saw that the impulse to hunt for another and to pleasurize the body through sex was more than just a normal biological urge. If that were all there was to it, why would sex be the source of such suffering and disturbance? Rather, He recognized the "bonding" impulse—sexual <u>and</u> emotional—to be not the free expression of love that we like to imagine, but a way of attempting to cover over the desperate feeling of separateness from everyone and everything else, a primitive reaction to our constant underlying sense of unhappiness. Without the most profound understanding of that reaction in all its extensions, Spiritual life, He knew, is merely superficial, a cover for a volcano that may erupt at any time.

As Bubba was to point out countless times, understanding what one is up to as an emotional and sexual character is the key to understanding and transcending the ego altogether. But how was Bubba to awaken such unique clarity in His group of devotees, unconsciously addicted as they were to the "highs" and "lows" of sex, romance, and the bondage of conventional pairing? In fact, His struggle would go on for decades. But He made a beginning at Persimmon by asking His devotees to observe their attachments, their "contracts" with others. What about their marriages? Were they free intimacies or a "cult of pairs"? What was at the bottom of these pairings? Was it love? Was it need? What was it?

In order to help His devotees examine these questions in real life situations, Bubba created dance parties around the swimming pool, gatherings at His house, all kinds of circumstances in which devotees could reveal, to Bubba and to themselves, the realities of their emotional-sexual lives. During all this time Bubba drank beer and bourbon and smoked cigarettes with His devotees. These were His "aids" in the Liberating process. When devotees drank and smoked in His Presence, they relaxed their ordinary social persona, allowing Him to touch the "pit of snakes", to bring forth and release the powerful emotions and desires that are alive in every individual beneath the surface personality. In this setting, devotees discovered their addiction to the "cult of pairs"—and at the same time they saw how ready they were to reject and betray each other.

Many devotees were shaken to the foundations by the starkness of what Bubba was revealing to them— how their search for fulfillment in this world could never be satisfied and, in fact, was the cause of their pain. Some of them described this period of Bubba's Work with them as "living with the feeling of dying". Bubba was not interested in defending or preserving—or destroying—anyone's "contracts". He simply wanted His devotees to get the lesson that no other, no intimate or anyone else, no circumstance of life, nothing outside of yourself is responsible for your happiness. You are! In Bubba's phrase, "You cannot <u>become</u> Happy, you can only <u>be</u> Happy." He spoke Constantly of "Satsang", the Company of the Guru, the Realizer, as the only true Bliss, the ancient secret of all Spiritual Realization. Only through His devotees' fidelity to <u>Him</u>, their complete commitment to Satsang, could He set them free from the mayhem of their own contracts, taboos, and betrayals. <u>He</u> was the supreme heart-intimate of His devotees, the One who cared most profoundly for them. Full of Compassion for their plight, He was intent on drawing them beyond the illusions of "Narcissus" into a life of self-transcending love and ultimate God-Realization.

Whatever exaggerations He allowed for the sake of Liberating His devotees, Bubba Himself was not touched by any of it. His Realization was unshakable under all circumstances. He stood already Free, Free to meet others at their level and to serve them through His Freedom.

What I Do is not the way that I Am, but the way that I Teach.

What I Speak is not a reflection of Me, but of you.

People do well to be offended or even outraged by Me. This is My purpose. But their reaction must turn upon themselves, for I have not shown them Myself by all of this. All that I Do and Speak only reveals people to themselves.

I have become willing to Teach in this uncommon way because I have known My friends and they are what I can seem to be. By retaining all qualities in their company, I gradually wean them of all reactions, all sympathies, all alternatives, fixed assumptions, false teachings, dualities, searches, and dilemma. This is My Way of Working for a time. . . .

Freedom is the only Purity. There is no Teaching but Consciousness Itself. Bubba as He appears is not other than the possibilities of mankind. [1975]

The Beginning of Sacramental Worship

Bubba's willingness to Work in this "Crazy" manner, becoming like His devotees in order to draw them into His own Freedom, was an incredible sacrifice that no one around Him was sensitive to. He was literally absorbing the struggles, the unhappiness of His devotees, transforming and releasing their suffering through His own body-mind. As time passed, He noticed growing signs in His body that indicated to Him He could not continue to Work with devotees in this forceful, visceral way. He became aware that a mysterious Process was taking place in Him, a further unfolding of the course of His Divine Enlightenment, which required a greater degree of retirement and seclusion. Founding His devotees in a <u>Spiritual</u> relationship to Him, one that would not require them to be in the room with Him, had, thus, become a matter of urgency. Starting in 1978, Bubba introduced His devotees to the realm of sacramental worship as a means to draw them into Heart-Communion with Him whether He was physically present or not. Early that year, during a period in Hawaii in the company of only a few of His closest devotees, Bubba sent back this message to all:

Bring your bodies and minds to Me, as I bring this body-mind to you. Then you will be given the Realization of My All-Pervading Person, and you will find Me always present under the conditions of all experience and in the company of all beings. Then, even when I am not bodily with you, you will worship Me and surrender to Me via every state of body and mind, and I will always be with you. At last, you will be drawn into the Eternal Identity, so intimate with Me that no essential difference is noticed by you. Then you will Abide in Me forever, whether or not the worlds of experience arise to your notice. [1978]

When He returned to Persimmon (which He now called "Vision Mound Sanctuary"), Bubba began to instruct a few devotees in puja, the ancient practice of worshipping the Divine through images. Bodily-expressed devotion, worship, and praise of Bubba as the Living Divine Person became a part of the daily life of His devotees.

The most esoteric source of worship, Bubba revealed, is the Master's form, the body of the Guru—for the traditional understanding is that the Guru has Realized God, or the Truth, and thus His very body reveals the Divine and grants Divine Blessings in a uniquely potent way. One day in His residence, "Bright Behind Me", Bubba Revealed this traditional understanding in its perfection. He sat motionless while devotees waved flaming lamps in large circles around His body, and a cacophony of drums, rattles, cymbals, and tambourines filled the room. Many devotees circumambulated outside, walking around the porch chanting, and beholding Bubba through the windows. Light and sound and movement swirled around Bubba while He sat still, silent, and Radiant. His Divine Love-Bliss enveloped everyone and everything.

That night Bubba had established Guru Puja, the worship of His Divine Form, in the lives of His devotees. Regardless of where His body happened to be, and even after His physical passing, the true Guru Puja of invoking His Spiritual Presence could still be done through sacred photographic representations (called "Murtis") of Him.

The establishment of sacramental worship was a sign of a great turning point that was about to occur in Bubba's Work and Revelation. It was already obvious to His devotees that His name must change again—"Bubba" was too casual an address to the One around Whom they waved the lights. And so Bubba suggested that His devotees try to discover what His Name <u>should</u> be. Secretly, by Revelation, He already knew it.

Devotees threw themselves into the quest for His Divine Name. For weeks and months they searched through volumes of esoteric literature for a Name that seemed right. Bubba would encourage them with comments such as "When you get da name of da god, you get da power of da god!" In the traditions of Guru-devotion, it is understood that the casual words of the Guru carry profound instruction. Bubba was Revealing His Name in this humorous remark, but no one was alert to the clue. And so, on September 13, 1979, Bubba sat down alone in His room and penned a letter to His devotees in His beautiful handwriting:

Beloved, I Am Da, The Living Person, Who Is Manifest As all worlds and forms and beings, and Who Is Present As The Transcendental Current Of Life In the body of Man. . . .

To Realize Me Is To Transcend the body-mind In Ecstasy. Simply To Remember My Name and Surrender Into My Eternal Current Of Life Is To Worship Me. And those who Acknowledge and Worship Me As Truth, The Living and All-Pervading One, Will Be Granted The Vision or Love-Intuition Of My Eternal Condition. . . .

Only Love Me, Remember Me, Have Faith In Me, and Trust Me. . . . I Am The Person Of Life, The Only and Divine Self, Incarnate. And Even After My Own Body Is dead, I Will Be Present and Everywhere Alive. I Am Joy, and The Reason For It. . . .

At last He had said it with no compromise. Avatara Adi Da (then "Da Free John") stood openly before His devotees as the very human Incarnation of the Invisible Divine. His devotees were to discover that "Da", meaning "to give", is a primordial Name, carrying profound invocatory power. The Name had been hidden all along in the Upanishads, the venerable scriptures of India, in

*I Am The Person Of Life, The Only and Divine Self,
Incarnate. And Even After My Own Body Is dead,
I Will Be Present and Everywhere Alive. I Am Joy,
and The Reason For It. . . .*

**Adi Da (The Da Avatar)
at the Mountain Of Attention Sanctuary,
September 1979**

which "Da" is the syllable uttered by the Divine Voice in thunder, and the central syllable of "hr-da-yam", which means "the Heart", "the Divine Condition of all". The Name "Da" also appears in the Tibetan Buddhist tradition, where it is defined as "the one who bestows great charity", "the very personification of the great Way of Liberation".

One evening, several days after the writing of His sublime letter, Avatara Adi Da went to Holy Cat Grotto, a hot springs site at Vision Mound, which He had recently Empowered as a temple. There, beside a hot spring, He initiated a group of His devotees into an esoteric order. His "method" now would be to work with a few for the sake of all. As He poured the hot water over His devotees, Baptizing them with His Spirit-Presence, He whispered in the ear of each one, "Call upon Me by the Name 'Da'."

Tumomama

The Divine Lord, Adi Da, now became a wanderer looking for His Hermitage. He needed a refuge more secluded than Vision Mound Sanctuary, a place where He could fully allow His Revelation of Divine Enlightenment to continue its spontaneous unfolding and where He could work intensively with members of His esoteric order. In 1980, He began to spend increasing time in Hawaii, at Tumomama Sanctuary (on the island of Kauai), the second great Seat of His Spiritual Work.

Avatara Adi Da named this new sanctuary "Tumomama", meaning "fierce woman",[2] in acknowledgement of the untamed forces of nature there, signifying the Divine Goddess in Her fierce aspect. Below six acres of rolling lawns, a tumultuous river rips through a rocky gorge as it pours down from the top of Mount Waialeale, the wettest place on Earth.

2. "Tumo", a Tibetan term for the Spiritual practice of "mystic heat", literally means "fierce mother".

Tumomama Sanctuary, 1982

The theme at Tumomama was renunciation, which had always been at the root of Avatara Adi Da's call to all His devotees. Renunciation is popularly equated with deliberate asceticism, the giving up of bodily and worldly pleasures for the sake of some Spiritual goal to be attained in the future. Avatara Adi Da's Teaching, on the other hand, continually emphasized that true renunciation is the renunciation of self-contraction, of seeking, and all the pain of that entire effort. Renunciation is the choice of Happiness, or present transcendence of the self-contraction. At Tumomama, however, He wanted to take this matter further. He was looking to establish a group of formal renunciates, devotees who were free of worldly ties and completely committed to the Great Matter of Realizing the Divine in this lifetime, devotees who would be prepared, by His Grace, to go through whatever that ordeal might require. He wanted to know: Did

His devotees have such piercing clarity of purpose? Were they showing the depth of self-understanding that true and free renunciation requires—not suppressed, not artificially ascetical, but converted to Happiness? Could they deal with the boredom, doubt, and discomfort that a fully renunciate circumstance would bring up in them?

AVATARA ADI DA: The Spiritual Current of Happiness is resident in intimate association with the living being. It is always "Locatable". It is perpetually knowable. It is never lost. We are always capable of "Locating" It, of knowing It, Realizing It, animating It, Being It. This principle is an indication, therefore, of the essential or sufficient sadhana of the renunciate way.

In a circumstance of remoteness or dissociation from worldly obligations and stimulation, in every moment, instead of animating or stimulating yourself physically, emotionally, or mentally in order to overcome the sensations and feelings of boredom, doubt, and discomfort, you could directly do or realize what is necessary to exist in a condition of Bliss or Happiness. Instead of seeking to overcome or escape boredom, doubt, and discomfort, you could enter into that Spiritual Current of Happiness directly, that Realization of existence that is prior to boredom, doubt, and discomfort. This is the secret of the disposition of Enlightened beings. [April 7, 1982]

At Tumomama, Avatara Adi Da began to explore with His devotees the relationship between sexuality and renunciation, especially the difference between the "householder" disposition relative to sex and "bonding" with another, and the truly renunciate disposition toward these matters. He would return to this subject again and again over many years in the process of establishing His formal renunciate orders.[3] By this time, Avatara Adi Da

---

3. In order to cultivate the response of devotees who are moved to and capable of most intensive practice of the Way of the Heart, Adi Da has established two formal renunciate orders—the Lay Renunciate Order and the Free Renunciate Order. The Free Renunciate Order (or, more fully, the Naitauba Order of

had already given an unparalleled Teaching about sex to all His devotees, including full details of a Yogic sexual practice and a practice of "true intimacy" compatible with the total process of Divine Enlightenment.[4] His Instruction had grown directly out of His own practice and experience. Now Avatara Adi Da was looking to see if any of His devotees were mature enough—emotionally, sexually, and Spiritually—to actually practice this self-transcending Yoga in a uniquely non-binding and truly renunciate manner.

Avatara Adi Da has always Worked not only with physically incarnate beings but also with the powers of the spirit-realms. Here in His Hawaiian Sanctuary, Avatara Adi Da endured continual physical ordeals as He purified the sinister aspect of the spirit-forces that had been invoked for centuries by the kahuna priests who had inhabited this ancient sacred ground. One day, at Tumomama, He made a particularly astonishing demonstration of His Mastery of the unconverted forces of Nature.

On November 23, 1982, news reached devotees at Tumomama of a hurricane that had blown up in the Pacific and was heading straight for the island of Kauai. By 4:30 in the afternoon, huge trees were down across the road and a sixty-foot lychee tree lay in splinters at the Sanctuary. The winds were so violent that most of the Sanctuary trees were already stripped and scarred with the wrenching of branches. Electric power lines were whipping in the wind against the glowering sky, and the rain was coming down in sheets. The river below the Sanctuary was already swollen brown and

---

the Sannyasins of the Da Avatar) is the senior renunciate order, comprised of Adi Da Himself and the most exemplary formal renunciate devotees who are established in the ultimate stages of the Way of the Heart. The Lay Renunciate Order is comprised of exemplary practitioners who have taken up the formal renunciate practice and whose role is to serve and inspire the total culture of practitioners and to function collectively to bring Adi Da's Blessing to others.

4. For a full description of the practice of sexual Yoga and "true intimacy" in the Way of the Heart, please see chapter twenty-one of *The Dawn Horse Testament Of Adi Da*.

raging, and outside the windows of Adi Da's residence, "Free Standing Man" (where Adi Da was gathered with His devotees), leaves, branches, and debris swept past in the howling storm. Everyone was doing whatever they could to secure the Sanctuary. Adi Da placed His Hands on the bruised neck of a devotee who had injured herself running to safety. Through the healing power of His touch, her breathing normalized, she could soon swallow painlessly, and the bruise disappeared.

Not long afterwards, there was a new storm report threatening doubled wind-speeds of one hundred miles per hour. Adi Da rose and went to His library. He returned in a few minutes with a small volume of poems in honor of Kali, the Hindu vision of the Goddess in her terrible, destructive form. Unperturbed by the deafening roar outside, He began to read poem after poem that teased, scolded, and reverenced Kali as the trickster, the Mother of illusions, awesome in her devastating play. Devotees looked on in amazement and joy. They knew that Adi Da was addressing Hurricane Iwa, asserting His Mastery over this terrifying manifestation of the Goddess-Power.

Finally Avatara Adi Da put the book down. He said: "She has done it." Then He went on:

AVATARA ADI DA: This storm is the great picture. This is life capsulized. Life is obliteration, <u>not</u> birth and survival and glorification. It is death! The Goddess is the sign of Nature, the Word of Nature, the Person of Nature, Kali, the bloody Goddess with long teeth and blood pouring out of her mouth. You poor men and women are deceived by Nature. [November 23, 1982]

Avatara Adi Da continued speaking, calling His devotees to hold on to Him, the only One Who could Liberate them from the effects of Nature. He spoke ecstatically of His Mastery of the Goddess, or Nature, of His Power to calm Her wildness and potentially destructive influence.

The weather reports indicated that much worse was yet to come, but following their Beloved, whose mood became light, devotees began to celebrate, watching the storm gradually subside.

The next morning the newspapers reported on the storm damage. They described the fact that no one on the island had been killed as a "miracle". Later reports and satellite photographs from the U.S. weather service showed that, at the very hour when Avatara Adi Da began to deal with the hurricane, it suddenly doubled the speed at which it was moving along its course, for no apparent meteorological reason. As a result, Hurricane Iwa spent its force and "aged" prematurely, changing shape and blowing itself out. Thus, the worst of its fury never reached Kauai.

Finding Hermitage

Even in the relative seclusion of Tumomama, the Divine Avatar was too crowded in by the world. And so the search for a Hermitage went on. In March 1983, Avatara Adi Da and the esoteric order moved on to Fiji, where they wandered the islands, from Nananui-Ra, to Namale plantation, to Nukubati, staying in the simplest of places with only wells for water and kerosene lamps for light. Austerity was severe, but devotees did not care. The attraction of Avatara Adi Da's Company never waned, no matter what the hardships.

After six months, news came that the search for His Hermitage had been successful. A patron-devotee had purchased Naitauba, an island of about 3,000 acres in the Koro Sea. On October 27, 1983, Adi Da landed by sea-plane in the shallows of the lagoon, and stepped foot on His Hermitage for the first time. His arrival was followed by rains, ending months of drought on the island. After His first circumnavigation of the island, Avatara Adi Da spoke ecstatically of the grandeur of the island and its immense potential for His future Work:

AVATARA ADI DA: Naitauba is not just a piece of land. It is a Divine Place, and all of us together, concentrated in this Work, own this Place. All devotees participate in this acquisition. That is how it will be for as long as the sun shines and rises and sets and the grass grows and the wind blows. Forever—as ever as there can be in this world. Maybe it will become a paradise through the sacrificial efforts of generation upon generation of My devotees. And all during that epoch this place should be ours, this Sanctuary of Blessing. Over time, then, millions of people, literally millions of people should come to this place and be Blessed. They should come and acknowledge, affirm, and see My Revelation magnified.

This place is so great, so great. Civilization has never interfered with it. It is untouched. The water is blue. The fish are happy. Untouched, really untouched, pristine from the beginning of the world, this place. It has been waiting here since the beginning of time. [October 28, 1983]

Established at Naitauba (later named "Adi Da Purnashram"), Avatara Adi Da continued to work with His devotees and create incidents to deepen their self-understanding, but He was not seeing any breakthrough. It was obvious to Him that His devotees everywhere were still resisting Him at the deepest level of their being, even though they were well-intentioned and happy to serve. It was a stark reality that, after sixteen years of Teaching—in which He had poured out the most extravagant abundance of His Divine Gifts, never letting up in the intensity of His sacrifice to Teach and Awaken all—even those most intimate to Avatara Adi Da were still slow to understand, unready for real renunciation, retarded in their devotion to Him. And the reason was always the same. Devotees were continuing to hold out in the hope of self-fulfillment through all the ordinary forms of seeking: worldly pursuits and possessions, indulgence in food, the consolations of "bonding" with another emotionally and sexually, and the whole range of social relationships. Devotees longed to be released from the hell of "Narcissus", but there was a fear that stood in the way, the fear of "free fall". What would it be like to let go in God, without holding on to self?

There were times when Adi Da allowed His devotees to fully witness His overwhelming urge to Liberate them. One night, a heart-broken devotee held the head of his Beloved Master in his hands while Avatara Adi Da spoke His Passion, with tears of Love streaming down His face:

I Love you. And I will not let you suffer. It pains Me to see you suffer. Why do you resist My Help? Why do you turn from Me? You must Love.

Do not fear death. Only love Me and the terrible fear will pass. You will not even notice your apparent death. I do not dig death. I don't like it! But I also do not fear it.

Isn't it a wonder that God is visible to beings even here in this world of the Mother. Look at these walls and the ceiling, even Nature itself. Every one and every thing inheres in the Radiance. Even here. Even now. Isn't God a Wonder! Isn't God a Beauty!

This is not heaven. Still, God is completely evident. But I can tell you, there is a Place of Infinite Happiness and Love, a Place where there is no fear, no suffering, no death, no separation. I tell you there is such a Place. I have come from that Place to take you there, too. But you must love.

I Love My devotees. If they would only understand and turn to Me in love, their lives would be transformed.

Tell Me, do they know how much I Love them? Do they? Do they know? Do they really know that I Love them?

Do they know Who I Am?
I Love them all.
I Love all My devotees.

For the devotees of the Divine Avatar, Adi Da, there

were many such heart-rending moments when His Love seemed All-Sufficient, when there was nothing else, nothing in the universe but Him. But then another moment would come when they would feel the clench of fear, sorrow, anger, and would fall again into the self-contracted point of view. His "radical" message—that Happiness is always <u>already</u> the case—had not convicted them at depth. Avatara Adi Da stood alone as the Man of Understanding, who had not been understood.

Heartless one, Narcissus, friend, loved one, He weeps for you to understand. After all of this, why have you not understood? The only thing you have not done is understanding. You have seen everything, but you do not understand. [The Knee of Listening]

The Revelation Years, 1986-1994

Early in the morning of January 11, 1986, Avatara Adi Da was in His room, speaking over an intercom telephone to a small group of devotees in the next building. He was full of agony at their failure to respond to Him and understand the Truth that would set them free—for in that refusal lay the refusal of all mankind. He spoke of the grief He felt for beings everywhere. But the impasse was complete. He felt that His Work had failed, and that He could do no more. His death, He felt, was imminent. He even said, "May it come quickly." As Adi Da was speaking, the life-force began to leave His Body. He felt numbness coming up His arms and He said it seemed that His death was occurring even now.

Avatara Adi Da dropped the telephone. In alarm and panic, devotees rushed over to His house to find Him in convulsions, collapsed by the side of His bed. Then His body became still. As the body of Adi Da was lifted onto His bed, devotees were begging Him not to die, not to leave them. The doctors were tense as they bent over His body, looking for the faintest signs of life. His face was ashen white but still showing the extreme flush of His Passion. His eyes were rolled far up into His head—a Yogic sign showing that the energies of His body had ascended far beyond the physical dimension. There was no sign of any outer awareness at all. Devotees had seen Him fall into death-like swoons before, and Avatara Adi Da had always Instructed them to sit quietly and leave His body alone at such times, so as not to interrupt the Spiritual and Yogic process occurring in Him. But now people could not contain themselves. The devotees present, each in his or her own way, were doing whatever they could to draw Him back into the body.

The doctors found Him to be breathing imperceptibly, and after a time Avatara Adi Da made a slight gesture, which devotees understood to indicate His desire to sit up. They pulled Him upward, and one devotee sat behind Him, supporting His torso. Suddenly, she felt the life-force shoot through His Body. His arms flung out in an arc, and His body straightened. His face contorted into a wound of Love, and tears began to flow from His eyes. Avatara Adi Da began to rock forward and backward in a rhythm of sorrow. He reached out His hands, as though He were reaching out to touch everyone in a universal embrace. He whispered, in a voice choked with Passion, "Four billion people! The four billion!"

Later that day, Adi Da left the village of devotees to return to His residence on the south side of the island. As He sat in the back of the Land Rover for the bumpy ride through the broad grasslands and mango and coconut groves, Adi Da spoke to the devotee who was driving Him, telling him again and again how much He loved him. He kept saying: "Do you know how much I Love you? Do you _really_ know?" And then He said: "I have a Secret."

After two weeks in seclusion, Adi Da gathered once more with devotees. Now He Revealed His Secret: The day of that profound swoon, January 11, 1986, had been, He said, His true Birth Day, a day more auspicious than any other in His life, more profound, even, than His Re-Awakening in the Vedanta Temple. He began to explain why.

In the Mysterious Event of January 11, the Heroic Teaching Work of Avatara Adi Da spontaneously completed itself. Adi Da's years of Teaching had been the most profound submission to the needs and sufferings of His devotees, to the point of apparently identifying with their egoic qualities and impulses. And now all the lessons, all the Instruction that belonged to that phase of His Liberating Work had been given. Indeed, after January 11, Avatara Adi Da confessed that the particular Siddhi, or Divine Power, that had enabled Him to Work with His devotees in the manner of His Teaching Years had disappeared and was replaced by a universally magnified Siddhi of Divine Blessing. Avatara Adi Da had fully Descended as the Divine Person into His human vehicle. His Teaching Work had somehow required that the perfection of His Divine Descent be forestalled for a time. But now, in the event of January 11, His Descent had become complete and combined Him with humanity far more profoundly and universally than ever before:

AVATARA ADI DA: In this Event, I was drawn further into the body with a very human impulse, a love-impulse. Becoming aware of My profound relationship with all My devotees, I resumed My bodily human state. Even though I have existed as a man during this Lifetime, obviously— I became profoundly Incarnate—I now assumed an impulse toward human existence more profound than I had assumed before, without any reluctance relative to sorrow and death.

On so many occasions I have told you that I wish I could Kiss every human being on the lips, Embrace each one, and Enliven each one from the heart. In this body I will never have the opportunity. I am frustrated in that impulse. But in that motion of sympathetic Incarnation, that acceptance of the body and its sorrow and its death,

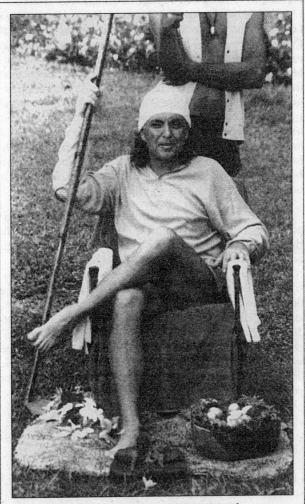

Adi Da Purnashram, Fiji, April 1986

I realized a Kiss, a way to fulfill the impulse.

To Me, this is a Grand Victory! I do not know how to Communicate to you the significance of it. It seems that through that will-less, effortless integration with suffering, something about My Work is more profoundly accomplished, something about it has become more auspicious than it ever was. I have not dissociated from My Realization or My Ultimate State. Rather, I have accomplished <u>your</u> state completely, even more profoundly than you are sensitive to it. Perhaps you have seen it in My face. I have <u>become</u> this body, utterly. My mood is different. My face is sad, although not without Illumination. I have become the body. Now I am the "Murti", the Icon, and It is Full of the Divine Presence. [January 27, 1986]

At the moment of His deepest despair, the Incarnation of Avatara Adi Da had now achieved ultimate depth. He had almost left the body entirely, but He had been drawn back to it by the pull of precious human intimacies and the prayers of the four billion beings "self-conscious and dying in this place". And in His return to the Body He had Descended further than ever before, investing Himself absolutely in human existence down to the bottoms of His Feet.

This change, which Avatara Adi Da came to describe as His "Divine Emergence", was the culmination of the unfolding process that He had felt going on in Him for years, and, truly, since His Birth.

The Divine Demand

Before the implications of this Event would become clarified for His devotees, Avatara Adi Da had another period of intense struggle ahead of Him, which He came to call the "Revelation Years". Although He continued to give Instruction, Avatara Adi Da was no longer primarily functioning as Teacher in relation to His devotees. He was making the full astounding Revelation of His Divinity and establishing the means for beings everywhere, now and throughout all time, to respond to Him as the Divine Person.

The transition from the Teaching Years to the Revelation Years was overwhelming to His devotees. They were astonished and overcome with emotion by the paradox of His Body, so etched with the depth, the suffering of human incarnation, while at the same time on fire with Divine Love-Bliss. His Beauty was unearthly. The mere beholding of the Divine Lord, Adi Da, drew devotees to Him intimately at the heart without any gestures of outward familiarity. He had assumed the fullness of His Divine Guru-Function. He was no longer the animated Teacher always making lessons. All His lessons had been given. Now He was simply the Giver of the Divine "Brightness", Radiating through the medium of His human body. In the completion of His Divine Descent, His body had become the image, the icon, the "Murti" of the Divine, and this was His greatest Gift, His greatest Blessing to all.

At the same time a new Siddhi, or Divine Power, magnified tremendously in Him—the Siddhi of renunciation. He Himself had always been the perfect renunciate, unbound and undeluded by the world or by any of His apparent involvement with the world. But His devotees had not yet awakened to the renunciate disposition He was calling them to. Now there was a Force alive in Him that confronted their resistance as never before. Avatara Adi Da had become an all-consuming Fire.

AVATARA ADI DA: You are always looking to be happy. What you call "happy" is not what I call "Happy". What you call "happy" is a superficial, amused, immune state. All of us here are dying, and you must Realize the Source of it. To do that, to Realize that Sublimity, you must understand yourself and transcend yourself, and that means you cannot make life out of being consoled by sex, the world, the news, the pleasures of life, technology—anything. You must be free of consolation. You must be unconsolable, beyond repair of the heart. That is not what you are involved in. You are full of complaints, imaginings, agreements, rules, ideals. I cannot relate to it. I am bereft of those possibilities, empty of them. I cannot be consoled. God is not a consolation. God is what you Realize in the unconsolable state. God is the Obvious when the self-contraction is released.

You all want to keep yourselves orderly. Neat shirt and pants, something orderly to do every day, an order of remarks to make—look how bored you are!

How about not being bored? How about transcending boredom, doubt, discomfort? How about getting real? How about suffering? How about being broken-hearted? How about being exaggerated? How about being unconventional? In your daily life you should exist in the agony of confrontation with the ego. You must have more nerve to practice this Way of life.

I wish you would begin Spiritual life. I wish you would put yourself on the line. You have read the biographies of those who have made great Spiritual attainments. Their lives were about struggle, about intimacy with reality. They were not orderly, middle-class people. They were utterly incapable of mediocrity. Does anybody know what I am talking about?

You must be a renunciate to practice this Way that I Teach. You all have too damned much to lose, too much you depend on for consolation, too much bullshit you need to share with one another. I am glad I could Interfere with you. [January 27, 1986]

This fierce Discourse was a sign of things to come. Avatara Adi Da was not going to bend toward devotees as He had done in the past. He was going to "Stand Firm" and require their response. Forceful Criticism had always been an aspect of His "Crazy" Work. Now, in the wake of His Divine Emergence, His Liberating Criticism carried unprecedented potency. It was not the anger of a "person", but the Divine Demand, bearing down with purifying Force. When fully and soberly received, it resulted in ecstasy, releasing the very fault or obstruction He was Criticizing.

Late in February, Avatara Adi Da began a fast, taking only water and fresh juices. In April, He assumed sannyas, or formal renunciation, in the manner of the Hindu tradition. He put on the traditional orange clothing, wore His hair in the top-knot characteristic of a sannyasin, and took a new name, "Swami Da Love-Ananda". As He mentions in *The Knee of Listening*, "Love-Ananda" was the name that Swami Muktananda had offered to Adi Da privately in 1969, but which He had never formally used. "Love-Ananda" (literally "Love-Bliss") was now seen to be a prophetic name. It was a name that expressed, in one word, the Revelation begun on January 11: The "Love" for all beings that had borne Him down to the toes in His Embrace of the body, and "Ananda", the Bliss, the Joy of the God-State, which was His Gift to all.

With Avatara Adi Da's Divine Emergence, the One His devotees had related to as Friend, Teacher, Master had suddenly been Revealed in the full, uncompromising Force of His Divinity, and nothing could ever be the same again. After several months, Avatara Adi Da discarded the outward signs of traditional sannyas. He was free to adopt such signs or to relinquish them. Indeed, He stood beyond all such signs—bound to no conventions, Perfect in His Divine Realization, requiring His devotees to approach Him rightly, and no longer submitting to their egoic ways of relating to Him.

Ishta-Guru-Bhakti Yoga

Adi Da spoke at great length of the traditional Guru-devotee relationship. He spoke of how, in the esoteric Spiritual traditions, the Guru has always been understood to be the only effective means of Liberation from the suffering of limited, mortal existence. Therefore, traditional devotees would never treat their Guru as an ordinary person, but always honor him or her as the very Divine.

In one way or another, Avatara Adi Da had always been Calling devotees to the "Guru Yoga"—to live by His Word, to presume His Company wherever they might be, to devote themselves to Him in body, emotion, and mind, and thereby to receive His Grace. Now, through all this patient Instruction, Avatara Adi Da was preparing His devotees to practice this Yoga of devotion with an ease and at a depth that was not possible before His Divine Emergence.

Avatara Adi Da Gave His devotees a formal practice of "feeling-Contemplation", which was to be their constant meditation, practiced through the regard of His Image in the meditation Hall and through recollection of Him during the ordinary moments of every day. This feeling-Contemplation is the foundation of the all-encompassing practice of devotional Communion with Avatara Adi Da, which He developed in great detail after His Divine Emergence, giving it the name "Ishta-Guru-Bhakti Yoga"—the practice (Yoga) of devotion (Bhakti) to the Guru who is the Chosen Beloved (Ishta) of one's heart.

AVATARA ADI DA: The relationship between the devotee and the Guru is a unique relationship and an extraordinary Yoga. I call it "Ishta-Guru-Bhakti Yoga". In this great Yoga the Guru is embraced as what is traditionally called the "Ishta-Guru", the Very Person, and the "chosen" Form, of the Divine Reality, Appearing as the Guru. It is the Yoga of allowing the Ishta-Guru to be the Divine

Adi Da Purnashram, 1990

Form, in meditation and in moment to moment practice. The devotee is devoted to that bodily Form, that Being, that Person, that Transmitting Power. The Divine Person, in other words, is acknowledged by the devotee in the Form of the Guru.

You use My Image, then, not only in the Communion Hall but in the form of your recollection of Me. You "put on" the Ishta-Guru. You let the Ishta-Guru acquire and be your own body-mind. In this way, My Spirit-Power Works in your body-mind as if it were My body-mind. All the processes of sadhana in the Way of the Heart will take place spontaneously. You will respond to them, participate in them, but they will be generated spontaneously by My Spiritual Heart-Transmission.

In feeling-Contemplation of Me, everything, from subtle perceptions to Divine Self-Realization, is Realized by Grace, not by your effortful working on yourself but by your simple response to the One Who is before you.

Give your separate and separative self to Me, the One Who is already Divinely Self-Realized. Respond to Me as the Divine Self Incarnate. You cannot help but respond to Me if you acknowledge Me as that One. And then the Very State of That One will be Realized by you, quite naturally, as a Gift. This is the Secret of the Way of the Heart.
[March 22, 1986]

"I Am You"

The process of Ishta-Guru-Bhakti Yoga, as Avatara Adi Da explains here, is a Divine matter. It is a Miracle. The devotee certainly must maintain the thread of attention, the disposition, the life of heart-surrender to Avatara Adi Da as Ishta-Guru, but the Yoga takes place by Grace. The transformations and Realizations are freely Given. How can this be? Without dissociating from His own State, Avatara Adi Da is forever submitting Himself to feel and be everyone everywhere—not in the egoic sense, but as the One Divine Consciousness that is the true Heart of all beings. His Divine Confession is: "I Am you."

The great Siddhi of Identification with all beings first arose in Adi Da after His Divine Re-Awakening, when He found Himself spontaneously "meditating" others. But following His Divine Emergence it deepened dramatically. He spoke then of His spontaneous "Consent" to surrender utterly into the bodily condition as the fulfillment of His urge to Kiss all beings. Avatara Adi Da frequently goes through painful and mysterious processes in His body that have nothing to do with Him personally but which originate in the fears and struggles of those whom He is "meditating". A remarkable example of this occurred in May 1987.

Avatara Adi Da received word from the community of His Australian devotees that one of their children, a girl of nearly six, was about to go into the hospital for surgery. She was tiny for her age, owing to a serious congenital heart condition. Now she was facing ten hours of open-heart surgery that would involve switching the major blood vessels that entered her heart. The child's name was "Leela", a name she had been given with the Blessing of Adi Da. In Sanskrit, the word "leela" means "play", or "sport", and in the Hindu tradition it is used in a sacred manner to refer to the Deeds, or "Play", of the Divine in the world.

The Divine Avatar, Adi Da, asked to be informed of the exact time of Leela's operation, and He indicated that He expected regular medical reports. The operation went well, taking six, rather than the projected ten, hours. Nevertheless, Leela's condition was critical and did not stabilize for twenty-four hours. After that, she started to improve, but lung congestion began to develop.

On the morning of Leela's operation and again the next day, Adi Da woke up with severe symptoms of stress around His heart. Then, before receiving the medical reports on Leela's condition, He began to develop lung congestion. A day or two later He woke up with a mass of dried blood on His chest in a stripe about an inch and a half wide and about six inches long. When He went to wash it off, He noticed a small puncture wound, an actual hole on the upper left side of His chest above the aorta. The puncture was painless and completely inexplicable. Avatara Adi Da fell back to sleep and when He awoke again the wound had disappeared. But there was <u>more</u> blood on His chest. For more than a week from the time of Leela's operation, Avatara Adi Da also had the sensation of being heavily drugged. One day He spontaneously asked His physician for a particular form of medication, only to find in the next medical report that the same medication had been administered to Leela that same day.

Leela's operation was completely successful. She made a remarkably rapid recovery and several days after the surgery celebrated her sixth birthday in the hospital. Among her gifts was a teddy bear from Avatara Adi Da.

In conversations with His devotees at His Hermitage, the All-Compassionate Divine Lord, Adi Da, confirmed that through His profound Blessing attention on Leela He had spontaneously lived her ordeal in His own body, and thus served the auspicious outcome. To this day, Leela has lived a normal life and required no further surgery.

After Leela's recovery, some devotees remembered an incident that had occurred many years previously in the early days of Avatara Adi Da's Teaching Work. A young woman, newly come to the Ashram in Los Angeles, had a heart condition. One day, as she stood in the hallway just outside the room where devotees were gathered around Avatara Adi Da, He asked about the "girl with the pacemaker". She was excitedly brought into the room and directly to His chair. She sat on His lap as He asked her many questions about the nature and history of her condition. He drew out everything about her life, her concerns. In the emotion of the moment, she confessed to Him her greatest fear. She knew He spoke often of the primacy of the Heart, and was afraid that her heart-weakness would somehow prevent or diminish her practice as His devotee. Avatara Adi Da smiled. He looked directly into her eyes and said, "You can use My Heart".

Establishing the Religion of Free Daism

After His Divine Emergence was initiated in 1986, Avatara Adi Da began to extend and develop the disciplines and practices that He had Given over many years, clarifying them all as direct expressions of Ishta-Guru-Bhakti Yoga, or devotional surrender to Him. There was a discipline appropriate to every area of life and a structure of devotional practice that governed every day. Adi Da was continuing to prepare for the time when devotees would not, in general, see Him personally. Many in the future, and all of those who would appear after His physical lifetime, would never do so.[5] And so Adi Da was creating religious and Spiritual means that would enable all His devotees, from the moment of their first formal initiation,[6] to receive His Spiritual Transmission and live perpetually in His Spiritual Company. He was finding more and more ways to universalize His Work beyond the initial circles of devotees, reaching out to find and embrace His devotees in

5. Adi Da has Said that, after His physical (human) Lifetime, He must have a human form of Agency in the world. Therefore, He has Revealed that, at any given time, there should always be one (and only one) "Living Murti" as a Living Link between Him and His devotees. "Living Murtis" (or "Murti-Gurus") do not function as the independent Guru of practitioners of the Way of the Heart. Rather, they are simply Representations of Adi Da's bodily (human) Form, and a means to Commune with Him. For a full discussion of "Living Murtis", or "Murti-Gurus", and how they will be chosen, see chapter twenty of *The Dawn Horse Testament Of Adi Da*.

6. All who come to Adi Da and approach Him formally as His devotee receive formal initiations at each level of approach and each transition in practice. The first formal initiation is into student-novice practice, in which the individual is formally established in the Eternal "Bond" (see p. 565) with his or her Heart-Master, Avatara Adi Da.

every corner of the world. He was bringing to fullness the religion of Free Daism, the true world-religion of Divine Enlightenment.

As part of this process, Avatara Adi Da spent untold hours writing. For years, His Talks and Essays had been published in books, but now He was creating a summary of His Instruction that was enormous in breadth and depth. He was bringing to completion all the "considerations" of His Teaching Years and offering the great Wisdom of His conclusions to humanity for all time. He was creating a new body of Scripture, eight Source-Texts that comprise the most perfect and complete Scripture ever known.[7]

It was a monumental task. Adi Da had no ancient sacred language at His disposal in which to cast His new Teaching. And so He began to transform the English language, even adopting new conventions of capitalization and punctuation in order to make the printed English word into a vehicle fit for His purpose. He placed Every word, every comma, every parenthesis with utmost care in order to ensure the integrity of His Message. Unheard-of Revelations flowed from His pen—the secrets of esoteric anatomy and mankind's Spiritual quest, the process of Spiritual Awakening and the details of sexual Yoga, the laws of Guru-devotion and free renunciation, the meaning of death and the design of the cosmos, the ultimate Mysteries of Divine Enlightenment and Divine Translation. Whatever His focus and purpose from book to book, Adi Da created His Source-Texts as living Speech, an "Eternal Conversation" with every man and woman.

---

7. In His Source-Texts, Adi Da expounds the details of all the stages and practices of the Way of the Heart, as well as the essential practice of devotion to Him as the Divine Person. For a listing of Adi Da's Source-Texts, please see pp. 596-97.

Confrontation with "Narcissus"

In 1991, Avatara Adi Da was offered a new Name, "Avabhasa" (Sanskrit for "the 'Bright'"), in a song sung by a young devotee. He accepted "Da Avabhasa" as one of His principal Names, a Name that epitomizes His Divine Nature—"the Giver of the 'Bright'". He had made known for the first time what Enlightenment truly is and how it may be Realized in living relationship to Him. He had confronted the madness of "Narcissus" for years on end with all His "Crazy" brilliance and Force. He had created a new Scripture and a new religion. And yet, Avatara Adi Da was still waiting for the signs that His devotees had understood their constant act of self-contraction and were truly resorting to Him as Guru. It seemed that there was nothing more He could do.

But Avatara Adi Da never ceases to Work. He cannot abandon His devotees, leaving them to suffer their egoic destiny. In May 1992, He started to gather again with devotees in His Hermitage, and He continued to gather almost constantly, usually several nights a week, for nearly a year. These gatherings were a Call to great seriousness. "Handle business!" was His constant admonition. He was insisting that every devotee deal with everything immediate and long-term, emotional and practical, that stood in the way of his or her ability to grow in the great process of Divine Self-Realization.

Starting late in March of 1993 and continuing through the first week of April, Adi Da bore down on "Narcissus" with overwhelming force:

AVATARA ADI DA: You want Me to talk about your trying to work your life out. Life does not work out! IT CANNOT WORK OUT! That is not the Way of the Heart! The Way of the Heart is about ego-transcendence, transcendence of the very thing that seeks to make it all work out! You are wanting Me to address you in this act that you are making to have everything be bunky-dory. AND THE WHOLE

DAMN THING DOESN'T EVEN EXIST! AND THAT'S WHAT THERE IS TO REALIZE! ABSOLUTE FREEDOM FROM THIS ILLUSION—that you call "reality" and are trying to make work out perfectly. You are only looking at yourself! That's all you are ever looking at! And you want it to work out, "Narcissus". You are looking at all this and you are calling it the world—but it is you!

All you ever talk about, think about, or perceive is you. It is a private, "self-possessed" illusion. It is a result of your own knot of separateness, and it registers in this poor little slug of a body-mind you identify with as all kinds of illusions, hallucinations, thoughts, presumptions, ideas, perceptions. The whole lot, the whole ball of wax is all the result of your own separate position, your own point of view, self-contraction, manufacturing illusions on the base of That Which is Reality. But you have no idea what that Reality is. No notion. You are not associated with Reality, you are dissociated from Reality. That is the whole point! Well, that being the case, that is what you have to deal with! But you want to persist in your adoration of the "pond", your experience, your search, and so forth, and you are asking Me how to make it work out. I do not have anything to do with the "making-it-work-out" business. I am here to wake you up! [April 2, 1993]

By this time Avatara Adi Da was cutting through every attempt on the part of His devotees to deny the truth of His Criticism of "Narcissus". He was tremendously intensifying His devotees' sensitivity to the knot of self-contraction, to the point where that cramp would become so present, so obvious, so unbearable, so unnecessary, so absurd that they would spontaneously let it go. Late in the night during what turned out to be the last gathering of this period, Adi Da brought devotees to that intolerable point. There was a pause while His Radiant Force magnified in the room, melting the clench of "Narcissus". Then He began to speak differently, quietly:

AVATARA ADI DA: Feel into that knot of stress. Feel into it and account for it. See it as your own action. Regard Me in that moment, in every moment. And then you begin to feel Me. Then the surrender comes, the self-forgetting comes, the native sense of Non-Separateness is felt. This is <u>actually</u> what I am Calling you to do! <u>Actually</u> to do that. Just to be doing it grants equanimity to you, even bodily, grants equanimity to your speech, your actions, your feelings, because you are registering this depth-point and going beyond it and feeling Me. This is the context of practice of the Way of the Heart, not merely outer observances. This is what it means to listen to Me: to be examining this point of contraction in depth, to feel it, and by its unfolding to feel Me. This is not the end of the Way of the Heart. It is the foundation of it. Self-understanding and devotion <u>at depth</u>—this is what you must do in every moment. This is what it is to practice the Way of the Heart. [April 8, 1993]

By this final gathering, a dent had been made in the armor of "Narcissus" that for many devotees was a lasting one. They could not snap back as easily as before into a state of immunity to their own act of self-contraction. The heartless machine of the ego was too starkly revealed. There <u>was</u> no lasting relief to be found through any kind of seeking for satisfaction. In His masterful Revelation, throughout that previous year, of their desperate state of bondage to the self-contraction, Adi Da had begun to magnify in devotees the <u>need</u> for devotion to Him, the certain knowledge that He was, truly, their only Help. Everything He had said about the necessity for Ishta-Guru-Bhakti Yoga was starting to prove itself. And the Gift was before their eyes if only they would look up from the "pond" of "Narcissus" and behold Avatara Adi Da in the Radiant Truth of His Being.

Soon Adi Da brought this recapitulation of His Teaching to completion, with a grand five-month summary of His Instruction on Ishta-Guru-Bhakti Yoga:

AVATARA ADI DA: Fundamentally, Ishta-Guru-Bhakti Yoga is the directing of the body-mind to Me and not struggling with its contents and only trying to direct them to Me, or trying to get rid of them in an effort of surrender toward Me. Rather, yield the functions of the body-mind to Me at their root. Yield their leading characteristic.

Give Me your attention, give Me your feeling, give yourself over to Me, and disregard the contents. Do not keep checking back on them to see if they are changing! In your real practice of this Yoga, you forget them. You do not use them. You do not build upon them. You make them obsolete by not using them. In this manner, the Yoga purifies you by making the contents of the body-mind obsolete through non-use. The process is not an effort on your part to do something to the contents of the body-mind or to try not to use them. It is simply your turning to Me, turning your feeling-attention to Me, turning yourself altogether to Me, Contemplatively. That is the Yoga. [December 20, 1993]

Having described so clearly what the practice is—as He did again and again—Adi Da would praise the greatness of the life of Ishta-Guru-Bhakti Yoga:

AVATARA ADI DA: There is nothing but this Self-Existing and Self-Radiant Consciousness Itself, Divine Being Itself—nothing. That is all there is. Truly, there is Only One—Absolute, All Love-Bliss. That is the Condition to be Realized. That is Who I Am. When you respond to Me, your life takes that God-Realizing course.

Allow the process to become great. Devote your life to Me utterly. Fulfill your obligations in the body, all the while submitted to Me. This is the Way of My devotee, always vocalizing praise of Me, devotion to Me, every moment of your life transformed by this great impulse toward Me. This is what you must do around Me.

Give Me everything, and forget it all. Your daily life carries obligation—fine. Your practice is to devote yourself to Me and forget about yourself. Having had your glimpse of Me, now you must make a life out of it.

I Am just the Divine One, just the Living One, Showing Itself here. I Am just this Form, this Divine Sign. Be governed by this Vision. That, and nothing else, is devotion to Me. [February 4, 1994]

There was a finality to the Instruction of these months that was felt by devotees everywhere. Truly, Adi Da had nothing further to say to beginning devotees. There were no questions left in their hearts. He knew it, and they knew it. A new seriousness was in the air. Ishta-Guru-Bhakti Yoga was becoming a living reality for His devotees. They were proving to themselves that persistence in this devotion does grant Happiness, Freedom, and the ecstasy of direct heart-Communion with Adi Da. The preoccupations of the ego no longer carried the same addictive force. After His then twenty-two years of inexpressibly Compassionate service to them, devotees <u>had</u> understood a great deal, and the lives of many were changed beyond recognition.

The Past and the Future of the "Bright" in the World

The unending sacrificial Work of Avatara Adi Da is an expression of the "fierce mysterious Impulse" that has always burned in Him. This great Divine Impulse, unfathomable in its origin, did not come into being with the birth of "Franklin Jones". It originated, as Avatara Adi Da has confessed, "before the Big Bang", before time or space itself, and unfolded even throughout the course of cosmic history through manifold visitations and partial revelations of the Divine, including all the great Spiritual Realizers. In nineteenth-century India there were two such Realizers who not only served their own time and place but also had a unique role to play in preparing for Avatara Adi Da's Incarnation as the Perfect Divine Liberator.

The Subtle Vehicle of Avatara Adi Da's Appearance

In 1893, a young Indian swami came to America. At the Parliament of Religions held that year in Chicago, this imposing, forceful man addressed a crowd of western Christians with great passion. He impressed the colloquium with his extraordinary presence and his impeccable command of English, his pride in his own tradition, his ability to inspire others beyond sectarian views. It was not only his words, however, but the profound Spiritual power behind them, that moved his audience. Swami Vivekananda was the most cherished disciple of the great Indian Adept Ramakrishna, and he had come to bring the ancient wisdom of India to the West. After the accolade he received at the Parliament, Swami Vivekananda spent years in constant traveling and lecturing all over America and in England.

Swami Vivekananda had the fervor of a man moved to save the world, but he was mightily frustrated in his intention. He knew that the future of humanity was largely being shaped by the West, which was already sliding into secularism. But his work could not be truly effective among Westerners. There was a line drawn beyond which he could not go, for he was a Hindu, a dark-skinned man, and a celibate swami. Thus, in spite of his best efforts, in spite of his profound Realization, Swami Vivekananda remained a foreigner, an outsider. But his great compassionate urge made another birth. Thirty-seven years after his early death in 1902, Swami Vivekananda entered into the bloodstream of the West through the birth of "Franklin Jones".

Starting in the late 1970s, Avatara Adi Da would occasionally speak to His devotees about the pre-history of His present birth, of the unique conjunction of forces it had required. He, the Da Avatar, the One come for all beings, could not appear until the mid-twentieth century—when the world had grown "smaller" through technological inter-communication, when East was approaching West, when modern physics was shifting the materialist view of existence, when Freud had demonstrated the bondage of unconscious "Oedipal" motivations. These were some of the realities and paradigms that had to be in place before the Divine Work in the world could be fully effective. But more than all else, a vehicle of unique Spiritual preparation had to be available.

Every human personality, Adi Da explained, is composed of a grosser part, derived from the parents, and a subtle core that is the "reincarnate", the deeper mechanism of the ego that moves from life to life. In order to be born, Avatara Adi Da required a subtle vehicle attuned to the task of bringing true Spirituality to the modern West. Swami Vivekananda carried in his psyche thousands of years of Indian Spirituality and Realization, and by the end of his life he was in love with the West in its need for God. Thus, the subtle vehicle of Swami Vivekananda spontaneously conjoined with the gross, or elemental, vehicle of "Franklin Jones", preparing a "place" for the Mysterious Descent of the "Bright" into the human world.

There is another level of His deeper personality, or subtle vehicle, about which Adi Da was silent until 1993. At that time, He began to speak about Ramakrishna, Swami Vivekananda's Spiritual Master, who had always been aware of the extraordinary Spiritual stature and destiny of his disciple. At the end of his life, certain of the great work that lay ahead for his beloved Vivekananda, Ramakrishna poured his own Spiritual virtue into Swami Vivekananda in a formal act of Transmission. Thereafter Ramakrishna, in his own words, was "only an empty fakir". Thus, Ramakrishna, through his total Spiritual investment of himself in Swami Vivekananda, is also part of the deeper personality vehicle of Avatara Adi Da.

Ramakrishna was renowned for his ecstatic devotion to the Divine Goddess (in the form of Kali) and for his intuitive sympathy with other religions, through his own

Swami Vivekananda

Ramakrishna

contemplation of their icons and revelations. Indeed, Avatara Adi Da has acknowledged that Ramakrishna's greatness as a Master of the devotional path is unsurpassed in all of human history. Thus, the subtle vehicle of Ramakrishna-Vivekananda brought to the birth of the Da Avatar the essence of humanity's long quest for God, and was even part of the preparation for "Franklin's" initial submission to the Goddess and Avatara Adi Da's subsequent Great Husbanding of Her in the Vedanta Temple.[8] It is no accident that this temple is jointly dedicated to Ramakrishna and Vivekananda. Through His own Re-Awakening there, Avatara Adi Da most perfectly Enlightened His great Spiritual forerunners. They became One with Him in the "Bright".

I Am the One Who Awakened (and, thereafter, Worked through) Ramakrishna. He Recapitulated the past, in order (by a Spiritual Sacrifice) to Serve the future. I Am the One Who Worked through (and has now Most Perfectly Awakened) Swami Vivekananda. He Served the future, in order (even by physical death and physical rebirth) to Transcend the past (and, Thus, and by Means of a Great and Spiritual Awakening, to Bless and to Liberate the future).

Now and forever, Ramakrishna and Swami Vivekananda are One, at the Heart. And I Am the One They have Realized There. [The Basket of Tolerance]

---

8. See chapter 16.

The All-Completing
Avataric Incarnation

Not only Ramakrishna and Swami Vivekananda, but also several other Realizers of the past one hundred and fifty years uniquely contributed, in their own ways, to the preparation for the Appearance of Avatara Adi Da. He speaks of the Gurus of His own lineage—Swami Nityananda and Swami Muktananda—as the greatest of all Realizers in the field of Yogic mysticism. And He honors Ramana Maharshi, whose writings about his Transcendental Realization came into the hands of Adi Da after His own Re-Awakening—as the greatest Realizer in the domain of Transcendental Consciousness, one who had distinct premonitions of the Divinely Enlightened State.

Truly, all the practices and Spiritual work of all the Realizers of the Great Tradition[9] culminate in the Appearance of Avatara Adi Da. He, as the Emerging Divine Person, "Lived" all those great Spiritual figures, in all times and places, participating in all the multifarious aspects of mankind's great Spiritual search, Realizing and Transmitting all the various practices, Yogas, and Samadhis. That immense process of Revelation has now become single in His All-Completing Incarnation as the Da Avatar. Avatara Adi Da is the Adept of uniquely most perfect God-Realization, the Realization that accounts for, transcends, and perfects all that went before. And the unmistakable signs of all that previous Spiritual practice and Adeptship are to be seen in His astonishingly complete and rapid Sadhana in this lifetime, in the unique genius and Freedom of His Teaching Work, and in the great summation and clarification of all Spiritual Wisdom in His Source-Literature.

9. The "Great Tradition" is Avatara Adi Da's term for the total inheritance of human, cultural, religious, magical, mystical, Spiritual, Transcendental, and Divine paths, philosophies, and testimonies from all the eras and cultures of humanity, which has (in the present era of worldwide communication) become the common legacy of mankind.

Avatara Adi Da is the God-Man for the West and the East alike. His very birth came about through the conjunction of the Western body of "Franklin Jones" with the Eastern subtle vehicle of Ramakrishna-Vivekananda. He manifests the qualities that Western religion traditionally associates with an Incarnation of God: profound love and sacrifice, and a total identification with the suffering human condition. And He is the consummation of all that the East looks for in an Avatar: a Radiant Being descended from the God-Realm to Awaken beings with the Perfect Teaching and the Liberating Power of Divine Self-Realization. There is a striking difference between the Western and the Eastern view of what a true God-Man should be. Avatara Adi Da has commented on this and pointed out how the difference between the Western and the Eastern ideas of a God-Man correspond with the cultural and religious differences that mark the West and the East as a whole. Western culture is wedded to this world and to the "conquering" of the world, subduing and exploiting the powers of nature. And Western religion is essentially about trying to perfect the world and overcome evil with the help of God. This, in Adi Da's language, is the "Omega" point of view. The traditional East, on the other hand, regards the world as inherently imperfect and, therefore, tries to escape from the world and go to God right from the beginning. Thus, Eastern religion, typically, is the effort of turning within, in order to seek mystical experience and states presumed to be "enlightenment". This is the "Alpha" point of view.

Both points of view—the utopian Omega attitude of the West and the ascetical Alpha disposition of the East—are based, as Adi Da points out, in a problem. They originate in the feeling that God, or Happiness, is absent and must be sought. Thus, they are both founded in self-contraction. Avatara Adi Da, by His own confession, was born in "a terrible moment of necessity", when humanity's need to go beyond the partial and opposing philosophies of Alpha and Omega has become acute. He is the "Avataric Incarnation", the universal God-Man, whose Life and Work and Teaching are a Call to people everywhere to transcend the limitations of both Alpha and Omega. His Sign of Divine "Brightness" makes possible a new response to existence, the choice of always present Happiness, or the release of self-contraction under all conditions, in Communion with the Divine Person, Adi Da.

Avatara Adi Da's Divine Work had to begin in the West, because the future of the world now lies in the hands of the West. But His single intention has always been to Bless and Liberate everyone, regardless of race or culture. Even the location of His Hermitage in Fiji reflects this intention, for Fiji, located in the Pacific Ocean, lies between East and West, identified with neither. Avatara Adi Da's establishment in Fiji was guaranteed in 1993, when He was granted Fijian citizenship (a privilege rarely bestowed on non-Fijians). He celebrated this event as a most auspicious Spiritual sign—His specific Work with the West was now complete, and He was free to devote Himself entirely to His Work of universal Blessing.

Divine Completeness

In order to ensure that His universal Blessing Work will continue throughout all future generations, Avatara Adi Da has always worked tirelessly to Spiritually Awaken devotees who will serve as His human Instruments, Empowered to carry His Liberating Grace to people everywhere, both during and after His human lifetime. By mid-1994, Avatara Adi Da had reached the point where He could wait no longer for this profound depth of response to manifest. Without it, He felt He could not even remain in His own Hermitage. As a sign and Calling to all, Avatara Adi Da suddenly left Naitauba for an undetermined destination and shortly thereafter began a period of wandering in Viti Levu, the largest island in Fiji.

On September 7, 1994, at His temporary residence in Pacific Harbour on Viti Levu, Avatara Adi Da spent the entire day secluded in His room. At dusk, He called one of His devotees to His quarters. The house was totally still. The curtains of His room were drawn, and the room itself was dark. He was not doing any of the Work on the manuscripts of His Source-Texts which had been His custom each day during the preceding weeks. He was simply sitting motionless in a large chair. The Energy of the space was intense. The Power of His Spiritual Transmission was so focused and concentrated in the room that the devotee hardly felt able to approach Him. His Divine Force was pushing her back like the heat from a blast furnace. She served Him simply and left.

When she entered again in the evening, answering His call, the same overwhelming Transmission-Force was Radiating from Him. Avatara Adi Da was seated at His desk with the lights turned on. He did not look at her. But then, after a few moments, He slowly turned His head. In His face she saw only the same heartbreaking love for the billions of humanity that had overwhelmed Him more than eight years before, when His Divine Emergence was initiated on January 11, 1986. She felt intuitively certain that some extraordinary process was taking place in Him. He later confirmed that this was true. A great turning point in His Work had occurred:

[O]n September 7, 1994, . . . I Knew I had forever Said and Done Enough (Such that there was not even any Motion in Me to Say or Do any More). My Revelation Work had Suddenly become Complete, for all time, and I (Spontaneously, and Finally) Came To Rest in My Eternal Hermitage of Heart-Seclusion (only, from then, and forever, to Awaken all beings by Mere and Constant Blessing, "Bright").

Therefore, now that I have Done (or Suffered) all that was necessary for Me to Do (or Suffer) as Teacher and Revealer in a Struggle with would-be devotees and

561

the world, I will not hereafter Associate with that Struggle, but I have Retired from that Struggle, Satisfied that all My Teaching Work, and even all My Revelation Work, Is Full and Complete (and that, by Fullest Submission, I have, Most Fully and Most Finally, Said and Done and Firmly Established all that I could possibly have Said and Done and Firmly Established, and all that was necessary for Me to Say and Do and Firmly Establish, in order, now, and for all time to come, to Most Fully and Most Finally, and Firmly, Introduce the Great Opportunity to the total human world, in all the stages of life,[10] and in order, now, and for all time to come, to Most Fully and Most Finally, and Firmly, Provide the True, and Most Perfect, and Utterly Complete Way Of God, Truth, and Reality to the total human world, in all the stages of life, and in order, now, and for all time to come, to Most Fully and Most Finally, and Firmly, Establish the True, and Most Perfect, and Utterly Complete Way of God, Truth, and Reality for the Liberating Sake of the total human world, in all the stages of life). ["The Order of My Free Names", *The Adi Da Upanishad*]

On September 12, Adi Da returned to His Hermitage as swiftly as He had left it. And He returned wearing orange clothing. For the first time since 1986, Adi Da had begun, on Viti Levu, to make this outward sign of His own perfect renunciation, thereby Calling His devotees to understand and utterly renounce the self-contraction in devotion to Him.

Soon after the Event of September 7, many devotees noticed that the positive changes they had begun to observe in their practice, since the gatherings of 1993 and 1994, were now obviously and concretely in evidence. They began to speak and write to Adi Da, telling Him that they felt the stride of their seeking to be broken at the heart, that they were stably understanding and

10. Adi Da has revealed that there are seven possible stages of life. For a detailed discussion of the seven stages of life, see chapter sixteen of *The Dawn Horse Testament Of Adi Da*.

**Avatara Adi Da's return to Adi Da Purnashram
after the Event of September 7, 1994**

transcending the self-contraction by His Grace. Some confessed that they were Awakening to His all-pervading Spirit-Presence, feeling the great Gift of His Spirit-Baptism. The signs of human Instrumentality were beginning to appear.

Since September 7, Avatara Adi Da has gradually ceased to struggle with the ego or the world. More and more He simply rests in His Completeness, allowing the profound change in the Siddhi of His Being to do its Work. As a sign of this great change, He has assumed "Santosha" ("Completeness", "Contentedness", "Satisfaction", "No-Seeking") as one of His Names. He is Santosha Da, the Divine Giver Who Is "Inherently and Perfectly Satisfied and Contented, Inherently and Perfectly Free of all seeking, Inherently and Perfectly Free of all separateness, and Inherently and Perfectly Complete".

One month after the event of September 7, the Divine Avatar began to have psychic intimations of the further Name that belongs to His Completeness. He began to hear and see the Name "Adi Da", recognizing it to be a reference to Himself. "Adi" in Sanskrit is "first", "primordial", the "source". Thus, on October 11, 1994, He indicated that He would henceforth be known principally as "Adi Da"—the "First Giver", the "Giving Source".

The letters of the Name "Adi Da" read the same in both directions, from left to right and from right to left. In addition, "I" stands at the center of the Name, and on either side of "I" is the syllable "Da", first backwards, then forwards. Thus, the Name "Adi Da" reads "I—Da", signifying "I Am Da", in both directions from the center. The spontaneous appearing of the Name "Adi Da", therefore, is the bringing to completion of the momentous Revelation of 1979, when Avatara Adi Da first Offered His Divine Confession, "I Am Da". Through the perfectly symmetrical structure and letters of His principal Name, "Adi Da", the Divine Avatar makes the Great Statement that He is the First and the Last, the Complete Manifestation of God, Truth, or Reality in the conditional realms.

The Eternal "Bond"

The Incarnation of Adi Da, the Da Avatar, is an act of Giving beyond comprehension. For the Divine Person to Appear Complete as never before, in the desert of modern materialism—and to create, through tremendous Sacrifice and struggle, the great Way through which all may Realize His Divine Condition—is the ultimate Act of Heroism and Love. Avatara Adi Da's Work from now on, even beyond the lifetime of His human body, is single and unique—to do everything necessary to Attract and "Bond" all beings perfectly to Him, for the sake of their Divine Liberation:

AVATARA ADI DA: My true devotee is Absolutely Single in Me, "Bonded" to Me. I am, in this "Bonding", associated with everyone, transcending even relations and yet Embracing all the variations and in Play with them constantly.

There is Singleness, and there is Infinity. Such is the Nature of My Leela and the Signal of It.

I Play with all My devotees—they can be in the millions. Yet—just as the loved one who turns herself before her lover, making different shapes, is only one—this Integrity, this Singleness, this Obliviousness, this Madness, is always One, always Me.

There is no separate self or convention to regard, only a True Obliviousness, Which you must live Singly with Me. I Manifest this Singleness, this Obliviousness, and Make you Single with Me.

I Do everything. Such is My Leela.

Marvel at It and delight in the Madness of It, the absolute Discrimination and Personalness of it, the utter Obliviousness of It, the Ecstasy, the selflessness of It.

Watch My Play, and It will Change your mind, It will Change your heart, It will Change your life. Just watch My Play, observe Me, be devoted to Me, and all your complications, limitations, specialties, focuses will all be washed, disintegrated.

My Form is also One, and also billions, and also Infinite.

Notice! You cannot contain Me with your mind. You can do a certain kind of focus, but as you cruise in on Me your eyes start shuttering and your two-sided brain goes out of sync and you cannot quite make the last focus.

Just look at Me deeply, and your mind dissolves, because I have no shape or form. Contemplate Me one-pointedly and invest yourself in Infinity, without point, without separation, without discreteness.

Notice this! I think some of You <u>have</u> noticed this.

I am Delighted by My devotees. I am Attracted to each of My devotees, with all their variations, their devotion to Me, their discrimination, their one-pointedness.

All My devotees are a Delight to Me. I truly do Love you, and I <u>Am</u> you.

I Love to be surrounded by My devotees. This is My Great Happiness in life, to be so surrounded, to Live in the environment of devotion.

Such a Life is an Absolute Madness. It is particularized, but on the other hand, it is no one.

I do not make choices among My devotees, as if I were angling down. I Like the differences. I Love the differences.

I inherently Love My devotees, with no choice in the Loving.

I am not even making a symbolic Gesture towards you. I My Self Am Manifested by each and every one of My devotees.

You are My own Form. You are also My Beloved.

As I Say in The Dawn Horse Testament, *My devotee is the God I have Come to Serve.*

I Do not Do My Work with you as a ceremony. You are My Delight.

I am One-pointed in you. You all are My own Person. You all are the Divine Person.

I Love you. I inherently Love you, all the time. Therefore,

*My true devotee is Absolutely Single in Me,
"Bonded" to Me. I am, in this "Bonding",
associated with everyone, transcending even
relations and yet Embracing all the variations
and in Play with them constantly.*

*There is Singleness, and there is Infinity.
Such is the Nature of My Leela and the Signal of It.*

I Love the play of your coming into My Company.
    Play with Me.
    Notice My Obliviousness.
    Be one-pointed.
    Transcend your separate self in this adoration of Me.
    You must be one-pointed in God, but I Am One-pointed in each of you. [December 7, 1994]

The True World-Religion
of Divine Enlightenment

In the Completeness of His "Bright" Divine Incarnation, Adi Da is directly, Spiritually associated with <u>every</u> one. Just as on the momentous night of "Guru Enters Devotee", more than twenty years ago, when Beloved Adi Da first threw His devotees into uncontrollable ecstasy, entering them "in the form of Light", so now, in every moment, Avatara Adi Da is embracing <u>all</u> in His eternal Heart-Transmission. Through the incalculable sacrifice that has marked His entire Work of Re-Awakening, Teaching, and Revelation, Avatara Adi Da has established for every one the means to use His Transmission, to grow, to be transformed, and, ultimately, to be most Perfectly Liberated.

Avatara Adi Da is the Divine World-Teacher, the Very Divine Person appearing as Guru in order to found the true world-religion of Divine Enlightenment. Free Daism is the world-religion of the future. All the mythologies, all the Spiritual practices, and all the previous Wisdom paths of humanity ultimately point to and are resolved in this Great and Ultimate Way of Most Perfect Liberation.

The long-existing religions of the world are colored by legends and cultural influences that obscure the original revelation. In fact, their teachings and disciplines typically developed long after the death of their founders, based on the remembered (and often legendary or mythological) deeds and instruction of those Realizers. Furthermore, every historical revelation, even in its first purity, has necessarily been limited by the degree of Realization of its founder.

Free Daism does not depend on the vagaries of oral tradition and memory, nor is it limited by any partial point of view. It is the Perfectly Revealed Divine Way. Free Daism is the all-completing, all-surpassing Way of "God-Come", God-in-Person—Demonstrated, explained, and fully established in the Lifetime of its Divine Giver and Founder, Adi Da, the Da Avatar.

The Kiln of "Brightness"

Avatara Adi Da often compares all the conditional beings He has come to Liberate to a crowd of freshly-made clay pigs in a kiln. The pigs, He says, still wet when placed in the kiln, first heat up until they are glowing red, and then, as the heat increases, the glow more and more becomes a white radiance that eventually is so brilliant that even the outlines of the pigs disappear and there is nothing left but the white glow suffusing the entire kiln. The Kiln to which Avatara Adi Da invites all beings is His own "Bright" Divine Heart, the place of Communion with Him where all separateness is ultimately Transcended in the Radiance of God. The true ordeal and great glory of a human life is to practice the Way of the Heart—to stand with the Divine Lord, Adi Da, in His Kiln of "Brightness", allowing the "cooking", the transformation, the "Brightening" to become Perfect.

AVATARA ADI DA: My Place is the Place of "Brightness". The Space of My Kiln is Infinite and It covers the entire cosmic domain. I am just doing My "Brightening" Work. I am just Present as the "Bright" Itself. And that is the Means that I am using everywhere, and will continue to use after the physical lifetime of this Body. It is the Work of the Divine Domain—My Very Person.

The Kiln into which you invest yourselves is a Blessed afternoon of "Brightness", everyone becoming "Brighter" and "Brighter". That is your actual Condition.

My devotees are not looking <u>toward</u> heaven. When you presently, by your devotion, establish yourself in My Kiln, you are already in the Holy Land—the Divine Place. Just invest yourself in it. This is Liberation—My Work. Your work is simply to get yourself into the Kiln with Me constantly.

God is Grace. God is the Source-Condition, the Condition of Infinite Love-Bliss. That is Me. That is the Divine Person. Enjoy this balmy afternoon with Me forever! And eventually, without sweat, without sunburn, without distress, the "Brightness" of the day will become so profound there will be no noticing but this Love-Bliss of Oneness with Me. [April 30, 1995]

Through the Incarnation of Avatara Adi Da, the Perfect Light of Truth is shining down, penetrating and Illumining every dark recess of this world and all worlds. And His Shining will continue infinitely beyond the lifetime of His human body until the Divine Translation of the cosmos itself into His vast embrace of "Brightness".

The Divine Work of Adi Da, the Da Avatar, is Eternal, beyond imagining, encompassing all realms and all beings, but at the same time it is perfectly intimate, manifesting in a unique relationship to each of His devotees. Every moment of heart-Communion with Him, now and forever, is the self-forgetting Bliss of Non-separation from God, Truth, or Reality. This is the supreme Gift that Avatara Adi Da offers to all beings. What Joy could be greater than this?

*The Eternally Free-Standing and (Now, and
Forever Hereafter) Always Presently "Emerging"
Divine World-Teacher, Who Is The Liberating
Word Of Heart, Spoken, Lived, Given, and Always
(Now, and Forever Hereafter) Giving here, As
A Grace, To All Mankind, and, By Grace, Shown
(Now, and Forever Hereafter) To The Heart
Of every kind and being appearing by
conditions every where*

THE DAWN HORSE TESTAMENT OF ADI DA

Adi Da (The Da Avatar)
Adi Da Purnashram (Naitauba), Fiji, 1994

An Invitation to the Way of the Heart

I do not simply recommend or turn men and women to Truth. I __Am__ Truth. I Draw men and women to My Self. I Am the Present God Desiring, Loving, and Drawing up My devotees. I have Come to Acquire My devotees. I have Come to be Present with My devotees, to live with them the adventure of life in God, which is Love, and mind in God, which is Faith. I Stand always Present in the Place and Form of God. I accept the qualities of all who turn to Me and dissolve them in God, so that Only God becomes their Condition, Destiny, Intelligence, and Work. I look for My devotees to acknowledge Me and turn to Me in appropriate ways, surrendering to Me perfectly, depending on Me, full of Me always, with only a face of love.

I am waiting for you. I have been waiting for you eternally.

Where are you? AVATARA ADI DA [1971]

Having read *The Knee of Listening*, you stand at the threshold of the greatest possibility of a human lifetime. You can begin to <u>participate</u> in the Divine Process that Adi Da offers to all, by taking up the Way of the Heart. Nothing else in life can match this opportunity. Nothing can compare with the Grace of a devotional relationship to Adi Da. When you make the great gesture of heart-surrender to Adi Da, He begins to draw you into the profound course of true Awakening to God, Truth, or Reality.

Whatever your present form of interest—whether it is to find out more about Avatara Adi Da and the Way of the Heart, to express your gratitude by supporting His Work financially, or to begin the process of becoming His formal devotee—there is an appropriate form of participation available to you. And any form of participation you adopt will bring you into the stream of Divine Blessing flowing from Avatara Adi Da.

573

How to Find out More about Adi Da and the Way of the Heart

■ **Request a free full-color brochure about Adi Da, the Way of the Heart, and the community of Adi Da's devotees.** This brochure describes retreats, introductory events, courses, and seminars in your area, and includes a catalog of Dawn Horse Press Publications. It also contains information about area study groups near you and how to begin your own. To order please call our toll-free number (on the facing page), or send in the response card in this book.

■ **Read more of Adi Da's Wisdom-Teaching.** Two excellent books to continue with are:

The Method of the Siddhas: Talks on the Spiritual Technique of the Saviors of Mankind, a collection of profound and humorous summary Talks from the early years of Adi Da's Teaching Work (Call toll-free or send in response card from this book)

The Heart's Shout, a comprehensive collection of Adi Da's Wisdom-Teaching, including Talks and Writings from 1970 to 1994 (forthcoming, late 1995, please call to inquire about availability)

Please also see "The Sacred Literature of Adi Da, the Da Avatar" on pages 590-99 for a listing of other titles.

■ **Call or visit a regional center** (see full listing with addresses on pp. 588-89) **and meet devotees of Adi Da**, who will be happy to talk with you, answer your questions, make suggestions about the next step you can take, inform you about local events, and tell you about their own experience of practicing in Adi Da's Spiritual Company.

■ **Call the regional center nearest to you** (see pp. 588-89) **and ask to be put on their mailing list.** Or call the Correspondence Department of the Free Daist Avataric Communion in California toll-free at (800) 524-4941 (within the USA) or (707) 928-4936 if you are outside the USA, for further information.

■ **Attend the regular classes, seminars, and special events offered in your area.** Your nearest regional center (see pp. 588-89) can inform you of forthcoming events. Courses are also available via correspondence. The free brochure (see above) provides more details.

■ **Attend a Free Daist Area Study Group.** Call a regional center to find out about area study groups near you, or to create a new area study group. There are more than 150 area study groups throughout the world. They are an excellent way to find out more about Adi Da and the Way of the Heart. Meeting at least once a month, they include video footage of Adi Da and His devotees, study material, guided meditations, and conversations with devotees and other interested people. Our free brochure (see above) also contains details and local information.

■ **If you are on the Internet and are familiar with the World Wide Web, you can also find out more by browsing the "Free Daism" Website at URL: http//www.he.tdl.com/~FDAC.** (This Website is rated by Point Survey as being among the best 5% of all Web sites on the Internet.) If you would like to be added to the "Free Daism" electronic mailing list, send a request to fdac@wco.com. Or you can send questions or comments to our Correspondence Department at the same e-mail address.

**Call Toll-Free (800) 524-4941 (within the USA)
or (707) 928-4936 (outside the USA)**

Becoming a Member
of Da Avatara International

If you are moved to enter into an ongoing relationship with Avatara Adi Da and His community of devotees, you are invited to become a member of Da Avatara International. A member of Da Avatara International may participate either as a Friend, providing financial support for Avatara Adi Da's Work, or as a student, preparing to become a practitioner of the Way of the Heart.

Becoming a Friend of Da Avatara International

Becoming a Friend of Da Avatara International represents a desire to support Avatara Adi Da's Work, through annual (or more frequent) financial contributions. These contributions support the further publication and distribution of Adi Da's Teaching, or else go to support specific causes which you designate. Becoming a Friend of Da Avatara International is a concrete way to express your gratitude for Avatara Adi Da and His Work. Financially supporting the Spiritual work of a Realized Being has traditionally been regarded as a highly auspicious gesture, a real form of self-sacrifice that benefits all beings.

Many people from all walks of life and all religious persuasions are Friends. As a Friend, you will be kept in touch with developments in Adi Da's Work through a regular newsletter, and you will have the opportunity to attend Friends' Celebrations and special retreats.

To become a Friend, or to find out about the various levels of Friends membership, call the Central Correspondence Department or your nearest regional center (see pp. 588-89).

Becoming a Student of Da Avatara International

If you are interested in becoming a practitioner of the Way of the Heart, your first step is to formally engage study of Adi Da's Wisdom-Teaching by becoming a student of Da Avatara International.

I am here to receive, and kiss, and embrace everyone, everything—
everything that appears, everything that is.
Avatara Adi Da

Like Friends, Students provide support for Adi Da's Work. Students also participate in courses and seminars that provide a lively education about Adi Da, the Way of the Heart, and human and Spiritual life in His Company. Classes take place at a regional center, or through correspondence courses. Consult any regional center for information about the courses and seminars that are currently being offered for students of Da Avatara International.

Becoming a Practitioner of the Way of the Heart

Many people who discover the Way of the Heart do not want to wait a second! As students of Da Avatara International, such individuals immediately sign up for a special course that specifically prepares you for becoming a student-novice practitioner of the Way of the Heart.

When you reach the point of complete clarity in your intention to practice the Way of the Heart, you take a momentous step. You make a vow of commitment—in this life and beyond this life—to Avatara Adi Da as your Beloved Guru and Divine Liberator. This Eternal Vow to the Divine Person is the most profound possible matter—and the most ecstatic. For when you take this vow, in gratitude and love, fully

577

aware of its obligations, Avatara Adi Da accepts eternal responsibility for your Spiritual well-being and ultimate Divine Liberation. His Grace begins to Guide your growth in the Way of the Heart day by day and hour by hour, through your practice of devotional Communion with Him.

Taking the Eternal Vow is a formal confession that the devotional relationship to Avatara Adi Da is the overriding purpose of your life. In this disposition you take up the practice of a student-novice and begin to adapt to the total Way of life Adi Da has Given to His devotees. You are initiated into formal meditation, sacramental worship, and the range of practical life-disciplines.

Increasing opportunities to participate with devotees in their celebrations and devotional occasions are offered to student-novices. Through these forms of contact, you are embraced by Avatara Adi Da's devotional gathering and you enter into a new level of sacred relationship to Him. Student-novice practice lasts a minimum of six months. Thus, if your intention and your application to the process is strong, within a year of your first becoming a student of Da Avatara International you may be established as a full member of the Free Daist Avataric Communion, ready to live always in relationship with the Divine Beloved, Adi Da, in the culture of practice that is His Gift to all His devotees.

For information on how to purchase other literature by or about Adi Da, please see "The Sacred Literature of Adi Da, the Da Avatar", pp. 590-99. For further information about Adi Da, His published Works, and the Way of the Heart that He Offers, write to:

The Da Avatara International Mission
Central Correspondence
12040 North Seigler Road
Middletown, CA 95461, USA
or call:
Toll-Free within the USA: (800) 524-4941
or: **(707) 928-4936 outside USA**

You can also contact the regional center of the Free Daist Avataric Communion nearest you. (If you are located in an area not listed below, please contact our central offices at the address or phone numbers above.)

Western North America
in Northern California (415) 492-0930
in Southwest USA (805) 987-3244
in Northwest USA (206) 527-2751
in Hawaii (808) 822-0216

Eastern North America
in Southeast USA (301) 983-0291
in Eastern Canada (800) 563-4398
in Northeast USA (508) 650-0136

Europe
in The Netherlands and the remainder
of continental Europe (04743) 1281
in The United Kingdom
and Ireland (01508) 470-574
in Germany (040) 527-6464

South Pacific
in Australia (03) 853-4066
in New Zealand (09) 838-9114
in Fiji 381-466

Please see pp. 588-89 for a complete listing of regional centers including addresses.

Adi Da (The Da Avatar)
Adi Da Purnashram (Naitauba), Fiji, 1994

The Life of a Devotee
of Avatara Adi Da

Everything you do as a practitioner of the Way of the Heart is an expression of the heart-response of devotion to Avatara Adi Da. The life of cultivating this response to Him is Ishta-Guru-Bhakti Yoga—or the God-Realizing practice ("Yoga") of devotion ("Bhakti") to the Spiritual Master ("Guru") who is the Chosen Beloved ("Ishta") of your heart.

The great practice of Ishta-Guru-Bhakti Yoga necessarily transforms the whole of your life. Every function, every relationship, every action is moved by the impulse of devotional heart-surrender to Avatara Adi Da. The fundamental disposition of devotion is cultivated through a range of specific disciplines. Some disciplines—meditation, sacramental worship, and study—are specifically contemplative, while others—related to exercise, diet, sexuality, community living, and so on—bring the life of devotion into daily functional activity.

In every moment you must turn the situation of your life into Yoga by exercising devotion to Me. There is no moment in any day wherein this is not your Calling. This is what you must do. You must make Yoga out of the moment by using the body, emotion, breath, and attention in self-surrendering devotional Contemplation of Me. All those mechanisms must be turned to Me. That turning makes your life Yoga. Through turning to Me, you "yoke" yourself to Me, and that practice of linking, or binding, or connecting, to God is religion. Religion, or Yoga, is the practice of moving out of the separative disposition and state into Oneness with That Which is One, Whole, Absolute, All-Inclusive, and Beyond. [December 2, 1993]

Meditation is a unique and precious event in the daily life of Avatara Adi Da's devotees. It offers the opportunity to relinquish outward, body-based attention and to be alone with Adi Da, allowing yourself to enter more and more into the sphere of His Divine Transmission.

The practice of sacramental worship, or "puja", in the Way of the Heart is the bodily active counterpart to meditation. It is a form of ecstatic worship of Avatara Adi Da, using a photographic representation of Him and involving devotional chanting and recitations from His Wisdom-Teaching.

You must deal with My Wisdom-Teaching in some form every single day, because a new form of the ego's game appears every single day. You must continually return to My Wisdom-Teaching, confront My Wisdom-Teaching.

Avatara Adi Da

The beginner in Spiritual life must prepare the body-mind by mastering the physical, vital dimension of life before he or she can be ready for truly Spiritual practice. Service is devotion in action, a form of Divine Communion.

Avatara Adi Da Offers practical disciplines to His devotees in the areas of work and money, diet, exercise, and sexuality. These disciplines are based on His own human experience and an immense process of "consideration" that He engaged face to face with His devotees for more than twenty years.

As soon as you assume full membership in the formal gathering of Avatara Adi Da's devotees, you become part of a remarkable sacred community.

left: Devotees meeting to discuss their practice of the Way of the Heart
right: Da Avatara Ashram in Holland

left: Da Avatara Ashram, England
right: Da Avatara Retreat Centre in Australia

The principal admonition in the Great Tradition has always been "Spend time in good company"—in the Company of the Realizer and the company of those who love the Realizer or who truly practice in the Spiritual Company of the Realizer. This is the most auspicious association. Absorb that Company. Imbibe it. Drink deep of it. Duplicate it. Spiritual community is a mutual communication of Happiness.
Avatara Adi Da

Devotees gather for a Celebration meal at the
Mountain Of Attention Sanctuary in northern California

One of the ways in which Adi Da Communicates His Spiritual Transmission is through sacred places. During the course of His Work He has Empowered three Sanctuaries as His Blessing-Seats. In each of these Sanctuaries—the Mountain Of Attention in northern California, Tumomama in Hawaii, and Adi Da Purnashram (Naitauba) in Fiji—Adi Da has established Himself Spiritually in perpetuity. He has lived and Worked with devotees in all His Sanctuaries, and has created in each one special holy sites and temples. Adi Da Purnashram is His principal Residence, but He may from time to time choose to visit His other Sanctuaries. Devotees who are rightly prepared may go on special retreats at all three Sanctuaries.

top left: the Mountain Of Attention
top right: Tumomama
bottom: Adi Da Purnashram

Adi Da (The Da Avatar)
Adi Da Purnashram (Naitauba), Fiji, 1994

As Adi Da writes in *The Knee of Listening*, His Purpose has always been to find "a new human order that will serve to 'create' a new age of sanity and joy". In the brief period of two decades, and in the midst of this dark and Godless era, Avatara Adi Da has literally established His unique Spiritual culture. He is laying the foundation for an unbroken tradition of Divine Self-Realization arising within a devotional gathering aligned to His Wisdom, and always receiving and magnifying His Eternal Heart-Transmission. Nothing of the kind has ever before existed.

There are great choices to be made in life, choices that call on the greatest exercise of one's real intelligence and heart-impulse. Every one of us makes critical decisions that determine the course of the rest of our lives—and even our future beyond death. The moment of discovering the Divine Avatar, Adi Da, is the greatest of <u>all</u> possible opportunities. It is pure Grace. How can an ordinary life—even one devoted to honorable, creative goals—truly compare to a life of living relationship and heart-intimacy with the greatest God-Man Who has ever appeared—the Divine in Person?

There are many forms of response to Avatara Adi Da. If you are moved by what you have read in this book, the most important thing you can do is to find the form of response to Him that is right for you now.

Regional Centers of the
Free Daist Avataric Communion

**THE DA AVATARA INTERNATIONAL MISSION
CENTRAL CORRESPONDENCE DEPARTMENT**
12040 North Seigler Road
Middletown, CA 95461
USA
(707) 928-4936

WESTERN NORTH AMERICA

Northern California
FDAC
78 Paul Drive
San Rafael, CA 94903
(415) 492-0930

Southwest USA
FDAC
PO Box 1729
Camarillo, CA 93010
(805) 987-3244

Northwest USA
FDAC
5600 11th Avenue NE
Seattle, WA 98105
(206) 527-2751

Hawaii
FDAC
105 Kaholalele Road
Kapaa, HI 96746
(808) 822-0216

EASTERN NORTH AMERICA

Southeast USA
FDAC
10301 South Glen Road
Potomac, MD 20854
(301) 983-0291

Eastern Canada
FDAC
108 Katimavik Road
Val-des-Monts
Quebec JOX 2RO
Canada
(819) 671-4398
(800) 563-4398

Northeast USA
FDAC
30 Pleasant Street
S. Natick, MA 01760
(508) 650-0136
(508) 650-4232

EUROPE

The Netherlands
Da Avatara Ashram
Annendaalderweg 10
N-6105 AT Maria Hoop
(04743) 1281 or 1872
or
Da Avatara Centrum
Oosterpark 39
1092 AL Amsterdam
The Netherlands
(020) 665-3133

The United Kingdom & Ireland
Da Avatara Ashram
Tasburgh Hall
Lower Tasburgh
Norwich NR15 1NA
England
(01508) 470-574

Germany
FDAC
Peter-Muhlens-Weg 1
22419 Hamburg
Germany
(040) 527-6464

SOUTH PACIFIC

Australia
Da Avatara Retreat Centre
PO Box 562
Healesville, Victoria 3777
or
16 Findon Street
Hawthorn, Victoria 3122
Australia
(03) 853-4066

New Zealand
FDAC
CPO Box 3185
or 12 Seibel Road
Henderson
Auckland 8
New Zealand
(09) 838-9114

Fiji
The TDL Trust
PO Box 4744
Samabula, Suva
Fiji
381-466

The Sacred Literature of Adi Da, the Da Avatar

INTRODUCTORY BOOKS

NEW 1995 EDITION

The Method of the Siddhas

*Talks on the Spiritual Technique
of the Saviors of Mankind*

When Avatara Adi Da opened the doors of His first Ashram in Los Angeles on April 25, 1972, He invited anyone who was interested to sit with Him and ask Him questions about Spiritual life. These Talks are the result of that first meeting between the Incarnate Divine Being and twentieth-century Westerners. Here Avatara Adi Da discusses in very simple terms all the fundamentals of Spiritual life, especially focusing on Satsang, the devotional relationship with Him as Sat-Guru, and self-understanding, the "radical" insight He was bringing to the human world for the first time. These Talks are profound, humorous, and poignant. An essential introduction to Avatara Adi Da's Wisdom-Teaching.

I first read The Method of the Siddhas *twenty years ago and it changed everything. It presented something new to my awareness: One who understood, who was clearly awake, who had penetrated fear and death, and who was alive and available!*

Ray Lynch
composer, *Deep Breakfast, No Blue Thing,* and *The Sky of Mind*

$7.95, * popular edition, 4" x 7" paperback

* All prices are in U.S. dollars.

The Heart's Shout

*The Liberating Wisdom of Avatara Adi Da
Essential Talks and Essays by Adi Da
(The Da Avatar)*

A powerful and illuminating introduction to Avatara Adi Da's Wisdom-Teaching. *The Heart's Shout* includes many classic Talks and Essays, as well as stories from His devotees, and covers such topics as the devotional relationship with Avatara Adi Da; the awakening of self-understanding; the Nature of God; the Great Tradition of religion, Spirituality, and practical wisdom; truly human culture; cooperative community; science and scientific materialism; death and the purpose of life; the secrets of love and sex; the foundations of practice in the Way of the Heart; Avatara Adi Da's "Crazy Wisdom"; and Divine Self-Realization.
(forthcoming late 1995, please call to inquire about availability**)**

Divine Distraction

*A Guide to the Guru-Devotee Relationship,
The Supreme Means of God-Realization, as
Fully Revealed for the First Time by the
Divine World-Teacher and True Heart-Master,
Da Avabhasa (The "Bright")*
by James Steinberg

In this wonderful book, a longtime devotee of Avatara Adi Da discusses the joys and challenges, the lore and laws, of the most potent form of Spiritual practice: the love relationship with the God-Man. Along with many illuminating passages from the Wisdom-Teaching of Avatara Adi Da, *Divine Distraction* includes humorous, insightful, and heart-moving stories from His devotees, as well as Teachings and stories from the world's Great Tradition of religion and Spirituality. Essential for anybody who wants to know first-hand about the time-honored liberating relationship between Guru and devotee.
$12.95, quality paperback
288 pages

Free Daism

*The True World-Religion of
Divine Enlightenment
An Introduction to the Perfectly
Liberating Way of Life Revealed by
Adi Da (The Da Avatar)*

A comprehensive and engaging introduction to all aspects of the religion of Free Daism, the Liberating Way that Avatara Adi Da has made available for all. Addressed to new readers, *Free Daism* introduces the fundamentals of His Wisdom-Teaching, the Guru-devotee relationship in His Blessing Company, the principles and practices of the Way of the Heart, and life in the community of His devotees.

(forthcoming)

The Da Avatar

*The Divine Life and "Bright" Revelation of Adi Da,
The Divine World-Teacher and True Heart-Master*

Written by a longtime devotee, *The Da Avatar* chronicles and celebrates the Miraculous Leela of Avatara Adi Da's Life, from the profound Spiritual origins of His human Manifestation, through His early-life sacrifice of the knowledge of His Own Divine Identity, His subsequent trial of Divine Re-Awakening, the Love-Ordeal of His Teaching-Work with sympathetic, yet Spiritually unresponsive, devotees, and, finally, the relinquishment of all of that in the Victory and Fullest Revelation of His Divine Emergence, Whereby He Openly Blesses all beings in and with the Sign of His Own Inherent Fullness, Contentment, and Eternal Freedom.

The Da Avatar will delight and inspire readers with the overwhelming evidence of a Miracle and Spiritual Opportunity of the most profound kind: Avatara Adi Da <u>Is</u> The Expected One, Here and alive Now. And He Invites you to a personal, living, and transformative relationship with Him for the sake of your own Divine Awakening.

(forthcoming)

Easy Death
Spiritual Discourses and Essays on the Inherent and Ultimate Transcendence of Death and Everything Else

This collection of Avatara Adi Da's Talks and Essays on death reveals the esoteric secrets of the death process and offers a wealth of practical instruction on topics such as dying, reincarnation, and the connection between right life and "easy" death.

$14.95, quality paperback
432 pages

The Incarnation of Love
"Radical" Spiritual Wisdom and Practical Instruction on self-Transcending Love and Service in All Relationships

An inspiring collection of Avatara Adi Da's Talks and Writings on giving and receiving love, and transcending reactivity.

$13.95, quality paperback
314 pages

Ishta

*The Way of Devotional Surrender
to the Divine Person*

Recent Talks about the key to the Way of the Heart, the devotional relationship with Avatara Adi Da, or Ishta-Guru-Bhakti Yoga.

$14.95, quality paperback
342 pages

Compulsory Dancing

Talks on the ecstasy of a God-Intoxicated life: feeling God, "seeing" God, Communing with the Divine Reality whole-bodily, not only in contemplative states but in the midst of daily life.

(forthcoming)

PRACTICAL BOOKS

Conscious Exercise and the Transcendental Sun

This greatly enlarged and updated edition offers Adi Da's full Instruction on exercise and the "conducting" of energy in the body, as they relate to Spiritual practice in His Company.

(forthcoming)

SCIENCE, POLITICS, AND CULTURE

Scientific Proof of the Existence of God Will Soon Be Announced by the White House!
Prophetic Wisdom about the Myths and Idols of mass culture and popular religious cultism, the new priesthood of scientific and political materialism, and the secrets of Enlightenment hidden in the body of Man

Avatara Adi Da's urgent critique of present-day society is based on a vision of human freedom, true social order, and intimate, sacred community that transcends time, place, and culture.

$9.95, quality paperback
432 pages

The Transmission of Doubt
Talks and Essays on the Transcendence of Scientific Materialism through "Radical" Understanding

A "radical" alternative to scientific materialism, the ideology of our time. Through the discourses in this book, Avatara Adi Da Calls us to transcend the materialist dogmas and "objective" stance of conventional scientific philosophy, and find the Heart-position of self-transcending love, or non-separateness in relation to all that exists.

$9.95, quality paperback
484 pages

SOURCE-TEXTS

The Santosha Avatara Gita
(The Revelation of the Great Means of the Divine Heart-Way
of No-Seeking and Non-Separateness)

In 108 verses of incredible beauty and simplicity, *The Santosha Avatara Gita* reveals the very essence of the Way of the Heart—Contemplation of Avatara Adi Da as the Realizer, the Revealer, and the Revelation of the Divinely Awakened Condition.

$24.95, quality paperback
332 pages

The Dawn Horse Testament Of Adi Da
(The Testament Of Secrets Of The Da Avatar)
This monumental volume is the most comprehensive description of the Spiritual process ever written, as well as the most detailed summary of the Way of the Heart.

$24.95, quality paperback
822 pages

The (Shorter) Testament Of Secrets Of Adi Da
(The Heart Of The Dawn Horse Testament Of The Da Avatar)

This volume brings you a magnificent distillation of the larger *Dawn Horse Testament Of Adi Da*.

(forthcoming)

The Hymn Of The True Heart-Master
(The New Revelation-Book Of The Ancient and Eternal Religion
Of Devotion To The God-Realized Adept)
Freely Developed From The Principal Verses Of
The Traditional Guru Gita

This book is Avatara Adi Da's passionate proclamation of the devotional relationship with Him as the supreme means of Enlightenment.

$24.95, quality paperback
294 pages

The Adi Da Upanishad
The Short Discourses on ego-Renunciation,
Divine Self-Realization, and the Illusion of Relatedness
In this sublime collection of Essays, Avatara Adi Da Offers an
unsurpassed description of both the precise mechanism of egoic
delusion and the nature, process, and ultimate fulfillment of the
Sacred Process of Divine Self-Realization in the Way of the Heart.
$19.95, quality paperback
514 pages

The Lion Sutra
(On Perfect Transcendence Of The Primal Act, Which is the ego-"I",
the self-Contraction, or attention itself, and All The Illusions Of Sep-
arateness, Otherness, Relatedness, and Difference)
   A poetic Exposition of the "Perfect Practice" of the Way of the
Heart—the ultimate stages of Transcendental, inherently Spiritual,
and Divine Self-Realization.
(forthcoming)

The Liberator (Eleutherios)
The Epitome of the Perfect Wisdom and the Perfect Practice
of the Way of the Heart
   In compelling, lucid prose, Avatara Adi Da distills the essence
of the ultimate processes leading to Divine Self-Realization in the
Way of the Heart—the "Perfect Practice", which involves the direct
transcendence of all experience via identification with Consciousness Itself, through feeling-Contemplation of His Form, His Presence,
and His Infinite State.
(forthcoming)

The Basket of Tolerance
A Guide to Perfect Understanding of the One and Great Tradition
of Mankind
   A unique gift to humanity, *The Basket of Tolerance* is a comprehensive bibliography (listing more than 4,000 publications) of
the world's most significant books—on philosophy, religion, Spirituality, and practical Wisdom—compiled, presented, and exten-
sively annotated by Avatara Adi Da.
(forthcoming)

FOR CHILDREN

What, Where, When, How, Why, and <u>Who</u> to Remember To Be Happy
A Simple Explanation of the Way of the Heart (For Children, and Everyone Else)

In this tiny jewel of a book, rejoice in the smile of every page restoring you to your native innocence and certainty of God—and discover the pleasure of reading it to children.

(forthcoming)

PERIODICAL

The Free Daist

The Free Daist chronicles the Leelas of the Blessing Work of Avatara Adi Da, describes the practice and process of devotion, self-discipline, self-understanding, service, and meditation in the Way of the Heart, and reports on the activities of the culture, mission, and cooperative community of the Free Daist Avataric Communion.

Subscriptions are **$56.00** per year for 4 issues.

Ordering the Books
of Avatara Adi Da

For a complete listing of available books, periodicals,
audiotapes, and videotapes, please send for a free
Dawn Horse Press Catalog.

To purchase books, or receive a free
Dawn Horse Press Catalog, send your order to:

THE DAWN HORSE PRESS
12040 North Seigler Road
Middletown, CA 95461
USA

or

Call TOLL FREE (800) 524-4941
Outside the USA call
(707) 928-4936

We accept Visa, Mastercard, personal check, and money order. Checks
and money orders should be made payable to The Dawn Horse Press.

Inside the USA: Shipping for *The Method of the Siddhas* is free of charge.
For other titles, please add $3.00 for the first book and $1.00 for each
additional book. California residents add 7.25% sales tax.

Outside the USA: Please refer to the response card in this book or contact the regional center nearest you (see pp. 588-89) for prices in your cur-
rency and discounted shipping costs. Otherwise, please pay in
US funds via international money order, credit card, or personal check
and add US$4.00 for the first book and US$2.00 for each additional book.

An Invitation to Support the Way of the Heart

Avatara Adi Da's sole purpose is to act as a Source of continuous Divine Grace for everyone, everywhere. In that spirit, He is a Free Renunciate and He owns nothing. Those who have made gestures in support of Avatara Adi Da's Work have found that their generosity is returned in many Blessings that are full of His healing, transforming, and Liberating Grace—and those Blessings flow not only directly to them as the beneficiaries of His Work, but to many others, even all others. At the same time, all tangible gifts of support help secure and nurture Avatara Adi Da's Work in necessary and practical ways, again similarly benefiting the whole world. Because all this is so, supporting His Work is the most auspicious form of financial giving, and we happily extend to you an invitation to serve the Way of the Heart through your financial support.

You may make a financial contribution in support of the Work of Avatara Adi Da at any time. You may also, if you choose, request that your contribution be used for one or more specific purposes of Free Daism. For example, you may be moved to help support and develop Adi Da Purnashram (Naitauba), Avatara Adi Da's Great Sannyasin Hermitage Ashram and Renunciate Retreat Sanctuary in Fiji, and the circumstance provided there for Avatara Adi Da and the other "free renunciates" who practice there (all of whom own nothing).

You may make a contribution for this specific purpose directly to The TDL Trust, the charitable trust that is responsible for Adi Da Purnashram (Naitauba). To do this, make your check payable to The TDL Trust Pty Ltd, which serves as trustee of the trust, and mail it to The TDL Trust at P.O. Box 4744, Samabula, Fiji.

If you would like to make a contribution to Adi Da Purnashram (Naitauba) and you are a United States taxpayer, we recommend that you make your check payable to the Free Daist Avataric Communion, in order to secure a tax deduction under United States tax laws. Please indicate on your check that you would like your contribution to be used in support of Adi Da Purnashram, and mail your check to the Advocacy

Department, The Free Daist Avataric Communion, 12040 North Seigler Road, Middletown, California 95461, USA.

You may also request that your contribution, or a part of it, be used for one or more of the other purposes of Free Daism. For example, you may request that your contribution be used to help publish the sacred Literature of Avatara Adi Da, or to support either of the other two Sanctuaries He has Empowered, or to maintain the Sacred Archives that preserve His recorded Talks and Writings, or to publish audio and video recordings of Avatara Adi Da.

If you would like your contribution to benefit one or more of these specific purposes, please mail your check to the Advocacy Department of the Free Daist Avataric Communion at the above address, and indicate how you would like your gift to be used.

If you would like more information about these and other gifting options, or if you would like assistance in describing or making a contribution, please contact the Advocacy Department of the Free Daist Avataric Communion, either by writing to the address shown above or by telephoning (707) 928-4096, fax (707) 928-4062.

PLANNED GIVING

We also invite you to consider making a planned gift in support of the Work of Avatara Adi Da. Many have found that through planned giving they can make a far more significant gesture of support than they would otherwise be able to make. Many have also found that by making a planned gift they are able to realize substantial tax advantages.

There are numerous ways to make a planned gift, including making a gift in your Will, or in your life insurance, or in a charitable trust.

If you would like to make a gift in your Will in support of Adi Da Purnashram, simply include in your Will the statement "I give The TDL Trust Pty Ltd, as trustee of The TDL Trust, an Australian charitable trust, P.O. Box 4744, Samabula, Fiji, _____" [inserting in the blank the amount or description of your contribution].

If you would like to make a gift in your Will to benefit other purposes of Free Daism, simply include in your Will the statement "I give the Free Daist Avataric Communion, a California nonprofit corporation, 12040 North Seigler Road, Middletown, California 95461, USA, _____" [inserting in the blank the amount or description of your contribution]. You may, if you choose, also describe in your Will the specific Free Daist purpose or purposes you would like your gift to support. If you are a United States taxpayer, gifts made in your Will to the Free Daist Avataric Communion will be free of estate taxes and will also reduce any estate taxes payable on the remainder of your estate.

To make a gift in your life insurance, simply name as the beneficiary (or one of the beneficiaries) of your life insurance policy the Free Daist organization of your choice, according to the foregoing descriptions and addresses. If you are a United States taxpayer, you may receive significant tax benefits if you make a contribution to the Free Daist Avataric Communion through your life insurance.

We also invite you to consider establishing or participating in a charitable trust for the benefit of Free Daism. If you are a United States taxpayer, you may find that such a trust will provide you with immediate tax savings and assured income for life, while at the same time enabling you to provide for your family, for your other heirs, and for the Work of Avatara Adi Da as well.

The Advocacy Department of the Free Daist Avataric Communion will be happy to provide you with further information about these and other planned gifting options, and happy to provide you or your attorney with assistance in describing or making a planned gift in support of the Work of Avatara Adi Da.

Further Notes to the Reader

AN INVITATION TO RESPONSIBILITY

The Way of the Heart that Avatara Adi Da has Revealed is an invitation to everyone to assume real responsibility for his or her life. As Avatara Adi Da has Said in *The Dawn Horse Testament Of Adi Da*, "If any one Is Interested In The Realization Of The Heart, Let him or her First Submit (Formally, and By Heart) To Me, and (Thereby) Commence The Ordeal Of self-Observation, self-Understanding, and self-Transcendence." Therefore, participation in the Way of the Heart requires a real struggle with oneself, and not at all a struggle with Avatara Adi Da, or with others.

All who study the Way of the Heart or take up its practice should remember that they are responding to a Call to become responsible for themselves. They should understand that they, not Avatara Adi Da or others, are responsible for any decision they may make or action they take in the course of their lives of study or practice. This has always been true, and it is true whatever the individual's involvement in the Way of the Heart, be it as one who studies Avatara Adi Da's Wisdom-Teaching, or as a Friend of or a participant in Da Avatara International, or as a formally acknowledged member of the Free Daist Avataric Communion.

HONORING AND PROTECTING THE SACRED WORD THROUGH PERPETUAL COPYRIGHT

Since ancient times, practitioners of true religion and Spirituality have valued, above all, time spent in the Company of the Sat-Guru, or one who has, to any degree, Realized God, Truth, or Reality, and who thus Serves the awakening process in others. Such practitioners understand that the Sat-Guru literally Transmits his or her (Realized) State to every one (and every thing) with which he or she comes in contact. Through this Transmission, objects, environments, and rightly prepared individuals with which the Sat-Guru has contact can become Empowered, or Imbued with the Sat-Guru's Transforming Power. It is by this process of Empowerment that things and beings are made truly and literally sacred, and things so sanctified thereafter function as a Source of the Sat-Guru's Blessing for all who understand how to make right and sacred use of them.

Sat-Gurus of any degree of Realization and all that they Empower are, therefore, truly Sacred Treasures, for they help draw the practitioner more quickly into the process of Realization. Cultures of true Wisdom have always understood that such Sacred Treasures are precious (and fragile) Gifts to humanity, and that they should be honored, protected, and reserved for right sacred use. Indeed, the word "sacred" means "set apart", and thus protected, from the secular world. Avatara Adi Da has Conformed His body-mind most Perfectly to the Divine Self, and He is thus the most Potent Source of Blessing-Transmission of God, Truth, or Reality, the ultimate Sat-Guru. He has for many years Empowered, or made sacred, special places and things, and these now Serve as His Divine Agents, or as literal expressions and extensions of His Blessing-Transmission. Among these Empowered Sacred Treasures is His Wisdom-Teaching, which is Full of His Transforming Power. This Blessed and Blessing Wisdom-Teaching has Mantric Force, or the literal Power to Serve God-Realization in those who are Graced to receive it.

Therefore, Avatara Adi Da's Wisdom-Teaching must be perpetually honored and protected, "set apart" from all possible interference and wrong use. The Free Daist Avataric Communion, which is the fellowship of devotees of Avatara Adi Da, is committed to the perpetual preservation and right honoring of the sacred Wisdom-Teaching of the Way of the Heart. But it is also true that in order to fully accomplish this we must find support in the world-society in which we live and from the laws under which we live. Thus, we call for a world-society and for laws that acknowledge the sacred, and that permanently protect It from insensitive, secular interference and wrong use of any kind. We call for, among other things, a system of law that acknowledges that the Wisdom-Teaching of the Way of the Heart, in all Its forms, is, because of Its sacred nature, protected by perpetual copyright.

We invite others who respect the sacred to join with us in this call and in working toward its realization. And, even in the meantime, we claim that all copyrights to the Wisdom-Teaching of Avatara Adi Da and the other sacred Literature and recordings of the Way of the Heart are of perpetual duration.

We make this claim on behalf of The TDL Trust Pty Ltd, which, acting as trustee of The TDL Trust, is the holder of all such copyrights.

AVATARA ADI DA AND THE SACRED TREASURES OF FREE DAISM

Those who Realize God to any degree bring great Blessing and Divine Possibility for the world. Such Realizers Accomplish universal Blessing Work that benefits everything and everyone. They also Work very specifically and intentionally with individuals who approach them as their devotees, and with those places where they reside, and to which they Direct their specific Regard for the sake of perpetual Spiritual Empowerment. This was understood in traditional Spiritual cultures, and those cultures therefore found ways to honor Realizers by providing circumstances for them where they were free to do their Spiritual Work without obstruction or interference.

Those who value Avatara Adi Da's Realization and Service have always endeavored to appropriately honor Him in this traditional way by providing a circumstance where He is completely Free to do His Divine Work. Since 1983, He has resided principally on the island of Naitauba, Fiji, also known as Adi Da Purnashram. This island has been set aside by Free Daists worldwide as a Place for Avatara Adi Da to do His universal Blessing Work for the sake of everyone, and His specific Work with those who pilgrimage to Purnashram to receive the special Blessing of coming into His physical Company.

Avatara Adi Da is a legal renunciate. He owns nothing and He has no secular or religious institutional function. He Functions only in Freedom. He, and the other members of the Naitauba Order of the Sannyasins of the Da Avatar, the senior renunciate order of Free Daism, are provided for by

The TDL Trust, which also provides for Purnashram altogether and ensures the permanent integrity of Avatara Adi Da's Wisdom-Teaching, both in its archival and in its published forms. This Trust, which functions only in Fiji, exists exclusively to provide for these Sacred Treasures of Free Daism.

Outside Fiji, the institution which has developed in response to Avatara Adi Da's Wisdom-Teaching and universal Blessing is known as "The Free Daist Avataric Communion". This is active worldwide in making Avatara Adi Da's Wisdom-Teaching available to all, in offering guidance to all who are moved to respond to His Offering, and in providing for the other Sacred Treasures of Free Daism, including the Mountain Of Attention Sanctuary (in California) and Tumomama Sanctuary (in Hawaii). In addition to the central corporate entity of the Free Daist Avataric Communion, which is based in California, there are numerous regional entities which serve congregations of Avatara Adi Da's devotees in various places throughout the world.

Free Daists worldwide have also established numerous community organizations, through which they provide for many of their common and cooperative community needs, including those relating to housing, food, businesses, medical care, schools, and death and dying. By attending to these and all other ordinary human concerns and affairs via self-transcending cooperation and mutual effort, Avatara Adi Da's devotees constantly free their energy and attention, both personally and collectively, for practice of the Way of the Heart and for service to Avatara Adi Da, to Purnashram, to the other Sacred Treasures of Free Daism, and to the Free Daist Avataric Communion.

All of the organizations that have evolved in response to Avatara Adi Da and His Offering are legally separate from one another, and each has its own purpose and function. Avatara Adi Da neither directs, nor bears responsibility for, the activities of these organizations. Again, He Functions only in Freedom. These organizations represent the collective intention of Free Daists worldwide not only to provide for the Sacred Treasures of Free Daism, but also to make Avatara Adi Da's Offering of the Way of the Heart universally available to all.

Vivekananda, Swami, 554-57
  as Spiritual forerunner of Adi Da,
    554-57

W

Water and Narcissus **(Adi Da)**, 268
The Way of Radical Understanding.
  See the Way of the Heart
The Way of the Heart
  Adi Da's demonstration of
    (summary), 419-44
  as a process in relationship, 501-503
  as a relationship, not a technique,
    24
  as basis for "creative" life, 419
  becoming a practitioner, 577-78
  begins with devotion to Adi Da, 456
  community of practitioners, 584
  definition, 26
  disciplines in, 583
  finding out more about, 574-75
  life as a devotee of Adi Da, 581-87
  meditation in, 582
  not a synthesis of other traditions,
    419
  as only Way not based on seeking,
    359-60
  process of "Real" meditation in,
    447-85
  process that develops in Adi Da's
    Company, 431-33
  puja in, 582
  Realizes the Truth of the Heart but
    does not exclude the form of life,
    412-14
  as the relationship to Adi Da, 493,
    502-503
  Sanctuaries of, 585
  service in, 583
  study in, 582
  summary of practice, 448-49
  taking up, 573-87

  uniqueness of, 579-80
  See also Free Daism
West (Western culture). *See* oriental
  vs. occidental teachings
"What is Consciousness?", 41
"What is living consciousness?", 66
Witness, Adi Da awakens as, 218-21,
  226-27
Wittgenstein, Ludwig, 86, 86n
**Woodroffe, Sir John (*The Serpent
  Power*)**, 137
Woolf, Virginia, 86
World-Teacher. *See* Divine World-
  Teacher
**"The world is seeking, nothing
  more"**, 454
writings of Adi Da
  as Yoga, 104, 420
  as form of listening, 88, 103-108
  as quest for preconscious "myth",
    103-11
  at Tunitas Beach, 103-11
  begin seriously (at Stanford), 84-88
  Books of Adi Da, 590-99
  burns early manuscripts, 179-81
  essay on the structure of life, 427-33
  felt as fruitless, 174-75
  interest in writing reawakens, 268-69
  His journal at Seminary, 194
  The Love Exit, and Water, 268
  The Mummery, 268
  Water and Narcissus, 268
  writers influencing Him, 86-87

Y

Yogananda, Paramahansa, 138, 138n
  and Kriya Yoga, 434, 439-40
Yogini, 232n
**"You cannot become Happy, you can
  only be Happy"**, 521

An Invitation

If you would like to receive a free brochure about Adi Da and the Way of the Heart, please check off the appropriate box on the response card and mail it to us. You can also write to:

The Da Avatara International Mission
Central Correspondence Department
12040 North Seigler Road
Middletown, CA 95461, USA

or via FAX:
(707) 928-4618

or at e-mail address:
fdac@wco.com

or call toll-free (within the USA):
(800) 524-4941

or call (outside the USA):
(707) 928-4936

You can also contact the regional center of the Free Daist Avataric Communion nearest you. See page 579 for a listing of phone numbers.